Reading Habermas

Reading Habermas

Structural Transformation of the Public Sphere

Michael Hofmann

LEXINGTON BOOKS
Lanham • Boulder • New York • London

Published by Lexington Books
An imprint of The Rowman & Littlefield Publishing Group, Inc.
4501 Forbes Boulevard, Suite 200, Lanham, Maryland 20706
www.rowman.com

86-90 Paul Street, London EC2A 4NE

British Library Cataloguing in Publication Information Available

Library of Congress Cataloging-in-Publication Data

Names: Hofmann, Michael, 1952- author.
Title: Reading Habermas : structural transformation of the public sphere /
  Michael Hofmann.
Description: Lanham : Lexington Books, [2023] | Includes bibliographical
  references and index. | Summary: "Reading Habermas: Structural
  Transformation of the Public Sphere provides comprehensive guidance to
  understanding the complex methodologies of Habermas's global academic
  best seller. This timely guide parallels Habermas's publications from
  2021 and 2022 about a new structural transformation of political
  will-formation caused primarily by the digital dominance of social media
  platforms"-- Provided by publisher.
Identifiers: LCCN 2022042094 (print) | LCCN 2022042095 (ebook) |
  ISBN 9781498590167 (cloth) | ISBN 9781498590181 (paperback) |
  ISBN 9781498590174 (ebook)
Subjects: LCSH: Democracy--Philosophy. | Habermas, Jürgen--Political and
  social views. | Social media--Political aspects.
Classification: LCC JC423 .H742 2023 (print) | LCC JC423 (ebook) |
  DDC 321.801--dc23/eng/20221104

LC record available at https://lccn.loc.gov/2022042094

LC ebook record available at https://lccn.loc.gov/2022042095

To the Memory of Art Evans
(1951 – 2017)
Professor of Sociology
Florida Atlantic University

Contents

List of Abbreviations

AS   Habermas, Jürgen. *Autonomy & Solidarity*. Interviews with Jürgen Habermas, edited and introduced by Peter Dews. London: Verso, 1986.

BFN   Habermas, Jürgen. *Between Facts and Norms: Contributions to a Discourse Theory of Law and Democracy*. Translated by William Rehg. Cambridge, MA: MIT Press, 1996.

CC   Koselleck, Reinhart. *Critique and Crisis: Enlightenment and the Pathogenesis of Modern Society* (1959). Translated by Berg Publishers Ltd. Cambridge, MA: MIT Press, 1988.

CCP   [On the Concept of Political Participation] Habermas, Jürgen. "Zum Begriff der politischen Beteiligung (1958)." First published in *Student und Politik*. Neuwied: Luchterhand, 1961. Reprinted in *Kultur und Kritik. Verstreute Aufsätze*. Frankfurt am Main: Suhrkamp, 1972, 9-60.

CPD   Schmitt, Carl. *The Crisis of Parliamentary Democracy*. With a preface to the second edition (1926): "On the Contradiction between Parliamentarism and Democracy." Translated and introduced by Ellen Kennedy. With a foreword by Thomas McCarthy. Cambridge, MA: MIT Press, 1985.

CR   Habermas, Jürgen. "Concluding Remarks."*Habermas and the Public Sphere*, edited by Craig Calhoun. Cambridge, MA: MIT Press, 1992, 462-80.

CT   Schmitt, Carl. *Constitutional Theory* (1928). Translated and edited by Jeffrey Seitzer. Foreword by Ellen Kennedy. Durham and London: Duke University Press, 2008.

DA   Horkheimer, Max, and Theodor W. Adorno. *Dialektik der Aufklärung. Philosophische Fragmente*. Completed in 1944. First published in 1947. Frankfurt am Main: S. Fischer, 1969.

DE   Horkheimer, Max, and Theodor W. Adorno. *Dialectic of Enlighten-ment* (1947). Translated by John Cumming. Completed in 1944. First English edition published in 1972. London: Verso, 1986.

DW   Habermas, Jürgen. "The Kantian Project and the Divided West. Does the Constitutionalization of International Law Still Have a Chance?" *The Divided West* (2004), edited and translated by Ciaran Cronin. Cambridge: Polity Press, 2006, 113-93.

EI   Habermas, Jürgen. *Erkenntnis und Interesse*. First published in 1968. With a new afterword. Frankfurt am Main: Suhrkamp, 1973.

EME   Habermas, Jürgen. "The Entwinement of Myth and Enlightenment." *New German Critique*, no. 26 (Spring-Summer 1982): 13-30.

FG   Habermas, Jürgen. *Faktizität und Geltung. Beiträge zur Dis-kurstheorie des Rechts und des demokratischen Rechtsstaats*. Frankfurt am Main: Suhrkamp, 1992.

FRPS   Habermas, Jürgen. "Further Reflections on the Public Sphere." Translated by Thomas McCarthy of the 1990 preface. *Habermas and the Public Sphere*, edited by Craig Calhoun. Cambridge, MA: MIT Press, 1992, 421-61.

HA   Habermas, Jürgen."The Horrors of Autonomy." *The New Conser-vatism: Cultural Criticism and the Historians' Debate*. Edited and translated by Shierry Weber Nicholson. Introduction by Richard Wolin. Cambridge, MA: MIT Press, 1989, 128-39. (Originally pub-lished under the title "Sovereignty and Führerdemokratie." *Times Literary Supplement*, September 26, 1986, 1053-54.)

HAM   Habermas, Jürgen. "Psychic Thermidor and the Rebirth of Rebel-lious Subjectivity" (1980). First published in the *Berkeley Journal of Sociology*. In *Habermas and Modernity*, edited by Richard J.Bernstein. Cambridge, MA: Polity Press, 1985, 67-77.

HB   Müller-Doohm, Stefan. *Habermas: A Biography*. First published in German as *Jürgen Habermas. Eine Biographie*. Berlin: Suhrkamp, 2014. Translated by Daniel Steuer. Cambridge: Polity Press, 2016.

HG   Corchia, Luca, Stefan Müller-Doohm, and William Outhwaite, eds. *Habermas global. Wirkungsgeschichte eines Werks*. Berlin: Suhrkamp, 2019.

HPS   Calhoun, Craig, ed. *Habermas and the Public Sphere*. Cambridge, MA: MIT Press, 1992.

HPSC   Hofmann, Michael. *Habermas's Public Sphere: A Critique*. Lanham: Fairleigh Dickinson University Press / Rowman & Littlefield, 2017.

KHI   Habermas, Jürgen. *Knowledge and Human Interests* (1968). First English edition published in 1972. Translated by Jeremy J. Shapiro. Cambridge: Polity Press, 1987.

KK   Koselleck, Reinhart. *Kritik und Krise. Eine Studie zur Pathogenese der bürgerlichen Welt.* First published in 1959. Third edition. Frankfurt am Main: Suhrkamp, 1979.

KUK   Habermas, Jürgen. *Kultur und Kritik. Verstreute Aufsätze.* Frankfurt am Main: Suhrkamp, 1973.

LC   Habermas, Jürgen. *Legitimation Crisis* (1973). Translated by Thomas McCarthy. Boston: Beacon Press, 1975.

LS   Habermas, Jürgen. *Legitimationsprobleme im Spätkapitalismus.* Frankfurt am Main: Suhrkamp, 1973.

NR   Habermas, Jürgen. "Naturrecht und Revolution" (1962). *Theorie und Praxis. Sozialphilosophische Studien.* First published in 1963. Fourth edition, corrected, enlarged, and with a new preface. Frankfurt am Main: Suhrkamp, 1971, 89-127.

NLR   Habermas, Jürgen. "Natural Law and Revolution" (1962). *Theory and Practice* (1963). Translated by John Viertel. Boston: Beacon Press, 1973, 82-120.

PCT   [Philosophy and Critical Theory] Marcuse, Herbert."Philosophie und kritische Theorie." *Zeitschrift für Sozialforschung* 6 (1937): 631-47.

PDM   Habermas, Jürgen. *The Philosophical Discourse of Modernity. Twelve Lectures* (1985). Translated by Frederick Lawrence. Cambridge: Polity Press, 1987.

SÖ   Habermas, Jürgen. *Strukturwandel der Öffentlichkeit. Untersuchungen zu einer Kategorie der bürgerlichen Gesellschaft.* First published in 1962. Fifth edition. Neuwied: Luchterhand, 1971.

STPS   Habermas, Jürgen. *The Structural Transformation of the Public Sphere: An Inquiry into a Category of Bourgeois Society* (1962). Translated by Thomas Burger with the assistance of Frederick Lawrence. Cambridge, MA: MIT Press, 1989.

TAHP   Habermas, Jürgen. "Taking Aim at the Heart of the Present: On Foucault's Lecture on Kant's *What Is Enlightenment?*" Originally translated by Sigrid Brauner and Robert Brown. *The New Conservatism: Cultural Criticism and the Historians' Debate*, edited and translated by Shierry Weber Nicholson. Introduction by Richard Wolin. Cambridge, MA: MIT Press, 1989, 173–79.

TAP   Habermas, Jürgen. *Theory and Practice* (1963). Translated by John Viertel. Boston: Beacon Press, 1973.

TCA   Habermas, Jürgen.*The Theory of Communicative Action.* Volume 2. *Lifeworld and System: A Critique of Functionalist Reason* (1981). Translated by Thomas McCarthy. Boston: Beacon Press, 1987.

TUP   Habermas, Jürgen. *Theorie und Praxis. Sozialphilosophische Studien.* First published in 1963. Fourth edition, corrected, enlarged, and with a new preface. Frankfurt am Main: Suhrkamp, 1971.

VL   Schmitt, Carl. *Verfassungslehre*. First published in 1928. Ninth edi-
        tion. Berlin: Duncker & Humblot, 2003.
VPM   Habermas, Jürgen. "Über das Verhältnis von Politik und Moral."
        In *Das Problem der Ordnung. Sechster Kongress für Philosophie
        München 1960*, edited by Helmut Kuhn and Franz Wiedmann.
        Meisenheim am Glan 1962.

Preface

The Social Media Transformation of the Public Sphere and the Crisis of Neoliberal Democracy

Only three decades separate Francis Fukuyama's triumphalist claim about the "universalization of Western liberal democracy as the final form of human government" from U.S. President Biden's declaration about the need to prove that this liberal model still works and that the Chinese and Russian leaders are wrong when asserting that "autocracy is the wave of the future and democracy can't function" under the complex and crisis-prone conditions that mark today's state of globalization (Fukuyama 2022; Schuessler 2022; Sanger 2021; Crowley and Kanno-Youngs 2021). Jürgen Habermas's not yet translated "Reflections and Theses on a New Structural Transformation of the Political Public Sphere" from August 2021 reflect this urge to reassess the strengths and weaknesses of liberal democratic principles which the "Constitutional Revolutions" of the late eighteenth century enshrined on the basis of free-market capitalism (Habermas 2021: 471).

Habermas's renewed reflections on the challenges for a rational-critical discourse in the political public sphere identify even greater dangers to democratic governance than his original study analyzed at the height of the Cold War in 1962. Gone is his cautious optimism expressed at the time of his "Further Reflections on the Public Sphere" from 1992, when he also published the German original of his Discourse Theory of Law and Democracy. By April 2022, he even has to tacitly withdraw his 1990s dictum that the terrifying "spiral of an armaments race" between the nuclear powers at least prevented "the outbreak of a hot war" (Habermas 1998: 313). Two months after the Russian invasion of Ukraine, his appeal to reason can only point out the danger of escalating the ongoing "hot war" into World War Three once Vladimir Putin sees his factual dictatorship threatened to such a degree that he authorizes the use of "tactical" nuclear weapons (Habermas, April 2022).

The Cuban Missile Crisis almost immediately vindicated Habermas's 1962 critique of the manipulation of democratic will-formation through political advertising and the imperatives of commercial television, as sections 3.2, 3.3, and 4.1. below analyze. Nevertheless, a bipartisan consensus about democratic deliberation and governance still prevented Republican Senator Barry Goldwater from being elected to the United States Presidency in 1964 as an advocate of extreme measures that did not exclude the use of "tactical" nuclear weapons in the Vietnam War (Jamieson 1993: 178, 183-84). One can easily imagine how today's essentially unregulated social media, further amplified by talk radio and right-wing populist cable channels, would have given his nationwide network of grass-roots supporters in the mold of the John Birch Society a megaphone big enough to significantly sway American public opinion.

Habermas concludes his reflections from 2021 with his call for a structure of the (social) media which facilitates "the inclusive character of the public sphere" as well "the deliberative character of the public formation of opinion and will" as the basis for democratic governance (Habermas 2021: 499). He can substantiate his assertion that this demand is not a decision of partisan politics but represents an imperative of constitutional law, because for sixty years the key criteria of his theory of the democratic public sphere have been his precise distinctions between the market and the public as well as between the consumer and the citizen. In the market, private property owners exchange goods and services while pursuing their individual interests as consumers of what they buy. In the public sphere, citizens exchange rational-critical arguments to reach conclusions about the general interest.

If the market and the public sphere are conflated, as is the case when using social media for political will-formation in the democratic process, neither inclusion nor deliberation can be safeguarded. As the headline of a *New York Times* editorial put it already in December 2014: "Facebook Is Not the Public Square," even though the U.S. Supreme Court would call social media "the modern public square" in 2017. Social media businesses do not constitute "the digital equivalent of the public square where opinions can be freely shared." Instead, these companies resemble privately owned shopping malls where "the management always reserves the right to throw you out if you don't abide by its rules" regarding the contents of your public statements (Kaminski/Klonick 2017). As Habermas would discuss in 2021, self-determined deliberation is even more curtailed by the use of sophisticated algorithms that imprison social media users in the echo chambers of their own prejudices (Habermas 2021: 488, 494, 498). For the business model of social media demands the perpetual captivity of user attention to continuously harvest personal data for instant sale to the highest bidder.

Ironically, the digital media as the ultimate communication technologies of freedom, proclaimed in the 1980s by authors like Ithiel de Sola Pool, have contributed to turning the original liberal pursuit of personal autonomy into the accelerating inequality and instability of democratic capitalism. What went wrong? A close reading of Habermas's 1962 classic goes a long way toward finding an answer. For his rational reconstruction of Immanuel Kant's ideal of the public use of reason as the method of Enlightenment *and* as the organizational principle of the bourgeois constitutional state is completely dependent on the presuppositions ascribed to the liberal phase of capitalism. By ignoring this historical specificity and applying the eighteenth century liberal model as the template for late-twentieth-century globalization, neoliberalism's "creative destruction" of the social fabric has reduced the number of autonomous citizens to the now proverbial 1 percent of the population.

This guide highlights already in section 2.3 what continues to be often neglected in the reception of Habermas's original paradigm of the public sphere, namely, the dependency of an absolute concept of the bourgeois constitution on natural laws of society which self-regulate the political economy of liberal capitalism. First posited by the Physiocrats and Adam Smith, these economic laws received their extreme stylization in Jean-Baptiste Say's "Law of Markets," which allegedly functions akin to Isaac Newton's natural "Law of Gravity." Just as the latter prevents the planets from colliding on their regular trajectories throughout the universe, the former allegedly keeps all solely market-based exchange relations of a capitalist society in principle harmonious and crisis-free.

It took more than a century of cyclical economic crises culminating in the global Great Depression of the 1930s, before John Meynard Keynes could disprove Say's Law in the eyes of the vast majority of citizens. Conversely, without the extreme inflationary pressures originating in the deficit-financed Vietnam War and amplified by the global oil crises of 1973 and 1979, Say's Law could not have been rehabilitated as the promising recipe to end stagflation through the supply-side economics of the Reagan Revolution. Early on in the 1980 presidential election, before Ronald Reagan's victory allowed the libertarian credo of neoliberalism to become an economic and political reality, his future running mate George Herbert Walker Bush had still denounced it as "voodoo economics."

In 2021, Habermas confirmed his analysis from 1962 about the crisis-prone character of capitalist democracies (Habermas 2021: 498). Lacking any natural laws as the guarantee of their complex economic presuppositions, their systemic instability has to be perpetually mitigated by governmental regulations and by taxpayer-financed state interventions. Without the Vietnam War quagmire of the Johnson administration, the early 1970s

Watergate cover-up of the Nixon administration, and the "malaise" that defined the domestic policy of the Carter administration in the crisis year of 1979, Reagan's neoliberal mantra that "government is the problem" would not have become a winning slogan in the 1980 presidential election.

One has to wonder which rational contribution an English edition of Habermas's 1962 classic could have made to the confused and confidence-lacking public discourse at that time. Such a translation would have been possible, because already a decade earlier Herbert Marcuse had been instrumental in arranging a contract with Beacon Press for seven English editions of Habermas's works (Mendieta/Randolph 2019). Arguably, it would have had a clarifying impact during a transitional period when even Irving Kristol as the key founder of the neoconservative counterrevolution against the liberating spirit of the sixties and seventies still lacked the full-blown bravado of his future ideological disciple Fukuyama and could muster only *Two Cheers for Capitalism* (Kristol 1978).

Clearly, Habermas in 1962 was prescient in the ideology-critical discourse about the legacy of the Enlightenment when he analyzed the commonality between Kant's idealism and Marx's materialism. In short, their shared trust in a "natural order" of social reproduction which the Physiocrats claimed to have discovered. As Isiah Berlin would later observe, Enlightenment philosophers were blended "by the spectacular successes of the natural sciences" and believed that with the right scientific method "truth of a fundamental kind could be uncovered about social, political, moral, and personal life" (Berlin 1998: 54).

In other words, Habermas's book that today is among the best sellers of MIT Press would have had more credibility than Daniel Bell's famous critique of Marxist ideology from 1960. For it would not have suffered from the huge blind spot in *The End of Ideology*. Namely, the failure to acknowledge the ideological presuppositions of democratic capitalism due to Bell's zeal as a convert to liberalism. Instead, Habermas's readers could have precisely distinguished between the normative strengths and the analytical weaknesses in Kant's seminal model of the liberal public sphere. Above all, its unacknowledged "presupposition of a natural basis of the juridical condition" (STPS 117). In short, Habermas's uniquely sophisticated immanent critique of liberal democracy and democratic capitalism from 1962 could have provided the precise criteria with which to analyze neoliberalism already at its inception as an ideology, pure and simple.

In 2021, Habermas identifies as the direct reason for the political public sphere's loss of functionality the coincidence between Silicon Valley's commercial exploitation of the Internet and the global dissemination of the economic principles of neoliberalism (Habermas 2021: 498). While the Reagan and Bush 41 administrations provided the foundations for this development, it was the Clinton administration's quest for free trade agreements, for deregulation of the financial industry, and for the "Information Superhighway" that really made it happen. This bipartisan faith in the tenets of neoliberalism lasted through the Bush 43 and Obama administrations. The latter negotiated as its crowning achievement the Trans-Pacific Partnership (TPP). Hillary Clinton, who praised it as the "gold standard" of free trade agreements, would have continued in this neoliberal tradition, if she had been elected as the 45th President of the United States.

In the 2016 presidential election, however, this decades-long ideological overreach faced its proverbial "tipping point." After millions of outsourced union jobs, billions of cuts in welfare support, and trillions of lost GDP during the Great Recession, caused by the financial industry's "reckless endangerment" (Gretchen Morgenson), the long predicted demagogue did arrive (see Introduction, VI). Given the peculiarities of the United States Electoral College, this tabloid celebrity and reality TV star only needed a winning margin of fewer than one hundred thousand mostly blue collar votes in the three "Rust Belt" states Pennsylvania, Michigan, and Wisconsin to clinch the decisive 46 electoral votes.

After the election, United Steelworkers president Leo Gerard acknowledged in a letter to the union's 600,000 members the role that the demagogic exploitation of labor's opposition to the TPP agreement played: "Trump used our own words to speak to these problems, and to the real suffering, fears and anxieties that so many felt" (quoted in Hofmann 2018: 11). Social media ads made this possible. For a fraction of the $100 million that the labor unions spent on a futile effort to educate their members about future President Trump's real views, like his support for outsourcing and his opposition to wage raises. Weaponizing algorithms for precision-targeting of union households with anti-TPP rhetoric was sufficient for him to win with a margin of barely 0.07 percent of the 134 million votes cast nationwide.

This outcome was not a fluke. In 2020, the margin of victory for the new President Biden was even slimmer. An advantage of only about 42,500 votes secured for him the decisive 37 electoral votes from Georgia, Arizona, and Wisconsin. Conversely, incumbent President Trump lost by less than 0.03 percent of the 160 million votes cast by the American electorate. In spite of his scandal-ridden tenure, culminating in his impeachment by the U.S. House of Representatives, he received about seven million additional votes compared to 2016.

The extreme polarization of the American electorate and these razor-thin margins of victory and defeat have created a fertile ground for conspiracy theories about stolen elections. Once inconvenient news about voter preferences is increasingly brushed aside as "fake news," cognitive perception in the political public sphere can gradually become deformed. Especially since the intentional production of false news about stuffed ballot boxes for dissemination on social media occurs more and more often. As Habermas emphasizes in 2021, the significant factor in this process of deformation is not the quantitative increase in the creation of false news, but the growing inability of voters to identify them as such and to distinguish them from only allegedly "fake news" (Habermas 2021: 497-98). To highlight the gravity of this challenge to political deliberation, he adds that in a world where through digital manipulation factual and false news can no longer be distinguished, "no child would be able to grow up without developing clinical symptoms" (Habermas 2021: 499).

Habermas takes this clear and present danger for the deliberative process of democratic formation of public opinion and political will so seriously that he is expanding his analysis of digital media and the crisis of democracy into a book-length study titled "A New Structural Transformation of the Public Sphere and the Deliberative Politics," to be published in Germany in September 2022. As section VII of the Introduction to this guide will discuss in more detail, there is an urgent need to do so. For the creation of "alternative facts," officially introduced by President Trump's aides on Inauguration Day 2017, has by now become the new normal for authoritarian regimes around the globe.

Social media like Facebook, TikTok, YouTube, and Twitter play a key role in this process of constructing an alternative reality. They allow to completely whitewash the history of a brutal and corrupt dictatorship, if in a country like the Philippines out of a population of nearly 110 million about 92 million are social media users and receive their political news mostly that way. Especially livestream videos of election rallies by Ferdinand Marcos, Jr. which are difficult to immediately fact-check and flag can be used to disseminate the most brazen lies about the 1986 "People Power" Revolution that ended the self-described "constitutional authoritarianism" of Ferdinand Marcos, Sr. and sent his family into exile. The cynical spreading of falsehoods is emblematic for a country that Facebook once called "patient zero" of disinformation and where 56 percent of eligible voters have no recollection of the popularity of Corazon C. Aquino in this hard-won fight for liberal democracy, because they are between 18 and 41 years old. Unable to remember how her husband was assassinated after he had exposed the corruption of the Marcos family, they can even be susceptible to the vile insinuation that Aquino herself was dishonest, because under her administration the debt of the Philippines allegedly doubled to $50 billion (Elemia 2022).

This example illustrates in a nutshell how social media can be used to corrupt the process of political will-formation itself. Already in 1940, the sociologist Karl Mannheim voiced his concern about the erosion of democratic procedures once citizens start looking at each other "through a tradesman's eyes" (quoted in Hofmann 2018: 14). This certainly was the case as early as 1905 when the powerful New York State Senator George Washington Plunkitt told a reporter: "I have a marketable commodity—one vote" (quoted in Riordon 1965). Today, social media influencers in the Philippines monetize their skill to spread political falsehoods by striking a responsive chord with the target audience. Their corruption is hidden, because there is no need for Marcos Junior to directly pay them. Instead, during the livestreams from his election rallies the attention of their followers is automatically auctioned off by the social media companies to consumer product brands for advertising *their* commodities. This way, a 27-year-old former Filipino salesman can earn close to $10,000 a month as a full-time YouTuber (Elemia 2022).

The main skill of these political manipulators on social media consists of appearing to be authentic by speaking the language of down-to-earth people in amateur-grade videos that can be produced by anybody who owns a smartphone and a selfie stick. Tragically, the other "skill" seems to be an ingrained cynicism acquired by witnessing the return of endemic corruption in Filipino governance that has already sent two former presidents to jail. At least this might be a plausible explanation for the response of a 44-year-old TikTok producer with 24,000 followers to a *New York Times* reporter. When informed about the correct figure of the national debt under Aquino, she remained unfazed: "So what if it's incorrect?" (quoted in Elemia 2022). After all, her video broadcasting the false $50 billion figure achieved 27,000 lucrative views.

In other words, the crisis in democratic governance that Habermas is warning about threatens to become systemic once the vast majority of citizens conducts their political discourse on social media as a digital shopping mall—thus replacing the public interest orientation of citizenship with the private gain mentality of salesmanship. At that point, fake news might become the new medium of public discourse. As the manager of the winning Marcos Junior campaign already claims today: "All candidates, all political parties engage in disinformation" (quoted in Elemia 2022).

Introduction

The Unique Significance of Structural Transformation of the Public Sphere *for the Theory and Practice of Democratic Deliberation*

I. THE RENEWED POLITICAL RELEVANCE OF HABERMAS'S GLOBAL ACADEMIC BEST SELLER

Sixty years after *Strukturwandel der Öffentlichkeit* [*Structural Transformation of the Public Sphere*] (1962/1989) was first published in West Germany, Jürgen Habermas's global academic best seller has been translated into 27 languages. In May 2022, it was listed on Google Scholar with nearly 33,600 citations. In the *Habermas Handbook* (2017), Nancy Fraser, the social philosopher and Habermas scholar with almost 14,700 citations for her essay "Rethinking the Public Sphere: A Contribution to the Critique of Actually Existing Democracy" (1990/1992), calls his *public sphere* theory "the most influential of Habermas's signature concepts." She then adds: "Unlike 'communicative action,' 'discourse ethics,' and 'the colonization of the lifeworld,' which are discussed principally by specialists, this concept has become a major focus of work ranging from history, law, politics, and sociology to literature, philosophy, gender studies, and media studies" (Fraser 2017: 245).

Written in English as the *lingua franca* of worldwide Habermas scholarship, *Reading Habermas: Structural Transformation of the Public Sphere* addresses readers in all these fields of academic study as well as educated citizens around the globe. As the recent voluminous study *Habermas global* (2019) about the international reception of Habermas's major works analyzes, *Structural Transformation* has for decades been a modern classic in academic curricula and in public discourse not only in German-language countries. Even before the book was translated into English in 1989, the geographical reach of its translations extended from Norway and Italy in 1971 to Japan in 1973, and from France in 1978 to Latin America by the mid-1980s after the publication of its Spanish (1981) and Portuguese (1984) editions (HG 854, 839–40, 845, 832, 871, 858).

In his famous Kyoto speech from November 2004, Habermas anticipated the key reason for the dramatically increased public and scholarly focus on *Structural Transformation* since Donald J. Trump's victorious social media campaign in November 2016, which itself had been foreshadowed by the Brexit campaign's demagoguery on Facebook. In Habermas's words, the vital state of a democracy "can be assessed by listening to the heartbeat of its political public sphere" (Habermas, November 2004). Already in the April 2017 issue of the *Boston Review*, the political scientist William E. Scheuerman emphasized that *Structural Transformation* not only "antici-pated the emergence of authoritarian populism" in countries like Turkey and Hungary, but "also sometimes makes for an illuminating reading of Donald Trump's United States" (Scheuerman 2017).

Of the more than 33,000 scholarly citations for *Structural Transforma-tion* in the 33 years since its English translation was first published, more than one third were accumulated during the four years of President Trump's tenure. In short, the annual average roughly tripled. Already these figures clearly demonstrate that the public *and* the academic discourse about the concrete responsibilities of democratic citizenship, which inform Haber-mas's classic, accelerated into top gear once the former reality TV host and *Fox & Friends* regular started using his tweets from the White House to discredit *The New York Times* and other liberal media of the bourgeois public sphere with the Stalinist label "enemies of the people." Trump & Brexit thus not only legitimized Russia's and China's Stalinist tendency to replace the public discourse of open minds with the social engineering of docile souls. This astounding Anglo-American turn, orchestrated by the oldest parliamentary democracy and by the first one to have a written con-stitution, very much encouraged authoritarian leaders around the globe in their persecution of journalists.

Of course, one has to differentiate. While currently authoritarian democracies like Brazil and India punish the pursuit of free speech "only" by incarceration, traditional dictatorships like Saudi Arabia do not refrain from the medieval dismemberment of a *Washington Post* columnist. They know full well that business as usual with the modern Western world will resume after a year of keeping up the appearances of deal-making abstinence. Even a CIA report with all the seamless forensic evidence imaginable is no match for the imperatives of military strategies for the Middle East and for the unique cynicism of *Realpolitik* (Hubbard 2020; Timur and Hubbard 2021).

II. AFTER *THE END OF HISTORY*: THE ADVANTAGES OF HISTORICAL SPECIFICITY IN HABERMAS'S ORIGINAL PUBLIC SPHERE CONCEPT

Ironically, after 1989, when its belated English translation facilitated the global distribution of *Structural Transformation*, the future seemed to look bright for a universal implementation of Habermas's Kantian concept of the public sphere as the core organizational principle of liberal democracies *and* as the method of Enlightenment for their citizens engaged in public discourse. After all, the Soviet leader Gorbachev's reform policy of *glasnost*, i.e. transparent governance, had initiated the unforeseen uprisings against the absolutism of the Warsaw Pact states. As the communication scholar John Durham Peters analyzed, the Russian term *glasnost* forms the precise equivalent of the Kantian understanding of *Öffentlichkeit* (publicness) as the process of exposing secrecy by making "the deliberations within the state visible to all citizens, and hence subject them to public criticism" (Peters 1995: 10).

Arguably, these first years after the fall of the Berlin Wall in November 1989 influenced Habermas's far-reaching revisions of his original public sphere concept, which he had researched since 1985 and published as his proceduralist discourse theory of law in Germany in 1992 under the title *Faktizität und Geltung: Beiträge zur Diskurstheorie des Rechts und des demokratischen Rechtsstaats*. In 1996, this "monumental work of philosophy and social theory" (Rosenfeld and Arato 1998: 1), was translated into English as *Between Facts and Norms: Contributions to a Discourse Theory of Law and Democracy*. By May 2022, it had gathered about 17,600 citations on Google Scholar. Twelve years before he would reflect on "The Kantian Project and the Divided West" (2004/2006) and voice in Kyoto his renewed concerns about the state of liberal democracy, Habermas emphasized in New York City that a "world-historical event like the collapse of the Soviet empire certainly requires us to rethink our political positions" (Habermas 1998: 442). During this "first comprehensive and in-depth public discussion of all major aspects" of *Faktizität und Geltung* at the Benjamin N. Cardozo School of Law in September 1992 (Rosenfeld and Arato 1998: 1), he agreed that "an heir to revolution" can only be found "in a political culture of unleashed communicative freedom," created in the lifeworld of civil society's social movements (Habermas 1998: 442). In other words, by liberating *glasnost* from its twin policy of *perestroika*, namely economic reform and reconstruction. As the constitutional law theorist and historian William E. Forbath remarked in retrospect: "More than once during this conference Habermas commented on the question of economic democracy as though the failure of socialism and the success of the American economy defined the limits of the possible" (Forbath 1998: 286).

It is perhaps emblematic for the failure of the neoliberal "shock doctrine" when trying to introduce democratic capitalism in Russia and for the subsequent rise of an equally corrupt and authoritarian oligarchy that the Russian translation of *Structural Transformation* appeared only in 2016 (HG 865). In other words, seventeen years *after* the book's publication in China (HG 826), where all hopes for a liberal democracy had been crushed as early as June 1989. This bloodbath that ended the democratic student movement for political reforms was, only three months later, on the minds of the participants at the legendary Chapel Hill conference that introduced the English translation of *Strukturwandel der Öffentlichkeit*. It also spawned *Habermas and the Public Sphere*, the seminal conference reader edited in 1992 by the sociologist and Habermas scholar Craig Calhoun. Widely used as a textbook, it has by now accumulated more than 5,300 citations on Google Scholar.

Significantly, the reader contains Habermas's "Concluding Remarks," in which he responded to the still highly relevant question about "the need to have a more contextually and historically specific analysis of social movements . . ." While insisting on "the institutional differentiation between the science system . . . and political action," Habermas nevertheless conceded that the questioner was "completely right to ask [him] why [he is] engaging in these abstract things, speech-act theory, moral theory . . . without entertaining a historically focused, straightforward analysis" (CR 471). This crucial acknowledgment dovetails with Calhoun's analysis in *Habermas and the Public Sphere* that "the historical specificity and grasp of concrete social-institutional foundations give *Structural Transformation* some advantage over Habermas's later theory" (HPS 33).

III. THE REWARDING CHALLENGES OF READING *STRUCTURAL TRANSFORMATION OF THE PUBLIC SPHERE*

In 2003, the philosopher Thomas McCarthy who as a leading Habermas scholar deserves the most credit for having introduced in the 1970s and 1980s Habermas's works to an English-speaking global audience, precisely identified the challenge that scholars face if they want to employ *Between Facts and Norms* to analyze the crisis of liberal democracy in the wake of globalization. As McCarthy concluded in the British philosophical journal *Mind* after analyzing the level of abstraction that Habermas's theory construction had reached: "[*Between Facts and Norms*] is not a work aimed directly at a critical theory of contemporary democracy; it is a work in *Rechtstheorie* intended to articulate and justify the normative standpoints from which such a critical theory might set out" (McCarthy 2003: 763–64).

Six years earlier, long before the full social and political impact of the North American Free Trade Agreement (NAFTA) and the admission of China to the World Trade Organization would become dramatically visible in the "Rust Belt" of the United States, this remoteness of *Between Facts and Norms* from the many concrete challenges of everyday democratic life was pointed out in the September 1997 issue of the journal *The American Political Science Review*. Interestingly, the author of that book review was Seyla Benhabib, the Yale philosopher who once witnessed in Starnberg the creation of Habermas's first magnum opus, *The Theory of Communicative Action* (1981/1984, 1987). After commenting on the book's "statesman-like optimism" that reflected "the euphoria of the democratic moment after 1989," Benhabib noted:

> What is missing in this work is a recognition of "democracy's discontent" (Michael Sandel). The rise of right-wing charismatic leaders such as Perot or Berlusconi, who exploit the circus of the electronic media; the surge of neo-fascist movements in Western Europe, which mobilize strong we-identities against foreigners, immigrants, and asylum seekers; the dismantling of the welfare state by neoliberal governments. . .; the tremendous sense of apathy, cynicism, and disillusionment with the political process. . .; the eclipse of popular sovereignty through the rise of new financial, capital, and communication networks–all are missing from Habermas's account of democracy. (Benhabib 1997: 726)

Viewed from this background perspective, it appears to be only logical to turn again to *Structural Transformation* as the seemingly straightforward historical analysis of the public sphere in the bourgeois constitutional state. However, readers of Habermas's first book on this topic face their own significant challenges. As Habermas warned in 1990: "Only to a superficial glance would it have appeared possible to write *Structural Transformation* along the lines of a developmental history of society in the style of Marx and Max Weber" (FRPS 442). Actually, for most readers even an in-depth look might not be sufficient. Contrary to Habermas's assertion in his "Further Reflections on the Public Sphere" (1990/1992), his book's dialectical structure and dazzling synthesis of conservative, liberal, and Hegelian-Marxist sources does *not* wear "the ideology-critical approach on its sleeve" (FRPS 442).

What McCarthy noted in his "Translator's Introduction" to *Legitimation Crisis* (1973/1975), Habermas's systems-theoretical interpretation of the public sphere in the context of the social and political crises of advanced capitalism, can in principle also be applied to *Structural Transformation*: "Habermas can be quite difficult to read, and the present volume is a case in point. It makes unusual demands on the reader, assuming some familiarity with a wide range of disciplines (from economics to ethics), authors (from Kant to Parsons), and approaches (from systems theory to phenomenology)" (LC viii). Moreover, in his "Further Reflections" Habermas himself acknowledged "that the original study [i.e., *Structural Transformation*] emerged from the synthesis of contributions based in several disciplines, whose number even at that time almost exceeded what one author could hope to master" (FRPS 421).

Not surprisingly, this sophisticated dialectical structure of *Structural Transformation* continues to be misunderstood quite frequently even by some Habermas scholars, if they are not well-versed in the Marxist critique of ideology by Herbert Marcuse, Max Horkheimer, Theodor W. Adorno, and Ernst Bloch. Habermas dialectically synthesized these different Marxist critiques into his key methodology, which allowed him to rationally reconstruct the Kantian ideal of the public sphere as "an illustration of what his idea of a 'philosophy of history with practical intent' might look like when worked out in greater detail," as the political philosopher Kenneth Baynes analyzed in 2016 (Baynes 2016: 21). In spite of the inherent challenges that Habermas's complex synthesis poses, he barely mentioned and certainly did not systematically explain his methodological sources. Above all, Habermas acknowledged only at the 1989 Chapel Hill conference that he "was at least not careful enough in distinguishing between an ideal type [of the liberal public sphere] and the very context from which it was constructed." Hence, "the collapsing of norm and description came into the book" (CR 463).

Writing in Germany in March 1990, Habermas further explained the magnitude of the methodological challenges for the reader when trying to untangle this intricate entwinement of normativity and facticity woven into *Structural Transformation*. Looking back on his elaborate and rarefied approach, he realized that his construction of a dialectical relationship between the "ideals of bourgeois humanism" and the "constitutional reality" of state institutions infused by them, in order to fuel the "dynamic of historical development" toward achieving these ideals, "makes it tempting to idealize the bourgeois public sphere in a manner going way beyond any methodologically legitimate idealization of the sort involved in ideal-typical conceptualization" (FRPS 442). But even this belated acknowledgment still takes it for granted that the reader is familiar with Max Weber's sociological concept of the "ideal type" and its application in Carl Schmitt's *Constitutional Theory* (1928/2008), a key source for *Structural Transformation*.

IV. ACCESSING THE DIALECTICAL STRUCTURE OF HABERMAS'S THEORY RECONSTRUCTION

My book *Habermas's Public Sphere: A Critique* (2017) set out to make a contribution to the interdisciplinary discourse on *Structural Transformation* by systematically analyzing all the complex and contradictory sources for the text, including the tacit ones. As I highlight in my 2020 review of the intellectual history *Der junge Habermas* ["The Young Habermas"] (2019) by Roman Yos about the period 1952 to 1962, Habermas early on adopted from the editors of the German public intellectuals journal *Merkur* the dialectical approach of "polarizing" with regard to "the selection of authors as well as of topics" (Yos 2019: 244n136; Hofmann 2020: 377). In other words, since his 1954 *Merkur* essay titled "Dialektik der Rationalisierung" ["Dialectic of Rationalization"], Habermas has demonstrated a "vital desire to controversially pair intellectual traditions," as one of his assistants in the 1960s, Ulrich Oevermann, would emphasize in 1999 when looking back on the occasion of Habermas's seventieth birthday (quoted in HPSC 21n24). Similarly, Rolf Wiggershaus, one of Habermas's former doctoral students, observes in his seminal work about *The Frankfurt School: Its History, Theory, and Political Significance* (1986/1994) that already in his 1958 essay "Zum Begriff der politischen Beteiligung" ["On the Concept of Political Participation"] (1958/1973), Habermas simultaneously juxtaposes and integrates Critical Theory's "idea of democracy" with texts by "conservative and authoritarian critics hostile to modern mass democracy —closed em dash Ernst Forsthoff, Carl Schmitt, Werner Weber and Rüdiger Altmann" (Wiggershaus 1986/1994: 548; CPP 16, 23–24, 25, 26–27, 28, 31n42, 36n47, 37, 38, 41, 43–44, 45, 49; cf. Specter 2010: 48–52).

Finally, in 1991 Richard Holub, a scholar of German literature, directly asked the key questions: "Why has Habermas over the past three and a half decades been so eager to enter into controversy? Why has he sought to challenge so many people in various disciplines, from philosophy and sociology to history and political science?"

Answering his own questions, Holub explained that through this approach "Habermas has advanced his own theory in 'dialectical' fashion." Specifically, while he "often rejects an adversarial position," Habermas "simultaneously incorporates significant dimensions of that same position into his own theoretical outlook" (Holub 1991:1).

Habermas's Public Sphere: A Critique analyzes in precise detail how both the structure and the substance of *Structural Transformation* employ exactly this approach especially with regard to *Critique and Crisis* (1959/1988) by Schmitt's student Reinhart Koselleck as well as regarding the following texts by Schmitt himself: *Constitutional Theory* (1928/2008), *The Leviathan in the State Theory of Thomas Hobbes* (1938/1996), *The Crisis of Parliamentary Democracy* (1923/1985), *The Concept of the Political* (1932/1976), and *Die Diktatur* (1921). My study systematically demonstrates how Habermas uses the Marxist critique of ideology in dialectical fashion for his theory reconstruction of Immanuel Kant's ideal of a rational-critical public by selectively appropriating key elements of Koselleck's and Schmitt's texts while simultaneously upending their conservative critique of liberalism and the Enlightenment. I also make *Structural Transformation*'s dialectical method transparent by filling in the unexplained theses and antitheses while clearly delineating the respective syntheses which form the building blocks of Habermas's narrative. As the sociologist Ralf Dahrendorf, Habermas's contemporary and early colleague at Horkheimer's Frankfurt Institute diagnosed in his 1962 review, *Structural Transformation*'s highly selective stylizations of French, English, and German intellectual, social, and political history are seamlessly "cast into one uniform mold" that seemingly forms *the* universal ideal type of the bourgeois public sphere (Dahrendorf 1962: 783).

In short, readers of this guide can benefit from the systematic unveiling of *Structural Transformation*'s key sources and methodologies in my previous book on Habermas's public sphere concept. After identifying and clarifying the main components of Habermas's complex scholarly endeavor, it is now possible to communicate the essence of his unique concept in a widely accessible language and to efficiently guide the reader to a fuller understanding of his lasting contribution to "critical social theory and democratic political practice" (Nancy Fraser 1992).

V. HABERMAS'S DISCOVERY OF THE PUBLIC SPHERE AS A CENTRAL CATEGORY OF MODERNITY

The overarching objective of this guide to reading *Structural Transformation* is to convey the magnitude of Habermas's project to ground his theory reconstruction of the Kantian ideal of the public use of reason in a political economy of seemingly uncoerced social relations, the modern basis for the realization of the ancient ideal of the *polis* where "everything was decided through words ... and not through force" (Arendt 1958). Hence, by designating "a central institution of modern society, one that previously lacked a name, Habermas's concept of the public sphere enjoys a status akin to that of a scientific discovery," as Fraser emphasizes (Fraser 2017: 245).

Simultaneously, introducing Fraser's analysis in this context guides the reader toward the recognition of Habermas's basic self-understanding expressed in *The Philosophical Discourse of Modernity* (1985/1987): "Modernity can and will no longer borrow the criteria by which it takes its orientation from the models supplied by another epoch: *it has to create its normativity out of itself*" (PDM 7, emphasis in the original). In other words, the modern *public sphere* with its rational-critical discourse about commodity exchange and social labor in the *political* economy categorically differs from the *polis* of antiquity, which excludes the private economy from the *res publica* (HPSC 3). Habermas's claim from 1962 is still valid: *Structural Transformation*'s historical interpretation and sociological clarification of the concept of the public sphere allows the reader to attain "a systematic comprehension of our own society from the perspective of one of its central categories" (STPS 4–5).

It was a fortunate coincidence that Arendt's seminal reflections on the "rise of the social" in modernity, defined by its intrusion into the ancient realm of the public matters, and C. Wright Mills's on the "eighteenth-century idea" about a parallel between the private autonomy in the markets and in the public were published in 1958 (*The Human Condition*) and 1956 (*The Power Elite*), respectively. Habermas could thus construct a synthesis between the Greek template of communication free from domination and liberal capitalism's ideal type of a "society solely governed by the laws of the free market," which presents itself "as one free from any type of coercion" (STPS 79). This foundational parallel between, in Mills's words, "the market composed of freely competing entrepreneurs" and "the public of [autonomous] discussion circles of opinion peers" continues to present the criteria with which to assess democratic capitalism's adherence to the original tenets of liberal democracy (quoted in HPSC 95).

Since Kant, liberal constitutional law has sought to guarantee the equal participation of all citizens in the process of self-legislation via the "economic laws" of free and open markets with just exchange relations. Habermas emphasized this already in 1958, when he wrote down his first reflections "On the Concept of Political Participation" (cf. CPP 17). The democratic legitimacy of the bourgeois constitutional state thus depends on the factual representation of all members of the electorate in the parliamentary discourse of self-government.

In the year of his Kyoto speech, Habermas implicitly offered criteria for evaluating the "heartbeat" of the political public sphere at the center of the democratic process. Reflecting on the "Kantian Project," he pointed out that their "innovative concept of autonomy" allowed Rousseau and Kant to trace the "rational content of a law" back to the "legitimacy-generating procedure of democratic legislation" (DW 131). As the essence of this vital procedure, the "productive ideas of self-consciousness, self-determination, and self-realization," in one word: autonomy, "continue to shape the normative self-understanding of modernity" (DW193).

VI. AUTONOMY UNDER SIEGE: HABERMAS ON A NEW STRUCTURAL TRANSFORMATION OF THE PUBLIC SPHERE

In August 2021, Habermas reestablished the enduring viability of his concept by contributing the crowning chapter to a 500-page German collection of essays on a new structural transformation of the public sphere under the triple threat of globalization, digitalization, and commodification, which was edited by Martin Seeliger and Sebastian Sevignani. Acknowledging that *Structural Transformation* sold the most copies of all his books, he now also embraces the fundamental impact that his political concept of the public sphere has had on the social sciences. Above all, Habermas analyzes "the central role of the political public sphere" for self-determination in democratic will-formation as being under even greater siege today than it already was in 1962.

The transition of the commercial broadcast media from analog to digital technologies of production, transmission, and reception culminated during the last two decades in the creation of global social networks, which facilitate a new dimension in the commodification of political communication. Although Habermas warned already in 1962 about the dangers the democratic process faces, if citizens are turned into compliant consumers unable to distinguish between new products and political proposals (cf. STPS 216–17), he now regards them as an existential threat to the future of liberal democracy. The social media's algorithmic manipulation of consumer attention by turning their technological platforms into echo chambers for increasingly autistic narcissism, addicted to seeing "selfies" go viral, has in Habermas's view the power *to deform* already the *"perception of the political public sphere as such"* (Habermas 2021: 471, emphasis in the original).

In other words, once market logic sets the agenda for political discourse, "rational-critical debate tends to be replaced by consumption," as Habermas first noted in 1962 (STPS 161; SÖ 194). Accordingly, the "idols of the marketplace," which Francis Bacon identified as early as 1620, can begin to generate a "'world' of Fake News" (Habermas 2021: 499) indistinguishable from true information. As pointed out above in the Preface to this guide, such a deformation of cognitive perception as the prerequisite for human orientation would have dire consequences.

Currently, Facebook's algorithms privilege a perception of the democratic process that is cunningly distorted by stunning conspiracy theories, which in turn are designed to perpetually capture the attention of citizens whose autonomy has been reduced to predetermined consumer choice. A century ago, the political philosopher and public intellectual Walter Lippmann was the first to systematically analyze this distortion of the democratic will-formation in his classic study *Public Opinion* (1922). Significantly, Lippmann's concept of the "stereotype" can be traced back to the nineteenth-century printing technology of the stereotype plate. Combined with the rotary press, it facilitated the high-speed printing of the mass-circulation press. Cast out of hot metal, it permanently molded the currency of attention-grabbing prejudices, the forerunners of today's "viral" social media posts, ready for large print runs and vast circulation.

By integrating the term "stereotype" with reflections by John Dewey and William James about "the acquisition of meaning" in the process of human cognition, Lippmann defined "the perfect stereotype" as the one that "precedes the use of reason." It can be used as a weapon against self-determination, because it "govern(s) deeply the whole process of perception." How does the perfect stereotype manipulate? By imposing "a certain character on the data of our senses before the data reach the intelligence" (Lippmann 1922/1965: 59, 65).

In other words, "Fake News" as such is nothing new. On a mass-circulation basis, it was first set in type in the 1890s by Joseph Pulitzer's *New York World* and its fiercest competitor, William Randolph Hearst's *New York Journal*. Stereotyping prejudices became their signature technique to successfully hawk in the city streets one of the most perishable commodities: news. To strike the strongest responsive chord with the largest number of consumers, news was at least exaggerated if not invented to fit the most emotionally charged stereotypes (cf. Hofmann 2019: 51-52).

However, Habermas uses the example of the storming of the Capitol on January 6, 2021, to clarify that manipulating citizens with conspiracy theories to obstruct the constitutional certification of a democratic election in the United States Congress cannot be orchestrated out of thin air. Instead, he argues that this cynical act of manipulation was unwittingly facilitated by "the political elites who for decades had disappointed the legitimate, constitutionally guaranteed expectations of a substantial portion of their citizens." Specifically, these elites ignored that the "normative core of a democratic constitution . . . has to be anchored in the implicit convictions of the citizens themselves," who "have to be able to *trust*" that their votes count and that they are participating in "a fair and lawful governance which is democratically legitimated" and equally serves the interests of all. Moreover, the elites failed to safeguard the "social and institutional preconditions" for equal citizenship under which the normative idealizations of the constitution "alone remain *credible*" (Habermas 2021: 474, emphasis in the original.).

These social and institutional preconditions for the autonomy of citizens are spelled out in Articles 21 to 26 of the "Universal Declaration of Human Rights," approved by the General Assembly of the United Nations on December 10, 1948. Only "eight Soviet bloc countries" abstained, as Lynn Hunt points out in *Inventing Human Rights: A History* (2007). Habermas's reflections in 2021 connect to lectures he gave on the *Universal Declaration* at Princeton and at Frankfurt University in 2010 (cf. HPSC 49, 83n80). The latter focused on the *Declaration*'s "Concept of Human Dignity," which is highlighted in its Preamble as well as in its references to "the economic, social and cultural rights indispensable for [human] dignity" (Article 22).

Article 23 (3) is quite specific about the economic rights necessary to achieve human dignity: "Everyone who works has the right to just and favourable remuneration ensuring for himself and his family an existence worthy of human dignity, and supplemented, if necessary, by other means of social protection." These economic rights defined "the politics of the American dream," equality of opportunity in the pursuit of affluence for all, for thirty years until the late 1970s. In 1993, after fifteen years of accelerating deregulation and globalization of the economy, Edward N. Luttwak concluded in his book about *The Endangered American Dream* that once these politics "become too blatantly unrealistic for most Americans," liberal democracy itself "must become fragile." In other words, if "better hopes are worn away by bitter disappointment," the way will be opened "for the strong, false remedies of demagogues" (Luttwak 1993: 127).

Significantly, these words were written even before NAFTA was signed. Five years after they had been published, Habermas's fellow political philosopher Richard Rorty would adopt Luttwak's dire prediction. He expressed it even more starkly: "Members of labor unions, and unorganized, unskilled workers, will sooner or later realize that their government is not even trying to prevent wages from sinking or to prevent jobs from being exported. . . . At that point, [they] will . . . start looking around for a strongman to vote for" (Rorty 1998: 89–90).

In October 2021, Farah Stockman, a Pulitzer Prize winner and member of the *New York Times* Editorial Board, used this Rorty quote published "at the height of what has been called 'free trade euphoria'" for the dramatic ending of her book chapter "A Strongman to Vote For" (Stockman 2021: 197). In that chapter, she describes her personal reckoning regarding her long-time unquestioning adherence to *New York Times* columnist Thomas Friedman's "cheerful manifesto about globalization," *The World Is Flat: A Brief History of the Twenty-first Century* (2005) (Stockman 2021: 193). What caused her epiphany was her meticulous and perceptive reporting of the outsourcing of factory jobs to Mexico and its consequences, observed from the perspectives of three blue-collar workers (one female, two males; one African American, two Whites) during the time period February 2017 to January 2021.

Published only two months apart, Stockman's bottom-up and Habermas's top-down analyses dovetail. Her ability to closely listen to union members who tweet and vote for Trump allows her to gather the forensic evidence to provide concrete illustrations of Habermas's claim that since "the neoliberal change of politics, the democracies of the West have entered into a phase of increasing internal destabilization" (Habermas 2021: 484). As he emphasizes, liberal democracies lose their democratic legitimacy, if, "from the perspective of political and social justice," they no longer satisfy the interest of broad segments of society in "the legal and material preconditions for the exercise of their private and public autonomy" (Habermas 2021: 483).

VII. A CLEAR AND PRESENT DANGER: HABERMAS'S CRITIQUE OF AUTHORITARIAN GOVERNANCE THROUGH DIGITAL SURVEILLANCE, DISINFORMATION, AND MANIPULATED MEDIA EVENTS

Almost a quarter century after Benhabib's critique of *Between Facts and Norms*, the necessary "recognition of 'democracy's discontent'" is no longer missing in Habermas's reflections on anew *Structural Transformation of the Public Sphere.* Without mentioning the authoritarian governments of Hungary and Poland, he now identifies the "divisions within the European Union" as well as the "completed Brexit" as indicators for a likely "exhaustion of democratic regimes." Moreover, such a weakening of democratic governance might even signify "the return to a new form of imperialism in the global politics of the great powers" to deal with "the changed global economic and political situation" after "the rise of China" and other developing countries (Habermas 2021: 484). In this context, one must now also point to Russia's invasion of Ukraine and to its attempts to militarily reassert itself as a global power.

In Habermas's analysis, the increasing internal destabilization of liberal democracies, due to libertarian economic policies and mounting external pressures in the wake of globalization, is further amplified by "the challenges of the climate crisis and the growing pressure of migration" (Habermas 2021: 484). In 1997, after the first two decades of globalization, Benhabib diagnosed "the eclipse of popular sovereignty through the rise of new financial, capital, and communication networks" (Benhabib 1997: 726).

In 2021, Habermas could draw on an abundance of empirical evidence to describe a key result of this anti-democratic process. Namely, the growth of "social inequality" within liberal democracies in direct correlation to the curtailment of each nation-state's sovereignty "through the imperatives of globally deregulated markets" (Habermas 2021: 484).

In December 2021, President Biden's "Summit for Democracy" called for safeguarding democracy and human rights by rallying the world's democracies against Russia and China's authoritarianism as "the defining challenge of our time." Specifically, his administration seeks to fight "digital authoritarianism" by strictly controlling the export of information technologies needed by "surveillance states" (Crowley and Kanno-Youngs 2021: A 6). However, his speech did not address the software needed for their surveillance practices. Namely, the techniques of "surveillance capitalism" introduced by Google in 2001 and developed into its current form since 2008 by Facebook.

The economist Shoshana Zuboff comprehensively analyzed these extremely sophisticated manipulation techniques in her seminal study *The Age of Surveillance Capitalism: The Fight for a Human Future at the New Frontier of Power* (2019). Habermas references her book. Arguably, her analysis might have motivated him to use harsh language in his critique of Silicon Valley start-ups, who were initially celebrated as the incarnation of "democratic capitalism." Google's and Facebook's systemic contempt for the private autonomy and "inalienable individuality" of all human beings using their search engine and social media services is captured in Habermas's wording that the initially "anti-authoritarian and egalitarian potential" of the Internet "soon petrified in the libertarian grimace of digital corporations that dominate the globe" (Habermas 2021: 472, 488).

On December 10, 2021, the 73rd anniversary of the United Nations "Universal Declaration of Human Rights," Maria Ressa, head of the digital news site *Rappler* in the Philippines, was one of two journalists who received the Nobel Peace Prize. *Rappler*'s reporters had investigated the extrajudicial killings of suspected drug dealers or users ordered by President Rodrigo Duterte as well as his government's disinformation campaign on Facebook. Afterward, Ressa was arrested ten times in two years and convicted of "cyber libel" in 2020 (Bengali and Santora 2021: A4; Hopkins 2021: A9; Hammer 2019 /2021; Ressa and Thompson 2021: SR 3).

As Ressa pointed out two days later in a *New York Times* opinion article, in the five years of President Duterte's tenure already 22 journalists had been killed in the Philippines. The most recent victim, one of her colleagues, was shot in the head coinciding with her arrival in Oslo. In the same week, the Committee to Protect Journalists noted in its annual report that such warnings by authoritarian governments to investigative reporters have become standard practice (Ressa and Thompson 2021: SR 3; Cohen, Wee, and Troianovski 2021: A 5; *New York Times* Editorial 2021: SR 8).

Nevertheless, the Filipino leadership was included in the wall of electronic screens that President Biden looked at during his virtual "Summit for Democracy." Seemingly, the strategic role of the Philippines in American efforts to contain China's military expansionism in the South China Sea defines the limits of the possible. For the country keeps its official designation as one of only 19 "major non-NATO" allies of the United States worldwide (Shear 2022: A 9), even if Duterte's prosecution of critical journalists is particularly provocative and getting worse. Already in 2020, his regime was ranked only 138th on a list of 180 nation states in a global survey of press freedoms conducted by Reporters Without Borders (Hopkins 2021, A 9).

In other words, President Biden's "Summit for Democracy" was challenged when trying to live up to the most enduring legacy of the Enlightenment and the constitutional revolutions of the 18th century, namely, the First Amendment to the United States Constitution. It is precisely in this context that Habermas's theory of democracy can make a difference by substantiating the necessary human rights orientation. His unwavering research program of reconstructing "the rational substance of the norms and practices," which through the ratifications of the republican constitutions of the late eighteenth century have achieved historical validity (Habermas 2021: 471), gains particular significance when applying it to the study of this constitutional norm and the process of implementing it.

As Hunt documents in her history of human rights, the "Virginia Declaration of Rights on June 12, 1776" was the first to include "a list of specific rights such as freedom of the press and freedom of religious opinion" (Hunt 2007: 121). In turn, the Marquis de Condorcet highlighted Virginia's Declaration in his essay "The Influence of the American Revolution on Europe" (1786). Significantly, he dedicated it to the Marquis de Lafayette, the prominent French veteran of the War of American Independence. Already in January 1789, six months before the storming of the Bastille on July 14, Lafayette in all likelihood worked with Thomas Jefferson, the American minister in France, on the draft for a French declaration. In the following weeks, Condorcet "quietly formulated his own." On August 27, the deputies of the revolutionary French National Assembly adopted the seventeen articles they had already voted on "as their Declaration of the Rights of Man and Citizen" (Hunt 2007: 128, 16). Article 11 opened by amplifying the right to freedom of the press in the Virginia Declaration in vigorous terms: "The free communication of thoughts and opinions is one of the most precious of the rights of man" (quoted in Hunt 2007: 222).

In this trans-Atlantic constitutional history, the final step toward the First Amendment was taken by James Madison. Prodded by Jefferson's letters from Paris, he saw to it that this gap in the United States Constitution from 1787 was filled with even more vigor: "Congress shall make no law . . . abridging the freedom of speech, or of the press. . . ." Moreover, he made an extra effort to ensure that all states ratified the Bill of Rights by December 15, 1791.

Ten days after the White House "Summit on Democracy," a *New York Times* editorial reminded President Biden that Madison had regarded "the freedom of the press" as "one of the great bulwarks of liberty." For it was not only the assassination of an investigative journalist in the Philippines that coincided with this media event. Directly underneath its article headlined "Accepting Nobel Prize, Two Journalists Warn of Perils to Democracy," the *New York Times* reported the ruling by a British court to extradite WikiLeaks founder Julian Assange to the United States. It noted that one set of charges against him "could establish a precedent that journalistic-style activities like seeking and publishing information the government considers classified may be treated as a crime in the United States." And the Knight First Amendment Institute at Columbia University concluded: "The message of the indictment is that these activities are not just unprotected by the First Amendment but criminal under the Espionage Act." Finally, Reporters Without Borders tacitly made the connection to the White House summit when warning about the indictment's "dangerous implications for the future of journalism and press freedom around the world" (*New York Times* Editorial 2021: SR 8; Specia and Savage 2021: A 9).

Habermas's analysis of the manipulation of political discourse among *citizens* through the "algorithmic steering of communication flows" under the imperatives of an economy that seeks to maximize the attention of *consumers* (Habermas 2021: 498, 494), confirms Ressa's critique from the perspective of a media practitioner caught between the threats of government persecution and economic annihilation by global digital behemoths. Her Nobel Prize speech emphasized that, on one hand, the American social media companies "controlling our global information ecosystem" spread a "toxic sludge" of disinformation and hatred—thus "dividing us and radicalizing us" to bind us to their websites in a state of heightened attention. On the other hand, we face "another existential point for democracy," where we have to decide whether to "descend further into fascism" or "to fight for a better world." In other words, Ressa consciously drew a parallel to the global political situation in 1935, when the Nobel Peace Prize was awarded to the German journalist Carl von Ossietzky, who later perished in a Nazi concentration camp (Hopkins 2021, A 9).

To quantify this clear and present danger of a totalitarian control of democratic will-formation and self-governance, one can reference Facebook's artificial intelligence capability of "producing six million behavioral predictions each second." Once they are "weaponized as targeting algorithms," it becomes possible "to reinforce or disrupt the behavior of billions of people." Zuboff thus concludes that the "abdication of our information and communication spaces to surveillance capitalism has become the meta-crisis of every republic, because it obstructs solutions to all other crises" (Zuboff 2021: SR 8).

Already during the Cuban missile crisis, Habermas's critique of the transformation of a rational-critical public sphere into "a show set up for purposes of manipulation" (STPS 221) achieved an almost tragic validity. Based on secret Soviet documents released in the era of *glasnost* as well as on newly unclassified American ones, the former RAND corporation and Pentagon nuclear war planner Daniel Ellsberg concluded in 2017 that sheer luck, and not an allegedly superb brinkmanship of the Kennedy administration, allowed humankind to survive in October 1962 (Ellsberg 2017: 211–17; cf. section 3.3 below). Given today's "disinformation and hatred" spread by social networks, which Ressa points to, and the meta-crisis brought about by "targeting algorithms," which Zuboff analyses, one has to wonder whether even the sheerest luck will be sufficient to avoid an accidental nuclear mistake during Cold War 2.0 which started in earnest in February 2022.

Chapter One

Structural Transformation's Normative Theses about a Dissolution of Domination in the Bourgeois Public Sphere

1.1 *STRUCTURAL TRANSFORMATION'S* FIRST NORMATIVE THESIS, ITS CONTEXT IN CRITICAL THEORY, AND ITS CONNECTION TO HABERMAS'S "NEW STRUCTURAL TRANSFORMATION OF THE PUBLIC SPHERE" FROM 2021

Primarily, *Structural Transformation of the Public Sphere* has to be classified as *the* seminal contribution to the critical theory of democracy, which originated in the 1930s writings of the constitutional law scholar and political scientist Franz Neumann. He developed it in the context of the Frankfurt School in exile on Morningside Heights near Columbia University, where he would become a professor. In 1958, Habermas adopted Neumann's dictum that "democracy works on achieving the self-determination of humankind" (CPP 11; cf. HPSC 12). In 1962, he expanded on it by viewing its quest for autonomy in the tradition of Rousseau and Kant through Marcuse's critical theory as his theoretical framework.

Structural Transformation presents the result of this analytical process in the book's first normative thesis. It is highlighted as the climactic ending of Section 11 on "The Contradictory Institutionalization of the Public Sphere in the Bourgeois Constitutional State." Specifically, Habermas applies Marcuse's Marxist critique of ideology to rationally reconstruct what in 1971 he would call "the fiction of a discursive will-formation that dissolves political domination" (TAP 4; TUP 11). In 1962, he defines this result of his search for normative potential inherent in the bourgeois formation of the public sphere during the liberal era of capitalism as *"ideology and simultaneously more than ideology"* (emphasis added):

On the basis of the continuing domination of one class over another, the dominant class has nevertheless developed *political institutions* which credibly embody as their *objective meaning* the idea of their own abolition. (STPS 88; SÖ 110, emphasis added)

After fifty years, Habermas *reaffirms* in 2021 that this quest for the self-determination of humankind "was institutionalized for the first time within the political system of the bourgeois constitutional state" (TAP 4; TUP 11). For he again posits as the task of the theory of democracy the rational reconstruction of "the substantial reason inherent in the norms and practices, which since the constitutional revolutions of the late 18th century have achieved positive validity and have thus become a part of the historical reality." Specifically, Habermas now emphasizes that through the "'Declaration' of Human and Civil Rights the substance of rational morality," in the tradition of Kant's *universal* moral laws, "has migrated into the medium of binding constitutional law, constructed out of subjective rights." A process he valorizes as "*historically unprecedented* acts of founding democratic constitutional orders" (Habermas 2021: 471, 472, emphasis in the original).

When Habermas in 2021 ascribes to these constitutional orders grounded in basic law a "normativity that points beyond the status quo" (Habermas 2021: 472), he factually reconnects to his preliminary study for *Structural Transformation* from 1958, "Zum Begriff der politischen Beteiligung" ["On the Concept of Political Participation"] (1958/1973). In turn, the last part of his 1958 essay opened with an implicit reference to Marcuse's original concept of counterfactual thinking from 1937. Its substance had been essentially adopted by Horkheimer and Adorno in 1944 in an appended note to *Dialektik der Aufklärung* (1947/1969), translated as *Dialectic of Enlightenment* (1972 / 1986). In 1958, Habermas quoted it in that form with a key change that revived the spirit of Critical Theory in 1937.

Following Horkheimer's first part, Marcuse's counterfactual concept is contained in the second part of Critical Theory's foundational text, titled "Philosophie und kritische Theorie," ["Philosophy and Critical Theory"] (1937). It is based on his dialectical reading of bourgeois philosophy. On one hand, Marcuse concedes that the criteria inherent in the "rational philosophy of [German] Idealism undoubtedly turn it into bourgeois philosophy." On the other hand, he emphasizes that "already its unique concept of reason" establishes this rational philosophy as "*more than ideology*" (PCT 635, emphasis added).

To access this utopian surplus, Marcuse in 1937 posits that Critical Theory "has to abstract from the *existing status*" and "look toward the future status of human beings." Only then can it reflect on "the autonomy of the individual" and "the idea of humankind" (PCT 642, 643, 644, emphasis added). In 1944,

Horkheimer and Adorno change the wording but not the meaning when they replace Marcuse's reference to the "existing status" with the term "status quo." In addition, they use the neutral term "philosophy" when writing about the essence of Critical Theory:

> [Philosophy] is immune to the suggestion of the *status quo* for the very reason that it accepts the bourgeois ideals without further consideration. These ideals may be those still proclaimed, though in distorted form, by the representatives of the *status quo*; or those which, in spite of their manipulation, are still recognizable as the *objective meaning* of existing institutions. . . (DA 218; DE 243, emphases added, translation modified)

It is Habermas's use of the term "status quo" in the above quote from 2021 that can alert the reader to this fascinating thread of intellectual history, spanning more than eight decades. It adds to the challenge of this forensic analysis that in 1958 Habermas left out the reference to "the status quo" ["*des Bestehenden*"]. Nevertheless, he tacitly communicated to his mentor Adorno and his employer Horkheimer that he had traced their quote back to the Frankfurt School's programmatic text from 1937. For Habermas changed their neutral term "Philosophy" from 1944 back to the designation "Critical Theory" they used in 1937 to identify their political commitment:

> The analysis of the development of the bourgeois constitutional state and its current form adheres to the rules of Critical Theory, whose freedom consists in "accepting . . . the bourgeois ideals, whether those, which their (bourgeois) representatives even in distorted form still proclaim, or those, which as *objective meaning of institutions* . . ., in spite of all manipulation, are still recognizable. . . (CPP 53, emphasis added)

Critical Theory's commitment to the bourgeois ideals that define the "rational philosophy of [German] Idealism" not only permeates Marcuse's opening statement. It is also expressed in even starker language in the last paragraph of Horkheimer's part of Critical Theory's basic text: "The martyrs of freedom did not search for the tranquility of their souls. Their philosophy was politics." In 1937, Horkheimer highlighted this political difference between philosophy and Critical Theory with complete certainty: "The philosophy that wants to find tranquility within itself or in whatever truth is available, has . . . nothing to do with Critical Theory" (PCT 631).

After following these analytical steps, the reader of this guide is now familiar with both the mission statement and the key methodology tacitly employed in *Structural Transformation*. Habermas's above claim from 1962 that his thesis about the dissolution of political domination in the rational-critical public sphere reflected (bourgeois) *"ideology and simultaneously more than ideology,*" was directly inspired by Marcuse's wording "more than ideology" in his part of Critical Theory's essay from 1937. Similarly, the book's key term "objective meaning" can be traced back to the above quote from Horkheimer and Adorno's text completed in 1944.

Significantly, readers do not find this crucial information in *Structural Transformation,* where it could help them to comprehend especially the term "objective meaning." For this term not only determines its central theses, but also serves as a cryptic reference at key junctures of its argument. Instead, it took 24 years before Habermas revisited the *Dialectic of Enlightenment* in his essay *The Entwinement of Myth and Enlightenment* (1982). In 1982, he would openly hint at the source for Horkheimer and Adorno's quote from 1944 by pointing out that it "reads like an intrusion from the earlier period of Critical Theory." Moreover, he would include the Marcusean reference to the "status quo."

Above all, Habermas would not only acknowledge the assertive character of Critical Theory's methodology which he had tacitly adopted from 1958 to 1962, but also highlight it in italics. However, even after 20 years there is no reference to its use in *Structural Transformation*. And he reversed his 1958 switch by changing his veiled reference to Horkheimer's commitment to Critical Theory in 1937 back to his 1944 reversal which now condoned "tranquil" philosophy:

> The passage claims that philosophy's "immunity to the influence of the status quo is due to the fact that it *accepts the bourgeois ideals without further consideration.* (EME 20, emphasis in the original)

Finally, three decades after *Structural Transformation*'s first publication, Habermas would for the first time identify the "dialectic of the bourgeois public sphere, which determines the book's structure." This broad reference to his 1962 methodology is contained in his "Further Reflections on the Public Sphere" (1992). However, only the German-language readers of the Suhrkamp edition of *Strukturwandel der Öffentlichkeit* (1962/1991) can access this text from 1990, originally written in German, as the Preface to that new edition. English-language readers have to look for it in *Habermas and the Public Sphere* (1992), if they want to find Habermas's clearest acknowledgment of his 1962 book's reliance on the bourgeois ideals first discussed in Critical Theory by Marcuse in 1937:

> The *ideals of bourgeois humanism* that have left their characteristic mark on the self-interpretation of the intimate sphere and the public and that are articulated in the key concepts of subjectivity and self-actualization, rational formation of opinion and will, and personal and political self-determination *have infused the*

institutions of the constitutional state to such an extent that, functioning as an utopian potential, they *point beyond a constitutional reality that negates them.* (FRPS 442, emphasis added)

Habermas's "New Structural Transformation" text from 2021 leaves hardly any doubt that there is a clear parallel between the "normativity that points beyond the status quo" and the "ideals of bourgeois humanism" that "point beyond a constitutional reality that negates them," which he refers to in his 1992 reflections. His four-page excursus within his 2021 book chapter analyzes the development of universal rational morality and rational constitutional law in the process of the "European Enlightenment." This development culminates in the normative power of universal human rights that "overshoot" the boundaries set by the status quo (Habermas 2021: 472).

In short, his 2021 reflections clearly connect to *Structural Transformation*'s Section 13 on Kant and Section 12 on the intellectual history of the French Revolution and its Constitution of 1791. Together with his classic's crucial Section 11, they form the center of Habermas's 1962 argument.

1.2 *STRUCTURAL TRANSFORMATION'S* SECOND NORMATIVE THESIS, KANT'S "MORALLY PRETENTIOUS RATIONALITY," AND CLASSICAL POLITICAL ECONOMY'S "FICTION OF A JUSTICE IMMANENT IN FREE COMMERCE"

As the wording *"transcends the status quo"* in *Structural Transformation*'s second normative thesis below indicates, it is closely connected to the book's first one. But its argument moves on a more generalized level of abstraction. Habermas first addressed the specific bourgeois ideal about a dissolution of political domination in discursive will-formation with the ultimate goal of abolishing political institutions as such. Now he places this ideal in the context of the genesis of bourgeois ideology during the liberal era of capitalism and the bourgeois constitutional state:

If ideologies are not only manifestations of the socially necessary consciousness in its essential falsity, if there is an aspect to them that can lay a claim to truth inasmuch as it *transcends the status quo in utopian fashion*, even if only for purposes of justification, then ideology exists at all only from this period on. *Its origin would be the identification of "property owner" and "human being as such."* (STPS 88; SÖ 110, emphases added)

To fully comprehend this thesis, readers have to be aware that since 1955 Habermas had pursued a federally funded research project titled "The Concept of 'Ideology' and the Ideology-Critical Procedure" (Yos 2019: 154). While he had already read Horkheimer/Adorno's book from 1944 (cf. Hofmann 2020: 378), this research allowed him to detect the texts by Marcuse and Horkheimer on Critical Theory from 1937 discussed under 1.1. above. It also led him to Karl Mannheim's sociology of knowledge and its use in Hermann Heller's constitutional state theory, published in 1934 after Heller's death in exile from Nazi Germany (HPSC 6–7). As the following quote demonstrates, Heller employed Mannheim's ideology critique to reveal what Habermas refers to above as "the socially necessary consciousness in its essential falsity":

> According to its foundational legitimation, bourgeois society functions as the uncoerced interaction of equal forces. Essentially, it thus cannot justify any [economic and political] domination, least of all a domination based on class rule. (quoted in CCP 13)

Amazingly, this quote can be found in "On the Concept of Political Participation" (1958). After all, already in 1937 Marcuse had denounced "the business of the sociology of knowledge" for solely focusing on "the falsities but not on the truth of [bourgeois] philosophy" (PCT 640). And in 1957 Habermas had implicitly agreed with him by even sharpening Marcuse's business metaphor when he claimed that Mannheim as the leading representative of "bourgeois sociology. . . became famous overnight due to his clearance sale of Marxism" (quoted in HPSC 20n19). Nevertheless, only one year later Habermas essentially contradicted Marcuse's critique (and his own) when he solely focused on "the falsities" of bourgeois philosophy and very strongly agreed with Heller's analysis: "Of course, *such a society has never existed*" (CPP 17, emphasis added). Moreover, he confirmed his agreement by quoting in a lengthy footnote Heller's analysis of the claims of justice and equality in free commerce as "justifying ideologies" (CPP 17n15).

Conversely, identifying this contradiction clarifies for the reader that for his rational reconstruction of Kant's ideal of the liberal public sphere, Habermas had to decide to adopt Marcuse's methodology and "think against facticity" (PCT 642). Hence, one of the most fascinating challenges created by the unique complexity of Habermas's scholarship is the enigmatic relationship between *Structural Transformation* and the book's preliminary study "On the Concept of Political Participation." While Adorno praised this introduction to the empirical study "Student and Politik" ["Student and Politics"] (1961) as a "tour de force," Horkheimer regarded it as so controversial that he refused to let the results of the research project be published under the auspices of his Institute for Social Research at the University of Frankfurt. Accordingly, the authors of the study had to search for a new publisher and the book appeared with a delay of about two years (cf. Wiggershaus 1986/1994: 554–55; Yos 2019: 417–18).

As will be discussed below, Habermas omits the crucial differences between these two texts when he writes in 1971 that in both of them he "analyzed the *historical* interconnection between the development of capitalism and the rise and dissolution of the liberal public sphere" (TAP 4; TUP 11). For only in the first part of his 1958 essay did he offer a straightforward historical analysis of the institutionalized *division of powers* between the rising bourgeoisie and the politically still dominant aristocracy in the Belgian Constitution of 1831, *the* liberal model for the bourgeois constitutional states in Continental Europe. It paradigmatically oriented the role of the liberal public sphere toward achieving a *compromise* between competing interests instead of a *consensus* about an alleged identity between the bourgeois and the national interest, as *Structural Transformation*'s Section 11 posits in its interpretation of the English Reform Bill of 1832 (HPSC 7–8; STPS 87). Significantly, the degree to which Habermas had to think against facticity in Sections 4 to 7 and 10 to 12 becomes apparent when he starkly qualifies his book's two normative theses at the very end of Section 11:

> *However that may be*, the developed bourgeois public sphere is bound up with *a complicated constellation of social preconditions*; *in any event*, they have soon and profoundly changed and with their transformation the contradiction in the public sphere of the bourgeois constitutional state comes to the fore: with the help of its principle, which according to its own idea was opposed to all domination, *a political order was founded whose social basis did not make domination superfluous after all.* (STPS 88; SÖ 110, emphasis added)

Readers thus face the challenge of correctly identifying the various components of this "complicated constellation of social preconditions," which was necessary to conceptualize in Habermas's Kantian ideal type of the bourgeois public sphere a "morally pretentious rationality" (STPS 54) that generated *"in the public competition of private arguments"* a *"consensus about what was practically necessary in the interest of all"* (STPS 83, emphasis in the original). At the center of this "morally pretentious rationality," which in public discourse "strove to discover what was at once [morally] just and [rationally] right" (STPS 54), stood classical political economy's "fiction of a justice immanent in free commerce" (STPS 111). This fiction was derived from the alleged exchange of equivalents in "the free market . . . as a sphere free from domination" (STPS 79). The other half of such a "morally pretentious rationality" was provided by the fiction of "anonymous laws functioning in accord with an economic rationality immanent. . . in the market" (STPS 46).

Only the "fiction of a justice immanent in free commerce" allows the selfish *bourgeois* to appear "in the guise of the unselfish *homme.*" According to *Structural Transformation*'s second normative thesis, it is this identification of 'property owner' and 'human being as such,'" which marks *the origin of bourgeois ideology*. In short, it seemingly turns self-interested private property owners into "autonomous individuals per se" (STPS 111). Hence, these "human being[s] as such" (STPS 88) can develop "the ideas of freedom, love, and cultivation of the person" (STPS 48) in the bourgeois intimate sphere at the core of the private sphere of commodity exchange and social labor.

In other words, only "*the ideological guarantee* of a notion that market exchange was just" and that the laws of motion immanent in markets enabled "justice to triumph over force" (STPS 46, emphasis added) allowed Kant to conceptualize a "morally pretentious rationality" inherent in his idea of the bourgeois public sphere. It also enabled Habermas to rationally reconstruct the "bourgeois idea of the law-based state" as "the binding of all state activity to a system of norms" (STPS 82). These legal norms are legitimated by an enlightened public opinion, which asserts that bourgeois society's sphere of commodity exchange and social labor follows "[natural] laws of its own versus the interventions of the state" (STPS 95). If a "society solely governed by the laws of the free market" could present itself as one "free from any kind of coercion" (STPS 79), then Habermas could claim, in parallel fashion, that the bourgeois law-based state "already aimed at abolishing the state as an instrument of domination altogether" (STPS 82 top).

Chapter Two

Habermas's Dialectical Use of Ideology Critique to Counterfactually Assert a Moment of Historical Credibility for the Bourgeois Ideal of the Public Sphere

2.1. *STRUCTURAL TRANSFORMATION'S* COMPLICATED RELATIONSHIP BETWEEN IDEOLOGY-CRITICAL PROCEDURE AND HISTORICAL ANALYSIS

As chapter 5 will systematically analyze, *Structural Transformation*'s ideology-critical procedure tends to dominate the book's historical analysis. Only in retrospect does the reader learn at the beginning of Section 10 that the previous two sections on the British "Model Case" and its "Continental Variants" could, as "historical excurses," describe *but not explain* the "political functions" the bourgeois public sphere takes on during the eighteenth century (STPS 73). Since its "morally pretentious rationality" hinges on the "fiction of a justice immanent in free commerce," its political functions can only be understood once the private sphere of commodity exchange and social labor becomes "largely emancipated from government directives (STPS 74).

This introduction of "free trade," defined as "the effectiveness of free competition at home and abroad," generates the hallmark of the liberal phase of capitalism. It issues "from a unique historical constellation in Great Britain at the close of the eighteenth century." But this liberal phase lasts "only for one blissful moment in the long history of capitalist development." Only during this "liberal era," which reaches its height "in the middle of the nineteenth century," can, in Habermas's ideology-critical theory reconstruction of Kant's liberal model, the political public sphere "attain its full development in the bourgeois constitutional state" (STPS 78, 79).

However, readers have to realize on their own that in this ideology-critical interpretationthe "unique historical constellation in Great Britain," facilitated

27

by the Industrial Revolution in interconnection with a specific level of capital accumulation, could only provide the necessary condition for the full development of the bourgeois public sphere. Without the unique historical event of the French Revolution, the British "Model Case" would have remained an insufficient basis for the development of a rational-critical public sphere in the bourgeois constitutional state. Above all, it took the Hegelian-Marxist philosophy of history to combine these two revolutions. For *Structural Transformation* had to "disregard national differences" between Great Britain and France as merely "differences in the level of capitalist development" (STPS 267n65), if the book wanted to implement its ideology-critical procedure.

As sections 5.5 and 6.1 will discuss, this hegemony of ideology-critique over historical analysis turns Habermas's reflections on the prehistory of the phrase *opinion publique* in Section 12 into an analytical stylization of what might be called "The Tacit Model Case of French Development." On one hand, *Structural Transformation*'s historical excursus on the political developments before and during the French Revolution is relatively brief and culminates in a detailed description of its failure to successfully implement the constitutional freedom of the press after August 1792. On the other hand, the book's chapter IV on the "Idea and Ideology" of the bourgeois public sphere devotes in its Section 12 more pages to this topic, culminating in Habermas's signature stylization of the French Constitution of 1791 as the fusion of rational-critical debate, practiced by the Physiocrats, and Rousseau's concept of autonomous democratic legislation (STPS 99).

The substance of Physiocratic rational-critical debate was classical political economy. They were the first representatives of this "specifically bourgeois science" (STPS 29) to posit the claim, referenced above under 1.2, that civil society followed "[natural] laws of its own versus the interventions of the state" (STPS 95). As Habermas would emphasize in "Naturrecht und Revolution" ["Natural Law and Revolution"] (1963/1973), the leading Physiocrat Francois Quesnay "scooped Adam Smith regarding the insight of 'laissez faire,' which Le Mercier celebrated as the 'glory of our century'" (NLR 100; NR 106).

As early as 1756, Quesnay had "advocated in his article 'Fermiers' in volume VI of the *Encyclopedie* the free trade in grain, his long-term program to 'lift the whole economy out of its low-price equilibrium which he saw as a cycle of perpetual poverty'" (cf. HPSC 31). In other words, he provided the seemingly scientific justification for the bourgeois demand in the political public sphere that the private sphere of commodity exchange and social labor had to be liberated from government directives in the interest of all. As Quesnay added "in his article on 'Natural Right' in the *Encyclopedie*, the 'absolute property right' of grain owners 'was crucial to creating the incentive for improvements to agricultural productivity.' Any governmental system of 'police which requisitioned grain from their owners' in times of bad harvests to safeguard the supply of the populace and avoid famine 'fatally compromised these incentive effects'" (cf. HPSC 34–35).

Structural Transformation focuses on the French Constitution of 1791, because its text evolved, as Habermas discusses in "Natural Law and Revolution" (NLR 96; NR 102), out of the National Assembly's "Declaration of the Rights of Man and Citizen" from August 1789. Article 2 of the "Declaration" guarantees the property right, which Quesnay had demanded 33 years earlier, as a "natural right." Its preservation, together with that of the rights of liberty, security, and resistance to oppression, defines for the "Declaration" the "purpose of all political association" (quoted in Hunt 2007: 221).

Once free trade as the seemingly natural law of motion of society has been recognized as a natural right in "the constitutional revolutions of the late 18th century" (Habermas 2021: 471), *Structural Transformation*'s ideology-critical procedure can identify the fiction of a justice immanent in free commerce as the origin of bourgeois ideology with its conflation of selfish property owner and selfless human being in the ideals of bourgeois humanism. Historical analysis then serves the purpose of *selecting* the empirical material that documents the progress of a morally pretentious rationality in the political public sphere and of celebrating free trade:

> At the industrial revolution . . ., capital accumulation and investment were faced, from each point of the economic compass, with ever-widening horizons to lure them on. (Maurice Dobb, quoted in STPS 277n4; see STPS xviii)

2.2. EMPLOYING THE IDEOLOGY-CRITICAL PROCEDURE IN THE SEARCH FOR NORMATIVE POTENTIAL

Arguably, Habermas's August 2021 essay marks the completion of a gradual course correction in his scholarly work with significant consequences for intellectual history. Twenty years earlier, at the end of the second volume of his *Theory of Communicative Action* (1981/1989), he suggested "that the normative foundations of the critical theory of society be laid at a deeper level" to bring "into the open the rational potential intrinsic in everyday communication" (FRPS 442). A decade later, "Further Reflections" reaffirmed this paradigmatic turn and emphasized that "a social science that proceeds reconstructively, identifies *the entire spectrum* of cultural and societal rationalization processes, and also traces them back beyond the threshold of modern societies" (FRPS 442, emphasis in the original). The author of the seminal work on *The Philosophical Discourse of Modernity*, translated into English only five years earlier, then pointedly added:

Such a tack no longer restricts the search for normative potential to *a formation of the public sphere that was specific to a single epoch.* (FRPS 442, emphasis added)

This statement was somewhat surprising for all readers who were aware that in the same year in which the English translation of "Further Reflections" appeared, 1992, Habermas had published the German original of *Between Facts and Norms.* In spite of replacing the Hegelian-Marxist philosophy of history with systems theory as its new theoretical framework, the latter remains connected to *Structural Transformation* through the umbilical cord of Kant's rational natural law theory of the bourgeois constitutional state. Since Kant's moral-practical theory of the republican constitution was focused on "the formation of the public sphere that was specific to a single epoch," the normative potential that *Between Facts and Norms* draws on remains largely tethered to the liberal era.

Similarly, in 1981, in the same year in which Habermas announced that the normative foundations of the critical theory of society should be laid at a deeper level than Kant's liberal model of the bourgeois public sphere could offer, he voiced the perhaps clearest expression of his lifelong valorization of Kant's cognitive and moral universalism, which would culminate in his legacy lecture at the University of Frankfurt on June 19, 2019. Responding to an interview question by Axel Honneth, his future successor on Horkheimer's Frankfurt chair in philosophy, Habermas critiqued Horkheimer and Adorno's "undervaluation" of the Kantian "theory of democracy." From his perspective, the "formal features of *bourgeois* systems of law and constitutions" demonstrate "a conceptual structure of *moral-practical thought* . . . which must be considered *superior* in relation to the built-in moral categories of traditional and political institutions" (Habermas 1981/1986: 101, emphasis added).

It speaks for the consistency and commitment of Habermas's scholarly work that forty years later this assessment from 1981 can still be connected to his August 2021 reflections on the moral and cognitive potential of Kant's universalism, which guarantees all human beings equal treatment of and esteem for their "inalienable individuality" (Habermas 2021: 472). This unique commitment to the Kantian ideals of bourgeois humanism spans even six decades, if one looks at *Structural Transformation*'s observation in Section 11, that the "constitutional norms," which since the constitutional revolutions established the rational-critical public sphere, "implied a model of civil society that by no means corresponded to its reality" (STPS 84). For in August 2021, Habermas explains how since that time "the *previously unknown* tension of a normative gradient has embedded itself in the political consciousness of legally free and equal citizens" (Habermas 2021: 473, emphasis in the original). Hence, he remains "interested in the normality of the self-evident idealizations implemented by these citizens," who have "no choice but to *participate* in their civic practices with the intuitive (and counterfactual) *assumption* that the civil rights which they exercise generally keep what they promise" (Habermas 2021: 473, emphasis in the original).

Significantly, with this statement Habermas has come full circle by essentially linking to his first reflections on political participation from 1958. At a time when even France was ruled by an "authoritarian regime" with "pseudo-parliamentary" features, he emphasized that such a government depends on the assumption of its citizens that its political domination is "mediated by the rational self-determination of enlightened citizens." Hence, it "has to make certain, even by using the means of directing public opinion, to create and maintain such a consciousness" (CPP 13).

In other words, Habermas's critical theory of democracy has been practicing "a social science that proceeds reconstructively" for more than sixty years. However, while his focus has not changed, it has broadened to include, beyond the normative principles which infused the positive law, the "intuitive expectations and understandings of legitimacy on the part of the citizens." He now regards it as the task of democratic theory to "*rationally reconstruct*" both, for the purpose of "explaining the justifying reasons, which actually provide legitimizing energy for the factually exercised rule in the consciousness of its citizens" and can thus shape their "normative self-understanding" (Habermas 2021: 474, emphasis in the original).

In short, Habermas's interest in normative potential remains unchanged. Moreover, he continues to search for it with Marcuse's method of thinking "against facticity," which is implied in his more recent term "counterfactual." Only the stark juxtaposition of constitutional norms and "a constitutional reality that negates them" (FRPS 442) has been replaced by "the tension of a normative gradient" (Habermas 2021:473) between normativity and facticity.

2.3. *STRUCTURAL TRANSFORMATION*'S HISTORICAL VALIDITY, ITS SECTION 15 NEGATION OF A NATURAL ORDER OF CIVIL SOCIETY, AND ITS DIALECTICAL USE OF THE IDEOLOGY-CRITICAL PROCEDURE

In his contribution to the 1989 Chapel Hill conference, the historian Geoff Eley first emphasized that *Structural Transformation*'s "conception of the public sphere amounts to an ideal of critical liberalism that remains historically unattained" (HPS 289). However, later in his text he began to wonder whether Habermas shared his analysis. For Eley, this remains an open question:

> It is perhaps unclear how far Habermas believes his ideal of rational communication, with its concomitant of free and equal participation, to have been actually realized in the classic liberal model of *Öffentlichkeit*. (HPS 293)

So far, Habermas has not answered this question from his own perspective. Instead, he has quoted assessments voiced by other scholars which only indirectly refer to that question. When writing the original German text of "Further Reflections" in 1990, he began his reflections on the "Genesis and Concept of the Bourgeois Public Sphere" with praise for Eley's "friendly assessment in his extensive and comprehensively documented contribution to the conference..." (FRPS 423). However, Eley's praise, which Habermas quotes, includes neither a reference to his conclusion that *Structural Transformation*'s ideal "remains historically unattained" nor one to his question about Habermas's view on that matter. Instead, it sidesteps these issues and remains on a rather general level:

> On re-reading the book . . ., it is striking to see how secure and even imaginatively the argument is historically grounded. (Eley quoted in FRPS 423)

Following this quote, "Further Reflections" posits that *Structural Transformation*'s "basic lines" of analysis "have been corroborated" by the German historian "H.U. Wehler's summarizing presentation of a wide body of literature." As proof, Habermas quotes Wehler's statement that by "the end of the eighteenth century there had emerged, in Germany, 'a public sphere, although a small one, where critical-rational discussion was carried on" (Wehler quoted in FRPS 423). However, readers of Section 13 on Kant will immediately realize that Wehler only confirms the role of "critical-rational discussion" as "the method of enlightenment" (STPS 104). He does not address the question whether it there and then also became "the organizational principle of the bourgeois constitutional state" (STPS 87, 104).

In other words, there cannot be any doubt that Kant's foundational and timeless essay "What Is Enlightenment?" in the December 1784 issue of the *Berlinische Monatsschrift* was the object of "critical-rational discussion" in many intellectual centers of Prussia and other German states. Nevertheless, readers have to wonder about the scope and stability of this discussion. As section 5.1 will analyze, the topics of such an enlightened discourse, as Kant defined them in the Preface to the first edition of his *Critique of Pure Reason* from 1781, were only admissible under the rule of the enlightened monarch Frederick the Great. After his death, Kant deleted in the second edition from 1787 this programmatic call for a critique of Church and State. Moreover, even Frederick the Great, in the same year in which "What Is Enlightenment?" was published, announced strict boundaries for such a critique (cf. STPS 25).

Above all, when Section 11 announces its crucial assertion that "during that phase of capitalism, the public sphere as the organizational principle of the bourgeois constitutional state had credibility" (STPS 87), *Structural Transformation* does not refer to Germany but to the British Reform Bill of 1832 (cf. STPS 74). As will be discussed below, Habermas issued this bold claim despite the fact that eleven years *earlier* Hegel's discovery of "the profound split in civil society" had *"decisively destroyed the liberal pretenses* upon which the self-interpretation of public opinion as nothing but plain reason rested" (STPS 118, emphasis added). At the center of these liberal pretenses stood, as discussed above under 1.2, "the fiction of a justice immanent in free commerce" (STPS 111).

Decisively destroying this *"ideological guarantee"* that a natural law of markets self-regulates the equality of uncoerced exchange relations, so that justice will always "triumph over force" (STPS 46, emphasis added), had consequences. In Section 15, Habermas states that "around the middle of the [nineteenth] century, when economic liberalism was reaching its peak, its social-philosophical representatives were forced almost to deny the principle of the public sphere of civil society even as they celebrated it" (STPS 130). Specifically, these liberals cast into doubt "the very presupposition of a natural basis [of civil society] upon which the idea of a political public sphere rested" (STPS 131).

Of course, readers will not be surprised by this turning point in Habermas's well-known narrative about the rise and fall of the bourgeois public sphere. Especially since his stylization presents it almost symmetrically exact at the half-way point of his text of 250 pages, before end notes. However, what so far has been mostly neglected, and not publicly commented on by Habermas, is his harsh critique of "the dialectically projected counter-model" to the bourgeois public sphere by Marx (STPS 130) which is presented in Section 14 (STPS 122–29).

After all, in 1958 Habermas agreed with Heller's analysis that a bourgeois society, in which "justice triumphs over force," never existed and that the fiction of a justice immanent in free commerce only served the purpose of covering up just the opposite (see 1.2 above). But three years later, when Habermas finished writing *Structural Transformation* in "Autumn 1961" (STPS xix), he classified John Stuart Mill's "liberalist apologetic," which did "not admit to itself the structural conflict of the society whose very product it was," as "superior to the socialist critique" in more than one respect (STPS 130). For Marx's "idea of the public sphere" shared with Kant's ideal of the bourgeois public sphere the same "problematic presupposition," namely, a "'natural order' of social reproduction" (STPS 140). Significantly, Habermas now distances himself from this idea by putting "natural order" in quotation marks.

On first thought, readers who detect *Structural Transformation*'s pivot might conclude that this summary withdrawal of all key assumptions of classical political economy underlying Sections 4 to 7 and 10 to 13 invalidates Habermas's narrative. However, once one comprehends his ideology-critical procedure one realizes that he *only calls out* Marx's critique of ideology for its "problematic presupposition" *but does not abandon it*. For he needs it to prolong his thinking against facticity for a time period of fifty years after Hegel had decisively destroyed the "natural basis" for *Structural Transformation*'s narrative.

In other words, readers have to reach Section 16 before they learn that the onset of the first global great depression in 1873 not only signified the beginning of the end of the liberal era, but also revealed in retrospect that the political economist Say's "famous Law" of self-regulating markets "was actually a function not of the system [of laissez-faire capitalism] as such, but of concrete historical circumstances" (STPS 143,144). Ironically, *Structural Transformation* thus has to rely on what Marcuse in 1937 called the "misery" of "the concrete" (PCT 642). Namely, the civilized barbarism that gave Great Britain a gargantuan economic advantage over all its competitors in the first half of the nineteenth century. If the capital accumulation necessary for the start of the Industrial Revolution was created by the labor of African American slaves in the sugar cane, cotton, and tobacco fields of the "New World," its implementation in what Marx called the "Grand Industry" of manufacturing was made possible by "White Slavery," that is, the most brutal exploitation of child labor imaginable (HPSC 194–5, 197–8; 114–8, 130–2 138–140).

In short, especially after achieving hegemony in global markets thanks to its military victories at Trafalgar in 1812 and Waterloo in 1815, Great Britain "had everything to gain" from free trade and "nothing to lose" (STPS 78). Nevertheless, this "unique historical constellation" (STPS 79) did not protect the country against severe economic crises that recurred already in the decade from 1816 to 1825. During all of them, the alleged self-regulation of markets failed (HPSC 107, 121–3). Hence, even the most favorable historical circumstances could not deliver what Say's Law had falsely promised. Namely, "an automatic tendency toward the equilibration of production and consumption on the level of the economy as a whole" (STPS 144).

However, not even this *double insufficiency* of alleged natural laws of civil society and the most favorable historical circumstances to avoid recurring economic crises is the real issue that *Structural Transformation*'s narrative is faced with after Sections 14 and 15. Instead, it has to find a substitute for classical political economy's disproven claim about a justice inherent in free trade.

Otherwise it cannot plausibly claim that, eleven years after Hegel's destruction of all Kantian fictions, the bourgeois and the national interest could still be *credibly* identified in the British Reform Bill of 1832.

It is at this point that Habermas has to apply, in dialectical fashion, the ideology-critical procedure to the Marxist critique of ideology itself. While he does not share the foundational presupposition of the Critique of Political Economy about natural laws of civil society, he can nevertheless tacitly use its "analysis of the value form" to ascertain that the claim about justice inherent in unregulated markets is a part of the "basic ideology of bourgeois class society" (LC 26), which can only be uncovered by the critique of commodity fetishism in the first volume of *Capital: A Critique of Political Economy* (1867/1976). Specifically, *Structural Transformation*'s unexplained methodology draws on *Capital*'s chapter about "The Transformation of the Value . . . of Labour-Power into Wages." It posits that this transformation creates "all the mystifications of the capitalist mode of production" in general and all the *incorrect* "notions of justice held by both the worker and the capitalist" about "the exchange of equivalents in exchange relations." In short, what Marx calls the "mystery of wages" (cf. HPSC 126).

In other words, *Structural Transformation* can seemingly acknowledge Hegel's insight from 1821 about "the at once anarchic and antagonistic character" of bourgeois society, but simultaneously adopt Marx's claim from 1867 that nevertheless this "mystery of wages" convinced both workers and capitalists that their exchange relations in the labor market were entirely just. In short, his dialectical use of the ideology-critical procedure allows Habermas to maintain that the bourgeois interest in 1832 *credibly* represented that of the workers and of the nation as such. Of course, for that purpose he has to bracket *Capital*'s chapter on "The Working Day," where Marx highlighted "a protracted and more or less concealed civil war between the capitalist class and the working class" in England during more than fifty years *before* 1867 (cf. HPSC 126–7).

Structural Transformation's systemic contradictions like this one strain even the book's most sophisticated use of the ideology-critical procedure. To mitigate the cognitive dissonance created by the book's fundamental reliance on alleged "natural laws" of society on one hand and the denial of their existence in Section 15 on the other hand, readers have to be constantly aware that Habermas's two normative theses discussed in chapter 1 were not only "bound up with a complicated constellation of social preconditions" that "soon and profoundly changed" (STPS 88; SÖ 110). Above all, one has to keep in mind that Habermas had to strictly follow Marcuse's approach of taking the bourgeois ideals at face value and thinking with them against facticity to reconstruct at least a "certain" foundation in reality for this "complicated constellation" during the "liberal phase of capitalism" (TUP 265). Only his dialectical use of the Marxist critique of ideology allowed him to otherwise bracket the fact that a society based on completely uncoerced competition in all markets "had never existed," as he himself had emphasized in 1958.

In other words, all these explanations are provided to assist readers around the globe who are not yet aware of *Structural Transformation*'s superbly complicated methodology. Habermas himself knew right from the start that this bourgeois ideal first espoused in the political economy of the Physiocrats remained historically unattained. However, he needed to operate with it. For Kant's rational natural law was based on these alleged "natural laws" of society. In short, if he wanted to assess the normative potential contained in republican constitutions with the Kantian ideal of the bourgeois public sphere at their core, his arguments had to dialectically move within these key fictions (cf. STPS 117).

Chapter Three

Structural Transformation's Cold War Origins

Habermas's Defense of Kantian Rationality, Human Rights, and the Enlightenment

3.1. KOSELLECK'S SCHMITTIAN ENLIGHTENMENT CRITIQUE, COLD WAR STIFLING OF DISSENT, AND MARCUSE'S RESURRECTION OF THE UTOPIAN POTENTIAL OF HUMAN RIGHTS

Arguably, Habermas was first motivated to fully adopt Marcuse's dialectical critique of ideology in 1959 in response to the publication of Koselleck's book and the one by Hanno Kesting titled *Geschichtsphilosophie und Weltbürgerkrieg* ("Philosophy of History and Global Civil War"). The forensic evidence to support this thesis can be found in Habermas's highly adversarial review essay in *Merkur* as well as in his correspondence with the two editors of the journal, Joachim Moras und Hans Paeschke. His November 1959 letter to Moras documents that Habermas not only asked to review these books of the two Schmitt students but also suggested to include in his review two other recently published ones that were extremely critical of Schmitt's Nazi past. In all likelihood, he wanted to expose Koselleck's and Kesting's rather problematic scholarly connection with Schmitt as the former "crown jurist" of the Third Reich (Müller 2003: 40). But the two editors must have sensed this and, shying away from certain controversy, denied his request to include in his review the critiques of Schmitt by Jürgen Fijalkowski and Christian Graf von Krockow (cf. Yos 2019: 443–46).

Moreover, while Paeschke in January 1960 was delighted that Habermas had submitted a polarizing, that is, attention-grabbing first draft, he nevertheless worried that it might trigger a serious explosion once the conservative authors featured in *Merkur* read it: "If one looks closely, one detects the dynamite in this text on almost every page" (quoted in Yos 2019: 446n114). Hence, Habermas had to spend some time revising his draft before the editors were willing to finally give their imprimatur in March 1960. Nevertheless, Moras and Paeschke did not interfere with the polemical tone of Habermas's critique, immediately visible in the wording of its title: "Verrufener Fortschritt—verkanntes Jahrhundert. Zur Kritik an der Geschichtsphilosophie. Replik R. Koselleck und H. Kesting." ["Maligned Progress —Misunderstood Century: On the Critique of the Philosophy of History. Reply to R. Koselleck and H. Kesting" (Habermas)] Significantly, Habermas shortened its title to "On the Critique of the Philosophy of History" when he included it in his 1973 essay collection *Kultur und Kritik*. He also deleted his reference from 1960 to the connection between Koselleck, Kesting, and Schmitt: "at least now we know through his pupils what Carl Schmitt is thinking these days" (cf. Müller 2003: 106, 266n15).

As the title of his response/review essay indicates, for Habermas nothing less than the process of Enlightenment and the progress of humanity in modernity had been fundamentally attacked by Koselleck and Kesting. What alarmed him was the fact, as he would put it even more strongly in 1970, that "the central topic of Carl Schmitt's lifework," that is, the unmasking of the "relationship between power politics and the 'ideology of humanism'" allegedly inherent in the "the bourgeois philosophy of Enlightenment," had been adopted by two scholars of his own generation whose works were "intelligent and excellent" (KK 371). In 1988, reprinted in 1996 as an appendix to *Between Facts and Norms*, he would still reiterate that Schmitt and his students "have denounced the discourse that converts power into word" by portraying it "as a mechanism that inevitably gives rise to the consensually veiled domination of intellectual spokespersons…" (BFN 470; cf. HPSC 61).

It is this perennial conservative attack on the Enlightenment legacy of universal human rights that can ultimately explain *Structural Transformation*'s sixty-year history of influence and "unusual impact" that Habermas acknowledged in August 2021 (Habermas 2021: 470). What continues to strike such a responsive chord with readers and bestows on his classic its timeless relevance, can be gleaned from Habermas's own reaction in 1956 to Marcuse's presentation of the Enlightenment ideals in his Frankfurt lecture commemorating the centennial of Sigmund Freud's birth. When reporting on Marcuse's lecture in the leading Frankfurt newspaper, he even crossed the line between news and opinion to express his deep appreciation:

[Marcuse's] courage to release utopian energies again, with the uninhibitedness of the eighteenth century, in times like ours makes a peculiarly strong impression. (quoted in HPSC 27)

The "times like ours" were marked by the policing of expression during the escalating Cold War amidst an atmosphere of fear, generated by the build-up of a nuclear arsenal of A-bombs and the introduction of the newly developed H-bomb. Dissenting voices were denounced as disloyal and branded as a security risk. The entwinement of American and West German Cold War politics, which manifested itself in a shared militant anticommunism, generated a political climate that "was stifling," as Habermas vividly remembered in the biographical references of his Kyoto speech from 2004. Calhoun thus emphasized in 2013 that Habermas "had more than enough reasons for worry in simple observation of the weaknesses of the public sphere in Europe and America in the 1950s":

> Adenauer's Germany was a country repressing discussion of both its recent history and anything more than the narrowest version of its future. The United States endured one of the greatest mass-mediated political panics in the McCarthy anticommunist witch hunts and as it recovered threw itself into apolitical, even antipolitical, popular culture and mass consumption. (Calhoun 2013: 76)

Structural Transformation's conceptual juxtaposition of constitutional norm and political practice reflects Habermas's firsthand experiences as a dissenting journalist in those repressive times. Readers have to take them into account, if they want to understand the roots of his book's thinking against facticity and his motivation to engage in Marcuse's conceptual approach to such an extent. His discontent with the state of liberal democracy in the 1950s grew out of a uniquely German constellation. This self-styled "nation of culture" (*Kulturnation*), drawing on its heritage as the country of Kant and Schiller, that is, of poets and philosophers (*Dichter und Denker*), had to face an unprecedented reckoning in 1945, when Habermas turned sixteen.

In 1979, he reflected on his reaction in that year when he watched "the first documentary films, the concentration camp films" in the movie theater of his West German hometown: "All at once we saw that that we had been living in a politically criminal system. I had never imagined this before" (quoted in HPSC 50). In turn, one can barely imagine just how profound the shock for him must have been when confronted with such unfathomable crimes against humanity. After all, he grew up in an educated family seemingly dedicated to the values of bourgeois humanism.

During the next decade Habermas witnessed the inability of most Germans, especially his country's ruling elites, to directly confront their past lives in the "politically criminal system" of the Nazis. Moreover, the more the Cold War intensified the greater the disconnect with the norms set down in 1948 in the United Nations "Universal Declaration of Human Rights" and in 1949 in the Basic Law of the Federal Republic of Germany became. Looking back on those times from his perspective of 1979, Habermas pointed out that he "primarily" wrote *Structural Transformation* to "clarify for himself" the "dark sides and mistakes" of West Germany's liberal democracy, whose "advantages he never doubted." Specifically, his book sought to identify the "potentially dangerous weaknesses," which, "in spite of its Basic Law," are "embedded in the political system of the Federal Republic," and can somehow turn its constitutional intentions into falsities (quoted in Horster/ van Reijen 1980: 76–77).

These weaknesses had become visible under Adenauer's Cold War authoritarianism, in which the electorate's democratic participation in the existential policy debates and decision-making about rearmament and the stationing of nuclear weapons in West Germany had been extremely restricted. As early as March 1953, Habermas reacted to this lack of democratic participation in a letter to the editor of a conservative weekly, which was printed under the heading "Democracy in the Slaughter-House." What triggered his letter was the fate of a liberal member of the West German parliament who had defied his party leadership by publishing a policy proposal that was not in lockstep with Adenauer's negotiations about a "European Defense Community." In retaliation, this liberal politician was isolated by his peers and stripped of all policy-making influence (cf. Yos 2019: 211–14). From Habermas's perspective, this curtailment of parliamentary debate was symptomatic for a lack of transparency in the legislative process. Increasingly, laws were written by party leaderships and business roundtables. As a result, "parliament turns into a hall of mirrors where members display their idle and boastful speechifying" (quoted in Yos 2019: 214).

By 1953, Habermas had already followed for three years the fate of Adenauer's former minister of the interior Gustav Heinemann, a leader in the Lutheran church, who resigned in October 1950 to protest Adenauer's rearmament plans (cf. Wiggershaus 1986/1994: 441). In 1952, Heinemann had been among the founders of an opposition party, which Habermas and his future wife Ute Wesselhoeft supported in the 1953 election (cf. HB 37). However, Adenauer, an exceedingly sly politician, was able to isolate Heinemann and many other liberal members of the bourgeoisie who opposed his rearmament policy.

Habermas thus witnessed early on how the power of the executive branch could ignore in January 1955 even the most respectable and sizable movement against rearmament to date. Lead by Heinemann as well as other prominent church and university dignitaries, together with the opposition Social Democrats and the trade unions, about one thousand representatives from all parts of West Germany met in Frankfurt's *Paulskirche*, the highly symbolic site of the national assembly during the bourgeois revolution of 1848/1849, to express their existential concerns in a "German Manifesto." However, Adenauer was solely focused on enforcing party discipline within his governing coalition to secure a majority for the final vote in the *Bundestag*, the West German parliament. Three months later, on May 5, 1955, the Federal Republic of Germany joined NATO as a member of the West European Union and was recognized as a sovereign state by the Western Allies (cf. Yos 2019: 51–64, 222–23; HB 54).

Simultaneously, Habermas experienced how the freedom of expression on controversial topics could be severely curtailed during the Cold War. Parallel to the event in the *Paulskirche* he had written an article about a loosely organized protest movement against rearmament and the reintroduction of the compulsory draft into militarily service. Called the *Without me* ["Ohne mich"] movement, it had been repeatedly denounced by members of Adenauer's cabinet as an alleged Communist front group. Habermas's article analyzed the difficulties one encountered when trying to overcome this stereotypical public perception. To illustrate the extent of these obstacles, he pointed to a discussion with high school students who were opposed to Adenauer's rearmament policy, in which the president of the *Bundestag* had accused them of having been brainwashed by Communist propaganda. Far from demonstrating their independence as the "Fourth Estate," the leading national newspapers at the time refused to print his article (cf. Yos 2019: 224–25).

Specifically, his correspondence with Karl Korn, the culture editor of the *Frankfurter Allgemeine Zeitung*, from February 9 and 21, 1955, documents that Korn had advocated for the article but that all other members of the editorial board had been opposed. A similar rejection had happened at the *Süddeutsche Zeitung*. Even his great success with his essay "Dialectic of Rationalization" in the August 1954 issue of *Merkur* did not help him when he offered his article to this monthly journal. Habermas's suggestion in his March 15 letter to *Merkur* co-editor Hans Paeschke that his article had been refused on political grounds turned into a self-fulfilling prophecy (cf. Yos 2019: 225n97). Only in May 1955, after Adenauer had won his rearmament victory, would his article be published in the *Deutsche Studentenzeitung*, a nationwide student paper, together with a debate in which the minister of defense, Theodor Blank, seemingly refuted all arguments raised by a select group of university professors against rearmament and the draft (cf. Yos 2019: 225).

As if these challenges for democratic dissent under Adenauer's authoritarian regime had not already been sufficient, the events between April 1957 and July 1958 turned out to be even more detrimental to the development of a democratic political culture in the Federal Republic of Germany. These yearlong protests against the stationing of nuclear weapons on West German soil were first defeated in March 1958 by Adenauer's absolute majority in the *Bundestag*, newly acquired in the September 1957 election (cf. Specter 2010: 62). Nevertheless, even after the *Bundestag* had ratified this controversial NATO decision, the *Kampf dem Atomtod* ["Fight against nuclear death"] campaign not only continued but also intensified. After all, fifty-two percent of adults polled in West Germany and West Berlin opposed this escalation of the Cold War. In Hamburg alone, 150,000 people joined a protest march on April 17, 1958. Against this background, the Social Democrats introduced a bill in the *Bundestag* that called for a plebiscite. While such a plebiscite would have been possible under the constitution of the Weimar Republic, it had been deleted in West Germany's Basic Law. Predictably, Adenauer's government rejected this initiative and filed injunctions with the Federal Constitutional Court when three federal states with Social Democratic governments tried to hold such plebiscites. On July 30, 1958, the Court ruled that these attempts violated the Basic Law (cf. Wiggershaus 1986 / 1994: 551; Specter 2010: 36).

Arguably, Habermas's worsening political experiences in those years as a citizen and as a journalist influenced the beginning conceptual shift *within* his preliminary study for *Structural Transformation* from 1958, that is, between its first parts and its last part. Clearly, a decade after the United Nations had enshrined in the Preamble to its "Universal Declaration of Human Rights" "peace in the world" and "freedom from fear" as among "the highest aspirations of the common people" (quoted in Hunt 2007: 223), these norms had not been achieved. On the contrary, the fear of a nuclear war with the Soviet Union was growing. It would reach its climactic phase with the building of the Berlin Wall in August 1961 while Habermas was adding the finishing touches to *Structural Transformation*. Small wonder that he thus ended the book's chapter VI on "The Transformation of the Public Sphere's Political Function" with an ominous reference to the "as yet unconquered state of nature in international relations." Given the size of the existing nuclear arsenal in the United States and the Soviet Union at the time, such a Hobbesian state of nature contained "a potential for self-annihilation on a global scale" (STPS 235).

3.2. HABERMAS'S EMBRACE OF KANT'S "PUBLIC USE OF REASON" IN HIS CRITIQUE OF NUCLEAR ARMAMENT AND VOTER MANIPULATION IN AN AUTHORITARIAN DEMOCRACY

Structural Transformation's Kantian essence originated in the context of this tension between the potential for nuclear "self-annihilation" of humankind and the primarily "propagandistic regard for the world public" by Cold War governance (STPS 295–96n133) concerning the human right to "peace in the world," as it was proclaimed in 1948 by all members of the United Nations with the notable abstention of the Soviet bloc. In this Cold War situation, Habermas argued that a global state of nature "has become so threatening for everybody that its specific negation articulates the universal interest with great precision." He thus adopted Kant's demand that "'perpetual peace' had to be established in a 'cosmopolitan order'" (STPS 235).

Habermas's reasoning was first expressed by the influential philosopher Karl Jaspers, "who after 1945 had advocated for the democratization of West German society like few others" (Yos 2019: 470). Emblematic for these reflections on the relevance of Kant's discourse on *Perpetual Peace* (1795) during the Cold War was the fact that Jaspers wrote a new introduction for Kant's essay in 1958, the same year in which he published *Die Atombombe und die Zukunft des Menschen* ["The Atom Bomb and the Future of Humankind"] in the context of the West German opposition to the stationing of nuclear weapons. Although Habermas had read key works by Kant even before beginning his academic studies of philosophy in 1949, the introduction by Jaspers to Kant's famous essay from 1795 arguably redirected his focus to Kant's ideal of the public use of reason. Specifically, Jaspers explained in his text that Kant's principle of *Öffentlichkeit* ("public sphere") is conceived as "the truth that emerges in the *Publizität* ("publicness") of communicating with each other" (quoted in Yos 2019: 471n173).

Significantly, when Jaspers focused on Kant's notion about truth emerging from publicly communicating with each other, he anticipated *Structural Transformation*'s designation of the Kantian dictum about the "public use of reason" as the "method of Enlightenment" in Section 13 (STPS 104). Moreover, Yos points to several recent sources which indicate that Habermas's thinking about "communicative reason" and "communicative competence" has been inspired by Jaspers (see Yos 2019: 471n173). Finally, Hannah Arendt's concept of "communicative power," in which the roots of Kant's "public use of reason" in the self-stylization of the Greek *polis* are spelled out, was first discussed by Habermas in 1976, with an English translation by Thomas McCarthy following in 1977 (Habermas 1977: 3–24). In the following two decades, Habermas would critically adopt key aspects of Arendt's concept.

It would be productive to analyze whether Habermas's Kantian turn, which *logically* followed from his adoption of Marcuse's dictum that bourgeois philosophy is "more than ideology," was *practically* motivated by experiencing what Marcuse had called the "misery" of the concrete (PCT 642). Arguably, this misery started in earnest on April 4, 1957, when the West German chancellor, in an act of sublime political cynicism, designated tactical nuclear weapons as "basically nothing more than an improved artillery" (quoted in Wiggershaus 1986/1994: 550–51). Publicly, Adenauer's callous disregard for human fear of nuclear annihilation would remain unmatched until 1963, when Goldwater declared that the atomic bomb was "merely another weapon" (quoted in Jamieson 1996: 203, cf. Preface above). However, during the 1964 election campaign not only the Democrats would use such Goldwater claims as the centerpiece of their campaign commercials against him. Already during the 1964 Republican primaries, New York Governor Nelson Rockefeller, the embodiment of his party's establishment, would authorize political advertising that "bludgeoned Goldwater with his own rhetoric" regarding "the possible use of nuclear weapons" (Jamieson 1996: 179). One of Rockefeller's mass mailings to registered Republican voters would quote a litany of Goldwater statements like "I don't see how [nuclear war] can be avoided" before rhetorically asking whether he would be fit to occupy the Oval Office: "Who Do You Want in the Room with the H Bomb Button?" (quoted in Jamieson 1996: 179).

In response to Adenauer's embrace of tactical nuclear weapons as "improved artillery," eighteen leading West German nuclear physicists declared in their "Göttingen Manifesto" not only their opposition but also their refusal to cooperate in any government-sponsored research related to that military program (cf. Wiggershaus 2004: 44, 45; Matustik 2001: 30). But their appeal to the public reason of the West German electorate suffered the same fate as the "German Manifesto" from 1955 against rearmament. For Adenauer also wielded the economic weapon of "higher benefits and retroactive payments" for "about 6 million retired people" (STPS 220). In short, the April 24, 1957 manifesto was almost immediately overshadowed in the news cycle by these increased payments starting on May 1. Moreover, Adenauer's popularity allowed him to simply rebuff in September 1957 the proposal advanced by "the Polish Foreign Minister Rapacki for a nuclear-free central Europe" (Specter 2010: 35).

Calhoun's observation of an "apolitical, even antipolitical, popular culture and mass consumption" as a more sustainable form of voter manipulation than McCarthyism after the downfall of the U.S. Senator from Wisconsin in the "Army-McCarthy hearings" of 1954 (cf. Kendrick 1969: 67–68), captures the essence of Adenauer's 1957 election campaign techniques. They provided abundant empirical data for *Structural Transformation*'s Section 22, titled "Manufactured Publicity and Nonpublic Opinion: The Voting Behavior of the Population."

Even before publishing his book in 1962, Habermas offered a systematic critique of Adenauer's comprehensive media manipulation in a January 1961 article for the magazine *Magnum*, titled "Die Bundesrepublik —eine Wahlmonarchie?" ["The Federal Republic—an Elected Monarchy?"].

In his essay, he summed up the undemocratic consequences of this substitution of manufactured publicity for public discourse (cf. HB 109–10; Yos 2019: 437). Namely, the demise of the citizen and the rise of the consumer: "Scientifically-led marketing turns political advertising into a component of consumer culture for the un-political [citizen]" (quoted in Specter 2010: 62).

This trend was inaugurated in 1952 by Rosser Reeves, who took a leave of absence from the Ted Bates Agency to work on BBD&O's Eisenhower campaign. Reeves was identified in the advertising industry with his "hard sell" TV commercials for mass market products like soap and toothpaste. In order to get the consumer's attention, his signature one-minute spots pounded in the message. Literally so, in the case of a headache relief pill, for which his eighteen-month ad campaign, featuring animated images of a pounding hammer and a jagged electrical bolt inside a human head, tripled yearly sales from $18 million to $54 million (Halberstam 1993: 226).

Applying this approach to a three-week campaign in "battleground" states leading up to Election Day 1952, Reeves saturated all available TV and radio channels with seemingly endless repetitions of about twenty different spots – all introduced by a booming voice (and in huge letters on TV) as "Eisenhower Answers America" (see photo in Diamond and Bates 1993: 60). Significantly, the spots introduced the techniques of manipulation into political advertising by faking the use of a Q&A format. In a studio, Eisenhower's scripted "answers" were filmed first. Afterwards a diverse cross section of "everyday Americans" was hand-picked from the lines of tourists waiting to visit Radio City Music Hall (Diamond and Bates 1993: 54–55).

These tourists from different parts of the United States, reflected in the regional fashions of their clothes and in their "wonderful native accents" (Rosser Reeves), would then be invited to come to a film studio (Diamond and Bates 1993: 54). There they would be handed cue cards with equally scripted "questions," which they had to recite to match Eisenhower's "answers" (cf. Diamond and Bates 1993: 54–60; Jamieson 1996: 81, 83–86; Halberstam 1993: 227–31). Their fake questions would then be spliced together with Eisenhower's perfect "answers," delivered with the sincerity and authority of a war hero and victorious general (cf. Jamieson 1996: 48). To the detriment of the Democratic candidate Adlai Stevenson who wanted genuine political debate and as a blow to the democratic process, these scripted and staged spots were highly effective. As a media specialist working for the Democratic National Committee (DNC) at the time would later tell political communication researcher Kathleen Hall Jamieson for her seminal book *Packaging the Presidency: A History and Criticism of Presidential Campaign Advertising* (1996):

They had all the money and bought all of this time and clobbered us. Some of our [state-level] polls showed that the only time there was any movement for Stevenson was before these spots were aired. The spots used a hammer to kill a fly but they worked and they set a horrible precedent. (Quoted in Jamieson 1996: 86)

Ironically, Eisenhower's attempt to retain a semblance of dignity and integrity within this hucksterism inadvertently helped Reeves to find an even shorter slogan when developing his trademark "unique selling position" (USP) for the Eisenhower campaign. Since the polling that George Gallup had conducted for Reeves had identified the stalemate in the Korean war as the primary concern of most Americans (cf. Jamieson 1996: 86, 47), Reeves wanted to position his candidate with the following USP: "Eisenhower, the man who will bring us peace." However, worried about his professional reputation, the general responded that nobody in the world could guarantee peace during the ongoing Cold War. Unfazed, Reeves simply shortened his USP and created an even simpler and more effective slogan: "Eisenhower, man of peace" (quoted in Halberstam 1993: 229).

It is plausible to assume that Habermas had the circumstances of Adenauer's September 1957 win of an absolute majority in the West German parliament on his mind when more than two decades later he reflected on the above quoted "potentially dangerous weaknesses" of the Federal Republic's political system as a motivating factor for writing Section 22 as well as Section 21 on "The Transmuted Function of the Principle of Publicity." For sufficient evidence can be found in his May 20, 1958, speech in front of Frankfurt's town hall, when he addressed a protest meeting against stationing nuclear weapons in West Germany (Matustik 2001: 30–31; see photo in Wiggershaus 2004: 46). In this speech, Habermas critiqued Adenauer's argument that plebiscites are incompatible with representative government. Specifically, he denied that the Federal Republic's factual *Kanzlerdemokratie* ["Chancellor Democracy"] (HB 110) fulfilled these criteria itself. Moreover, he argued that if West Germany had a representative democracy in the classic sense," elections to the *Bundestag* "would not be veiled plebiscites." Since "the advertising consultants of the Christian Democratic Union asked on September 15 for a referendum about a *person*," there is the need for a demonstration of political will-formation regarding the key *issue* of nuclear armament that Adenauer carefully avoided during his re-election campaign (quoted in Wiggershaus 2004: 47, emphasis added).

This downhill trajectory of Habermas's first-hand experiences with West Germany's democratic process from the failure of the "German Manifesto" in 1955 to the futility of the "Göttingen Manifesto" in 1957 continued after his May 1958 speech. When it was printed in the June 1958 edition of *Diskus*, a paper published by Frankfurt University students, it appeared next to a diatribe by Franz Böhm, a professor and former rector of the university, who also was a Christian Democratic member of the German *Bundestag*. Habermas's speech was titled "Unrest—the Citizen's First Duty" ["Unruhe erste Bürgerpflicht"]. Böhm's article looked like a response under the heading "Provoked Nuclear Panic" ["Provozierte Atompanik"]. This impression was reinforced by Habermas's explicit critique of the advertising techniques which the Christian Democrats had employed in the 1957 elections, especially since Böhm accused the speakers at the protest meeting of "class baiting" ["Klassenhetze"] directed against the Christian Democratic party (quoted in Wiggershaus 2004: 46; cf. Yos 2019: 441–42).

Böhm's throwback to McCarthyite rhetoric targeted not only Habermas but also other speakers like the distinguished political scientist Ernst Fraenkel who had only recently returned from his exile in the United States (cf. Yos 2019: 429, 429n85). There he had published an analysis of the Nazi regime titled *The Dual State: A Contribution to the Theory of Dictatorship* (1941). However, these credentials did not save Fraenkel from Böhm's indictment of all speakers for their alleged "brutalization of political discourse plus hollowing out of the Basic Law" ["Verrohung der politischen Diskussion plus Grundgesetzaushöhlung"], which allegedly *paved the way for a new National Socialism* (quoted in Wiggershaus 2004: 46). This bitter irony does not end here. Böhm also included Fraenkel in his vile denunciation that the speakers allegedly "turned against the Western Allies while one-sidedly cooperating with [Communist] dictators and oppressors" (Wiggershaus 2004: 46).

Given his untenured status as an assistant at Horkheimer's Institute of Social Research, Habermas in 1958 took a very courageous stand when reasoning in public against nuclear armament. Especially since he sharply criticized Adenauer and the Christian Democrats for misleading and manipulating the voters with regard to this existential issue. After all, Böhm at that time headed the executive committee of the Institute's Foundation (Wiggershaus 2004: 46).

3.3. *STRUCTURAL TRANSFORMATION'*S KANTIAN RATIONALITY VERSUS THE IRRATIONALITY OF NUCLEAR BRINKMANSHIP AND "OVERKILL" IN THE COLD WAR

As a member of the West German movement against nuclear armament, Habermas could feel vindicated by the events in 1961 and 1962 when in the words of Robert McNamara, the then U.S. Secretary of Defense, the United States and the Soviet Union "came very, very close" to mutually assured nuclear destruction, taking much of the globe with them as collateral damage. Specifically, Daniel Ellsberg, who in spring 1961 drafted as a RAND corporation consultant the Kennedy administration's "Basic National Security Policy," that is, the civilian guidance for nuclear war planning, confirmed in 2017 that by then "the Soviets had hundreds of medium- and intermediate-range missiles within range of Europe, along with medium-range bombers— *more, in fact, than we had ever predicted.*" In short, at the time of the Berlin crisis in 1961, "the Soviets had . . . a medium-range missile force capable of making one deep smoking hole of West Germany. . ." (Ellsberg 2017: 151, emphasis added).

This sense of vindication could only be heightened once the public received access to many classified documents from that period. In hindsight, *Structural Transformation*'s argument turns out to have been *too reasonable* when claiming that faced with the potential for global self-annihilation "divergent interests can be relativized *without difficulty*" (STPS 235, emphasis added, translation modified). In December 1960, while Habermas was working on his book, the Joint Chiefs of Staff presented at the U.S. Strategic Air Command their latest "Single Integrated Operational Plan" for nuclear war to a high-ranking military audience. Only the then Secretary of Defense and a few of his civilian staff members were admitted. One of them was John H. Rubel, the deputy director of defense research and engineering. As he recalled in *Doomsday Delayed: USAF Strategic Weapons Doctrine and SIOP-62, 1959-1962* (2008), he learned at the meeting that the deaths from radioactive fallout alone would number 100 million in the Soviet Union and 300 million in China (quoted in Ellsberg 2017: 100). Conversely, as Ellsberg estimated, "it was in reality quite possible . . . that not a single nuclear warhead would land on U.S. territory after such an American first strike." But "*our Western European allies in NATO would be quickly annihilated twice over*: first from the mobile Soviet medium- range missiles and tactical bombers targeted on them, which our first strike couldn't find and destroy reliably, and second from the close-in fallout from our own nuclear strikes on Soviet bloc territory" (Ellsberg 2017: 99, emphasis added).

While President Eisenhower was reportedly "distressed" about "the tremendous amount of 'overkill' in the plan," he nevertheless endorsed it and passed it on to the newly elected President John F. Kennedy (Ellsberg 2017: 103). Only in his farewell speech in January 1961 would Eisenhower famously warn about the proliferating influence on American social and political life by an exponentially growing military-industrial complex. However, it is unlikely that John Foster Dulles, until 1959 the U.S. Secretary of State, would have shared Eisenhower's distress. For he had already made his own contribution to the ultimate irrationality of nuclear war strategy. In a 1956 interview with *Life* magazine, he had defined the concept of "brinkmanship" as the essence of the Cold War:

> Some say that we were brought to the verge of war. Of course we were brought to the verge of war. The ability to get to the verge without getting into the war is the necessary art. If you cannot master it, . . . if you are scared to go [to] the brink, you are lost. (quoted in Halberstam 1993: 410)

Only by coincidence was *Structural Transformation* published in the year of the Cuban missile crisis as the supreme example of nuclear brinkmanship. Nevertheless, the timing by Habermas's publisher could not have been better. For citizens concerned about the state of democratic participation at the height of the Cold War could directly apply Habermas's analysis to this ultimate case study about the manipulation of public opinion. Above all, this unsurpassed example of avoiding global nuclear annihilation only through sheer luck, after all democratic safeguards had been circumvented in a misinformed and miscalculating gamble of the executive branch, has only increased in relevance due to today's dysfunctional state of global affairs under conditions of growing nuclear proliferation.

In 1999, McNamara would further upgrade the likelihood of global nuclear annihilation. He now realized that "our brush with nuclear catastrophe in October 1962 was *extraordinarily* close." In addition, he would finally acknowledge that "we had seriously underestimated those dangers" (McNamara, Blight, and Brigham 1999: 10 bottom, emphasis added, 9 bottom). For the CIA had mistakenly reported that there were no tactical nuclear warheads on Cuba that could be "used against U.S. invasion forces." Instead, there were at least ninety. Moreover, Khrushchev had authorized the Soviet commander in Cuba to use these tactical nuclear weapons in case of a U.S. invasion and the warheads had been moved from their storage facility inside a hill south of Havana into position. (McNamara, Blight, and Brigham 1999: 10 top; cf. Ellsberg 2017: 209).

Above all, at an international conference that reassessed the Cold War in 1992, Fidel Castro's response to a question by McNamara was clear-cut: "Now, we started from the assumption that if there was an invasion of Cuba, nuclear war would erupt" (quoted in McNamara, Blight, and Brigham 1999: 11 top).

Arguably, it is difficult to imagine a more existential example of human fallibility than this one. The level of "misinformation, miscalculation, and misjudgment" of the U.S. military and the executive branch of the American government in October 1962 that McNamara would identify retroactively, has remained unsurpassed. McNamara's own reaction to the response of his former enemy was revealing: "Castro's answer sent a chill down my spine" (McNamara, Blight, and Brigham 1999: 9, 10).

McNamara's chill would become even more intense when he learned at the next Havana conference in 2002 that the nuclear apocalypse had only been "a hair's breadth away" in the early evening of Saturday, October 27, 1962. Unknown to the CIA or anybody else in the United States government, the four Soviet submarines hunted by the U.S. Navy in the Caribbean each carried a "torpedo with a Hiroshima-size nuclear explosive power." According to a "brand-new signaling arrangement" sent to the Soviets, these submarines were supposed to surface once hand grenades were exploded next to their hulls. However, their captains never received that message and thought they were being attacked. One of the submarines, having been harassed by these intensifying explosions for four hours under conditions of lack of oxygen and extreme heat of around 120 degrees Fahrenheit inside the hull (three duty officers and other crew members had already fainted), unable to communicate with the General Staff and thus not knowing "whether the war has already started up there," would have fired its nuclear torpedo, if sheer luck had not intervened. The submarine commander had already instructed the officer assigned to the nuclear torpedo "to assemble it to battle readiness." The political officer in possession of the other half of the key with which to launch the weapon had agreed to firing it. Only by sheer coincidence was the chief of the brigade traveling on that submarine and not on one of the other three. He stopped the two by reminding them that Moscow had only authorized the Soviet commander on Cuba to launch his tactical nuclear weapons under his own discretion but not the submarine commanders (Ellsberg 2017: 211–17).

As Ellsberg analyzed that situation in 2017, if the torpedo had been fired, "there is every reason to believe that the carrier USS *Randolph* and several, perhaps all, of its accompanying destroyers would . . . have been destroyed by a nuclear explosion." Lacking any knowledge about the nuclear torpedo, Navy commanders and the Executive Committee assembled in the White House would have had to assume that the source of the nuclear explosion "would have been a medium-range missile from Cuba whose launch had not been detected." Ellsberg's logical conclusion: "That is the event that President Kennedy had announced on October 22 would lead to a full-scale nuclear attack on the Soviet Union" (Ellsberg 2017: 217).

Chapter Four

Participatory Democracy
versus
Political Manipulation

*The Role of Habermas's
"Celebrated Coffee Houses" (Todd Gitlin)
in the Modern Public Sphere*

4.1. *STRUCTURAL TRANSFORMATION'S* ANALYSIS AS A GUIDE TO EXPOSING POLITICAL MANIPULATION IN PRESIDENTIAL POLITICS

To this day, the successful manipulation especially of the American press has made it possible to perpetuate the myth, elaborately launched by Arthur Schlesinger, Jr., the Harvard historian and member of the Kennedy administration, that Kennedy's "brilliantly controlled" and "matchlessly calibrated" brinkmanship had faced down the Soviet threat (quoted in Bird 1998: 246). Only in 1988 would McGeorge Bundy, Kennedy's special assistant for national security affairs, admit that "we misled our colleagues, our countrymen, our successors and our allies." By keeping secret the withdrawal of United States missiles in Turkey in exchange for the withdrawal of Soviet missiles on Cuba, "[w]e allowed them all to believe that nothing responsive had been offered. . . ." (Bundy 1988: 434). In the words of the historian Kai Bird, this "appearance of uncompromising toughness sent a message to the American people that a confrontational policy against communists was necessary at all times" (Bird 1998: 241, emphasis added). In reality, Khrushchev had achieved two key objectives, the removal of the U.S. missiles from Turkey and the agreement by the U.S. government not to invade Cuba (cf. Bundy 1988: 432-33, 435; Bird 1998: 240).

Nevertheless, Kennedy's politics of appearances, greatly influenced by his counselor Ted Sorensen, the discrete mastermind behind his razor-thin victory in the 1960 Presidential election, succeeded in the short term. One week before the midterm election, Kennedy could enjoy a steep rise of his approval rating in the Gallup polls by twelve percentage points (Bird 1988: 246.) As a detailed content analysis of press coverage by major American newspapers during the Cuban missile crisis documents, "Kennedy gained immeasurably in public esteem and emerged from the ordeal a national hero." Above all, the conclusion by the political scientists and historians who conducted the study confirms the successful manipulation of the media by the Kennedy White House. As Montague Kern, Patricia W. Levering, and Ralph B. Levering sum up in *The Kennedy Crises: The Press, the Presidency, and Foreign Policy* (1983): "The press, by giving full credence to the administration's *interpretation* of events, had played a major role in [Kennedy's] multi-faceted triumph" (Kern, P. W. Levering, and R. B. Levering 1983: 139, emphasis added).

Similar to the veiled plebiscite about Adenauer in 1957, which Habermas had critiqued in his 1958 speech, the 1962 elections to the U.S. Senate as well as to the House of Representatives were a referendum about *a person*, about Kennedy's brinkmanship. Even the conservative *Chicago Tribune*, his staunch critic, could be manipulated by seemingly confirming its own Cold War logic of "peace through strength." The paper's unconditional praise was unprecedented: "For the first time in twenty years, Americans can carry their head high because the president of the United States has stood up to the premier of Russia and made him back down" (quoted in Kern, P. W. Levering, and R. B. Levering 1983: 138).

In the long run, however, not even informing Vice President Lyndon B. Johnson about this Kennedy deception significantly contributed to Johnson's military escalations since 1964, which resulted in the "Vietnam Tragedy" (Robert McNamara). As Bundy, who continued in his position in the Johnson administration, reiterated to the international relations scholar Gordon M. Goldstein shortly before his death in September 1996: "Johnson didn't want to be a coward" (quoted in Goldstein 2008: 3).

Moreover, Sorensen made certain that President Richard M. Nixon also continued to regard the standard that Kennedy had seemingly set in October 1962 as the one he would be judged by with regard to his conduct of the war in Vietnam. When Sorensen edited *Thirteen Days*, Robert Kennedy's diary of the Cuban missile crisis for posthumous publication, he consciously deleted, as he would admit in a 1989 conference, the "very explicit" description of the secret deal to withdraw the missiles in Turkey (quoted in Bird 1998: 238–39).

Finally, in a memo from March 1965, the Harvard Law School professor and assistant secretary of defense for international security affairs, John McNaughton, assigned Cold War image politics a seventy percent share in all Vietnam decision-making. This is how he quantified for McNamara the hierarchy of U.S. interests in Vietnam—*before* about 57,500 *additional* American soldiers would lose their lives:

> *70%—to avoid a humiliating US defeat (to our reputation as a guarantor).* 20%—to keep SVN [South Vietnam] (and the adjacent territory) from Chinese hands. 10%—to permit the people of SVN to enjoy a better, freer way of life. (quoted in Goldstein 2008: 168, emphasis added; cf. Bird 1998: 311)

Structural Transformation's Section 21 analyzes such a state of political manipulation and its consequences. Specifically, it observes that publicness, created through the public use of reason, "loses its critical function in favor of a staged display, even arguments are transmute into symbols to which one cannot respond by arguing but only by identifying with them" (STPS 206). According to Cold War logic, the *appearance* of successful brinkmanship, of going "toe-to-toe" with the enemy, of making him flinch and back down, constitutes the key symbol that determines a Super Power's prestige and credibility on the international stage as well as its legitimacy and support at home. In the words of columnist William S. White after the Cuban missile crisis: Failure to confront the Soviet Union "would have been an *unmanly* betrayal of this nation" (quoted in in Kern, P. W. Levering, and R. B. Levering 1983: 138, emphasis added).

On October 22, 1962, in his televised prime time address to the nation and the world, Kennedy pioneered the staging of brinkmanship as a media event. Significantly, Habermas's analysis was published at exactly the time when the vast majority of households in the United States had acquired television sets and public debate started to move from the printed newspaper page to the electronic screen. In short, the following quote from *Structural Transformation*'s Section 22 turned out to have been highly prescient:

> For inasmuch as important political decisions are made for manipulative purposes (without, of course, for this reason being factually less consequential) and are introduced with consummate propagandistic skill as publicity vehicles into a public sphere manufactured for show, they remain removed *qua political* decisions from both a public process of rational argumentation and the possibility of a plebiscitary vote of no confidence in the awareness of precisely defined alternatives." (STPS 220–21, emphasis in the original)

Shaped primarily by his stellar rhetorician Sorensen, Kennedy's speech preempted any public discourse about precisely defined alternatives regarding the removal of the Soviet missiles from Cuba by presenting a doomsday scenario about "clearly offensive weapons of sudden mass destruction" that could only be tackled (and hopefully resolved) in absolute secrecy in order to safeguard not only national security but also at least a chance of survival for the human race.

To keep his "fellow citizens" on tenterhooks for the duration of the crisis, his ominous warnings created an apocalyptic atmosphere: "No one can foresee precisely . . . what costs or casualties will be incurred. Many months of sacrifice and self-discipline lie ahead." Immediately after the speech, McNamara further stoked the fears of the nation in a not-for-attribution backgrounder for the press. Withholding any specific information about the detected Intermediate Range Ballistic Missiles and their launch sites on Cuba, he nevertheless presented to the reporters a map of the United States with the impact ranges of the missiles superimposed on it. These predictions of potential nuclear annihilation were already scary enough: "The outer ring covers for all practical purposes all of the United States except a small slice of Washington and the northern part of the Pacific Coast" (quoted in in Kern, P. W. Levering, and R. B. Levering 1983: 126, 128).

Nevertheless, their effect was further enhanced by McNamara's carefully staged display. As the late Columbia Journalism professor Todd Gitlin, a former president of Students for a Democratic Society (SDS) remembered, McNamara cultivated his public image as "the former Harvard Business School professor with the steel-rimmed glasses," radiating "technocratic reason and cynical vigor (to use one of Kennedy's favorite words) in person." Small wonder that, as Gitlin reports, at "colleges in New England, some students piled into their cars and took off for Canada until further notice" (Gitlin 1987: 91, 98).

Exactly one week before Kennedy's televised doomsday warnings, Bundy's actions had supported Habermas's thesis that "political decisions are made for manipulative purposes," even when they can be factually consequential to the most dangerous degree. As Bird described it in 1998, when Bundy received a call from the deputy director of intelligence at the CIA on Monday, October 15, at 8:30 PM, he "knew right away that the news was political dynamite." How could the Kennedy administration announce to the American public that a U-2 spy plane had now gathered photographic evidence of Soviet medium-range missile sites on Cuba, just one day after Bundy had told a nationwide TV audience in an interview that the Republican U.S. Senator Kenneth Keating's secret sources were wrong when claiming that the Soviets were building six such sites? After all, on September 13, Kennedy had promised in "a high-visibility press conference" that he "would take action," if such "ground-to-ground missiles," classified by him as "offensive" nuclear weapons, would be installed. And Bundy had reiterated in his TV interview on October 14 that there was neither "present evidence" nor "present likelihood" that the Soviets would build launch sites for such offensive weapons on Cuba (Bird 1998: 226, 227; Kern, P. W. Levering, and R. B. Levering 1983: 107–108).

In short, as Bundy knew only too well, in the eyes of the consummate politician Kennedy the fate of the Democrats in the upcoming midterm election was hanging in the balance—and thus his own reelection in 1964. Even without any knowledge of the CIA evidence about the missile sites, the *Washington Post* would report on October 18 that 344 news editors and 208 members of the United States Congress regarded the existence of a Communist government in Cuba as "the primary campaign issue." Since 1961, Louis Harris, Kennedy's pollster and political advisor, had been conducting focus group research on the President's job performance across the nation. In his report on October 4, he confirmed that throughout 1962 the majority of the American public disapproved of his policies toward Cuba. On average, Kennedy received a 62 percent negative rating regarding this issue. That's why the Bay of Pigs disaster had been identified by Sorensen as Kennedy's "Achilles' heel" (Kern, P. W. Levering, and R. B. Levering 1983: 122, 116–17, 100).

Not surprisingly, the audiotape recording of the second executive committee (ExComm) meeting on the Cuban missile crisis that Kennedy convened in the White House on October 16 at 6:30 PM contains his assessment that "this is a political struggle as much as military." To which McNamara responded in the course of the discussion: "I don't think there is a military problem here." Earlier, when answering a question from Bundy, he had already confirmed that the Soviet missiles do "not at all" change "the strategic balance." Kennedy himself believed at that time "that the strategic gap was more than five to two against the Russians." As Bird documents, it was actually "more like nine to one" in favor of the United States. McNamara thus analyzed the Cuban missile crisis as "a domestic political problem" for the Democrats (Bird 1998: 229, 228, 230).

Already on August 31, the Republican Keating had warned in the U.S. Senate, based on rudimentary evidence, that the Soviets "might be constructing a missile base" (Kern, P. W. Levering, and R. B. Levering 1983: 107). Since then, the Republicans had done their utmost to keep the issue way up on the public agenda of election year issues. Now, as McNamara put it, it was "just exactly this problem, that if Cuba should possess a capacity to carry out offensive actions against the U.S., . . . we said we'd act. . . . Well, how will we act?" (quoted in Bird 1998: 230).

Actually this dilemma of the Democrats was even more serious than the tape recordings reveal. In a twist of morbid irony, Kennedy was hoisted with his own petard. Two years earlier, on the night before his second TV debate with Vice President Richard M. Nixon in the 1960 presidential election, he had accused the Eisenhower administration of having "lost Cuba." His campaign knew that such a controversial charge was tailor-made for commercial television with its systemic need to produce attention-grabbing drama. In the first debate, CBS producer Don Hewitt had introduced the high-impact reaction shots of Nixon, ill and in pain, wiping off his sweat triggered by the hot studio lights. Hewitt's live manipulation created the appearance that Nixon's was sweating and distorting his face under the pressure of Kennedy's arguments (Seltz and Yoakam 1977: 89–90; Jamieson 1996: 158–61). Hewitt had borrowed this production technique from the extremely popular but rigged NBC quiz show *21*, which turned off the ventilation in the booth of the predetermined loser, so that he could dramatically pat his sweaty brows with his handkerchief (Mc-Fadden 2020, D7). Now, Kennedy's political decision to introduce the Cuba issue as one of his "publicity vehicles into a public sphere manufactured for show" (Jürgen Habermas) had come to haunt him.

Predictably, the question whether Eisenhower and Nixon "must take responsibility for the loss of Cuba" opened the second TV debate in October 1960 (Debate Transcript, in Kraus, ed. 1977: 369). Dramatically, the staunch anti-Communist Nixon had unexpected difficulties to defend himself against the implied charge of suddenly being "soft on Communism." For he could not reveal the covert planning by the CIA of the Bay of Pigs operation.

In October 1962, tables had turned. Obviously, Kennedy could not publicly admit that in the preceding nine months he had spent $50 million of taxpayer money on "hit-and-run attacks" to sabotage the Cuban economy. They were a part of his covert CIA-operation "Mongoose." Since February 1962, the CIA had been following "a detailed, six-phase plan for the removal of the Castro regime" by October 20 (Bird 1998: 242; cf. Bundy 1988: 416).

Significantly, Bundy, who chaired a "highly secret . . . interagency group of CIA, State and Defense Department aides," had dedicated "an inordinate amount of his time in the spring and summer of 1962" to coordinate this proverbial "October surprise" in time for the November midterm elections. As Bird analyzes, on one hand these incessant disruptions of everyday life were designed to create serious hardships for the Cuban people with the intent of fomenting a "popular revolution." On the other hand, Bundy and Kennedy signed off on "Mongoose" planning documents which clearly stated that "final success will require decisive U.S. military intervention" (Bird 1998: 242).

Finally, on October 1, the commander in chief of the U.S. Atlantic fleet followed McNamara's instructions to prepare not only for a blockade of Cuba but also for air strikes by October 20. Simultaneously, U.S. Army commanders were alerted to the "imminence of a possible implementation" of the plans for a "full-scale invasion of Cuba" (Bird 1998: 244). In 1999, McNamara would confirm that these "contingency plans called for a 'first-day' air attack of 1,080 sorties." In his words, "a huge attack." Moreover, an "invasion force totaling 180,000 troops" had been assembled in ports on the Atlantic and Gulf Coasts of Florida. In comparison, the failed Bay of Pigs invasion had been attempted by about 1,500 Cuban exiles without any U.S. Air Force support (McNamara, Blight, and Brigham 1999: 9).

This chilling example of the inadvertent consequences of Cold War brinkmanship clearly demonstrates that Habermas's analysis of the manipulation of democratic decision-making is not an academic exercise but an immensely practical one. *Structural Transformation*'s detailed study of the manipulation of public discourse to deceive voters is derived from Habermas's astute observation of the growing dysfunction of Western democracies since the birth of their nuclear Cold War with the Soviet dictatorship and its Warsaw Pact satellites. This threat to the self-determined participation of citizens in the democratic process was most visible in West Germany where under Adenauer's restoration republic former Nazis could perpetuate their authoritarian governance. However, manipulating the public in the name of a need for secrecy during the Cold War also became the new normal in an increasingly imperial U.S. Presidency. After the Cuban missile crisis, McNamara's chief press officer Arthur Sylvester even "brashly proclaimed that the government had the right to deceive the press in the interest of national security" (quoted in Kern, P. W. Levering, and R. B. Levering 1983: 139).

During the Vietnam war, he continued to practice what he preached. Already in 1964, when a young *New York Times* reporter argued with him in Saigon over "the government's lack of credibility" in its statements about the progress of the war, Sylvester responded "that although it was unfortunate, there were times when a government official had to lie" (Halberstam 1972: 527). Not surprisingly, this practice gradually dissolved trust in government among a large portion of the electorate like acid. Emblematic for this development was the response to McNamara's 1995 book *In Retrospect: The Tragedy and Lessons of Vietnam* by the head of the Veterans Administration under President Jimmy Carter, Max Cleland, who had lost both legs and one arm in Vietnam: "It sure would have been helpful in May of 1967, when I volunteered for Vietnam, if he had said then that the war was unwinnable" (quoted in *The New York Times*, April 15, 1995, A 2, "Quote of the Day").

4.2. THE INFLUENCE OF NEUMANN, JASPERS, AND MARCUSE ON *STRUCTURAL TRANSFORMATION*'S DEMOCRATIC THEORY IN THE CONTEXT OF HABERMAS'S PARTICIPATORY POLITICAL PRACTICE FROM 1958

On Saturday night, October 27, 1962, in the climactic hours of the Cuban missile crisis, John F. Kennedy told his brother Robert in the Oval Office that the "thought that disturbed him most" was "the specter of death of . . . the young people . . . who had no say . . ., but whose lives would be snuffed out like everyone else's." They would "never have a chance to make a decision, to vote in an election, to run for office. . ." (quoted in Ellsberg 2017: 219). Since he was a father of two young children, Kennedy's thought seemed genuine. He also knew that his words would find a responsive chord with his brother, who had several children of his own. However, a sizable number of these young people wondered whether the Kennedy brothers were living up to their parental responsibilities.

Earlier that week, at the University of Michigan, about 400 college students, members of SDS and Women for Peace, had demonstrated *against* the provocative move by the Soviets to install nuclear missiles and *for* Cuba's safety from a potential invasion by the United States. Their leaflet implicitly referred to a popular James Dean movie about juvenile delinquents who raced their cars to the edge of a cliff and jumped out before getting airborne. The winner of this test of vigor and courage jumped at the very last moment. The loser was too scared to go to the brink—or tried to demonstrate so much virility that he ignored the margin of error or mishap, like the sleeve of his leather jacket getting caught on the door handle. In short, the young protesters urgently called on Washington and on Moscow to end the ongoing "game of chicken," with humankind "on the bumpers" (quoted in Gitlin 1987: 99).

This astute metaphor captured the disconnect in Kennedy's ruminations about nuclear death potentially keeping the young people from ever having "a chance to make a decision." For even those who had reached voting age in 1960 and cast their ballot for the charismatic young candidate who as United States President would appeal to their altruism and enlist them in his "Peace Corps," were not allowed to participate in a democratic decision-making process about their potential nuclear annihilation. Neither were almost all of their parents and grandparents. Figuratively speaking, the vast majority of voters and office holders were "on the bumpers" while only the innermost civilian and military leadership of each "Super Power" was "in the driver's seat."

In his biographical remarks in Kyoto in November 2004, Habermas highlighted that for him *democracy* was "the magic word, not the Anglo-Saxon liberalism." For in his view the concept of democracy united the "tradition of natural law with modernity's spirit of awakening and its promise of emancipation." Needless to say, there was no energizing democratic magic in Adenauer's paternalistic authoritarianism (cf. Hofmann 2020: 379).

Habermas's equally precise and withering critique of the West German chancellor from May 1958 dovetails with his Kyoto remarks almost four decades later: "What kind of image of democracy does it take to justify treating the mass of citizens as an immature mass—in order to decide all questions regarding the political fate of the nation *for* the people but not together *with* the people" (quoted in Yos 2019: 214n72, emphasis added). He also exposed Adenauer's focus group tested euphemism about "peace through strength" as the boilerplate saber rattling it was. Regarding the Cold War rhetoric about a "muscular defense" to achieve "peace through strength," Habermas introduced a particularly biting parallel to Nazi propaganda:

> Some time ago the Nazis spoke of 'fresh milk without cream' when selling skimmed milk to the people. Today the politicians arguing for strength speak of the 'most advanced weapons' when selling A- and H-bombs to the people. (quoted in Yos 2019: 214n72)

Small wonder that in this suffocating atmosphere of political cynicism Marcuse's "courage to release utopian energies again, with the uninhibitedness of the eighteenth century," struck such a responsive chord with Habermas. The Marcusean core from 1937 in Horkheimer and Adorno's 1944 testimonial about accepting the bourgeois ideals, no matter how distorted or manipulated they have become, "without further consideration," allowed him to access Kant's rational natural law in conjunction with Rousseau's democratic theory which fueled modernity's "spirit of awakening and its promise of emancipation." In 1958, Habermas practiced in front of Frankfurt's town hall the democratic political participation he reflected on and advocated for in the same year in his introduction to *Student und Politik*.

This text not only referenced Horkheimer and Adorno's past acceptance of the bourgeois ideals but also Neumann's ongoing commitment to them, when he defines the self-determination of humankind as the essence of the democratic process. In the sixth volume of the *Zeitschrift für Sozialforschung* from 1937, fewer than thirty pages separated the last page of Neumann's article on the functional transformation of law in the right of bourgeois society from the first page of the foundational reflections by Horkheimer on philosophy and Critical Theory, which were followed by Marcuse's. In 1958, the writings by Jaspers reinforced Habermas's orientation toward Kant, while Neumann's text from 1937 offered the essence of the political economy presuppositions for Rousseau's democratic theory.

Structural Transformation's Section 12 highlights that Rousseau's theory "provided the foundations for the public's democratic self-determination" with "all desirable clarity" (STPS 96). In time for the bicentennial of the French Revolution, Habermas would add that "Rousseau, the forerunner of the French Revolution, understands liberty as the autonomy of the people, as the equal participation of each person in the practice of *self-legislation*" (BFN 472, emphasis in the original). Before emphasizing in the next sentence the connection between Rousseau and Kant, who was "a philosophical contemporary of the French Revolution." And referencing the famous quote in which Kant admitted that Rousseau "set him straight" in terms of democratic theory.

It is no coincidence that the political scientist and intellectual historian James Miller first published *Rousseau: Dreamer of Democracy* in 1984, before following up three years later with his history of Students for a Democratic Society (SDS), titled *"Democracy is in the Streets": From Port Huron to the Siege of Chicago* (1987). Rousseau's ideal of direct democracy was an intellectual foundation and "the magic word" for the SDS *Port Huron Statement* from June 1962 as much as for *Structural Transformation,* published in the same year. Both texts envisioned self-governance without political domination. The only slight difference occurred with regard to the location where Rousseau's "idea of a plebiscite in permanence" would take place. For Habermas this idea "presented itself to Rousseau in the image of the Greek *polis,*" where citizens would assemble in the *"place publique"* (STPS 99), like the one in front of Frankfurt's town hall. For SDS members who came out of the civil rights movement in the South and were transitioning to community organizing in the ghettos of the North, the image of participatory democracy was closer to Rousseau's own experience with the *"Montagnons* near Neufchatel in the Swiss Alps, which he had known since his youth":

> Hence, his description of the democratic form of government in the *Social Contract* (1762/1959) features a very small public, where citizens can easily congregate and where all know each other. The members of this public have to live by very simple mores, own equally distributed wealth, and not have any knowledge of luxury. Above all, "nobody must be sufficiently wealthy to buy somebody else, and nobody may be so poor to have to sell oneself." (Fetscher 1960: 218; cf. HPSC 32–33)

Neumann's analysis of Rousseau's draft for the Constitution of Corsica anticipates *Structural Transformation*'s discussion of the "bourgeois idea of the law-based state" that "already aims at abolishing the state as an instrument of domination altogether" (STPS 82). Since Rousseau's "model of a society of petty commodity producers" leaves "hardly any room for domination," Neumann concludes that in "Rousseau's system the law is the real sovereign" (Neumann 1937: 576; cf. HPSC 32). Emblematic for Rousseau's ideal of direct democracy is the notion of the "virtuous citizen," *Structural Transformation*'s "moral person" (STPS 85,111) at the core of the book's second normative thesis discussed above under 1.2.

Conversely, "Habermas's theory evolution from participatory democracy in *Structural Transformation* to deliberative democracy in his fully developed discourse theory of law and democracy" (Hofmann 2021: 956) dissolves the identification of *bourgeois* and *homme*. It can thus end "the moral overburdening of the virtuous citizen" (BFN 473). In this process, it also moves closer to the "Anglo-Saxon liberalism" that *Structural Transformation*'s Section 15 still took to task:

> The liberalist interpretation of the bourgeois constitutional state is reactionary: it reacts to the power of the idea, *initially* included in its institutions, of the self-determination of a reasoning public, *as soon as* this public is subverted by the propertyless and uneducated masses. (STPS 136, emphasis added)

In this context, readers have to keep in mind that *Structural Transformation* restricts its democratic theory to Kants's "liberal model," which is informed by Rousseau. Habermas also draws via Schmitt's *Constitutional Theory* on Condorcet, although *Structural Transformation* does not reference him. In stark contrast, John Stuart Mill is not regarded as a liberal, because he supposedly converted to liberalism.

This distinction can easily lead to misunderstandings. After all, *On Liberty* (1859) is universally taught as the classic liberal text on individual liberty. Moreover, Mill's *Principles of Political Economy* (1848) was the canonical textbook at the height of liberal capitalism in the nineteenth-century. Finally, Section 15 classifies Mill's "reactionary" *On Liberty* as "superior to the socialist critique," even though it shares with Marx's alternative to the liberal model of the public sphere the "problematic presupposition" of a "natural order" of social reproduction.

Nevertheless, readers can find the criteria for *Structural Transformation*'s distinction between "liberal" and "liberalist" in Section 15, if they juxtapose Rousseau, the "Dreamer of Democracy," and Mill, the Anglo-Saxon political economist. Mill is content with the separation of powers. Rousseau dreams of the abolition of power. *Structural Transformation* has adopted Neumann's definition of "true democracy" as "the self-determination of humankind." In short, after power has been abolished, truth alone makes the laws. This dream fueled the rise of the bourgeois public sphere up to Section 13 on Kant. With the "liberalist" turn in Section 15, the idea of the dissolution of power is withdrawn. Instead, the *dissolution of the bourgeois public sphere itself* begins. As Habermas's sums up after extensively quoting *On Liberty*:

> The political public sphere no longer stands for the *idea of the dissolution of power*; instead, it has to serve its division; public opinion becomes *a mere limit on power.* (STPS 136, emphasis added)

4.3. HABERMAS'S "CELEBRATED COFFEE HOUSES" (TODD GITLIN) AS UNIVERSAL SYMBOLS OF FREE SPEECH AND PARTICIPATORY DEMOCRACY IN THE MODERN PUBLIC SPHERE

The historical specificity of London's coffee houses, originating in the 1650s, is perhaps the most striking feature of Structural Transformation's narrative about the rise of free speech and the public use of reason in modernity. As concrete examples of historical spheres for democratic debate of news and public matters, these social institutions go a long way toward explaining why Habermas's classic continues to strike such a responsive chord among students, faculty, media professionals, and members of an educated public around the globe. Even in today's online world, their roots in republican dissent, expressed in the unlicensed printing during the second half of the seventeenth century, capture the imagination of public-minded intellectuals concerned about the violation of constitutional rights by the economic and political powers that be.

In short, these foundations of the modern public sphere remain highly relatable, even though the free access to newspapers was replaced by the free Wi-Fi connection to the global news on the internet. A recent report from the site on Russell Street in Convent Garden, where Button's Coffee House took a star turn in Habermas's British "model case" (STPS 33, 42) illustrates this continuity. Now morphed into a Starbucks, it can still harbor the "same enthusiasms, the same passions, the same heated discussions." Only today the arguments start with "a tap-tap-tap on keyboards" while the counter-arguments are announced by the "pings and dings and whooshes" of recipient and response notifications (IMP Media. "Roarings of the Lion: The Starbucks that's on the site of social media history," www.impmedia.co.uk/2017/03/11).

In 1962, *Structural Transformation* highlighted a Royal Proclamation from the 1670s, which accused coffee house debaters of having "assumed to themselves a liberty . . . to censure and defame the proceedings of the State" (STPS 59). Already in 1960, the historian Christopher Hill had praised them for having preserved "'a popular republican tradition' in a hostile political culture after 1660." Between the lines, he was writing about the present. His article valorized the Partisan Coffee House opened on Carlisle Street in London's Soho district in October 1958 by the editors and supporters of *Universities & Left Review*. The new journal had been founded at Oxford University. It published its first issue in spring 1957. *ULR* and its Partisan Coffee House quickly became havens for political dissent in a hostile Cold War culture, observed by Special Branch" government spies—echoes of the Restoration period from 1660 to 1688. They played key roles in the Campaign for Nuclear

Disarmament as well as the "Committee of 100," presided over by the phi-losopher Bertrand Russell, which organized acts of civil disobedience like a sit-down demonstration by about four thousand protesters at the Ministry of Defense in Whitehall in February 1961.

In 2017, when a London art gallery was about to open an exhibition on the long-gone *ULR* Partisan and its upstairs bookstore, *The Guardian* posted an online article about its history under the headline "How a Soho coffee house gave birth to the New Left" (Thorpe, April 2017). This is only slightly exag-gerated. After all, in 1960 C. Wright Mills mailed his famous "Letter to the New Left" to Carlisle Street, where *ULR*'s successor, the *New Left Review*, published it in its September–October issue. His groundbreaking letter estab-lished the trans-Atlantic connection of the New Left. For it was reprinted by *Studies on the Left, a journal of research, social theory, and review*, which graduate students had founded one year earlier, in fall 1959, at the University of Wisconsin, Madison. Several of them were students of Mills's mentor, the sociologist Hans Heinz Gerth, whom they asked to contribute the lead article for their first issue. Its title was "The Relevance of History to the Sociological Ethos" (Hakim 1990: 257; cf. HPSC 25n46).

In the 1940s, Gerth, who until 1933 had been Karl Mannheim's second assistant at Frankfurt University, connected Mills to the same German intel-lectual history tradition that informs *Structural Transformation*'s application of Weber's "ideal-type" to the concept of the public in constitutional theory (cf. HPSC 15–16). The result was Mills's 1950 article "The Sociology of Mass Media and Public Opinion" for the U.S. Department of State's Russian language journal *Amerika*, whose publication was prohibited by Soviet authorities. In 1956, it would form the basis for Mills's reflections on "the classic public of democratic theory" in *The Power Elite*, which very much influenced a young Habermas (see above: Introduction, V).

Mills's academic best seller had an even greater impact on a group of University of Michigan, Ann Arbor students, whose "love of coffee and serious conversation" let them congregate "at the Michigan Union Grill, where they could linger for a dime." In his history of the SDS, referred to above in 4.2, James Miller describes how in 1958 these avant-garde non-conformists assisted Robert Alan Haber, a member of their circle, in getting elected to a seat on the Student Government Council (Miller 1987: 28). Haber, only seven years younger than Habermas, was named after the legendary Wisconsin senator Robert La Follette who, after his historic address "Free Speech in Wartime," was almost expelled from the United States Senate, so that he could be prosecuted under President Woodrow Wilson's May 1918 Sedition Act. His crime? Making "disloyal" statements like "The 'right of the people freely to discuss all matters pertaining to the Government' must always be protected because 'the people are the rulers in war not less than in peace'" (quoted in Kazin 2017: 302; cf. Hofmann 2019: 60–61).

Haber and Habermas were attracted to the same quote from *The Power Elite*. It can be found in *Structural Transformation*'s Section 25, which is titled "A Sociological Attempt at Clarificaton." On his book's next-to-last page, Habermas refers to it as providing his Weberian ideal-type, derived from Kant's ideal of the "public use of reason," with "empirically usable criteria for a definition of public opinion":

> In a *public*, as we may understand the term, (1) virtually as many people express opinions as receive them. (2) Public communications are so organized that there is a chance immediately and effectively to answer back any opinion expressed in public. Opinion formed by such discussion (3) readily finds an outlet in effective action, even against – if necessary – the prevailing system of authority. And (4) authoritative institutions do not penetrate the public, which is thus more or less autonomous in its operations. (Mills 1956: 303-304; quoted in STPS 249, emphasis in the original; cf. Miller 1987: 83–86, 87, 93–95)

When Haber was elected as the first SDS president at a national convention in New York City titled "Student Radicalism—1960," his commitment to the face-to-face communication at the core of Mills's above characteristics of "participatory democracy" had already energized his university's Political Issues Club. Now his activism was validated by Mill's message to the New Left: "The Age of Complacency is ending. . . . We are beginning to move again" (quoted in Miller 1987: 87). To make certain that these inspiring words were not only discussed abroad at a Soho coffee house but also at home in places like the Michigan Union Grill, SDS immediately mimeographed the text and sent it out to all eight chapters to be read by its 250 members at the time. Mills was prescient: That number would grow to 100,000 by 1968 (Miller 1987: 65, 259).

In a 1994 interview, Stanley Fish, the postmodernist professor of English, accused Habermas of preaching "the theology of talk" (quoted in Stephens 1994: 10). The *Los Angeles Times Magazine* article that included Fish's verdict presented seemingly corroborating evidence. A regular participant in these discussion sessions by professors and students about philosophy and politics at the Greek restaurant "Dionysus" in Frankfurt/Main was willing to go on the record: "Habermas is someone who really has to be pulled out of a restaurant at midnight." However, Habermas did not deny this. On the contrary, he confirmed that he enjoyed these discussions so much that his wife had to regularly remind him of his teaching obligations the next morning (quoted in Stephens 1994: 9).

With midnight approaching on December 31, 1961, forty-five chapter representatives from around the country were trying to wrap up at Ann Arbor two days of discussions about the future of SDS. Earlier that year, Haber had finally succeeded in recruiting Tom Hayden, the editor of the student news-paper *The Michigan Daily*. Now Hayden was tasked to write the draft for "a political manifesto of the Left." At the next SDS convention in June 1962, it would become the Port Huron Statement. As Miller learned in his interviews with participants, the atmosphere of these discussions had been exhilarating:

> In the preceding months, Haber and Hayden had both written about their yearning for face-to-face politics and their desire to be part of a public with common values and commitments. They longed for a vital sense of democ-racy, a living sense of community. Now, they were discovering it among themselves. (Miller 1987: 77; cf. Gitlin 1987: 101)

The only drawback: New Year's Day was a few minutes away and the lively debates continued unabatedly. Finally, "with no end in sight," Hayden's wife "broke out champagne and forced the group to stop talking" (Miller 1987: 77).

The "sovereign public—both deliberative and rational—stands at the heart of the Enlightenment ideal of a democratic republic" (Gitlin 1998: 168). This is how in 1998 Gitlin summed up the essence of *Structural Transformation*'s Kantian ideal. In 1963, after graduating from Harvard with a B.A. in math-ematics, he moved to Ann Arbor to go to graduate school at the University of Michigan. As he describes it in *The Sixties: Years of Hope, Days of Rage* (1987), his motivation for this move was "not so much to study political science ([his] ostensible purpose) as to breathe the air of the SDS circle" (Gitlin 1987: 103). Through his own political activism at Harvard, he had met and been impressed by Haber, Hayden, and other leading SDS members. In June 1963, Gitlin was elected president of SDS, succeeding Hayden (Miller 1987: 178; Gitlin 1987: 104).

Gitlin's eyewitness account confirms Miller's assessment of the exhila-rating experience SDS members shared when living, face-to-face, the ideal of a democratic community through their joint political engagement. This momentary fusion of democratic theory and practice is exemplified by the degree to which Hayden's research on Mills's concept of the public and par-ticipatory democracy for his M.A. thesis informed his draft of the Port Huron Statement.

Conversely, the spontaneous democratic protest that started the Free Speech Movement at UC Berkeley on October 1, 1964, can serve as a text-book example for Mills's above thesis that the opinion of a self-determined public "readily finds an outlet in effective action, even against—if necessary—the prevailing system of authority." After University of California administrators outlawed the recruitment of civil rights workers on campus, Mario Savio and Jack Weinberg, who had helped register African American voters in Mississippi during the Freedom Summer of 1964, became the catalysts for a thirty-two-hour sit-in protest. In a history-making act of civil disobedience, hundreds of students blocked a police car from taking away Weinberg, a Ph.D. student in Mathematics, who had been arrested after setting up his unauthorized recruitment table (Gitlin 1987: 164; J. Morrison and R. K. Morrison, eds. 1987/2001: 225–31).

To achieve and sustain its autonomy, the public "needs *rights* of political organization, speech and assembly; it needs *deliberation*" (Gitlin 1998: 168, emphasis in the original). Gitlin's 1998 explication of Habermas's concept connects its Kantian origins with the emancipatory practices of the Free Speech Movement inspired by Mills. *Structural Transformation* highlights Kant's conviction that, in contrast to the inability of isolated individuals to overcome their prejudices, "the *public* should enlighten itself. . ., if only freedom is granted" (quoted in STPS 104).

Gitlin's conclusion that this public requires "in short, a way to take shape, to become itself" (Gitlin 1998: 168), reflects his experiences from the early SDS community in Ann Arbor to the communal quest for Berkeley's "People's Park in the Northern California spring" of 1969. For him, the "harmonious combination" of "the spirits of the New Left and the counterculture. . . redeemed visions of the cooperative commonwealth" from seventeenth-century England. At the time, he regarded "this improvised utopia" of squatters on a university lot off Telegraph Avenue as "substance and sign of a possible participatory order" (Gitlin 1987: 355).

The "regular, freely circulating supply of information occupies a special place in the Enlightenment ideal of autonomous individuals engaged in the practice of self-government. At one end of the ideal stands the French Encyclopedia; at another, the newspapers and coffee houses celebrated by Jürgen Habermas. . ." (Gitlin 1998: 168). During the many years that Gitlin worked and lived in Berkeley as a journalist, political activist, Ph.D. student, and professor, this ideal literally had the spatial dimension his wording from 1998 implies. To this day, one can move back and forth between the UC Berkeley campus and the coffee houses that surround it.

In the course of the first English Revolution, the combination of newspapers and coffee houses had spawned *The Penny Universities* (1956) which the historian Aytoun Ellis examined two years before the Partisan Coffee House would open. In January 1660, Samuel Pepys walked the short distance from his clerkship in Exchequer Yard to "the Turk's Head Coffee-House in New Palace Yard, a location in the vicinity of Parliament and the government offices at Whitehall" (M. Ellis 2004: 49, 45). There he paid even more than the customary penny entrance fee to join the Rota Club regularly convened by the political philosopher James Harrington. As he noted in his famous diary, the "admirable discourse" and "exceeding good argument" of the participants who included the mathematician and political economist William Petty were worth his time and money (M. Ellis 2004: 49, 50; cf. A. Ellis 1956: 37–39, 41–42, 55).

Once the Commonwealth period of English history was terminated, Harrington's bold attempt to continue his coffee house club ended with his imprisonment in the Tower of London in December 1661. He was accused of having advanced "treasonable Designs and Practices." Government spies had reported that in his club, established in *"Bowstreet in Coventgarden"* in March 1661, "twenty people debated the dissolution of Parliament and the bringing in of a new one" (M. Ellis 2004: 54).

Harrington's fate can be regarded as rather emblematic for dissenting intellectuals and journalists in modernity, from the unlicensed printing during the Restoration to the "war against the unstamped" British press in the early nineteenth century. Arguably, an important factor why Daniel Ellsberg could avoid being sentenced during the continuing reign of Wilson's Espionage Act in the United States since 1917 was his decision to give the "Pentagon Papers" to *The New York Times* instead of to San Francisco's *Ramparts* magazine or another print forerunner of *Wiki Leaks*.

Chapter Five

Understanding Habermas's Public Sphere Concept by Dissolving Its Monolithic Stylization

Structural Transformation's *Interpretation of a Sociological and Political Category with the Norms of Constitutional Theory and Intellectual History*

5.1. THE FACTICITY OF SOCIAL AND POLITICAL HISTORY VERSUS THE NORMATIVITY OF CONSTITUTIONAL LAW THEORY AND INTELLECTUAL HISTORY

The most efficient approach to comprehending *Structural Transformation*'s complex theses is the dissolution of the book's monolithic stylization by reading Sections 1 to 18 in an order that allows to correctly identify and clarify them. For readers have to know *from the beginning* of their reception of Habermas's book, that only Sections 12 to 15 about the *liberal* bourgeois idea and ideology of Öffentlichkeit in its meaning of "publicness" *implicitly* explain why his stylized presentation of the social and political history of Öffentlichkeit in its meaning of the "public sphere" in Sections 4 to 11 is so highly selective. In other words, Habermas presents his analysis of the public sphere as "a category of bourgeois society" through the lens of "publicness" as a *norm* of Kant's modern rational natural law, institutionalized in the bourgeois constitutional state.

Starting one's reception of *Structural Transformation* with Section 4 "The Basic Blueprint" allows to productively take on this intriguing intellectual challenge. The opening sentence of that section seemingly provides the book's central thesis about the bourgeois public sphere as a *sociological* and *historical* category, which explains how the public discourse about developing and regulating the complex political economies of modernity has been facilitated:

The bourgeois public sphere may be conceived above all as the sphere of private people come together as a public; they soon claim the public sphere regulated from above against the public authorities themselves, to engage them in a debate over the general rules governing relations in the *basically privatized but publicly relevant sphere of commodity exchange and social labor*. The medium of this *political* confrontation was peculiar and without historical precedent: people's public use of their reason. (STPS 27, emphasis added)

However, in 1971, Habermas implicitly confirmed that *Structural Trans-formation*'s seminal thesis about the modern public sphere was not his main focus, even though Section 3 "On the Genesis of the Bourgeois Pub-lic Sphere" seems to give this impression. For that section is informed by Arendt's juxtaposition of the *polis* of antiquity and the "the rise of the 'so-cial'" in modernity, i.e., the fact that the *"private sphere of society . . . has become publicly relevant. . ."* (STPS 19, emphasis in the original). Moreover, Habermas's "Author's Preface" ranks "sociology and economics" first and second regarding his interdisciplinary research for *Structural Trans-formation* (STPS xvii). Nevertheless, these disciplines primarily *assist* in reconstructing an ideal type of modern rational natural law inscribed in bourgeois constitutions that, in Habermas's view, "aims at dissolving domination altogether" (STPS 81). Above all, his 1971 foreword to *Theory and Practice* (1963/1973) claims that *Structural Transformation*'s theory reconstruction of Kant's constitutional law detected such an intention and its inscription in the political institutions of modernity.

Significantly, Habermas first published the essence of this thesis in spring 1960, *before* completing his work on *Structural Transformation*. While conceding in his adversarial review of Koselleck's *Critique and Crisis* (1959) that the (Kantian) notion of making politics rational through the "principle of publicness" was "in its function sheer ideology," he simultaneously emphasized that it contained the *idea* of dissolving political into rational authority in the medium of a rational-critical public sphere—thus transforming domination as such. This idea entered into the norms of "the bourgeois constitutional state" in a "contradictory fashion." (KUK 358). In other words, what has remained unchanged over more than fifty years is Habermas's goal, as he stated in his foreword to the 2013 Italian edition of *Between Facts and Norms*, "to rationally reconstruct (in Hegelian terms: reduce to the concept) the normative substance *already present* in the constitutions of existing democracies." (Habermas quoted in Floridia 2017: 299–300, emphasis in the original).

To correctly understand *Structural Transformation*, its readers thus have to constantly keep in mind this underlying relationship between idea and ideol-ogy as well as the unique tension between facticity and Habermas's search for normative potential. Especially since he only addresses these topics randomly, mostly cryptically, even in his book's part IV, which is explicitly titled "The Bourgeois Public Sphere: Idea and Ideology." This missing identification of his ideology-critical procedure even obscures what Habermas himself acknowledged in 1989, namely, his book's "collapsing of norm and description" (CR 463). The impact of this obstacle to achieving a correct understanding of *Structural Transformation* is further enlarged by his methodological decision to conduct the "sociological investigation of historical trends. . . on a level of generality," which interprets "unique processes and events . . . as instances of a more general social development" (STPS xviii). In short, by using Max Weber's "ideal type" and, above all, the Hegelian-Marxist philosophy of history without identifying these methodologies.

Section 4 presents readers with the resulting challenges already on its first page. On one hand, that section emphasizes that in Great Britain, other than on the continent, "the prince's power was relatively reduced by a parliament" (STPS 27). Accordingly, its emerging public sphere of bourgeois society (STPS 23) also developed differently. On the other hand, Section 8 posits its rise in England from the end of censorship in 1695 to the election reform of 1832 as "The Model Case of British Development." How can the English exception of, for example, Daniel Defoe's and Jonathan Swift's *political* reflections on parliamentary debate in the early eighteenth century be simultaneously typical for both the French and Prussian variants of the emerging bourgeois public sphere during that time period? The answer can be found on page 267, where endnote 65 of Section 11 reminds the reader of the methodological prerogative stated in the "Author's Preface":

> At this level of generality we disregard national differences between Great Britain, France, and Germany, which are simultaneously differences in the level of capitalist development. (STPS 267n65)

Conversely, *Structural Transformation* did not find sufficient normative potential for its signature concept of a uniquely *critical* public opinion in England as the most advanced capitalist country at the time. Instead, Habermas had to turn to 1760s France and to 1780s Prussia. There he could dialectically reconstruct the Physiocratic and Kantian definitions respectively.

Contrary to its title "The Basic Blueprint," Section 4, which opens the book's chapter II "Social Structures of the Public Sphere," does not include this *basic* information. Neither does Section 9 about "The Continental Variants" in chapter III "Political Functions of the Public Sphere." The reader only finds it in chapter IV, which discusses the "Idea and Ideology" of the term *opinion publique* in Section 12 about "Public Opinion–*opinion publique*—*Öffentliche Meinung*: On the Prehistory of the Phrase." Above all, chapter IV analyzes the central Kantian term

Publizität ("publicness") in Section 13 about "Publicity as the Bridging Principle between Politics and Morality (Kant)."

By using this guide, the reader can realize that the bourgeois and aristocratic members of the Physiocrats were "the private people come together as a public" to engage the French public authorities "in a debate over the general rules governing relations in the basically privatized but publicly relevant sphere of commodity exchange and social labor" (STPS 27). In the process, as Habermas emphasizes in Section 12, the term *opinion publique* received its "strict meaning of an opinion purified through critical discussion in the public sphere to constitute a true opinion." As "exponents of a public that now also debated about *political* matters," the Physiocrats "were the first to assert that civil society followed laws of its own versus the interventions of the state" (STPS 95, emphasis added).

This turn in intellectual history occurred in 1767, when Pierre-Paul Le Mercier de la Riviere, a disciple of Francois Quesnay, the founder of the Physiocratic political economy, became the first to present "the rigorous concept of *opinion publique*" (STPS 95) in his book "The Natural and Essential Order of Political Societies." This date gains additional significance, because in the same year the Physiocrat Pierre-Samuel Dupont de Nemours, Quesnay's close collaborator, coined the term "Physiocracy." It designates the political implementation of their economic doctrine as the universal and peaceful "rule of nature" (HPSC 31).

In comparison, it took England until the beginning of the Industrial Revolution before the most advanced capitalist country entered the term "public opinion" into its *Oxford Dictionary* in 1781 (STPS 95). In the same year, when "conditions in Prussia looked like a static model of a situation that in France and especially in Great Britain had become fluid at the beginning of the century" (STPS 25), Kant nevertheless became the exponent of a public formed by "private people" who "readied themselves to compel public authority to legitimate itself before public opinion" (STPS 25–26). This happened when Kant published his Preface to the first edition of his *Critique of Pure Reason* from 1781, as Koselleck highlighted in 1959 (CC 121).

Since *Structural Transformation* does not include this crucial quote, this guide presents it in its entirety. Readers will realize that it succinctly explains *why* "the medium of this *political* confrontation" between the private people and the public authorities "was peculiar and without historical precedent" (STPS 27, emphasis added):

> Our age is, in especial degree, the age of criticism, and to criticism everything must submit. Religion through its sanctity and law-giving through its majesty may seek to exempt themselves from it. But they then awaken just suspicion, and

cannot claim the sincere respect which reason accords only to that which has been able to sustain the test of free and open examination. (Quoted in CC 121)

In short, this medium, "people's public use of their reason" (STPS 27), triggered such political controversy that after the death of Frederick the Great in 1786 Kant deleted the above quote in the second edition of his *Critique* from 1787 (CC 121n59). Moreover, even Frederick as the famous example of an enlightened monarch seemingly felt compelled to respond to this challenge. The following quote from 1784, contained in Section 3, reads like His Majesty's direct rebuttal:

A private person has no right to pass *public* and perhaps even disapproving judgment on the actions, procedures, laws, regulations, and ordinances of sovereigns and courts, their officials, assemblies, and courts of law, or to promulgate or publish in print pertinent reports that he manages to obtain. For a private person is not at all capable of making such judgments, because he lacks complete knowledge of circumstances and motives. (Quoted in STPS 25, emphasis in the original)

Finally, the juxtaposition of these quotes in this guide demonstrates the advantages of *not* reading the sections of *Structural Transformation* in sequential order *and* of systematically drawing on the sources that inform Habermas's book. For more than 75 pages separate the above quote from Habermas's discussion of Kant's seminal exposition of the private "people's public use of their reason" in his legendary essay "What Is Enlightenment?" from the same year, 1784, in Section 13 (STPS 104). Moreover, his article, published in the *Berlinische Monatsschrift*, is not even mentioned in the discussion of Prussia's "static" public sphere in Section 3 (STPS 25) or in the one in Section 9 about the German "public's rational-critical debate of political matters" in "the last decades of the eighteenth century" (STPS 72).

The above guidance about systematically connecting the first sentence of Section 4 to Sections 3, 11, 9, 12, 13 is not contained in *Structural Transformation*'s "Basic Blueprint," even though it addresses not only the *social* structures of commodity exchange and social labor that shape the emergence of the bourgeois public sphere. Habermas's introductory thesis also explicitly identifies the *political* functions of developing and regulating the political economy as well as legitimating public authority in this sphere of critical public opinion. In short, the "Basic Blueprint" does not focus on these social structures to analyze the *facticity* of social and political history. Instead, Section 4 invokes the *normativity* of legal theory and intellectual history to find in these social structures evidence that can advance

Structural Transformation's central thesis about the dissolution of domination in the rational-critical discourse of the public sphere.

For that purpose, Habermas's graphic schema on page 30 divides the private sphere of property owners between the "civil society" of commodity exchange and social labor in the Hegelian sense and the conjugal family's intimate sphere. The crucial importance of the latter for Habermas's signature notion about the dissolution of domination is foregrounded already on page 28. There he claims that the "public's understanding of the public use of reason was guided specifically by such private experiences as grew out of the audience-oriented subjectivity of the conjugal family's intimate sphere" (STPS 28, translation modified; SÖ 43).

Such an explicit and specific causality is *not* included in Kant's signature thesis about "the public use of reason." Instead, Habermas introduces this unique causality into his theory reconstruction of Kant's liberal model of the public sphere. Like his rational reconstruction of "the normative substance *already present* in the constitutions of existing democracies" quoted above, Habermas also applies this Hegelian reduction "to the concept" to Kant's ideal type of the bourgeois public sphere. In 1989, Tom Rockmore further explained the logic behind Habermas's 2013 claim about "the normative substance *already present*," namely, Hegel's "understanding of the growth of knowledge through the reconstruction of earlier, imperfect theories in order to better attain their goals" (quoted in HPSC 18n13).

Structural Transformation's key sources for rationally reconstructing the role of the conjugal family's intimate sphere in developing the public's understanding of the public use of reason were Koselleck's following three chapters in *Critique and Crisis*: I.2, "Hobbesian Rationality and the Origins of Enlightenment; II.4, "Locke's Law of Private Censure and its Significance for the Emergence of the Bourgeoisie," and II.8, "The Process of Criticism (Schiller, Simon, Bayle, Voltaire, Diderot and the *Encyclopedie*, Kant)." They are based on Koselleck's highly sophisticated elaboration of Schmitt's "civil war topos" in *The Leviathan in the State Theory of Thomas Hobbes*. In addition, Koselleck's chapter on "The Process of Criticism" draws on Schmitt's stylizations in *Die Diktatur* (1921), specifically on those about "Legal Despotism as the Dictatorship of Enlightened Reason: Voltaire, the Physiocrats, especially Le Mercier de la Riviere" (HPSC 9).

Section 4 neither identifies these sources nor connects the reader to Section 12, where Koselleck's book from 1959 and Schmitt's from 1938, but not these specific chapters, are referenced in the endnotes (STPS 267n2, 268n8, 268n9, 268n11). Moreover, the "Author's Note" obscures this crucial importance of intellectual history for *Structural Transforma-*

tion's domination dissolution thesis by relegating it to the sixth and last position among the book's interdisciplinary sources, behind political science and social history (STPS xvii). In reality, its influence on Habermas's theory reconstruction has to be ranked second, behind the decisive one of constitutional law theory.

Finally, even when readers consult the above endnotes to Section 12, they do not learn that Koselleck's intellectual history turns Schmitt's Hobbes interpretation about a "moral inner space" within the "Absolutist State" (CC 39) into the "specific point of origin" (CC 38) for the "bourgeois Enlightenment" (CC 53)—facilitated by the "secret and tacit consent" (CC 55) of John Locke's moral law of private censure. And they do not find a clear identification of this "civil war topos" as Schmitt's intellectual creation—beyond the general reference that such a "moral inner space" was needed, because England's "religious civil war . . . could not be settled politically" and thus had to be ended "under the dictate of a state authority neutralized in religious matters" (STPS 90). Only in 1986 would Habermas tacitly follow up on his 1962 book and confirm in a review article of two English-language translations of Schmitt texts, that in Schmitt's paradigm this "moral inner space" is "turned inside out and extends to become the bourgeois public sphere" (HPSC 6, 19n17, 9, 21n27).

As *Habermas's Public Sphere: A Critique* clarifies, *Structural Transformation* tacitly follows Koselleck's intellectual history of the Reformation with its Lutheran claim, in the tradition of Thomas Aquinas, of a Divine superiority of "inward thought" (Hobbes) in this "moral inner space" (HPSC 190, 222n67). Readers need this explanation (see 5.2 below) to understand why Section 6 on "The Bourgeois Family and the Institutionalization of a Privateness Oriented to an Audience" can define "the intimate sphere" of the "patriarchal conjugal family" as the area where "the experience of 'humanity' originates," namely, "in the humanity of the intimate relationships between human beings who, under the aegis of the family, are nothing more than human" (STPS 48). And why Habermas can claim in Section 11 to "have designated the historical and social location" in which the future bourgeois public sphere germinated, namely, in the "formless humanity" of the bourgeois family as "simply" human beings, that is, *moral* persons (STPS 85). In short, why *Structural Transformation* can use its central claim about a "morally pretentious rationality" to distinguish bourgeois humanism from "the humanism of the Renaissance" (STPS 260n47) in Section 7 about "The Literary in Relation to the Political Public Sphere" (STPS 51, translation modified; SÖ 69).

In this context, the influence of Koselleck's sophisticated elaboration on Schmitt's "civil war topos" in *The Leviathan in the State Theory of Thomas*

Hobbes stands out. This intellectual construct posits a "moral inner space" excluded from the sovereignty of the "Absolutist State" that had been reserved for "humans" as nothing but "human beings" to end England's religious civil war of the seventeenth century. It provided Habermas with the template to conceptualize the genesis of bourgeois humanism's morally pretentious rationality in the "intimate sphere of the bourgeois family" as "humanity's genuine site."

5.2. THE ROLE OF CONSTITUTIONAL LAW THEORY AND INTELLECTUAL HISTORY IN HABERMAS'S RECONSTRUCTION OF A "MORALLY PRETENTIOUS RATIONALITY" OF THE BOURGEOIS PUBLIC SPHERE

In its specific interpretation of legal theory, Section 4 introduces its following claim as a given:

> Needless to say, the power of control over one's own capitalistically function-ing property, being grounded in private law, is *apolitical.* (STPS 28, emphasis added, translation modified; SÖ 42–43)

Section 7 already acknowledges that, "from the beginning," the "character" of the bourgeois public sphere, when challenging "the established authority of the monarch," is also "polemical" (STPS 52; SÖ 70). However, Habermas would only concede (in brackets) in 1990, that the allegedly "apolitical" operation of the capitalist means of production was both "publicly relevant" (STPS 19, 27) *and* quite political. In retrospect, "Further Reflections" (1990/1992) informs the reader that this universal claim was developed by the "liberal theory of constitutional rights" for a specific country, Germany, and in a specific period, during the *Vormärz* leading to the failed Revolution of 1848/49, because at that time it insisted "(with obvious *political* intentions) on a strict separation of public and *private* law" (FRPS 431, emphasis added).

Habermas's implicit correction of his claim in Section 4 also helps to better understand the decisive influence that Koselleck's analysis of the "Process of Criticism" had on *Structural Transformation*'s introduction of "a public sphere in *apolitical* form—the literary precursor of a politically function-ing public sphere" (STPS 29, emphasis added, translation modified; SÖ 44). As Habermas explains only in Section 12, this "Process of Criticism" started in 1695 with Pierre Bayle's introduction of "criticism as such" (STPS 92) through his *Dictionnaire Historique et Critique* (CC 107). Following Koselleck, Habermas emphasizes that "'critique' for Bayle is a private matter and without consequence for public authority," even though "truth is discovered in public discussion among critical minds" (STPS 92, translation modified; SÖ 115). In short, Bayle defines "critique" as *apolitical*: "Criticism that becomes guilty of overstepping the borderline into the political realm, degenerates into pamphleteering" (STPS 92, translation modified; SÖ 115).

Structural Transformation's insistence in Section 4 on its claims about an *apolitical* sphere of commodity exchange and social labor as well as an *apolitical* literary public sphere is necessary to defend its core thesis in Section 13, that the rational-critical discourse in the bourgeois public sphere "aims at rationalizing politics in the name of morality" (STPS 102) through the medium of Kant's rational natural law as the hallmark of a modern republican constitution. For this thesis depends on successfully reconstructing in Section 6 the conjugal family's intimate sphere as the site where, according to "the Anglo-French humanism of the Enlightenment" and "the neohumanism of the German classic period" (STPS 260n47), "the experience of 'humanity' originates" and spawns "the ideas of freedom, love, and cultivation of the person" (STPS 48). Only when this "concept of humanity that is supposed to inhere in humankind as such" (STPS 47), permeates the bourgeois public's understanding of the public use of reason, can a "morally pretentious rationality that strives to discover what is *at once just and right*" develop (STPS 54, emphasis added). As Section 7 explains, this "morally pretentious rationality," that is "intrinsic to the idea of a public opinion born of the power of the better argument" (STPS 54), thus adds a "substantive rationality" to the law's "formal criteria of generality and abstractness" (STPS 55).

This distinction is grounded in Schmitt's *Constitutional Theory* which further juxtaposes the *legal norm* "with certain qualities" like "righteousness, rationality, justice, etc." (CT 63) and the *command* "based on mere will." In *Structural Transformation*'s Section 11, Habermas uses this Schmittian distinction to first prioritize the definition of constitutional law "as an expression of reason" over the one that restricts it to an expression of mere political will. Next, he posits what he calls a "typically bourgeois idea" (STPS 81), namely, that acts of political sovereignty "are considered apocryphal per se" (STPS 82), since, in its intention, "the rule of law aims at dissolving domination altogether" (STPS 81).

Readers have to realize that this is a highly selective Schmitt interpretation regarding "the binding of all state activity to a system of norms legitimated by public opinion" (STPS 82; see HPSC 47, 82n73). It exclusively privileges what *Constitutional Theory* classifies as the fiction that "constitutional norms ... are sovereign" (CT 154-155). This fiction forms the core of the "Absolute Concept of the Constitution," which posits the bourgeois constitutional state as "a closed *system of norms*," conceived as an "*ideal unity*" of the "highest and ultimate *norms*" (CT 59, 62, emphasis in the original; VL 3,7).

As *Constitutional Theory* explains, this ideal-typical assumption regarding a sovereignty of constitutional norms has to transcend their *formal* character and assign *substantial* qualities to them. Schmitt identifies two qualities, namely, "reason and justice." Their specific blending in the bourgeois constitutional norms ideal-typically unites rationality and morality. It thus forms the "rationally right" (CT 63, VL 8). In other words, readers can now identify this ideal-typical construct as the source for *Structural Transformation*'s core thesis about a "morally pretentious rationality" of the bourgeois public sphere.

Significantly, Schmitt's ideal-typical stylization of the "Absolute Concept of the Constitution" with its *substantial* norms of "reason and justice" unites them in the *neutral* wording "the rationally right." It is unclear why Habermas's theory reconstruction of Kant's aim to rationalize politics in the name of morality through the public use of reason defines the result of this rational-critical process in the bourgeois public sphere as a morally *pretentious* rationality—in spite of a possible pejorative connotation implied in the translation of the German-language term "prätentiös" as "pretentious." For both German and English dictionaries assign opposed meanings to the term. It can be understood either as *exacting* and *ambitious* ("anspruchsvoll") or as *presumptuous* ("anmassend").

In the English edition of *Structural Transformation* from 1989, Thomas Burger (with the assistance of Frederick Lawrence) translated "prätentiös" as "pretentious." The "Translator's Note" (STPS xv-xvi) does not alert the reader to the ambiguity of the term. One has to assume that Habermas signed off on the English translation as it was published in the United Kingdom by Polity Press and in the United States by MIT Press. Two years later, in the new edition of *Strukturwandel der Öffentlichkeit* (1991) by Suhrkamp, Habermas also left his use of the term "prätentiös" in the original 1962 edition by Luchterhand unchanged.

It would help the scholarly discourse about *Structural Transformation* to learn why Habermas did not define Kant's ideal as a morally *exacting* or *ambitious* rationality. After all, his later reflections on "Popular Sovereignty as Procedure" included in *Between Facts and Norms* partially imply that meaning when he refers to Rousseau's "moral overburdening of the virtuous citizens" (BFN 473) which influenced Kant. Moreover, such a clarification could avoid any interpretation of *pretentious* as *presumptuous*.

Obviously, the decisive difference between *ambitious* and *presumptuous* directly affects *Structural Transformation*'s core argument. If the book's wording allowed the kind of rationality that is "intrinsic to the idea of a public opinion born of the power of the better argument" to be interpreted as morally *presumptuous* instead of morally *ambitious*, then the "insight" of this public opinion could not be classified as "compelling" (STPS 54, 88). In short, "the idea of a dissolution of domination" itself would be at stake, if it could be regarded as a *presumptuous* assertion. Needless to say, without the "compelling insight of a public opinion," the "constraint that prevails" when this insight is implemented as binding law could not be universally accepted as "easygoing" (STPS 88).

The question whether this idea of an "easygoing constraint" of the better argument is an ambitious or a presumptuous one has remained highly relevant to this day. For Habermas in his later works essentially doubled down on it. Today, his proceduralist discourse theory of law and democracy even posits the *uncoerced coercion* ("zwanglose Zwang") of the better argument.

Arguably, *Structural Transformation* marks the inception of this signature idea in Habermas's works. In 1962, it evolved from the tacit adoption of *Constitutional Theory*'s ideal-typical stylization. Specifically, Schmitt traces the history of this idealized "binding of all state activity" to a closed "system of norms," which represent "reason and justice," back to the French Revolution's inauguration of a "rationalistic faith in the wisdom of the law-maker." As discussed below under 5.6, in the French National Assembly "one entrusted oneself with formulating a conscious and complete plan for the entire social and political life" based on a legally binding "normative frame-work" (CT 65, 62; VL 10–11,7; see HPSC 44–45). This absolute rationalism of the French Revolution was rejuvenated about three decades later by liberal parliamentarians like Pierre-Paul Royer-Collard.

As the first leader of the so-called French Doctrinaires, he summed up the "liberal idea of an absolute constitutional state" in his claim about a "sovereignty of the constitution." The claim was adopted by Alexis de Tocqueville with regard to the Constitution of 1830. He "consistently advocated its inal-terability" and "emphasized that all the rights of the people, of the king, as well as of parliament are derived from the constitution and that outside of the constitution, all their political powers are nothing." Moreover, Francois Guizot, who became Royer-Collard's successor as leader of the Doctrinaires, directly expressed the legacy of absolute rationalism by coining the phrase "sovereignty of reason" (CT 63, 65; VL 8,11; see HPSC 45–46).

This constitutional law theory and intellectual history will only be partially and implicitly revealed in Section 12, when *Structural Transformation* intro-duces Guizot's "classic formulation of the 'rule of public opinion'" (STPS 101). However, these ideal-typical manifestations of an absolute rationalism *tacitly* inform already Section 4 for its claim that the rising bourgeoisie did not demand that "the powers of command" be "'divided.'" Instead, the pri-vate property owners ideally sought "to change domination as such" through "publicness" as the "principle of control" that "undercut the principle on which existing rule was based" (STPS 28).

Although Section 4 refers in this context to Section 7 in general, it does not guide the reader to the specific role of the Physiocrats in undercutting Thomas Hobbes's principle *auctoritas non veritas facit legem* (authority not truth makes law), which had defined the rule of the "Absolutist State" (CC 31, CC 23). Significantly, they went beyond Montesquieu who had reversed the principle of "absolute sovereignty" by grounding law in human reason. For the Physiocrats were the first to "relate the law *explicitly* to *public opinion as the expression of reason*" (STPS 53-54, emphasis added).

Section 7 provides the reader with a vivid example of *Structural Transformation*'s fusion of constitutional law theory and intellectual history under the misleading chapter heading "Social Structures of the Public Sphere." Only Section 5 "Institutions of the Public Sphere" contains references to the social institutions of the public sphere like the growing number of coffee houses in London since the middle of the seventeenth century (STPS 32–33). Paradoxically, the book's rigid separation of social structures and political functions delays a reference to the *sociological* analysis of these coffee houses until Chapter III "Political Functions of the Public Sphere."

Moreover, while Habermas credits Hans Speier's journal article "The Historical Development of Public Opinion" (1950) with having established "the connection between the coffee houses and public opinion" (STPS 262n5), he "nevertheless reverses Speier's ranking regarding their sociological functions" by selecting only their use as institutions of "literary criticism, which Speier ranks fourth and last—behind 'news-gathering,' 'news dissemination,' and 'political debate'" (HPSC 14). Emblematic for Habermas's privileging of his category of a "literary public sphere" is his focus on a German book from 1924 about "English coffee houses as rallying points for the literary world in the age of Dryden and Addison" (see HPSC 14–15).

Section 4 introduces Habermas's intellectual construct of a "literary public sphere" as "the training ground for a critical public reflection" of private people engaged in "a process of self-clarification," in which an audience-oriented subjectivity "communicated with itself" in diaries and through the exchange of letters (STPS 29). Section 6 detects in this process "the origin of the typical genre and authentic literary achievement" of the eighteenth century: "the domestic novel, the psychological description in autobiographical form" (STPS 49). Already Section 4 reminds the reader that "next to political economy, psychology arose as a specifically *bourgeois science*" during that century (STPS 29, emphasis added).

As Section 4 implicitly documents, both bourgeois sciences are needed to analyze the "status of private man," which combines "the role of owner of commodities with that of head of the family, that of property owner with that of 'human being' per se" (STPS 28–29, cf. STPS 88; see 1.2 above). In the words of Section 7, as "a privatized individual, the bourgeois is two things in one," namely, "*bourgeois* and *homme*" (STPS 55, translation modified; SÖ 74). Section 6 draws on political economy as well as on psychology to analyze why, in this bourgeois self-interpretation, "the higher plane of the intimate sphere" furnishes "the foundation for an identification of those two roles" (STPS 29):

> *In a certain fashion*, commodity owners can view themselves as *autonomous*. To the degree that they are emancipated from governmental directives and controls, they make decisions *freely* in accord with the standards of profitability. In this regard they owe obedience to no one and are subject only to the *anonymous laws* functioning in accord with an *economic rationality, so it appears*, in the market. These laws are backed up by the *ideological guarantee* of a notion *that market exchange is just*, and they are altogether supposed to enable *justice to triumph over force*. (STPS 46, emphasis added, translation modified; SÖ 63–64)

In other words, bourgeois political economy supposedly provides the "substantive rationality" of the legal norm by facilitating both rationality *and* justice. In turn, "the autonomy of property owners in the market" is psychologically reflected in their "self-presentation" as "human beings in the family." For the "latter's intimacy, *apparently* set free from the constraint of society," is "the seal on the truth of a private autonomy exercised in competition" (STPS 46, emphasis added). In short, thinking the *bourgeois* as one with the *homme* facilitates the unique intellectual construct of a "morally pretentious rationality" that seeks to discover what is *at once just and right*.

However, readers have to be aware of the qualifiers Habermas inserts into these claims. Yes, commodity owners can view themselves as *autonomous*. But only *in a certain fashion*. Yes, the *anonymous laws* are functioning in the market in accord with an *economic rationality*. At least, this is how *it appears*. Yes, the bourgeois family's intimacy is set free from the constraint of society. But only *apparently* so. Finally, *Structural Transformation* explains these qualifiers. But only in Section 13 on Kant:

> The *fiction of a justice* immanent in unfettered commodity exchange renders plausible the conflation of *bourgeois* and *homme*, of self-interested, property-owning private people and autonomous individuals per se. (STPS 111, emphasis added)

Alerting the reader to Habermas's tacit use of the Hegelian-Marxist critique of ideology in his quest to detect the emancipatory potential in this Kantian fiction is highly relevant. For *Structural Transformation*'s theory reconstruction of Kant's idea of a rational-critical public sphere in the bourgeois constitutional state rests on these background assumptions about the private people who engage in their "public use of reason." Each private member of that public has to simultaneously reason as *bourgeois* and as *homme* (cf. STPS 88; see 1.2 above).

This explains why Habermas emphasizes directly at the outset of Section 13 on Kant that it "was no coincidence," that *the* political economist of the eighteenth century, Adam Smith, "held a Chair of Moral Philosophy." For in that century, "the Aristotelian tradition of a philosophy of politics was reduced in a telling manner to moral philosophy." Not only was "the moral" thought as one "with 'nature' and reason,'" but it also "encompassed the emerging sphere of 'the social'" (STPS 103).

In other words, Habermas explains to the reader *with a delay of more than 75 pages*, and only *indirectly* so, why *Structural Transformation*'s part II about "The Social Structures of the Public Sphere" was *primarily* written from the perspective of moral philosophy and not from one of a social history of public institutions like the coffee houses.

Accordingly, *Structural Transformation*'s readers have to be aware that Habermas's designation of the *historical and social* location of this self-interpretation does *not* address a topic in *social history* but one in *intellectual history* and *constitutional theory*. *Habermas's Public Sphere: A Critique* has analyzed that this designation was inspired by the writings of "the *young* Marx," especially by "A Critique of the Hegelian Philosophy of Right" (1844/1926) and his essay "On the Jewish Question" (1844/1926). Habermas's combination of the role of property owner with the one of human being *per se* in the status of private man mirrors Marx's juxtaposition of "the egoistic, independent individual" in bourgeois society on one hand and the citizen, namely, "the moral person," on the other.

In Marx's words, the "German conception of the modern State" abstracts from "real men" and posits the "true man" under the influence of Rousseau's ideal of the nation as the medium of human emancipation: "He who dares undertake to give instruction to a nation ought to feel himself capable as it were of changing human nature; ... of substituting a social and moral existence for the independent and physical existence which we have all received from nature" (quoted in HPSC 99, 142n12).

Habermas's privileging of intellectual history and constitutional law theory is reflected in *Structural Transformation*'s "Model Case of British Development." Figuratively speaking, it superimposes Schmitt's "Historical Overview of the Development of the Parliamentary System" in section 25 of his *Constitutional Theory* onto Koselleck's chapter II.8 "Process of Criticism." Arguably, Habermas *primarily* starts his discussion of his "model case" in 1695, because, as mentioned above, in that year Bayle introduced the process of "criticism as such" through his *Dictionnaire Historique et Critique.*

Significantly, Bayle's insistence on an allegedly *apolitical* nature of criticism, and his sharp critique of pamphleteering, reflect his lifelong experience with censorship, first with the Catholic Church and the Absolutist State in France, and later in Rotterdam, after particularly dogmatic Calvinists among the Huguenots had taken over the Dutch consistory (cf. HPSC 204).

In other words, the publication of Bayle's dictionary in 1695 was more important for the development of *Structural Transformation*'s thesis about a "morally pretentious rationality" than the end of censorship in England in the same year. For, as Speier analyzed, the latter advanced *political* debates and relegated literary criticism to the last ranking in the sociological functions of the coffee houses as centers of the reading and debating public. Habermas thus contrasts Bayle's *apolitical* criticism and the "press devoted to the debate of political issues," which, at the same time, developed in England "out of the pamphlet" (STPS 92).

Structural Transformation's focus is clear. Defoe's political journalism and Swift's political satire receive only a few lines in its "model case" in Section 8 (STPS 59, 60). Moreover, they are excluded from Section 5, where Habermas devotes more than one page to the "moral weeklies," like the *Tatler*, the *Spectator*, and the *Guardian*, as the "key phenomenon" of the rising literary public sphere (STPS 42, 43).

By simultaneously drawing on Section 8 and on Section 5, readers can learn that Joseph Addison's and Richard Steele's "combination of literature and journalism" (STPS 59) in these "moral weeklies" allows the bourgeois individuals to come to a self-understanding of their own humanity through reading and debating such "periodical essays," as well as through responding to them in their own letters (STPS 42).These weeklies define themselves as *moral*, because, as an author, Addison also views "himself as a censor of manners and morals" (STPS 43). And as *apolitical*, because he adopts the role of an "impartial spectator" who has "no interests but those of Truth and Virtue" when facilitating "the emancipation of civic morality from moral theology" (STPS 43; HPSC 193).

To fully understand the role that *Structural Transformation* ascribes to this emancipatory process within the developing bourgeois public sphere, readers should turn to Section 12, where Habermas implicitly responds to Koselleck's interpretation of Locke's *Essay Concerning Human Understanding* (1690). Following up on Schmitt, *Critique and Crisis* introduces Locke as "the spiritual father of the bourgeois Enlightenment" (CC 53) and classifies his *Essay* as one of the "Holy Scriptures of the modern bourgeoisie" during the eighteenth century (CC 54). Koselleck's polemic thus highlights that, in Habermas's words, the *Essay*'s signature "secularized morality" was "obtained from its origin in privatized religious faith" (STPS 91).

Connecting the moral weeklies to Locke's influential *Essay* clarifies for the reader why this literary genre achieved a similar popularity. According to *Structural Transformation*'s endnote 39 on page 260, in the course of the eighteenth-century Great Britain could count 227 examples of this genre and Germany 187. Moreover, this connection illuminates Addison's goal of emancipating "practical wisdom from the philosophy of the scholars" (STPS 43).

In the 1660s, Locke had been "Censor of Moral Philosophy" at Christ Church College in Oxford. Of his *Essay*'s three moral laws, namely, the Divine Law, the Civil Law, and the Law of Opinion or Reputation, only the last one allowed the rising bourgeoisie to pass judgment on public authorities. In short, it was grounded in the "consent of private men who have not authority enough to make a [civil] law" (Locke quoted in STPS 91; see CC 56).

A Whig politician out of parliamentary power under the reign of Queen Anne, Addison literally applied this power of moral censure when publishing, together with Steele, "the first issue of the *Tatler* in 1709" (STPS 42). He praised as virtuous all "civilized forms of conduct," culminating in a "cultivated refinement." Conversely, his polemics attacked vices like fanaticism and pedantry in his quest to humanize dogmatic Puritans and avoid the appearance of "moral tyranny" on the part of quintessential bourgeois individuals like Defoe. When publishing his political *Review* from 1704 to 1713, Defoe regularly insulted the gentry as "bred boors, empty and swinish sots and fobs" (STPS 43; quoted in HPSC 193 and 196).

In other words, Addison and Steele were devoted to making the rising bourgeoisie look respectable in the eyes of a "courtly-noble society" (STPS 29). In this context, readers face the additional challenge of having to think through a structural tension already inherent in Section 4 with regard to the sociological prerequisites of educating the emerging bourgeois intellectuals in "the art of critical-rational debate" (STPS 29). On one hand, "The Basic Blueprint" informs the readers that the literary public sphere is "not, of course, autochthonously bourgeois." Instead, the "bourgeois avant-garde of the educated middle class" preserves "a certain continuity" with the public representation "enacted at the prince's court" through its "contact with the 'elegant world'" of this courtly noble society (STPS 29).

On the other hand, the graphic representation of social spheres in the same "Blueprint" places the bourgeois intellectuals not even in the clubs and press of the literary public sphere in the middle of the diagram. Instead, they appear in the conjugal family's intimate sphere on the *opposite* side of the courtly-noble society. While the former is located in the *private* sphere of bourgeois society, the latter belongs to the sphere of *public* authority. The diagram makes this opposition quite clear by using two vertical lines to mark the separation of bourgeois society and the feudal state (STPS 30).

This juxtaposition reveals in a nutshell *Structural Transformation*'s permanent tension between the facticity of social and the normativity of intellectual history. For the diagram in Section 4 gleans its location of the bourgeois intellectuals from Schmitt's intellectual construct elaborated on in Koselleck's *Critique and Crisis*, while the other part of Habermas's "Blueprint" follows social histories of culture, like the ones by Arnold Hauser and Raymond Williams (see STPS 37). Arguably, the *original* blueprint for *Structural Transformation*'s key thesis about the rise of the bourgeois public sphere in the eighteenth century can be found in this stylization at the beginning of chapter II.4 in *Critique and Crisis*:

> The *bourgeois intelligentsia* set out from the *private inner space* within which the State had been confining its subjects. *Each outward step was a step towards the light*, an act of enlightenment. The movement which blithely called itself *"the Enlightenment"* continued its *triumphal march* at the *same pace* at which *its private interior expanded into the public domain*, while *the public, without surrendering its private nature*, became the *forum of society that permeated the State*. In the end society would knock on the doors of the political powers, calling for attention there, too, and demanding admission. (CC 53, emphasis added)

What fuels this "triumphal march" of "the Enlightenment" in Koselleck's Schmittian view, tacitly adopted by *Structural Transformation*, is a *moral superiority* of "the *inner-worldly* opposition of a privatized society to political authority" (STPS 268n8, emphasis in the original). In this endnote to Section 12, Habermas approvingly quotes Schmitt's Hobbes interpretation from 1938: "At the moment when the distinction between inward and outward is acknowledged, the *superiority of the inward* over the outward and hence *of the private* over the public is, at its core, already decided" (STPS 268n8, emphasis added). For, as Koselleck adds, the "authority" of the moral conscience remains "an *unconquered* remnant of the state of nature, protruding into the formally perfected [Absolutist] State" (CC 39, emphasis added).

Without guidance to this rather cryptic and implicit explanation in Section 12, readers cannot understand why Section 4 "The Basic Blueprint" can designate "the conjugal family's intimate sphere" as "the historical point of origin" for "privateness in the modern sense of a saturated and free interiority" (STPS 28). Just how difficult it is for the reader of *Structural Transformation* to access this interpretation of intellectual history in the writings of Schmitt,

Koselleck, and Habermas, is inadvertently evident in Calhoun's following comment in his Introduction to *Habermas and the Public Sphere*:

> It is remarkable that *Habermas's account* of how the family helped to give rise to a notion of 'pure' and undifferentiated humanity *does not betray any sense of the role of religion in helping to produce this result*. Yet the *tradition of interiority* was *pioneered by Augustine*, and during the *Protestant Reformation* it was given decisive new form as something shared equivalently among all people. (HPS 43n16, emphasis added)

Arguably, Calhoun's misunderstanding in his highly influential synopsis of *Structural Transformation* occurred, because Habermas does not *sufficiently* discuss "the role of religion" in creating the notion about the bourgeois family's pure and formless humanity in its intimate sphere. His short endnote (7 lines) about the shifting meaning in "the [Protestant] Reformation's distinction between the *regnum spirituale* and the *regnum politicum*" along intellectual history's path "from Luther and Calvin to Hobbes" (STPS 268n8), which is *tacitly* based on Koselleck's lengthy one (81 lines) in *Critique and Crisis*, does indeed leave out Augustine. In comparison, as *Habermas's Public Sphere: A Critique* analyzes, Koselleck traces the intellectual history of this consequential idea from Luther back to Augustine (HPSC 222n87):

> The separation of inward and external, or as Hobbes phrases it, of "externall acts" and "*inward thought*," . . . is rooted in the Christian world-view, and in *Augustine's two-world doctrine* it was part of the Middle Ages. Thomas Aquinas assumed that man could judge only external acts, that the *inner realm* was God's . . . The contrast of *inwardness* and externality is essentially the theme of Luther's [1523] pamphlet. (CC 29n27, emphasis added)

Calhoun's statement about the role of religion in Habermas's theory reconstruction of a saturated and free inwardness as the hallmark of the bourgeois family's intimate sphere becomes particularly relevant in the context of *Structural Transformation*'s following claim in Section 7 about "The Literary in Relation to the Political Public Sphere":

> The representation of the *interests of the privatized domain of a market economy* is interpreted with the aid of ideas grown in the soil of the intimate sphere of the conjugal family. (STPS 51, emphasis added)

Section 6 identifies this "soil of the intimate sphere" as "the permanent intimacy of the new family life," which turns "in on itself" (STPS 44) in a process of self-reflection that seems "to permit that non-instrumental development of all faculties that marks the cultivated personality" (STPS 46–47). Since "free in-dividuals" also seem to establish this family life "voluntarily" and maintain it "without coercion," while it seems "to rest on the lasting community of love on the part of the two spouses," *Structural Transformation* defines the intimate sphere of the bourgeois conjugal family as "humanity's genuine site" (STPS 52). In other words, the interests of the privatized domain of the market economy are interpreted as the interests of humanity as such.

Although *Structural Transformation* does not contain a single reference to Max Weber's analysis of *The Protestant Ethic and the Spirit of Capitalism*, Habermas's theory reconstruction of "humanity's genuine site" in modernity nevertheless dovetails with what Weber identifies "as the pride of the Puritans "in their own superior middle-class business morality" (quoted in HPSC 190, see HPSC 222n88). Moreover, their seemingly superior morality also defined the public interactions of bourgeois individuals when the permanent intimacy of their conjugal families was "played off against courtly conventions." Fre-quently, these courtly conventions included among "the urban nobility" sepa-rate households for the spouses and, of course, the mistress as "an institution" (STPS 35,44).

The Protestant inwardness of *Structural Transformation*'s bourgeois intellec-tuals allows them to have the best of both world-views by combining the alleged moral superiority of the bourgeois family's intimate sphere with the Renaissance humanism that informs and permeates the public representation of the courtly-noble society in the tradition of the Greek *polis*. The book's readers only find this out, if they follow a reference (in brackets) at the beginning of Section 7 to Section 18 titled "From a Culture-Debating to a Culture-Consuming Public." In this reference, Habermas reminds his audience that "the Greek model," which the concept of the bourgeois public sphere draws on, contains a fundamental difference. It stipulates that "the public sphere itself," and not the private house-hold, is "humanity's genuine site" (STPS 51–52).

The "peculiarly normative power" that the "ideological template" of the "Hellenic public sphere" has assumed in intellectual history, is first addressed in Section 1 on "The Initial Question." But the crucial importance of their "private autonomy as masters of households," which allowed Greek citizens to partici-pate in public life (STPS 4, 3), is only fully explained *more than 150 pages later* in Section 18. Significantly, Habermas waits until the demise of the bourgeois public sphere in *Structural Transformation*'s narrative, before postulating, in retrospect, that the bourgeoisie could develop the *idea* of humanity, because its *literary public sphere* "possessed . . . a 'political' character in the Greek sense of being emancipated from the constraints of survival requirements." In other words, the "rational-critical debate of private people in the salons, clubs, and reading societies was not directly subject to the cycle of production and consumption, that is, to the dictates of life's necessities" (STPS 160). Already Habermas's 1954 essay "Dialectic of Rationalization" addressed the ancient prerequisite for private autonomy and public humanity, namely, that without slave labor at his disposal, the Greek citizen would have been unable to create either the *polis*, or the temples and statues, or philosophy (Habermas 1954: 720).

Moreover, the bourgeois intellectuals thus had to be aware that one of the characteristics of their intimate sphere which defines bourgeois humanism, namely, cultivation of the person, originated in the *studia humanitatis*. Since the fifteenth century, Renaissance humanism had contemplated the requirements for fully developing one's humanity. Nevertheless, bourgeois humanism regarded itself as superior to its Greek model. For the private autonomy of the commodity owners was seemingly not based on the *exercise of force* inherent in a "patrimonial slave economy" (STPS 3).

Instead, the "fiction of a justice immanent in free commerce" when contracting with wage workers in the labor market bestowed through the "mystery of wages" (Marx) the *aura of sheer benevolence* on the bourgeois property owners (STPS 111). Conversely, in the Greek model individual freedom only existed in the public sphere, because "the private status of the master of the household . . . rested on *domination without any illusion of freedom*" (STPS 52, emphasis added). In comparison, such an "illusion of freedom" was evoked by the human intimacy of bourgeois family life. In turn, this human intimacy was the expression of the "community of love" between the spouses, with its religious overtones of holiness.

It is this self-stylization of being the heir to the Greek template, while simultaneously replacing domination with freedom in all human relationships, that defines the "neohumanism of the German classic period" (STPS 260n47). The hallmark of this stylization is "the all-around development of the individual person," *the* bourgeois ideal of the German *Bildungbürgertum*. In his essay "The Idea of the University—Learning Processes" (1987), Habermas would quote from F.W.J. Schelling's "Lectures on the Methodology of Academic Study" to illustrate a genuinely bourgeois version of the Greek and the Renaissance templates about the "cultivation of the person."

In Schelling's view, the rational philosophy of German Idealism not only "commended itself as a form which reflected the whole of culture." Its "self-reflexive basis" also "promised the unity of science and enlightenment." It can thus facilitate "the all-around development of the individual person" (Habermas 1987: 11, 10).

Moreover, while "ideas are comprehended," they "simultaneously enter into the knower's moral character." In other words, the bourgeois cultivation of the person is stylized as the unity of rationality and morality. The process of acquiring knowledge frees the individual's *moral* character "from all one-sidedness" (Habermas 1987: 10).

In *Structural Transformation*'s narrative, the experience of an "interiorized human closeness" between family members in the intimate sphere at the core of the private sphere indirectly served a political purpose in the public sphere. It provided the rising bourgeoisie with the strength to challenge "the established authority of the monarch" in the public sphere with regard to the "political task" of regulating the private sphere of commodity exchange and social labor (STPS 52). In short, Habermas tacitly adopts Koselleck's dictum that "the moral striving to become political will be the great theme of the eighteenth century" (CC 39).

Accordingly, Habermas's stylization first lets the joint reflections on the subjective experiences of "human beings pure and simple" in the bourgeois intimate sphere facilitate the humanity of an apolitical "literary public sphere." Only after its morally pretentious rationality has been fully established, does *Structural Transformation* transition it into a "political public sphere." Toward the end of Section 7, the motivation for this complex theory reconstruction becomes quite transparent:

> As soon as privatized individuals in their capacity as human beings cease to communicate merely about their subjectivity but rather in their capacity *as property-owners desire to influence political power* in their common interest, *the humanity of the literary public sphere serves to increase the effectiveness of the political public sphere.* (STPS 56, emphasis added)

5.3. THE LIBERALIZED MARKET AS ECONOMIC PRECONDITION FOR PRIVATE AUTONOMY AND THE FULLY DEVELOPED POLITICAL PUBLIC SPHERE

Sections 5.1 and 5.2 of this guide have used *Structural Transformation*'s Section 4 "The Basic Blueprint" and its connections to Sections 3, 11, 8, 9, 12, 13, 6, 7, 5, 18, and 1 as the first step toward accessing Habermas's theory reconstruction of the "morally pretentious rationality" that allows the rational-critical public opinion inherent in Kant's liberal model of the public sphere in the bourgeois constitutional state *to rationalize politics in the name of morality* (STPS 102). For the second step, this guide will use Section 10 on "Civil Society as the Sphere of Private Autonomy: Private Law and a Liberalized Market" and Section 11 as a framework. Section 10 logically follows up on Habermas's key thesis, outlined in Section 4 (STPS 28-29) and developed in Section 6 (STPS 46) and Section 7 (STPS 55–56), about the *private autonomy* of the commodity owner in the markets of liberal capitalism.

Habermas's thesis posits that this private autonomy allows the *bour-geois* to 1) present himself in the intimate sphere of the bourgeois conjugal family, *and thus* also in the literary public sphere, as the *homme,* "'the human being *per se*;'" 2) learn the art of rational-critical discourse in the *literary* public sphere and use it to develop the universal idea of humanity; 3) use the humanity of the literary public sphere, expressed in its "morally pretentious rationality," to increase the effectiveness of the *political* public sphere when seeking to influence political power regarding the regulation of the private sphere of commodity exchange and social labor.

Structural Transformation restricts its "Basic Blueprint" (Section 4) to an outline of Sections 5, 6, and 7, with only limited (and implicit) references to the other sections of the book. If one read the sections of the book in sequential order, one would only learn at the beginning of Section 10, that Section 8 on "The Model Case of British Development" and Section 9 on "The Continental Variants" did *not* continue to discuss the key theses first introduced in Sections 4 to 7. Instead, Sections 8 and 9 were "historical excurses" about "the institutional interrelations of public, press, parties, and the parliament" (STPS 73).

According to Habermas, they could *only* "document *that* the public sphere takes on political functions during the eighteenth century" (STPS 73, emphasis in the original). For the specific *substance* of these political functions can seemingly *only* be grasped within the totality of "the devel-opmental history of civil society," once "commodity exchange and social labor largely emancipate themselves from governmental directives" (STPS 73–74, translation modified; SÖ 95). As mentioned in chapter 1 of this guide, such an emancipation occurred *only* "in Great Britain at the close of the eighteenth century," due to "a unique historical constellation," that "lasted only for one blissful moment in the long history of capitalist devel-opment," namely, during the "liberal" phase of capitalism (STPS 79, 78).

Section 10 defines this functional *substance* of the *political* public sphere as "the *normative status* of an organ for the *self-articulation of civil society* with a state authority corresponding to its needs" (STPS 74, emphasis added). The *social* precondition for such a "'developed' bourgeois public sphere" is rooted in the *economic* sphere of commodity exchange and social labor as the domain of *private* property owners.

This social precondition is a "market that tends to be liberalized." It thus leaves the "private people" and their "interactions in the sphere of *social* reproduction as much as possible to themselves." Since this liberalized market is largely emancipated from the directives and interventions of *public* authorities, it "completes the *privatization* of civil society" (STPS 74, emphasis added, translation modified; SÖ 95).

In this *liberal* interpretation, the private autonomy of the *bourgeois*, his ability to engage in the rational-critical discourse of the political public sphere as the *homme* who seeks "Truth and Justice" (Joseph Addison), depends on the liberation of the seemingly "natural" laws of the market from governmental regulations. Only then can "social relationships assume the form of exchange relationships" of "freely competing owners of commodities," whose interactions are autonomous and "basically harmonious" (STPS 74, 75, 130). To achieve this private autonomy, the bourgeois has to be granted "free power of control" over his property "that functions in capitalist fashion," namely as private means of production (STPS 74, translation modified; SÖ 96).

In short, the legal control of these *social* relationships has to be switched from public to *private law*. Section 10 gives the example of the deregulation of the labor market in England between 1757 and 1813. It started with the liberation of the textile industry from "state-imposed wage regulations" by "the justices of the peace." It ended with the introduction of "free wage labor ... in all branches of industry" (STPS 77). In the *liberal* interpretation, this deregulation facilitated "the free declaration of will" (STPS 75) for both contractual parties in the labor market, namely, the owner of the means of production *and* the owner of the labor power needed to operate them.

Moreover, by ascribing the *status naturalis* to all legal subjects, private law can bracket the social differences of "rank and birth," namely, the lower ranking of the bourgeoisie as the "Third Estate" in comparison to the aristocracy and the clergy, and thus legalize a "fundamental parity among owners of commodities in the market" (STPS 75). Section 10 acknowledges that this transition to private law first "advanced in the mercantilist phase" of capitalism (STPS 75), when the feudal state authorities essentially regulated the private sphere of commodity exchange and social labor into existence. In the famous words by Karl Polanyi from 1944 in *The Great Transformation*: "[C]otton manufactures—the leading free trade industry—were created by the help of protective tariffs, export bounties, and indirect wage subsidies, *laissez-faire* was enforced by the state" (quoted in HPSC 105).

Nevertheless, at the close of the eighteenth century the bourgeoisie had accumulated sufficient economic power to engage the public authorities "in a debate over the general rules governing relations in the basically privatized but publicly relevant sphere of commodity exchange and social labor"—to quote from the opening sentence of *Structural Transformation*'s "Basic Blueprint" (STPS 29). The "classic work of bourgeois private law," the French "Code Civil of 1804," thus "originated not only in the interest of civil society but also in its specific medium," namely, the political public sphere, even though parliament "remained ineffective … in Napoleonic France" (STPS 75, 76). To facilitate the rational-critical discourse, "in Paris the proposed legal code was in 1800 submitted for critical assessment to the public" (STPS 76).

However, this transformation of social relationships into their new normative status of exchange relationships, formalized in private law, fulfilled only the necessary condition for the realization of private autonomy when exchanging commodities. To sufficiently liberalize all markets, the *laissez faire* doctrine of classical political economy had to be actually implemented. As Section 10 delineates, based on an *orthodox* interpretation about *The Progress of Capitalism in England* (1916), only after the "victory of Trafalgar" in 1812 had established "the unrivalled maritime power of Britain," and thus control of global trade, did the country "have everything to gain . . . and nothing to lose" from deregulation (STPS 78):

> . . . when the nineteenth century opened public opinion was inclined to leave the capitalist *perfectly free* to employ his wealth in any enterprise he chose, and to regard the profit which he secured as the best proof that his enterprise was beneficial to the State. (Cunningham 1916: 107, emphasis added, quoted in STPS 265n49)

In stark contrast, other countries did not deregulate their international trade "without reserve, even in the middle of the nineteenth century when the liberal era was at its height" (STPS 79). Needless to say, it takes the Whig interpretation of history to conflate the utopia of a Weberian ideal type ("perfectly free") with the actually existing public opinion in England in 1800. Habermas himself acknowledges that the landed interests, with their political economist Malthus, successfully disagreed by keeping the Corn Laws in place until 1846 (STPS 81).

Regarding the laboring poor, Parliament was forced to regulate the labor market already in 1802 with the "Health and Morals of Apprentices Act." Since 1795, the Manchester Board of Health had called for these legislative restrictions to curtail the fever epidemics caused by highly unsanitary conditions in the cotton mills (cf. HPSC 114–15). In other words, readers have to view *Structural Transformation*'s selection of the quote by Cunningham as another example of the book's "collapsing of norm and description" (CR 463).

In retrospect, the reader now realizes the significance of the qualifiers in Section 6 and of the level of generality in Section 4 when *Structural Transformation* first discusses its postulated private autonomy of the members of the bourgeoisie, which allows them to simultaneously act in "*the role of property owners and the role of human beings pure and simple*" (STPS 56, emphasis in the original). Since their self-determination in the market depends on "the degree" of their emancipation "from government directives and controls" (STPS 46), it only becomes possible to acquire this double identity of *bourgeois* and *homme* once the alleged natural "laws of motion immanent in society," with the one about the "self-regulating market" at their core (STPS 130, 132), are given free reign. Hence, the "political public sphere could attain its full development in the bourgeois constitutional state" (STPS 79) only in one country and only for a limited time period.

Specifically, the fact that it took several decades of intense fights in parliament and in the public against the "landed interest," before the Corn Laws were repealed in 1846 (STPS 78), illustrates the enormity of this challenge for the bourgeoisie to achieve private autonomy. Moreover, the freedom of capital to contract with labor solely on market terms was substantially curtailed only one year later by the Ten Hours Bill of 1847. These *new* regulations, imposed by the factory legislation that the British parliament passed (see HPSC 126–141), are *left out* of Section 10.

However, the reader needs this information to better understand the tensions within the argument advanced in Section 10. They are only addressed 50 pages later, and only partially so. Namely, in in the enigmatic Section 15, already alerted to in chapter 2. Habermas titled it "The Ambivalent View of the Public Sphere in the Theory of Liberalism (John Stuart Mill and Alexis de Tocqueville)":

> . . . under the altered social preconditions of 'public opinion' *around the middle of the* [nineteenth] *century*, when *economic liberalism was just reaching its peak*, its social-philosophical representatives were forced almost to deny the principle of the public sphere of civil society even as they celebrated it. (STPS 130, emphasis added)

The state of these "altered social preconditions" is only identified with all desirable clarity more than 60 pages later, when Habermas introduces a veiled reference to Benjamin Disraeli's novel *Sybil, or the Two Nations* (1845) in Section 20:

> In a phase of more or less unconcealed class antagonism, *about the middle of the* last [i.e., nineteenth] *century*, the public sphere itself was torn between "the two nations." (STPS 192, emphasis added)

In short, in the middle of the nineteenth century, when the "political public sphere could attain its full development in the bourgeois constitutional state," because "the liberal era was at its height" and "economic liberalism was just reaching its peak," the public sphere itself was already torn between "*the two nations*" (STPS 79, 130, 192, emphasis added). Nevertheless, according to Section 11, "in the first half of the nineteenth century . . . the interest of the bourgeois class could be identified with the general interest and the third estate could be set up as *the nation*" in the

Electoral Reform Bill of 1832 (STPS 87, emphasis added). Once readers become aware of these tensions in *Structural Transformation*'s argument, they will begin to understand just how contradictory the "Institutionalization of the Public Sphere in the Bourgeois Constitutional State" had to be in the book's narrative, if it still wanted to advance its key thesis that "during that phase of capitalism, the public sphere as the organizational principle of the bourgeois constitutional state had credibility" (STPS 87).

5.4. NATURAL ECONOMIC LAWS AS PRESUPPOSITION FOR KANT'S RATIONAL NATURAL LAW OF THE BOURGEOIS PUBLIC SPHERE

Section 10 refers to natural economic laws, intrinsic in all markets, that first need to be liberated from governmental regulations before the political public sphere can attain its full development. However, only Section 11 discusses these "natural" laws, posited in the classical political economy of the Physiocrats and of Smith, in more detail. Conversely, in Section 13 on Kant readers need to remember these explanations on their own as well as try to connect them to largely unexplained references like the one to "Mandeville's slogan (*Slogan*), 'private vices, public benefits'" (STPS 109; SÖ135). That "slogan" was the inspiration for Smith's famous dictum about the "invisible hand" that allegedly self-regulates all markets as well as the capitalist economy as a whole (see HPSC 211–212, 201–203).

Only in December 1961, after the typescript for *Structural Transformation* had been sent to his publisher, would Habermas precisely address the fundamental role of political economy for the development of Kant's modern rational natural law inherent in the idea of the rational-critical public sphere as the organizational principle of the bourgeois constitutional state. He did so in his Inaugural Address at the University of Marburg, titled "The Classical Doctrine of Politics in Relation to Social Philosophy." Specifically, he explained that, almost a full century after Locke, Kant could now present an "economic answer" to the challenge of grounding the political organization of society in the natural rights of citizens.

While Locke's natural law "made the legal order of property (*Eigentumsordnung*) of bourgeois society as such the natural basis of state power founded on contract," Kant could draw on the political economy of "the second half of the eighteenth century, which declared these laws to be the natural laws of society itself." For "in the advanced Western societies the sphere of commodity exchange and social labor had, in the meantime, sufficiently liberated itself from the regulatory regime of state authority." Accordingly, the "natural order" of political society "could now be understood in the categories of the laws of motion of civil society in the modern sense" (TAP 76, translation modified; TUP 80).

Section 11 identifies these laws of motion as the *natural* "laws of the free market," which are "intrinsic" in a "self-regulating" system of "free competition." It functions harmoniously as long as there is no interference from an "extra-economic agency." Above all, the "society *solely* governed by the laws of the free market presents itself not only as a sphere *free from domination* but as one *free from any kind of coercion*" (STPS 79, emphasis added, translation modified; SÖ 101).

While the liberation from "the regulatory regime of state authority" achieves this freedom from *political* domination, the private autonomy of the bourgeois in exchange relations also has to be protected against *economic* and *social* coercion. Kant refers to the latter when he is quoted in Section 13 regarding the qualification required to become a citizen: ". . . he must be his *own master* (*sui juris*)." For his self-determination rests on *not* "allowing others to make use of him." Only then can he "in the true sense of the word *serve* no one but the commonwealth" (quoted in STPS 110, emphasis in the original). Section 11 adds that to guard against *economic* coercion, "the economic power of each commodity owner" must be insufficient to influence "the price mechanism" in order to gain an unfair advantage over the other market participants (STPS 79).

This explains what Section 6 is referring to when it requires that to achieve the private autonomy of the *bourgeois*, which allows him to act in the role of the *homme*, there has to be an "ideological guarantee. . . that market exchange is just" (STPS 46, translation modified; SÖ 63-64). In other words, only because Section 11 posits "a private sphere *neutralized as regards power*," could there be a "*triumph of justice over force*" already in Section 6 (STPS 79, 46, emphasis added). In retrospect, this also illustrates for the reader "the collapsing of norm and description" (CR 463) in Section 4.

In short, the private sphere of commodity exchange and social labor, where the *bourgeois* exercises control over his "capitalistically functioning property," is *not* apolitical. Based on the principles of classical political economy, "The Basic Blueprint" only *conceptualizes* the private sphere as neutralized regarding all influence of power. Even if this normative claim is asserted as "needless to say" (STPS 28), "ja" in the German original (SÖ 43), it still does not acquire the status of facticity.

As Max Weber delineates in *The Methodology of the Social Sciences* (1904/1949), the use of the "ideal-type" in classical political economy "is an attempt to analyze historically unique configurations ... by means of genetic concepts." This "abstract economic theory" thus "offers us an ideal picture of events on the commodity-market under conditions of a society organized on the principles of an exchange economy, free competition and rigorously rational conduct," which are "conceived as an internally consistent system." Such a "construct in itself is like a *utopia* which has been arrived at by the analytical accentuation of certain elements of reality." In its "conceptual purity," an ideal type "cannot be found empirically anywhere in reality." (Weber 1904/1949: 93, 89/90, 90).

Readers need this specific information about Weber's methodology of the ideal type. For *Structural Transformation*'s connection between the natural economic laws posited by bourgeois political economy and Kant's rational natural law construction of the ideal bourgeois public sphere is tacitly based on Schmitt's ideal-typical construct of a "general liberal principle." He first articulated it in *The Crisis of Parliamentary Democracy* (1923/1985). In this ideal-type, Liberalism is presented as "a consistent, comprehensive, metaphysical system" that equates competition in a self-regulating market and in the rational-critical public:

> It is exactly the same: That the truth is generated through an unrestrained clash of opinions and that economic competition will automatically produce harmony. (CPD 35, see HPSC 15)

Schmitt's wording in this quote reveals that he implicitly traces this "general liberal principle" all the way back to John Milton's seminal valorization of a free press in 1644, titled *Areopagitica: For the Liberty of Unlicenc'd Printing*:

> And though all the winds of doctrine were let loose to play upon the earth, so Truth be in the field, we do injuriously by licencing and prohibiting misdoubt her strength. *Let her and Falsehood grapple*; *who ever knew Truth put to the worse, in a free and open encounter.* (Milton 1644/1959: 561, emphasis added, spelling modified; see HPSC 44)

Moreover, the connection between Milton's wording "free and open encounter" and Kant is contained in the preface to the first edition of *Critique of Pure Reason* quoted above in 5.1, which argues for "a free and open examination" of the affairs of church and state.

The reader can find *Structural Transformation*'s equivalent of Schmitt's wording "that economic competition will automatically produce harmony" in Section 16. There Habermas sums up the essence of Say's Law, which he first detailed in Section 11. Namely, that the unregulated competition of "free market" capitalism generates an "automatic equilibration of production and consumption on the level of the economy as a whole" (STPS 144, translation modified; SÖ 175).

Arguably, Say's Law is not only the most important "natural" economic law introduced in Section 11. It also plays the decisive role in the book's stylization of a rise of the bourgeois public sphere and its fall, which starts in Section 16. In Section 10, readers learn that the fully developed political public sphere could have only existed in Great Britain during the liberal phase of capitalism. However, they have to wait until Section 16 before being informed that the liberalized market, that seemingly made its development possible, was *not* generated by Say's Law as an intrinsic "natural" law of markets, but by the *same* unique "historical circumstances" (STPS 144) first introduced in Section 10.

Habermas's description of Say's Law in Section 11 is straightforward. There is no indication that it will "come to grief" in Section 16 during the first global crisis of capitalism in 1871 and the first "Great Depression" starting in 1873 (STPS 144, 143; SÖ 175, 173). Moreover, in Section 14 *Structural Transformation* ascribes the verdict that the bourgeois public sphere is "mere ideology" solely to Marx (STPS 125, SÖ 153).

Otherwise, readers might only sense in Section 15 that, in Habermas's view, there could be a problem with Say's Law. As discussed under 2.3 above, at the beginning and at the end of Section 15 they are told that the theory of Liberalism *questions* "foundational presuppositions" underlying "the classic model of the bourgeois public sphere." Specifically, the natural economic law presupposition, first advanced in the political economy of the Physiocrats, about a "'natural order' of social reproduction" (STPS 130,140; SÖ 159, 170).

Admittedly, Section 13 already alerts the reader that a "series of fictions in which the self-understanding of the bourgeois consciousness as 'public opinion' is articulated extends right into the Kantian system." Hence, already "Hegel will explicitly doubt that civil society could ever function as this kind of *natural order*" (STPS 117, emphasis added; SÖ 143). Nevertheless, at least the readers familiar with bourgeois political economy will be surprised when Section 15 confronts them with its assertion that John Stuart Mill and Tocqueville *also* question the core presupposition of a "natural order" of commodity exchange and social labor in civil society.

After all, Mill consistently refused to question Say's "natural law" of markets. Even in 1871, in the seventh edition of his *economic* Liberalism classic *Principles of Political Economy* (1848/1965), he would still express his trust in the validity of Say's doctrine. Above all, Mill's *political* Liberalism classic *On Liberty* (1859/1929), which Section 15 focuses on, calls for "leaving the producers and sellers perfectly free" and *equates* the solidity of this "so-called doctrine of Free Trade" with that of "the principle of liberty asserted in this Essay" (quoted in HPSC 16, 25n48)

Anybody who has ever taught *Structural Transformation* knows that this discussion about the role of Say's Law in Habermas's theory reconstruction of Kant's liberal model of the bourgeois public sphere is hardly academic. After all, in mainstream Economics it only "came to grief" during the *second* "Great Depression," when John Maynard Keynes deconstructed it in *The General Theory of Employment, Interest, and Money* (1936/1964). Needless to say, the "Last Hurrah" of Keynesianism occurred in 1971, when President Richard Nixon, after enacting wage and price controls, declared that "We are all Keynesians now!"

Only one year later, a highly sophisticated counter-offensive of Libertarianism, in the tradition of the Austrian School of Economics, came to fruition. It had been started already in the thirties, when a young Friedrich Hayek helped at the London School of Economics to defend against the Keynesian onslaught from Cambridge University (cf. HPSC 152n92). Finally, in 1972, Thomas Sowell's seminal book *Say's Law: An Historical Analysis* provided the credible capstone in the Chicago School's development of libertarian neoliberalism, spearheaded by Hayek and Milton Friedman.

In 1974, Hayek still had to share the Nobel Prize in Economics with Gunnar Myrdal. It was a sign of the changing times that this perceived need for balance would soon be regarded as obsolete. Only two years later, Friedman could receive his Nobel Prize in full.

It is well known that for the "Progressive Neoliberalism" (Nancy Fraser) that has guided and legitimized the corporate policies of most Silicon Valley start-ups during the last forty years, the *principles* of Say's Law are a given. Especially, if their respective spectacular successes seem to provide proof positive that nearly unlimited deregulation is economically sound and its results are morally just, because judging by consumer demand they seemingly are in the interest of all. In short, the following description of Say's Law in Section 11 would mostly receive only a quick nod:

> . . . under conditions of *complete* mobility of producers, products, and capital, supply and demand will always be in equilibrium. This means that no production capacities shall be idle, that labor reserves shall be fully utilized, and that the system shall be in principle crisis-free and, at any given time, in equilibrium on a high level commensurate with the state of development of the forces of production. (STPS 86, emphasis added, translation modified; SÖ 109)

Structural Transformation does not quote Say directly and does not identify any other source for its definition of Say's Law. Based on the literature that Habermas quotes, his most likely source is John Galbraith's *American Capitalism: The Concept of Countervailing Power* (1952/1956). However, the relevant passages of Galbraith's book do not contain such an ideal-typical reconstruction of Say's equilibrium theory. As Sowell points out, the standard English translation of Say's Law is based on the fourth French edition of 1821, which does not include the changes Say himself made in the fifth edition (1825), namely, tacitly incorporating aspects from J.C.L. Simonde de Sismondi's equilibrium theory (cf. Jean Baptiste Say. *A Treatise on Political Economy* [1834] and HPSC 19n14).

Readers have to be aware of these dates, because one of *Structural Transformation*'s enigmas is the book's pairing of Say's Law with Kant's public use of reason as the expression of "[e]ighteenth-century bourgeois consciousness [that] had conceived the idea of making political domination rational within the framework of a philosophy of history" (STPS 130). Simply put, Kant was already ill and slowly approaching his death in February 1804 when Say published the first edition of his treatise in 1803. Moreover, it only contained a "few sketchy pages" about his future law of markets. According to Sowell, it took until the fourth edition of 1819 before they evolved into a "substantial chapter" (quoted in HPSC 120).

Surprisingly, *Structural Transformation* did not select Smith's famous passage about "an invisible hand" that allegedly advances "the interests of society," which he first published in his *Theory of Moral Sentiments* in 1759. As Emma Rothschild points out in her brilliant analysis in *Economic Sentiments: Adam Smith, Condorcet, and the Enlightenment* (2001), it remained "unchanged throughout Smith's subsequent revisions of the work" (quoted in HPSC 211). Moreover, it influenced the development of the political economy of the Physiocrats, especially when during his extended stay in Paris in 1766 Smith regularly attended their club meetings at Quesnay's (HPSC 35). Section 9 refers to these meetings (STPS 69) but does not connect them to Smith. Conversely, the Physiocratic thesis about a "natural order" of social reproduction, first advanced in Quesnay's diagrams about harmonious circular motions of all factors of production and consumption, akin to the blood circulation, informed *The Wealth of Nations* (1776).

Structural Transformation presents Say's Law in Section 11 at the bottom of page 86. However, readers learn only in Section 15 on page 130 that this information would have helped them on pages 82 and 83 when trying to understand the book's definitive presentation of its core thesis about a dissolution of domination in the bourgeois public sphere. In the public competition of private arguments, the "public opinion born of the power of the better argument" (STPS 54) is supposed to dissolve domination "into that easygoing constraint that prevails on no other ground than the compelling insight" that this public opinion offers (STPS 88, see 5.2 above). In this concept, the public competition of private people is defined as not only "free from domination," but also "free from any kind of coercion" (STPS

79). However, does the same freedom exist when it comes to selecting the "better argument" or the more "compelling insight?"

Readers will find an answer to this question by consulting Sections 7, 12, and 15. In Section 7, the Physiocrats "declare" that they can offer the more compelling insight that can add a "substantive rationality" to the law's "formal criteria of generality and abstractness," because *"opion publique* alone recognizes and makes visible the *ordre naturel* so that, in the form of general norms, the enlightened monarch can then make this natural order [of society] the basis of his action—in this way domination shall be brought into convergence with reason" (STPS 55, translation modified; SÖ 73). *Structural Transformation* expands on this argument in Section 12, where the Physiocrats assert "that it is the monarch's task to watch over the *ordre naturel*; he receives his insights into the laws of the natural order through the *public eclaire* [enlightened public]" (STPS 95; SÖ 119).

In Habermas's words from 1962: *"L'opinion publique* is the enlightened outcome of the joint and public reflection on the foundations of the social order. It encapsulates the latter's natural laws; it does not rule, but the enlightened ruler will have to follow its insight" (STPS 96, translation modified; SÖ 119).

In short, the natural laws of society, which the Physiocrats claim to have discovered, present to the monarch the better argument and the more compelling insight for bringing his political rule into convergence with reason. Since the "abstract economic theory" that the Physiocrats present, is "conceived as an internally consistent system," in the sense of Weber's ideal-type, the public competition of private arguments does not proceed in the dialectical fashion of thesis, antithesis, and synthesis. Instead, it signifies a process in which the Physiocrats educate the public. Once the members of the public correctly understand this economic doctrine, they are enlightened. Consequently, the consensus about what is necessary in the interest of all is *predetermined* (cf. HPSC 37–50).

Section 15 generalizes this educational principle of consensus-building by opening up this process beyond the education of the monarch and by no longer restricting it to the economic doctrine of the Physiocrats. Hence, it becomes applicable to all doctrines of classical political economy, including Say's idealized version of the ideals inherent in equilibrium theory. Since these doctrines claim to have discovered a "natural order" of society, there should also exist a "natural basis of the [bourgeois] public sphere, which basically guarantees an autonomous and in principle harmonious course of social reproduction." Accordingly, *"public opinion would,* on one hand, be set free from structural contradictions, and, on the other hand, *in the degree in which it recognizes and takes into account the laws of motion immanent in society, be able to decide in accord with binding criteria which regulations are practically necessary in the interest of all"* (STPS 130, emphasis added, translation modified; SÖ 159).

In other words, *Structural Transformation*'s foundational thesis about the dissolution of domination "into pure reason" (STPS 88) is predicated on the existence of those natural laws of society that classical political economy claims to have discovered. Once readers have become aware of this reasoning underlying the book's narrative, they now know what public opinion's "own intention" and the public's "own idea" allegedly are. In short, they can finally access and understand the following cryptic passage in Section 11:

> According to *its own intention*, public opinion wants to be neither a check on power, nor power itself, nor even the source of all powers. Within its medium, rather, the character of executive power, domination (Herrschaft) itself, is supposed to change. The "domination" of the public is, according to *its own idea*, an order in which domination itself is dissolved; *veritas non auctoritas facit legem* [truth not authority makes law]. (STPS 82, emphasis added, translation modified; SÖ 104)

In *Structural Transformation*'s narrative, adopting and implementing the doctrines of classical political economy allows to dissolve domination into pure reason. The Physiocrats surely saw it that way. Readers have to draw on the information from this guide and connect the respective passages in Sections 9 and 12 to realize that in France in 1774, seven years after the Physiocrat Mercier de la Riviere had developed the "rigorous concept of *opinion publique*" (STPS 95), his fellow Physiocrat Turgot had the opportunity to implement these doctrines when he was "called into government" as the first exponent of such a rational-critical "public opinion" (STPS 69). To highlight the magnitude of this event for his theory reconstruction of Kant's idea of the bourgeois public sphere, Habermas introduces a key quote from *Critique and Crisis*, in which the Physiocrat La Harpe says of Turgot that he "is the first among us to transform the acts of sovereign authority into works of reason" (STPS 96, STPS 269n25; CC 147).

The rationality of these posited natural economic laws is an expression of the "rigorously rational conduct" (Weber) practiced by the commodity owners in the exchange relations of the "free market." To emphasize this point, Section 11 even goes so far as to momentarily dissolve the unity of morality and rationality in Habermas's signature "morally pretentious rationality." It does so by fleetingly awarding first place to rationality when severely criticizing state activities that violate the binding norms of the law-based state when interfering in the market. Such acts are judged as "blameworthy primarily *not because they violate principles of justice* laid down by natural right *but simply because they* are unpredictable" and thus *"preclude* exactly the kind and measure of *rationality"* required in "a system in which exchange transactions proceed in accord with calculable expectations" (STPS 80, emphasis added, translation modified).

Nevertheless, *Structural Transformation* is only too aware that Kant's norms of truth and justice in his modern rational natural law are predicated on both the rationality of exchange relations *and* the justice allegedly inherent in them. Otherwise justice could not "triumph over force" (STPS 46) in the book's narrative. Hence, the *bourgeois* could not assume the role of the *homme*, politics could not be rationalized in the name of morality (STPS 102), and the rational-critical discourse in the bourgeois public sphere could not serve as both "the principle of the legal order and as the method of Enlightenment" (STPS 104).

As Horkheimer analyzed, in Kant's philosophy of history the ideas of truth, justice, and freedom are derived from his ideal of reason whose "triumph" was "the hidden yet certain trend of world history notwithstanding all retrogression, interludes of darkness, deviations" (quoted in HPSC 27). His Kant interpretation from 1941 dovetails with Koselleck's, who received it from Schmitt. In *Critique and Crisis*, the "bourgeois intelligentsia" set out on a "triumphal march" for reason in their "Enlightenment" movement (CC 53) from Bayle's dictionary to Kant's reflections on *Perpetual Peace* (1795/1970) one hundred years later.

Readers have to be constantly aware that this stylization structures and informs *Structural Transformation*'s narrative from Section 4 "The Basic Blueprint" to Section 13 on Kant. The latter tacitly adopts Schmitt's claim that Kant's essay from 1795 contains the "clearest and final expression" of "principal ideas of the bourgeois Enlightenment" like "freedom" of all members of society as human beings, "equality" among them, and "autonomy" for all of them as citizens" (CT 126).

Conversely, all three categories of Kant's rational natural law reflect the presuppositions of classical political economy that Section 11 refers to regarding natural economic laws. Already Section 10 ascribed to the natural "laws of the free market" a "model character" for defining the formal and general legal standing of the person. This equality before the law thus corresponded to the "fundamental parity of commodity owners in the market and among educated individuals in the public sphere" (STPS 75)

As emphasized in Section 11, the validity of the "presuppositions of classical economics" decided whether everybody had an "equal chance" to acquire "property and education" as "the qualifications of a private person" (STPS 87) for admission to the political public sphere and to realize the autonomy of citizenship. These economic presuppositions were "the guarantee of free competition," "the model of a society of petty commodity producers" with "relatively widely and evenly distributed ownership of means of production," and Say's Law (STPS 86). *Structural Transformation* follows *Constitutional Theory*'s ideal type of the parliamentary system in the bourgeois constitutional state based on the two presuppositions of "*property and education*" (CT 334, emphasis in the original):

> According to its own idea, the bourgeois parliament of the nineteenth century is an assembly of educated human beings, who represent . . . the education and the reason of the entire *nation.* (CT 334, emphasis in the original)

To better understand this liberal idea of parliament, the reader should consult the reference in Section 12 to Francois Guizot, introduced by Schmitt as the "typical representative of bourgeois liberalism," due to his belief in "parliament as a representation of reason" (CT 335). For this Guizot reference explains Karl Mannheim's dictum in *Ideology and Utopia* (1929/1936), that "the original conception of parliamentarism was, as Carl Schmitt has so clearly shown, that of a debating society in which truth is sought by theoretical methods" (quoted in HPSC 16).

Already the 1923 German original of *The Crisis of Parliamentary Democracy* included the seminal Guizot quote that Schmitt's interpretation is based on. It defines parliamentarism as the system, which compels "the whole body of citizens" to continuously "seek after reason, justice, and truth" in order to regulate "power." This search for truth should occur 1) jointly in "discussion"; 2) publicly, "under the eyes of the citizens"; 3) through "the liberty of the press, which stimulates the citizens themselves to seek after truth and to tell it to power" (quoted in STPS 101).

5.5. THE DOMINATION OF INTELLECTUAL HISTORY IN SECTION 12 OVER POLITICAL HISTORY IN SECTIONS 9 AND 8

Sections 5.3 and 5.4 of this guide have used *Structural Transformation*'s Sections 10 and 11 as well as their connections to Sections 4, 6, 7, 8, 9, 15, 20,13, 16, 14, and 12 as the second step toward identifying, clarifying, and understanding the key theses of Habermas's book. To briefly recap, the first step traced under 5.1 and 5.2 the origins of the book's Kantian thesis about a "morally pretentious rationality" inherent in the bourgeois public sphere back to the "civil war topos" in Schmitt's constitutional theory and to Koselleck's intellectual history of the Protestant Reformation. In this theory reconstruction, Luther's contrast of inwardness and externality in the tradition of Augustine's two-world doctrine imbues the conjugal family's intimate sphere with the privateness of a "saturated and free interiority" (STPS 28), which bestows on the bourgeois family a moral superiority over the political authority of the Absolutist State. Habermas locates this "superiority of the inward over the outward and hence of the private over the public" in Schmitt's Hobbes interpretation (STPS 268n8).

This moral superiority gains political relevance once the "representation of the interests of the privatized domain of a market economy" is interpreted in the political public sphere "with the aid of ideas grown in the soil of the intimate sphere of the conjugal family" (STPS 51). Since these ideas of human beings "pure and simple" constitute the *humanity* of the literary public sphere and are expressed in the double identity of the property-owner as *bourgeois* and as *homme*, they serve "to increase the effectiveness of the political public sphere." In short, once "property-owners desire to influence political power in their common interest" (STPS 56), they can do so in the name of "Justice," which allegedly is inherent in all exchange relations of a market economy.

In its second step, this guide analyzed under 5.3 and 5.4 *Structural Transformation*'s concept of "rationality" as the coequal component in the "morally pretentious rationality" of the bourgeois public sphere, which "strives to discover what is *at once just and right*" [in German: "*das Rechte und das Richtige*"] (STPS 54, emphasis added, translation modified; SÖ 73). From the perspective of Kant's rational natural law, Addison's quest for "Truth and Justice" in his moral weeklies had to be limited to the latter, because his secularized Puritan morality did not yet cover the former. Only in the last third of the eighteenth century will the classical political economy of the Physiocrats and Smith declare as "Truth" that natural rights of citizens like Freedom, Equality, and Justice, are guaranteed by "natural" laws of society itself, if all markets are completely liberated from governmental regulations.

What makes it even more challenging for the reader to correctly understand *Structural Transformation*'s complex theory reconstruction, is the book's choice to substitute the terms "Truth" [*Wahrheit*] and "Justice" [*Gerechtigkeit*] with ones that can lead to misunderstandings. This is likely to occur in a crucial passage of Section 11 when Habermas asserts that "the critical public debate of private people *convincingly* claims to be in the nature of a noncoercive inquiry into what is at the same time *correct* and *right*" (STPS 82 emphasis added, translation modified; SÖ 104). While in Section 7 "right" stands for the German term "*das Richtige*," ["Truth"], in Section 11 it is used to translate the other German term, namely, "*das Rechte*" ["Justice"]. In other words, "right" on page 54 means "correct" on page 82. Conversely, "right" on page 82 means "just" on page 54.

In this context, readers might wonder whether, for example, the principles that Say's Law declared to be "right" were really supposed to represent the

"Truth?" They thus might want to find out how its author answered this question himself. In his *Letters to Mr. Malthus on Several Subjects of Political Economy and on the Cause of the Stagnation of Commerce* (1821), first published throughout 1820 in the *New Monthly Magazine*, Say defended during a prolonged period of "general glut" in the markets his proposition "that it is production alone which opens markets to produce." In the 1980s, advocates for the "supply-side economics" of the Reagan administration would confidently sum up this proposition as "Supply creates its own demand."

In comparison, Say opened his letter on a less assertive note. Given the "gloomy and distressing" business news which *Blackwood's Edinburgh Magazine* had already reported in October 1819, he initially acknowledged that this core proposition of his Law of Markets had a "paradoxical appearance." For *Blackwood's* had documented in great detail that due to "the immense extension of our manufactures we have indeed overstocked almost every market" around the globe. Say thus could not deny that the economic doctrine of "underconsumption," advanced especially by Thomas Malthus, "has indeed appearances on its side" and "may be supported by arguments." Nevertheless, Say brushed aside that given all this misery Malthus may be able to "interpret facts" in his favor. His letter defiantly concludes with the following assertion that compares his economic law to the laws of the natural sciences and ascribes to both the same level of "Truth":

> But, Sir, when Copernicus and Galileo first taught that the sun (although it was daily seen to rise in the east, ascend majestically to the meridian, and decline at evening in the west) never moved from its station, they also had to contend with universal prejudice, the opinion of antiquity, the evidence of the senses: ought they have renounced the demonstrations resulting from sound philosophy? (quoted in HPSC 123)

In other words, the unique historical condition of Great Britain's liberalized market as the result of the Industrial Revolution and of militarily enforced global trade hegemony seemingly allowed Say's Law to equate the "rigorous rational conduct" (Weber) in exchange economies with the rationality of the natural sciences. Nonetheless, such an advanced degree of idealization also underlies Schmitt's "general liberal principle," which transfers this market rationality onto public discourse and the deliberations in parliament. For its theory reconstruction, *Structural Transformation* needs both just exchange relations and harmony in the commodity markets.

Otherwise Habermas cannot rationally reconstruct the liberal ideal of "Truth and Justice" in the political public sphere of parliament as the organizational principle and the "substantial rationality" of the bourgeois constitutional state. This "binding of all state activity to a system of norms legitimated by [the morally pretentious rationality of] public opinion" can then "aim at abolishing the state as an instrument of domination altogether" (STPS 82; SÖ 104). In short, the rising fusion of Morality and Rationality reaches its climax on the final page of Section 11 with the proclamation of *Structural Transformation*'s *telos* of a dissolution of domination "into pure reason" (STPS 88; SÖ 111; see 1.1 and 1.2 above).

Based on its first two steps, the third step of this guide offers its readers the insight that the intellectual history of a "rising" bourgeois public sphere in Section 12 largely determined the *selection* of events in its social and political history in Sections 8 and 9. According to the logic of *Structural Transformation*'s narrative, a morally pretentious rationality as the hallmark of a political public sphere that serves as the organizing principle of the bourgeois constitutional state could only be achieved in a process that started around 1780. Symbolized by the invention of the steam engine as the "universal agent" of the "Grand Industry" (Marx), the Industrial Revolution in a "feedback loop" with the growing influence of classical political economy, brought about the liberalized market which "the laws of motion of civil society in the modern sense" (TAP 76) needed to function akin to the laws of natural science.

Arguably, David Ricardo, author of the *Principles of Political Economy and Taxation* (1817), became the eminent representative of an enlightened public opinion in the British Parliament. Endowed with the financial means to buy his seat before the Reform Bill of 1832 would have granted him access through open and fair elections, Ricardo served from March 1819 until his death in September 1823. He used his access to this "strong public sphere" (Nancy Fraser) with the power to legislate for grounding his 129 speeches recorded in Hansard in his following maxim:

> "Political Economy . . . is only useful, as it directs Governments to right measures in taxation" and provides to the public "the knowledge that Agriculture, Commerce, and Manufactures flourish best when left without interference on the part of Government." (quoted in HPSC 120)

Readers have to keep in mind this logic of *Structural Transformation*'s narrative when trying to understand why the book privileges in Section 12 Edmund Burke's reflections from the 1780s about "the general opinion of those who are to be governed" (quoted in STPS 94) over Bolingbroke's publication of *The Craftsman* from 1726 to 1735. For it had looked like Section 8 already wanted to locate the origin of the political public sphere in this journal of the opposition to the Walpole ministry. However, Sections 10 to 12 let readers know in retrospect that only at first glance could Habermas's following analysis regarding Bolingbroke's *The Craftsman* be taken at face value:

. . . the press was for the first time established as a *genuinely critical* organ of a public engaged *in critical political debate*: as the fourth estate. (STPS 60, emphasis added)

Moreover, the same happens to the valorization of Montesquieu in Section 7, which is effectively demoted in Section 9 by an intrusion of *Structural Transformation*'s interpretation of intellectual history. As this guide pointed out above in section 5.2, Habermas initially praises Montesquieu for reducing the "publicly promulgated law" altogether to human reason (STPS 54). He even goes so far as to credit *The Spirit of the Laws* (1735/1949) with introducing a specific rationality into its definition of "law" as "the quintessence of general, abstract, and permanent norms." In this inherent rationality, "what is right converges with what is just." (STPS 53; SÖ 71–72). In other words, Montesquieu's law definition anticipates the "morally pretentious rationality" inherent in Kant's rational natural law, which is implicitly introduced only on the following page (STPS 54; SÖ 73). In stark contrast, Section 9 seemingly deletes Montesquieu from its preferred trajectory of the criticism of the *philosophes*:

In the first half of the [eighteenth] century, the criticism of the *philosophes* is preoccupied, *Montesquieu notwithstanding*, with religion, literature, and art; only at the stage of its encyclopedic publication does the *moral* intent of the *philosophes* develop into a political one, at least indirectly. The *Encyclopedia* is planned as a publicist undertaking in the grand style. . . *Robespierre can later celebrate it as "the introductory chapter of the Revolution."* (STPS 68–69, emphasis added; SÖ 89)

The last sentence in this quote anticipates the essence of the intellectual history displayed in Section 12. Both strands of it seem to inevitably lead to the French Revolution. Moreover, they originate as the two faces of the "bourgeois Enlightenment" in the same "moral inner space" that, in Koselleck's reading of Schmitt's Hobbesian thesis, the Absolutist State had granted to end the religious civil war. Their common basis is Locke's moral Law of Opinion or Reputation which emerges from this inner space by "a tacit and secret consent."

Locke's Law is grounded in "the informal web of folkways." These folkways represent a "secularized morality," because they originate "in privatized religious faith." In the first strand of this common trajectory referred to in the above quote, Bayle's *Regime de la Critique* replaces Locke's Law. It thus functions as the predecessor of the author of the Encyclopedia, who since 1751 seek to "dissolve . . . through a critique of ideology" the "opinion of the people supported by tradition and *bon sens*" (STPS 90–92, 95).

In dialectical fashion, the second strand starts with Jean-Jacques Rousseau's *Discourse on the Arts and Sciences* from 1750, in which he defends exactly this "opinion of the people." Initially, he preempts the Physiocrats by using their future term *opinion publique* to denote this opposite of a rational-critical public opinion. According to *Structural Transformation*'s narrative, in 1762 Locke's Law "became sovereign by way of Rousseau's *Contrat Social*" (STPS 93, 95, 97).

Moreover, *both* alleged intellectual origins of the French Revolution, the Encyclopedia *and* Rousseau's *Social Contract* (1762/1959) as well as his *Discourse on the Arts and Sciences*, were first asserted by Maximilien Robespierre. Already in his National Convention speech on May 10, 1793, he praised, in "language very close to Rousseau's own," the vast majority of the people, uncorrupted by the race for wealth and luxury, for protecting the public good because only "labor, austerity, and poverty . . . are the guardians of virtue." His moral rhetoric culminated in his speech to the Convention on February 7, 1794, when he celebrated "the sovereignty of that eternal justice," which is based on "laws . . . inscribed in the hearts of all human beings."

But in his speech on May 8, 1794, he equally valorized the role of reason in educating all citizens about the moral laws that safeguard republican virtue: "The world has changed, it has to continue to change. One half of the global revolution has been accomplished. Reason resembles the globe, the home to humankind: One half is steeped in darkness, yet the other one is brightly lit" (quoted in HPSC 91n143, see HPSC 69).

Above all, in Habermas's theory reconstruction the power of the reason that Robespierre refers to goes beyond the one that informs the Encyclopedia. It incorporates both the insights of classical political economy and of Kant's rational natural law. Once again, already Section 9 introduces this reasoning underlying Section 12. With regard to the connection between the ideology critique of the Encyclopedia and the political economy of the Physicocrats with its alleged "natural laws of society," Section 9 presents the following sweeping assertion:

In the last third of the [eighteenth] century, . . . the philosophes changed from belles lettrists into economists. (STPS 69)

Regarding the posited connection between Kant's modern rational natural law and the French Revolution, Section 9 is even more emphatic. Its presentation stands out, because this aspect of intellectual history almost entirely substitutes for social and political history. The latter is essentially reduced to one sentence, which opens on a rather laconic note: "The Revolution created overnight, *although with less stability*, what in Great Britain had taken more than a century of steady evolution: the institutions . . . for critical public debate of political matters" (STPS 69-70, emphasis added). In comparison, the following quote demonstrates the emphasis on constitutional law theory and foreshadows a core thesis in Section 12:

> *At least as important* as the factual institutionalization of the political public sphere is its anchoring in legal norms. *The revolutionary event is immediately interpreted and defined in terms of constitutional law.* (STPS 70, emphasis added, translation modified; SÖ 90)

It also anticipates the explanation of this thesis in lectures on "Natural Law and Revolution," which were presented in October 1962. They were published in 1963 in *Theory and Practice* (1963/1973). In these lectures, Habermas's heavy emphasis on constitutional law inadvertently functions as a sort of saving grace for the Terror in the French Revolution's Jacobin phase:

> . . . as learned disciples of Rousseau, the Jacobins conceive of democracy, even in its most radical form, in such a way that the general will *exercises its sovereignty* by means of *formal and general laws.* (NLR 105, emphasis added, translation modified; NR 110)

Section 12 devotes a total of more than three pages to Rousseau's theory of democracy. This emphasis reflects Habermas's general preference for the "democratic culture" invented through the French Revolution, which "reveals to the world one of the foundational postures of conscious historical action," as he approvingly quotes Francois Furet in "Popular Sovereignty as Procedure" (BFN 466–67). The comprehensive summary of Rousseau's *Social Contract* in Section 12 focuses on its use of the term *opinion publique*, which is in "almost verbatim agreement with Locke's 'Law of Opinion.'"

However, in contrast to Locke's Law, *opinion publique* has "the additional task of legislation." This task presents a crucial challenge. On one hand, the "general will is always right." On the other hand, "the judgment that guides it is not always enlightened." Hence, it is "necessary to present matters as they are, sometimes as they are supposed to appear." In short, "Rousseau's democracy of unpublic opinion ultimately postulates the manipulative exercise of power" (STPS 98–99, translation modified; SÖ 122).

Given the identity between Locke's definition of "opinion" and Rousseau's definition of *opinion publique*, Section 12 asks why Rousseau does not simply adopt Locke's term? Actually, there is a twofold answer to this question, which goes beyond the requirement that in a direct democracy, like in the Greek *polis*, the sovereign "is actually present" for the legislative process. Readers thus have to add a second part to *Structural Transformation*'s explanation. As stated above, Locke's Law of Opinion or Reputation functions by a "secret and tacit consent" and not as a *public* display. Nevertheless, Section 12 clarifies that *opinion publique* derives its legal norm of "publicness" from its spatial attribute of "the *place publique*," where "the citizens assemble for acclamation," and "not from the rational-critical public debate of a *public eclaire*" (STPS 99, translation modified; SÖ 122).

At this point in the book's narrative, both strands of intellectual history emanating from the "moral inner space" within the Absolutist State meet head-on. In 1762, Rousseau's *Social Contract* had postulated "democracy without public debate" (STPS 99). In 1767, the Physiocrats, in the tradition of Bayle's *Regime de la Critique* and the Encyclopedia, presented the "rigorous concept" of *opinion publique*, in which a rational-critical discourse "purifies" Locke's and Rousseau's "opinion" to constitute "Truth" akin to that in the findings of the natural sciences. However, they do so within the anti-democratic framework of an Absolutist State. In the next two decades, these fundamentally different meanings of *opinion publique* "become particularly polarized in prerevolutionary France" (STPS 99).

In Rousseau's concept, the legislative process of the democratic sovereign is uncritical and even potentially manipulated. In the Physiocratic concept, the legislative process is grounded in the rational-critical discourse of an enlightened public, but is enacted by the sovereignty of the monarch. To dissolve the head-on confrontation between these two concepts in 1789, Section 12 advances its boldest claim:

> . . . *the Revolution itself* combines the two sundered functions of public opinion, the critical and the legislative. (STPS 99, emphasis added, translation modified; SÖ 123)

Arguably, Habermas was aware of the magnitude of his assertion. After he published "Natural Law and Revolution," he added an endnote to *Structural Transformation*'s claim, in which he also refers to this essay (see STPS 269n38). It contains a detailed discussion of the "competing natural law constructions" of Rousseau and the Physiocrats (NLR 96; NR 102). However, its analysis of the debate in the National Assembly in August 1789 regarding the Declaration of Human Rights demonstrates that the Revolution did *not* resolve the fundamental differences between Rousseau and the Physiocrats as the above quote seems to indicate.

Among the delegates, the exponents of Physiocracy agree with Rousseau's disciples only with regard to the existence of "human rights *as* the rights of citizens" and of "freedom solely *within* a political state" (NLR 101, emphasis in the original; NR 106). They continue to differ regarding the legislative process which legitimizes the exercise of political power. For them, "political power proceeds *on the basis of laws which have been established from philo-*

sophical insight into the nature of the things themselves" (NLR 101, emphasis added; NR 106–107). The following quote from Section 12, which directly follows on the one above, sidesteps this continuing fundamental difference:

> The Constitution of 1791 integrates the principle of popular sovereignty with that of the parliamentary constitutional state, which provides a constitutional guarantee for a public sphere as an element in the political realm. (STPS 99, translation modified; SÖ 123)

Sections 10 and 11 define *the critical function* of public opinion in the bourgeois public sphere, in accord "with its own intention," as the medium in which the character of domination changes and will eventually be dissolved. Accordingly, it neither wants to be "power itself" nor "the source of all powers" (STPS 82). However, Section 12 further illustrates its claim about the implementation of this critical function in the French Constitution of 1781 by using a quote from the delegate Bergasse who, "in a discussion in the National Assembly about the constitutional significance of *opinion publique*" (STPS 99), emphatically stated:

> You know that it is *only through public opinion* that *you can acquire any power* to promote the good; . . . you know that *before public opinion all authorities become silent.* (Quoted in STPS 99, emphasis added)

Far from wishing to dissolve all power in the rational-critical discourse of the political public sphere of parliament, Bergasse, on the contrary, regards *opinion publique* as the highly desirable source of all powers (HPSC 42). In the scholarly discourse about the French National Assembly the views of Bergasse have been regarded as representative. They were already quoted in 1912 in a book by Robert Redslob about the constitutional theories underlying the debates in the National Assembly. In 1958, the political scientist Ernst Fraenkel (introduced in section 3.2 above) vetted them again when he published his German-language essay "Parliament and Public Opinion" (HPSC 80n55, 81n56).

In short, the French authors of the Constitution of 1791 did not share *Structural Transformation*'s future claim that it is the intention of the bourgeois constitutional state to institutionalize a critical function of public opinion that changes and eventually dissolves all political power.

To fully realize that such a claim is unsubstantiated, readers not only have to compare the book's statements on page 99 (Section 12) with the ones on page 82 (Section 11), but also with those on pages 70 to 71 (Section 9). Only Section 9 provides the *specifics* of the "constitutional guarantee for a public sphere as an element in the political realm" in the Constitution of 1791. While this Constitution's paragraph 11 confirms that the "free communication of ideas and opinions" is one of the "most precious rights" of humankind, this guarantee for everyone to "speak, write, and print freely," is only granted with an accompanying strong qualifier. Citizens can exercise this "most precious" right of humankind only "with the proviso of responsibility for the *misuse of this liberty* in the cases *determined by law*" (quoted in STPS 70, emphasis added).

A comparison of the *constitutional law theory* in Section 11 with one of the references to the *political history* of the French Revolution in Section 9 reveals that in fact this proviso could severely restrict the citizen's public use of reason. On page 71 readers learn that in August 1792, "two days after the storming of the Tuileries," the Paris Commune used its political power to issue an edict that denounced conservative opponents of the Revolution as "poisoners of public opinion" and had their presses confiscated" (STPS 71). Moreover, Section 9 leaves out that already in the months following "the massacre at the Champ de Mars in July 1791" various political journals, "of both pro- and counter-revolutionary persuasion," were repressed by law.

Jack Richard Censer's comprehensive research for his book *Prelude to Power: The Parisian Radical Press, 1789-1791* (1976) further documents this. Only *after* the *Declaration des Droits de l'Homme et du Citoyen* in 1789, but *before* the Constitution of 1791, could its paragraph 11 about the "free communication of ideas and opinions" as one of the "most precious rights" of humankind become a *constitutional reality*. During those two years alone was the "rising popular interest" in national politics and "the growing number of people who wanted to publicize their own opinions" reflected in the increase in the number of political journals (quoted in HPSC 81n57).

This tension and partial disconnect between Section 12 and Section 9 only increases when the former presents a seemingly linear development from the Constitution of 1791 to Guizot's claim about a "sovereignty of reason" (CT 8) in his *"classic formulation* of the 'rule of public opinion'" quoted above in 5.2. Readers thus get the impression that Guizot's "lectures on the origin and history of the bourgeois constitutional state," which he held "from 1820 on," could actually present such an uninterrupted rise of the bourgeois public sphere (STPS 101, emphasis added, translation modified; SÖ 125). In stark contrast, the selective references in Section 9 to the political history of France until the July Revolution of 1830 contain the following sobering statements:

1) "On 17 January 1800, two days after the coup d'etat, Napoleon eliminated the freedom of the press"; 2) "From 1811 on he allowed only three papers besides the official *Moniteur*, and even these were under strict censorship"; 3) "The Bourbons, upon their return, [proclaimed] that they would

respect the freedom of the press. . . . But the opposition could express itself only with great caution" (STPS 71).

Nevertheless, what might be called *Structural Transformation*'s *"tacit model case of the French development"* still benefits from an inverse ratio between attention and valorization, if one compares Section 12 to Section 9 and Section 8, respectively. While Section 8 The Model Case of British Development, from the perspective of social and political history, is *more than ten pages long*, its influence on the book's stylization of intellectual history and constitutional law theory in its core Section 12 is *less than secondary*. In the section's trajectory toward 1789, only the appeal to "the public spirit of the people" in Bolingbroke's political journalism is credited with "the Enlightenment characteristics of what would soon be called 'public opinion.'"

However, even these "principles of public criticism" (STPS 93) with which Bolingbroke established for the first time the press as "a genuinely critical organ of a public engaged in critical political debate" (STPS 60), were not sufficient to save him from being overshadowed by Burke in the section's intellectual history. For Section 12 charges Bolingbroke's public criticism with harboring "a piece of anticipated Rousseauism" (STPS 93), i.e., "the direct, undistorted sense for what was *right and just* and the articulation of 'opinion' into 'judgment' through the public clash of arguments" (STPS 94, emphasis added). Only in the 1780s, when Burke encouraged his electors to engage in "public discussion" of their "private reflections upon public affairs" to "form the general opinion of those who are to be governed" (STPS 94), could the latter according to Section 12 achieve the status of the enlightened public opinion of the Physiocrats and of Kant's rational natural law construction of the bourgeois public sphere.

Still, to fully understand this argument, readers have to move back 30 pages from Section 12 to Section 8, where the *political history* of press, parliament, and the public sphere is selected according to the prerogatives of this *intellectual history*. Specifically, the fact that Bolingbroke's *Craftsman* as the "genuinely critical organ of a public engaged in critical political debate" played "more than once" a key role in forcing "Walpole and his parliamentary majority to concessions" must "of course, not be construed *prematurely* as a sign of a kind of rule of public opinion" (STPS 64, emphasis added). Similarly, "the demanded dissolution of Parliament" in connection with "the agitation of Wilkes" between "1768 and 1771" is only mentioned in passing, because even the "dissolution of Parliament in 1784," when the King famously "stated that he felt obliged 'to recur to the sense of the people'" was, in the *ideal typical* interpretation of Section 8, "not due chiefly to the pressure of this 'opinion of the people'" (STPS 65).

Structural Transformation thus has to leave out John Wilkes's struggle for the freedom of the press in 1763, for the rights of the Middlesex electors in 1768, and for the open reporting of Parliamentary proceedings in 1771. In addition, it must not "prematurely" include Wilkes's plea in the House of Commons in 1776, to give "the meanest mechanic, the poorest peasant and day labourer . . . [some] share in the power of making those laws which deeply interest them" (quoted in HPSC 113). Instead, Section 8 has to wait until 1792 when, "three years *after* the outbreak of *the French Revolution*," Fox could introduce into Parliament "*public opinion in the strict sense*" of Kant and the Physiocrats (STPS 65, emphasis added). Only then is the "sense of the people" replaced by an enlightened "public opinion." It "is formed in public discussion *after* the public, *through education and information*, has been put in the position to arrive at a *reasoned opinion*. Hence, Fox's maxim, 'to give the public the means of forming an opinion'" (STPS 66, emphasis added, translation modified, SÖ 86).

It is at this point of *Structural Transformation*'s stylization when readers have to wonder whether their reasoning is only admitted if it can be poured into "one uniform mold," the one Ralf Dahrendorf referred to in his book review. Yes, in 1726 Bolingbroke founded a "genuinely critical organ of a public engaged in critical political debate." No, *objectively* it could not really be rational-critical, because the objective truth about the natural laws of society would only be detected three decades later by Quesnay, the leading political economist of the *Encyclopedie*. In other words, the development of the forces and relations of production was not yet sufficiently advanced for the discovery of these natural laws which would form the presupposition for Kant's rational natural law of the bourgeois constitutional state.

However, readers of this guide already know from section 2.3 above that Kant built his rational natural law theory on fictitious presuppositions (STPS 117) and that classical political economy's key assumption about natural laws of society was mistaken (STPS 130, 131, 140). When confronted on page 64 with the bold assertion that it would be *premature* to ascribe real communicative power to Bolingbroke's *Craftsman* for its influence in forcing "Walpole and his parliamentary majority to concessions," they can now question this claim. *Without* natural laws of society, the "true [political] power constellation" regarding a "rule of public opinion" (STPS 64) did not fundamentally differ in the 1730s from the one in the 1770s when the Physiocrats sought concessions from the absolute monarch regarding the free trade in grain.

As mentioned in section 5.4 above, according to *Structural Transformation*'s Section 12 *opinion publique*, defined as "the enlightened outcome of common and public reflection on the foundations of social order," lacks any *political* power. In short, it "does not rule." However, the "enlightened monarch will have to follow its insights (STPS 96, translation modified, SÖ 119).

Section 5.4 also pointed out that such a transformation of the communicative power of a rational-critical public opinion into political power occurred when the Physiocrat Turgot was appointed controller general in 1774. However, it is debatable whether he transformed "the acts of sovereign authority into works of reason" (STPS 96, STPS 269n25; CC 147). As Istvan Hont and Michael Ignatieff acknowledged from a liberal perspective in their essay on "Needs and Justice in *The Wealth of Nations*" (1983), this first grand attempt to implement the bourgeois political economy of free trade in grain as "conscious historical action" was "exploded in the *guerre de farines* of 1775" (quoted in HPSC 31).

It takes Koselleck's conservative perspective to praise Turgot as "a champion of enlightened Absolutism" who used the despot's powers to "speedily . . . put down the grain riots of 1775" (CC 141–42). Nevertheless, Louis XVI dismissed Turgot in 1776 and brought back the feudal police of the grain trade. After losing their political power, the Physiocrats also ended up with a diminished communicative power in the rational-critical public sphere. According to Hont and Ignatieff, "the Physiocratic school disintegrated" (quoted in HPSC 31).

Arguably, *Structural Transformation* leaves out this social and political history, because it does not fit into the uniform mold of its stylization. Contrary to the book's assertion quoted above that after 1767 the "philosophes changed from belles lettrists into economists" (STPS 69), leading Enlightenment philosophers like Voltaire and Diderot remained "genuinely perplexed by the grain question" in spite of being "very well informed" about it, as Steven L. Kaplan points out in his seminal work *Bread, Politics and Political Economy in the Reign of Louis XV* (1976). While agreeing with Quesnay regarding the importance of free trade in "creating the incentive for improvements in agricultural productivity," they also realized that in "an economy dogged with poor transport" the deregulated flow of grain often reached areas of scarcity only *after* people had died of hunger (quoted in HPSC 35, 36).

Emblematic for this split among the authors of the *Encyclopedie* was Turgot's claim in a private letter to his fellow Physiocrat Dupont de Nemours "that Voltaire was 'talking complete nonsense about economics.'" Conversely, Diderot did not see how the free trade in grain could be reconciled "with the humane ideals which the Enlightenment embodied" (quoted in HPSC 36). In other words, Turgot's "works of reason" lived up to the "rigorous rational conduct" in Max Weber's ideal type of the *bourgeois* but not to the "morally pretentious rationality" in Habermas's bourgeois ideal of the "cultivated personality" (STPS 47) as the synthesis of the *bourgeois* and the *homme*.

Chapter Six

Structural Transformation's Tacit Model Case of the Bourgeois Public Sphere

The French Revolution, Kant's "Unofficial" Philosophy of History, Condorcet's Absolute Rationalism, and Schiller's Expressive Subjectivism

To understand the reasoning behind *Structural Transformation's* core arguments, readers have to keep in mind that Habermas shares with the philosophy of German Idealism its foremost dictum, also adopted by Marx and Friedrich Engels, that Kant provided the constitutional theory for the French Revolution. In his July 1962 inaugural address at the University of Heidelberg, Habermas strongly agrees with Hegel's valorization of the French Revolution "as the world-historical event which for the first time had conferred real existence and validity" on the "reason of rational natural law." This modern rational natural law that informs Kant's conception of the republican constitution as well as Habermas's theory reconstruction of the rational-critical deliberation in the bourgeois public sphere, accepts only "the abstract freedom of the legal person in the equality of all men under formal and general laws" (TAP122; TUP 129).

Commemorating the bicentennial of the French Revolution more than 25 years later, Habermas reinforces Hegel's argument about this "world-historical event" from July 1789: "Unlike the American Revolution, which was, so to speak, the *outcome* of events, the French Revolution was *carried forward* by its protagonists in the consciousness of a revolution" (BFN 466, emphasis in the original). Moreover, this quote and the following one implicitly reveal a key reason why *Structural Transformation* neglects the role of the political public sphere in all earlier bourgeois revolutions: "One could even say that the bourgeois revolutions—the Dutch, English, and American—became aware of themselves *as* revolutions only in the French Revolution" (BFN 466, emphasis in the original).

Above all, Habermas's philosophical *telos* of a dissolution of domination in discursive will-formation is rooted in his valorization of the "innovative concept of autonomy" by Rousseau and Kant. As alerted to above in the Introduction, in 2004 Habermas confirmed his commitment to this core concept of rational natural law which informs "the normative self-understanding of modernity." In turn, these "productive ideas of self-consciousness, self-determination, and self-realization" (DW 193, cf. FRPS 442) infuse the modern concept of democracy with a "spirit of awakening" and carry with them "the promise of emancipation."

6.1. THE PROCESS OF CRITICISM AND THE FRENCH REVOLUTION: THE TACIT ORIGINS OF HABERMAS'S PRIVILEGING OF KANT'S "UNOFFICIAL" PHILOSOPHY OF HISTORY—TOCQUEVILLE, KOSELLECK, SCHMITT

Habermas's enthusiastic adoption of Hegel's admiration for "the unheard-of occurrence" of the French Revolution when "human beings had made philosophical thought their basis and had constructed political reality according to it" (NLR 82) informed *Structural Transformation*'s theory reconstruction of Kant's ideal of the public use of reason in the bourgeois constitutional state. This rational reconstruction is guided by the "idea of the political realization of philosophy—namely the *autonomous* creation, by contract, of legal compulsion springing solely from the compulsion of philosophical reason" (NLR 86, emphasis added). As Habermas emphasizes in "Natural Law and Revolution," the autonomous human action of realizing philosophical reason "is the *concept of revolution* which follows *immanently* from the principles of modern natural law" (NLR 86, emphasis added).

Accordingly, in its fourth step this guide will identify the kind of "education and information" *Structural Transformation* thinks the bourgeois public needs "to arrive at a reasoned opinion" about "the principles of modern natural law." Drawing on Sections 12, 11, 9, and 8 will also allow to clarify which autonomous political action seems to be necessary for the realization of this reasoned opinion. In the process, it will become apparent that The Model Case of British Development does not fulfill the criteria of Habermas's theory reconstruction, unless it is quite selectively interpreted from the perspective of a Tacit Model Case of French Revolutionary Development.

Section 10 described the systemic and historical character of a liberalized market in Great Britain in the first half of the nineteenth century as the economic precondition for the private autonomy of property owners in their roles as *bourgeois* and *homme*. In turn, these private people have to play these roles in the political public sphere to guard the private but publicly relevant sphere of commodity exchange and social labor against governmental regulations.

Section 11 delineated the natural economic laws which, according to bourgeois political economy, facilitate a harmonious self-regulation of all factors of capitalist production and reproduction.

However, only after *Structural Transformation* was published will "Natural Law and Revolution" explain that they require, *contrary to the claims of Say's Law*, "legal regulation and despotic revolutionary enforcement, because the natural laws of society do not operate with the absolute inviolability of the laws of physics, but rather are laws which must be made to rule by political means in the face of the corruption of human nature" (NLR 119; NR 123).

Needless to say, such "despotic revolutionary enforcement" did not take place in Great Britain. Readers thus have to realize that, in *Structural Transformation*'s narrative, it took the outbreak of the French Revolution on July 14, 1789, before the French National Assembly could *politically* implement the natural laws of society through its "construction" of rational natural law, which was "inspired equally by Rousseau and the Physiocrats" (NLR 118). Once again, one has to draw on Habermas's endnote 65 on page 267 and remind oneself that at "this level of generality" his book disregards "national differences between Great Britain, France, and Germany, which are simultaneously differences in the level of capitalist development."

Significantly, this proposition of the Hegelian-Marxist philosophy of history was applied in the same year by Eric Hobsbawm's *The Age of Revolution, Europe 1789-1848* (1962). In his book, Hobsbawm presents the concept of "the dual revolution," the Industrial Revolution in England and the "rather more political one in France." He does so not without coining a rather memorable phrase. His imagination pictures this dual revolution as "the simultaneous eruptions" of "the twin craters of a rather larger regional volcano" (quoted in HPSC 73).

In comparison, the "Glorious Revolution" of 1688/1689 is so insignificant for *Structural Transformation* that the British Model Case is only allowed to start in 1694/1695. The reasoning behind this decision is implicitly revealed in "Natural Law and Revolution." Following Burke's distinction in his famous critique of the French Revolution, Habermas regards the "Glorious" one as a Revolution in name only. In stark contrast to its predecessor, the "Great Rebellion" with its regicide and civil war, it was "not credited to political acts of [revolutionary] actors themselves" (NLR 83, emphasis added; NR 90).

Instead, in "their objectively oriented concept of revolution" the *contemporaries* of the "Glorious Revolution" allegedly compared this political act of revolutionary treason by leading Whigs in their elaborately planned cooperation with King William of the Dutch Republic to the "magnitude and inevitability of an astronomically controlled destiny." The "revolutions of the planets" were self-regulating. In the interpretation of this Whig history, which Habermas adopts for his purposes of stylization, these forces of nature "did not know any revolutionaries" (NLR 83, translation modified; NR 90).

According to "Natural Law and Revolution," a key source for understanding *Structural Transformation*'s reasoning, only *rational natural law* "could ignite the concept of revolution which enters *as such* into the consciousness of active revolutionaries and which can be carried to its conclusion by these revolutionaries alone" (NLR 83, emphasis in the original, translation modified; NR 90). However, in Habermas's view this power to "ignite the concept of revolution" did not apply to the influence of Locke's rational natural law, developed in the Dutch Republic during his exile, on the events of 1688/9. Accordingly, *Structural Transformation* sees no need to analyze the impact of Locke's thought on the consciousness of those "Modern Whigs" who outsourced their revolution to William and Mary by advancing a loan over 6 million guilders for a Dutch invasion undertaken in the grand style. Needless to say, afterward they saw to it that they were reimbursed with interest by unprecedented taxes on the British landed interest and on the laboring poor (see HPSC 173–74).

Instead, the reader has to realize that Habermas, following Hegel, distinguishes between Locke's rational natural law underlying the American Revolution and the far more sophisticated one by Rousseau and Kant that supposedly ignited the French Revolution. Only in vain could Thomas Paine emphasize the commonalities between the two revolutions, namely, "the universal foundation of the state in natural law." He was strongly rebuffed by Robespierre, who "always reserved this fundamental claim of the bourgeois revolution for the French Revolution alone." The following quote not only contains the reasons why in *Structural Transformation* the French *revolutionary* development of the bourgeois public sphere towers over the British *evolutionary* one, but also why Habermas still feels justified to exclude the *American Revolution*:

> The Anglo-Saxon tradition of natural law, derived from Locke, on which the fathers of the American constitution based themselves, and to which Thomas Paine then appealed explicitly to justify a revolution, was *never taken seriously* as an essentially revolutionary doctrine—not only by a French *competitor* like Robespierre, but also by neither Burke nor Hegel. (NLR 86, emphasis added, translation modified; NR 93)

Specifically, the French "Declaration of Human and Civil Rights" is not just added to the Constitution in the form of amendments, like in the American case. As a preamble, it precedes the French Constitution, because it intends to posit for the first time the validity of fundamentally new rights. Its revolutionary meaning is "to lay the foundation for a new constitution," based on rational natural law, "'for one of the oldest nations on earth which for 1400 years has given itself its own form of government'" (NLR 87, 90; NR 94, 96). In America, however, the revolutionary meaning of the "Declaration of Independence" is restricted to justifying the political actions of a colonial people breaking "'the bonds of a distant government'" (NLR 87, 90; NR 94, 96). Hence, "Natural Law and Revolution" describes in detail how, in July and August 1789, the National Assembly had to analyze these differences before it could decide whether a Declaration of basic rights was necessary and, if so, which form it should take. Finally, the majority of the Assembly agreed that such a Declaration was needed, because *the public required effectively publicized enlightenment*" about the natural rights of humankind. For ignorance about these rights and their neglect "'are the universal causes of public misfortune and the corruption of the regime" (NLR 91, emphasis added; NR 97).

This justification for a "Declaration of Human and Civil Rights" dovetails with the core commitment of Physiocratic theory to "the public instruction of the people." For "the evidence of the natural order [of society] which *rose to power through publicity* is the sole basis on which a correct constitution can be founded" (NLR 89, emphasis added, translation modified; NR 96). Accordingly, the three Physiocrats "Le Mercier, Mirabeau, and Dupont each drew up a plan for organizing the education of the people." Moreover, in the National Convention the Marquis de Condorcet, one of the most distinguished Physiocrats, would continue this core commitment as "the Chair of the Commission for the Enlightenment of the People" (NLR 89, 292n20, translation modified; NR 96, 125n19).

In this context, readers have to remember that like in the American Constitution in this French usage, too, "people" refers solely to the bourgeoisie. In January 1789, as a member of the Constituent Assembly, the Abbe Emmanuel-Joseph Sieyes "published perhaps the *most famous pamphlet* of the Revolution, *What Is the Third Estate?*, in which he argued that so long as the *nobility and clergy* refused to share common rights and burdens with their fellow citizens they were *not part of the nation* and so should enjoy no rights of any sort," to quote this traditional assessment in William Doyle's history *Origins of the French Revolution* (1999) (quoted in HPSC 85n100, 85n101, emphasis added).

This pamphlet explicitly informs "Natural Law and Revolution," where it receives more than a full page of attention. Its influence on *Structural Transformation* reveals itself in the wording of the central claim in Section 11 that in Great Britain in 1832 "the third estate could be set up as the nation" (STPS 87). In short, The Tacit Model Case of French Revolutionary Development shapes the stylization of the British one after 1789. After all, in his election campaign for a seat in the Third Estate of Paris, Sieyes, the *vicaire general* of Chartres, had answered the rhetorical question of his pamphlet in praise of his constituents—they are the nation (cf. HPSC 55, 85n101).

Remarkably, in January 1789, only six months before the storming of the Bastille, Sieyes had to acknowledge just how undeveloped the bourgeois consciousness of the third estate still was. Not only was it in its knowledge of natural human rights "still far behind" those few authors who had "studied the [natural] order of society, but also behind the mass of common ideas which form *public opinion*" (quoted in NLR 88, emphasis added; NR 95). In light of this gap, the philosopher has the task "to use his influence on *the power of public opinion* to secure political validity for reason itself" (NLR 88, emphasis added, translation modified; NR 95). Following the doctrine of the Physiocrats, Sieyes concludes that this "duty to declare the truth is incumbent on the philosopher all the more when '*public opinion finally even dictates the laws to the lawgivers*'" (quoted in NLR 89, emphasis added; NR 95).

The reader will remember that this core Physiocratic notion about the *power of public opinion* would be echoed by the delegate Bergasse when the French National Assembly debated "the constitutional significance of *opinion publique*" (cf. HPSC 42). On the eve of the French Revolution, it was popularized by Jacques Necker, controller general and author of *A Treatise on the Administration of Finances in France* (1787). He consciously moved the information about the budget out of the *arcanum* of the Absolutist State to submit it to the *opinion publique* of "the individuals of a higher class," which he carefully distinguished from the *opinion du people*, that is, those without property and education. *Structural Transformation*'s Section 9 quotes Necker's highly consequential claim that further illuminates the role French revolutionary development plays in Habermas's book:

> For the majority of foreigners it is difficult to obtain a correct idea of the *authority that public opinion exercises in France*. Only with difficulty do they understand that there is *an invisible power* that, without treasury, without bodyguard, without army, *lays down laws*—laws obeyed even in the palace of the King: and yet there exists nothing that would be more true. (quoted in STPS 263n28, emphasis added)

Habermas quotes Necker's widespread assertion from Wilhelm Bauer's German-language classic about "Public Opinion and Its Historic Origins" (1914). Speier draws on *Kritik der* öffentlichen Meinung (1922) by Ferdinand Tönnies for the following quote from Count Vergennes in a confidential report to Louis XVI, which further illustrates the impact Necker's claim had:

> If M. Necker's public opinion were to gain ascendancy, Your Majesty would have to be prepared to see those command who otherwise obey and to see those

obey who otherwise command. (quoted in Speier, "The Historical Development of Public Opinion" [1950], 327)

Above all, Necker's claim about this *invisible power of public opinion* influenced the famous chapter 1 in book 3 of Tocqueville's *The Old Regime and the Revolution* (1856/1998) titled "How Around the Middle of the Eighteenth Century Intellectuals Became the Country's Leading Politicians, and the Effects Which Resulted from This." Tocqueville's chronology is mirrored by *Structural Transformation*'s central thesis, following Robespierre, that the French Revolution originated in 1750 with Diderot's *Prospectus* for the Encyclopedia and Rousseau's *Discourse on the Arts and Sciences*, which introduced *his* concept of *opinion publique* into the debates of the rising bourgeois public sphere. Both Diderot and D'Alembert consciously followed in the tradition of Bayle's Republic of Letters by addressing their introductions to an enlightened public as their audience (STPS 68–69, 253n26).

Section 9 even echoes Tocqueville's wording "around the middle of the [eighteenth] century" in his chapter heading when introducing the Abbe Coyer's critique of *La Noblesse Commercante*, which triggered "a storm of pamphlets" about this "parasitic, economically and politically functionless, yet socially eminent nobility" (STPS 68, 69). The parallel is significant. While, "from the bourgeois standpoint of productive labor," this nobility only represented "a parasitical stratum" of society, it nevertheless served as "the womb," in which future bourgeois intellectuals like the "plebeian d'Alembert" and "sons of watchmakers," including Rousseau, "had risen socially" (STPS 68, 33, 69). Moreover, these "forerunners" of the Revolution were not only socially but also intellectually dependent on access to the *salons* of this controversial nobility. For its members were "more receptive to the enlightened mode of thought of bourgeois intellectuals than the bourgeoisie itself" (STPS 68). From Tocqueville's perspective, the "upper classes of the old regime thus aided in their own destruction" with "strange blindness" (quoted in HPSC 53, cf. HPSC 84n96).

Tocqueville gives two key reasons why, in his view, these "*men of letters, who possessed neither rank, nor honor, nor wealth, nor responsibility, nor power*" and who were excluded from government, not only became "the *chief statesmen of the time*" but also *the only ones who had authority*. First, the increasing lack of justification for the "abusive or ridiculous privileges" as well as for the unequal taxation decreed and enforced by the old regime made "the *philosophes* of the eighteenth century" receptive "towards the *idea of the natural equality of ranks*" and the condemnation of "all privileges whatsoever … *by reason*." In turn, every "public passion" was allegedly "inflamed by writers' ideas" and *wrapped up in philosophy*." He thus claims that "*political life was violently driven back into literature*" (quoted in HPSC 53, emphasis added, see HPSC 84n94, 84n95).

Second, the French nobility had lost its political power and thus its "moral authority": "An aristocracy in its vigor not only runs affairs, it still directs opinion, sets the tone for writers, and lends authority to ideas." Instead, the nobility joined the writers in philosophizing "almost without restraint on the *origin of societies*, on the *essential nature of government*, and on the primordial *rights of the human species*." These "general theories" were treated as "very clever intellectual games"—not as "*doctrines*," which, "*once accepted*, inevitably end up turning themselves into *political* passions and *actions*." At that climax of his increasingly dramatic narrative, Tocqueville thus conspicuously joins Burke who was the first to see "the unfortunate Louis XVI . . . perishing in the democratic flood" (quoted in HPSC 53, emphasis added, cf. HPSC 84n96).

Tocqueville's references to nobility and bourgeois intellectuals philosophizing about the *origin of societies* and the *essential nature of government* directly invokes Physiocratic theory about natural laws of society and, specifically, Le Mercier de la Riviere's book on "The Natural and Essential Order of Political Societies." As mentioned above, *Structural Transformation* follows Schmitt's analysis in *Die Diktatur* ["The Dictatorship"] who credits Le Mercier's book with the term and the strict concept of the Legal Despotism of the enlightened monarch which is derived from "the most general principles of reason" (Schmitt 1921: 109). In turn, Habermas locates in this context "the rigorous concept of *opinion publique*" (STPS 95), in which an enlightened public led by the Physiocrats recognizes that the "true interest of the sovereign is identical with the true interest of the subjects" once the "true laws of social order" have been discovered (Schmitt 1921: 109; see STPS 269n22).

Tocqueville and Habermas thus select the same way stations in their respective narratives about the inevitable development toward the French Revolution. The "men of letters" came into their own while publishing the articles of the Encyclopedia. At the same time, but on a parallel track, Rousseau started his quest for a democratic political culture, based on *the natural equality of ranks*. In 1762, it would permeate his social contract theory. Five years later, the Physiocrats would launch their elaborate system that posits a harmonious "rule of nature" based on natural laws of society. Since these economic laws are supposed to self-regulate *like* the law of gravity but are *not identical* with the physical forces of nature, they have to be legally implemented through political acts. The *opinion publique* of an enlightened public thus has to communicate to the monarch as well as to the nation that these "true laws of the social order" are in their "true interest."

From the perspective of both authors, these two narratives become one in the Revolution. Regarding the Physiocratic theory that informs Sieyes, both make extensive use of his pamphlet and regard it as typical. Regarding Rousseau, Habermas shares Tocqueville's following claim: "In the beginning they quoted and commented Montesquieu; in the end they talked of no one but Rousseau" (quoted in HPSC 55). In the words of "Natural Law and Revolution": "With respect to what is to be understood by a democratic sovereign, the *Contrat Social* at that time enjoyed canonical authority" (NLR 102; NR 107).

Critique and Crisis equally highlights "the middle of the [eighteenth] century" as the beginning of a four decades long countdown toward the French Revolution. Specifically, the publication of the first seven volumes of the Encyclopedia between 1751 and 1757 marks the watershed in Koselleck's presentation of "The Process of Criticism," which also draws on Tocquevlle and anticipates Habermas. For Koselleck (and Habermas) "victory over the religion of Revelation appears to have been achieved in the middle of the century." A claim that *Kritik und Krise* (1959/1973), but not its English translation, backs up by quoting Frederick the Great's statement from 1768 about religion having visibly "reached its turning point and moving toward its decomposition" (KK 203n185, translation M.H.). *Criticism* can thus assume "the functions, which Locke had at one time assigned to *moral censorship*, it becomes the *spokesperson of public opinion*" (CC 115, emphasis added, translation modified; KK 96).

In other words, around the middle of the eighteenth century, *Structural Transformation*'s narrative switches from its overt British to its tacit French model case. The moral weeklies, with Addison as the self-declared "censor of manners and morals" (STPS 43), are superseded by a more advanced form of criticism. *Critique and Crisis* quotes from "Marmontel's long essay about criticism" in the Encyclopedia to emphasize that "by definition" it has gone "far beyond arts and letters and already encompasses State and society" (CC 115n44, translation modified; KK 203n186). In short, Koselleck provides the source for Habermas's already quoted claim that with the launching of the Encyclopedia "the moral intent of the philosophes develop[s] into a political one, at least indirectly" (STPS 68).

Structural Transformation's mission to rebut Koselleck's charge about the moralization of politics in the process of Enlightenment with the counterclaim that, instead, a rationalization of politics in the name of morals was intended, tethers the book to this stylization of the process of criticism in *Critique and Crisis*. Since Bayle excludes the flourishing political criticism in early eighteenth-century England from the impartial critique practiced in the Republic of Letters, only bourgeois moralists like Addison as the "impartial spectator," solely dedicated to "Truth and Virtue," can be truly admitted to Habermas's narrative without any tacit reservations. His elaborate stylization of the rise of a bourgeois public sphere, defined by its "morally pretentious rationality," cannot alert the reader to the revealing fact that Defoe's *Review*, his thrice-weekly *political* journal, had already been published for five years *before* the first *moral* weekly by Addison and Steele would appear in 1709.

Accordingly, readers face the challenge of only realizing in retrospect in Section 12 that Defoe's achievements as "the first professional journalist" who "defends the cause of the Whigs not only in the pamphlets. . . but also in the new journals" were strictly limited. Compared to the French National Assembly during the Revolution, he helped to create an only *unenlightened* political public sphere. Although he is "the first to really turn the 'party spirit' into a 'public spirit,'" he nevertheless still lacks the knowledge of the Encyclopedia's criticism, of Rousseau's social contract theory, of the "natural order" discovered by the Physiocrats, and, above all, of Kant's rational natural law (STPS 59, translation modified; SÖ 78).

Structural Transformation's selective perception of its British model case is guided by such seeming deficits in the public use of reason not only with regard to Defoe but on a bipartisan basis. The chronology of the process of criticism it adopts from *Critique and Crisis* also affects Swift's *Examiner*, the Tory journal. His famous essay on "The Conduct of the Allies" dominated coffee house discussions in 1711, in spite of the popularity of the moral weeklies at the time. Nevertheless, political essays like his have to be neglected, because they do not sufficiently advance the future rationalization of politics in the name of morality within a rising bourgeois public sphere (see HPSC 182–83).

6.2. SEPARATION OR DISSOLUTION OF POWERS: CONDORCET'S ABSOLUTE VERSUS KANT'S RELATIVE RATIONALISM IN THE CONSTITUTIONAL REVOLUTION

In *Structural Transformation*'s stylization, it takes until 1751 before the publication of the first volume of the Encyclopedia starts planting the seeds for the enlightened French National Assembly of 1789. As "Natural Law and Revolution" emphasizes, at that terminal stage in the process of criticism the "philosophers had become law-givers." Already "the first report of the committee constituted to draft the Declaration of Rights (presented by Meunier)" was regarded by contemporary observers as "more appropriate for a philosophical society than for a National Assembly." In this discussion of the Rights of Humankind the transition from a literary public sphere to an enlightened political public sphere is finalized. In the bourgeois self-interpretation of that time, "the assembly was transformed into 'en école de Sorbonne'" (NLR 90, NR 96). Readers who look for a political event that comes closest to the realization of the book's Kantian ideal of the rationalization of politics in the name of morality can find it in these deliberations leading up to the Declaration of Human and Civil Rights by the French National Assembly.

However, this empirical reality of parliamentary and legislative history does not offer similar evidence for Habermas's claim that *the fiction of a dissolution of political domination in discursive will-formation* had been effectively institutionalized in the bourgeois constitutional state at that time (see 1.1 above). Article 16 in the Declaration of Human and Civil Rights, which is repeated in the French Constitution of 1791, only "demands the separation of powers," but not their dissolution. *Structural Transformation* leaves out the crucial information that the Constitution of 1791 thus *only* "provides a constitutional guarantee for a politically functioning public sphere" (STPS 99), but not one for the dissolution of political domination, not even only in principle and for a distant future (VL 127, 185).

Readers who want to understand how Habermas might have tried to rationally reconstruct the fiction of a dissolution of political domination in discursive will-formation as inscribed in the Constitution of 1791, can compare the respective references in *The Crisis of Parliamentary Democracy* and in *Constitutional Theory*. As documented in its footnotes, Habermas drew on both books already in 1958 when writing *On the Concept of Political Participation*. He again refers to both Schmitt texts in *Structural Transformation*.

Obviously, he could not use the reaffirmed Article 16 itself in the process of his theory reconstruction. For already *The Crisis of Parliamentary Democracy* emphasized in 1923 that the liberal identification of the bourgeois constitution with the division of power "held an absolutely dominant position in West European thought since the middle of the eighteenth century." Above all, Article 16 contained "the most famous proclamation" of that liberal thought: "Any society in which the separation of powers and rights is not guaranteed has no constitution" (quoted in CPD 41).

Moreover, as *Constitutional Theory* analyzes, the Constitution of 1791 moved beyond Montesquieu's term *division* of powers and, for the first time, emphasized in a more forceful expression their *separation* (CT 222). This liberal Constitution also conformed strictly to "the relative rationalism" of Montesquieu's "balance theory." While identifying "law with truth," the legislative deliberations in parliament can, in the discourse of "argument and counterargument," only arrive at a "relative truth" (CPD 46).

For *Structural Transformation* the idea that *truth and not authority makes law* is thus "lost in the attempt to conceive of the function of public opinion . . . in the constitutional law construction of the *pouvoirs*" (STPS 82), namely, in the separation of powers and its inherent relative rationalism. Instead, in Habermas's ideal-type from 1962 the issue of "pouvoir as such" is "subjected to debate in a politically functioning public sphere" (STPS 82–83; SÖ 105). But not in the Constitution of 1791. Its "constitutional guarantee for a politically functioning public sphere" (STPS 99) does not contain language that could be interpreted as subjecting "pouvoir as such" to public debate. Once again, the reader is faced with a fundamental tension in the text, this time between Section 11 and Section 12. And, one more time, a plausible explanation can be located and teased out in a close reading of "Natural Law and Revolution."

This time readers will notice that when discussing the natural rights constructions of Rousseau and the Physiocrats, Habermas matter-of-factly replaces the Constitution of 1791 with the Jacobin Constitution from 1793, which no longer mentions a separation of powers (CT 171). In a detailed analysis of the "Security" guarantees in the Jacobin Constitution's Article 8, which preserves for all citizens their personal safety, rights, and property, Habermas emphasizes that this protection is "accorded *by the society* to every one of its members" (NLR 103, emphasis in the original). Specifically, he refers to Rousseau's concept of a *corps social* and the Physiocratic *societe politique*.

In both cases, their natural law constructions signify "a total constitution organized by the institutionalization of natural rights, which politically embrace state and society" (NLR 103). In other words, with its Jacobin Constitution of 1793 the French National Convention attempted to consciously create a political society, whose rational natural law was informed by principles of a "natural order." In short, such an abolition of the separation of powers combined with grounding the legislative process in the reason of an enlightened public opinion certainly subjected pouvoir as such to political debate.

Arguably, Section 12 did not include any reference to the Jacobin Constitution, because upon publication it immediately clashed with the "constitutional reality" (STPS 71) which was now shaped "in the shadow of the guillotine" (NLR 107). In comparison, the "constitution of 1793" was referenced in Section 9 regarding its protection of the "right to communicate one's ideas and opinions, whether through the press or in any other manner" (STPS 70–71). However, *Structural Transformation* omitted the potentially lethal constitutional reality at the time it was published. Instead, the less lethal one from August 1792, with its confiscation of the conservative presses, was substituted to illustrate the really existing press censorship. This scrambling of the chronology further obscures for the reader the Jacobin phase of the French Revolution.

Against this background, readers will find it even more surprising that Habermas did not include a single reference to the draft for the "Gironde constitution," presented to the National Convention in February 1793. In short, *before* the onset of the Jacobin terror. After all, this draft comes closest *to effectively institutionalizing in the bourgeois constitutional state the fiction of a dissolution of political domination in discursive will-formation.*

Condorcet's draft of the Gironde constitution, presented on behalf of the Convention's Constitutional Committee, which included the Abbe Sieyes, calls for a single national assembly with the power to make laws. Moreover, while Montesquieu only defines the judiciary as "the mouth that pronounces the words of the law," Condorcet also restricts the executive to "the application of the law." Their agents no longer command, but may only reason (CPD 44). Above all, the draft does not contain a single word about a division or separation of powers. Article 29 of its rights declaration is "content to state the necessity of 'a limitation of public functions by law' and of guaranteeing the responsibility of all public officials" (CT 171; VL 127; see HPSC 42).

Regarding the concept of law in the bourgeois constitutional state, Schmitt's *The Crisis of Parliamentary Democracy* already called Condorcet "the typical representative of enlightened radicalism, for whom everything concrete is only a case for the application of a general law." As Schmitt emphasizes when quoting from the Gironde constitution, its design intended to firmly establish that the "'characteristic that distinguishes the laws is to be found in their generality and unlimited duration'" (CPD 44). Instead of relying on the separation of powers for the "inherent negotiation and moderation of state powers," Condorcet's "absolute rationalism" wants to bind every activity, "the whole life of the state . . . in law and the application of law" (CPD 46, 44).

In other words, Condorcet dismisses Montesquieu's system of separating and balancing powers as a constitutional theory that was not "born in an enlightened age." Already in 1788, he argued that a "declaration of the rights of man and the citizen drawn up by enlightened men is the true barrier against every power." Since truth and justice "are the same in all countries and for all men," a "perfectly free" public use of reason will find out "what justice consists in"—thus allowing for its universal and uniform implementation in political society (quoted in HPSC 41). For his absolute trust in reason had convinced Condorcet that such a consensus could be reached.

Significantly, *Constitutional Theory* no longer refers to Condorcet when discussing the absolute rationalism that, in Schmitt's view, dominated the constitutional debate in the National Assembly during the French Revolution. Neither does the book's section 1, titled "The Absolute Concept of the Constitution" identify the Gironde constitution when essentially describing it as a "closed system of laws that encompasses the state in its totality and will be forever correct." Nor does Schmitt explicitly refer to Condorcet when he clearly includes him among those lawmakers who "even had reservations about merely contemplating changes and revisions" regarding such a complete constitutional plan "for the entire political and social life" (CT 65; VL 10).

Accordingly, *Structural Transformation* was presented with the option to veil both the Gironde constitution and its author Condorcet by only referring to Schmitt's discussion of "The Absolute Concept of the Constitution." However, the book also does not identify *Constitutional Theory* as its source when it discusses the "bourgeois idea of the law-based state, namely, the binding of all state activity in a system of norms" (STPS 82). Section 11 does not contain an endnote referring to the respective section 13 in Schmitt's book, titled "The Legal Concept of the Law-Based State (*Rechtsstaat*)" (CT 181; VL 138). Readers thus have to search on their own before they find the respective quote: "It continues to be the ideal of the law-based state to encompass all possible state activities in a system of norms, thus binding the state" (CT 190: VL 150).

It is even more challenging for readers to find the origin of *Structural Transformation*'s claim that "binding the state" through such "a system of norms" (CT 190: VL 150) "already aims at abolishing the state as an instrument of domination altogether" (STPS 82; SÖ 104). Not only does Section 11 fail to give its source in an endnote. It also engages in a rather idiosyncratic interpretation of Schmitt's text when giving as the evidence for its claim that allegedly "[a]cts of sovereignty are considered apocryphal per se" (STPS 82).

In this case, readers have to consult section 11 in *Constitutional Theory*, which is titled "Concepts to Be Derived from the Concept of the Constitution" (CT 147; VL 99). In this context, Schmitt identifies the difficulty that "the bourgeois constitutional state (*Rechtsstaat*) assumes that it is able to comprehend and to limit the entire exercise of all state power, without exception, in written laws. Political action of any given subject . . ., even sovereignty itself thus becomes impossible" (CT 154; VL 107). As a result, "a diverse range of fictions has to be set up," for example, that "constitutional norms are sovereign" (CT 154–155; VL 107–108).

Precisely at this point *Structural Transformation*, in search of normativity to substantiate its *fiction of a dissolution of political domination in discursive will-formation* detects an opening in Schmitt's following analysis: "The fiction of the absolute normative quality then has no result other than that such a fundamental question like the one regarding sovereignty is left unclear." Schmitt thus concludes that for "the inevitable acts of sovereignty, a method for *apocryphal acts of sovereignty* develops" (CT 155, emphasis in the original; VL 108). However, Habermas does not share Schmitt's assumption that there are "inevitable acts of sovereignty." Reversing Hobbes, he wants to substitute the truth of the law for the authority of the sovereign. In short, he is not interested to learn that a *method* for these "*apocryphal acts of sovereignty* develops." Instead, in *his* interpretation acts of sovereignty "are considered apocryphal per se" (STPS 82)

Readers are not only confronted with a "white whale" of a challenge by having to rely on such forensic evidence to understand the reasoning behind *Structural Transformation*. They also have to ascertain on their own whether this key example discussed above constitutes exhibit A for Habermas's acknowledgment in *Further Reflections* that his book idealized "the bourgeois public sphere in a manner going way beyond any methodologically legitimate idealization of the sort involved in ideal-typical conceptualization" (FRPS 442). While he now also concedes that "the model of the contradictory institutionalization of the public sphere" in Section 11 "is conceived too rigidly," he nevertheless does not even include these methodological errors in his following conclusion:

> Still, *a* mistake in the assessment of the significance of *certain aspects* does not falsify the larger outline of the process of transformation that I presented. (FRPS 430, emphasis added)

In any event, *Constitutional Theory* assists its reader by connecting its analysis in section 11 of the fiction that "constitutional norms are sovereign" (CT 154–155; VL 107–108) to page 8 in its section 1 about "The Absolute Concept of the Constitution." There one can find the above discussed conceptions by Royer-Collard about a "sovereignty of the constitution" and by Guizot regarding a "sovereignty of reason" (CT 63; VL 8). In turn, section 16 of Schmitt's work, titled "Bourgeois Constitutional State (*Rechtsstaat*) and Political Form" (CT 235; VL 200) precisely distinguishes between these two conceptions by classifying the former as a *principle* of the law-based state and the latter as an *abstract* norm (CT 235; VL 201).

Moreover, when comparing the "state theories of bourgeois liberalism" from Kant to Benjamin Constant, Guizot, Tocqueville, J. S. Mill, and so on, Schmitt expands on Guizot's abstract constitutional norm of the "sovereignty of reason" to include "justice." He does so by again connecting to "The Absolute Concept of the Constitution," where the reader can find the normative context for this Kantian construct of a "sovereignty of justice and reason" (CT 235–236, 62–63; VL 201, VL 7). In other words, for the constitutional law underpinning of *Structural Transformation*'s central category of a "morally pretentious rationality" as the hallmark of the bourgeois public sphere analyzed above under 5.2.

After teasing out these compatibilities between Condorcet's absolute rationalism and his absolute concept of the constitution as a "united, closed system of highest and ultimate norms" (CT 62; VL 7) on one hand, and *Structural Transformation*'s ultimate claim that the "bourgeois idea of the law-based state . . . already aims at abolishing the state as an instrument of domination altogether," because "acts of sovereignty are considered apocryphal per se" (STPS 82, SÖ 104) on the other, the reader arrives at a crucial insight. *Habermas's theory reconstruction of Kant's ideal of the bourgeois public sphere has to go beyond Kant's rational natural law construction of the bourgeois constitutional state and rely on Condorcet's absolute concept of the constitution.*

Contrary to Habermas's theory reconstruction, Kant did *not* consider acts of sovereignty apocryphal per se. For him, these "inevitable acts of sovereignty" did *not* constitute inauthentic and erroneous violations of his republican ideal. As *Perpetual Peace: A Philosophical Sketch* (1795/1970) states: "*Republicanism* is that political principle whereby the executive power (the government) is separated from the legislative power." This separation of powers is detailed in *Constitutional Theory*'s section 12 on "The Principles of the Bourgeois Constitutional State (*Rechtsstaat*): "For Kant, every state contains three intrinsic powers, the 'generally unified will in the form of a person divided in three parts as legislator, governor, and judge' (*Rechtslehre*, part II, Das *Staatsrecht*, section 45, Vorländer, p. 136)" (CT 170; VL 127).

Structural Transformation thus faces the key challenge that Kant, who "provided the constitutional theory for the French Revolution," as well as Rousseau, its "forerunner," regarded "the ideal form of the state created by the social contract as a republic," defined by its signature *separation* of powers. This essential quote is taken from the chapter "Social Progress or Political Freedom?" in *Constitutional Revolution: The Link between Constitutionalism and Progress* (1990 /1995) by the constitutional law theorist Ulrich K. Preuss. Not only did the French Constitution of 1791 confirm this separation, but "after the abolition of the monarchy on September 21, 1792, the nation was [also] declared a republic" (quoted in Preuss 1990/1995: 49).

In stark contrast, for Rousseau's social contract theory a democracy "is characterized by a union of the legislative and executive powers." In his own words, it represents "'a government without government, so to speak.'" Kant's definition in *Perpetual Peace* is even more specific:

Of the three forms of sovereignty, *democracy*, in the truest sense of the word, is necessarily a *despotism*, because it establishes an executive power through which all the citizens may make decisions about (and indeed against) the single individual without his consent, so that decisions are made by all the people and yet not by all the people; and this means that the general will is in contradiction with itself, and thus also with freedom. (Kant 1795/1970: 101)

Only Condorcet's absolute concept of the constitution, based on his absolute rationalism, trusted that the general will could always be enlightened. A "perfectly free" public use of reason would facilitate the universal and uniform implementation of a sovereignty of truth and justice in political society. Accordingly, a declaration of human and civil rights drawn up by enlightened citizens would thus form "the true barrier against every power" (quoted in HPSC 41).

Even without a reference to Condorcet's Gironde constitution of 1793, "Natural Law and Revolution" clearly reveals *Structural Transformation*'s tacit dependency on the revolutionary French development. Arguably, the mathematician and philosopher Condorcet personifies the process of criticism from the Encyclopedia to the Physiocrats, which informs the transition from a literary to the political public sphere in Habermas's narrative based on the blueprint provided by *Critique and Crisis*. Condorcet's first mentor was d'Alembert who orchestrated his rise in the Paris Academy of Sciences, culminating in his appointment as permanent secretary in 1776. His second mentor was the statesman and social reformer Turgot who in 1757 had joined Quesnay in contributing articles on the political economy of the Physiocrats to the Encyclopedia. From 1774 to 1776, when Turgot, as Controller–General, was transforming "the acts of sovereign authority into works of reason" (Le Harpe quoted in STPS 96), Condorcet was his advisor.

The missing acknowledgment of Condorcet is another one of the enigmas in *Structural Transformation* that the reader has to contemplate. One plausible explanation can be found in the section on "The presuppositions of a materialist philosophy of history" in Habermas's essay "Between Philosophy and Science: Marxism as Critique" (1960/1963). It contains a critique of Turgot and Condorcet's "conception that it would only require a Newton of history in order to comprehend the law of history's progress as a natural law" (TAP 246; TUP 273). This view is regarded as inferior to Kant's philosophy of history:

> Subjected to the critical distinctions of Kantian philosophy, however, every attempt to subsume the laws of history under the universal laws of nature soon revealed the equivocal character of its presuppositions. That reason which made these presuppositions, as nature, the basis of the development of the human race, now was painstakingly distinguished from *the* reason, which an enlightened and autonomous humankind still has to historically realize on its own in the future. (TAP 246, emphasis in the original; TUP 273)

Nonetheless, beyond Condorcet's draft for the Gironde constitution, his contribution to the "education and information" *Structural Transformation* thinks the bourgeois public needed "to arrive at a reasoned opinion" about "the principles of modern natural law" should have been sufficient to *explicitly* include him in the book. For Condorcet himself reflected in exemplary fashion on the role of the public philosophers in facilitating the process of Enlightenment. As he wrote in a famous passage of his *Sketch for a Historical Picture of the Progress of the Human Mind,* which was posthumously published in 1795:

> Soon there was formed in Europe a class of men who were concerned less with the discovery or development of the truth than with its propagation, . . . using . . . all the weapons with which learning, philosophy, wit, and literary talent can furnish reason . . . from the vast erudite encyclopedia to the novel or the broadsheet of the day . . . never ceasing to demand the independence of reason and the freedom of the press as the right and the salvation of humankind . . . and finally, taking for their battle cry—*reason, tolerance, humanity.* (quoted in Baker, ed. *Condorcet: Selected Writings* ix, emphasis in the original)

Of course, there might have been one final reason for veiling Condorcet's influence on *Structural Transformation*'s own absolute rationalism. For the book was conceived as a veiled response to *Critique and Crisis*. This adversarial position also motivated its writing. Actually, while directed against Koselleck its real target was his teacher Schmitt. For "Carl Schmitt seeks," as Habermas wrote at that time, "to prove that the political substance will revenge any attempt to dissolve politics into rational administration, due to the entwinement of the revolutionary initiative and the totalitarian rule which was supposed to be abolished" (TAP 199; TUP 232).

Needless to say, the Jacobin Terror qualified as such a "totalitarian rule." Accordingly, Koselleck could dramatize Condorcet's tragic death as the ultimate proof of a causality between *Critique and Crisis*. Condorcet's role as a victim of the Terror was exploited in a conservative morality tale:

> The process set in motion by the critics finally engulfed them, too, and swept them into the abyss. It was only through suicide that Condorcet eluded this verdict, immediately after completing his sketch about eternal progress. (CC 120)

6.3. REVOLUTIONARY "MORAL POLITICS" AS THE FUSION OF KANT'S COGNITIVE/MORAL UNIVERSALISM AND SCHILLER'S EXPRESSIVE SUBJECTIVISM

No pecuniary rewards could inspire the opponents of the revolutionaries with that zeal and greatness of soul which the concept of right alone could produce in them. [The French Revolution] is . . . too intimately interwoven with the interests of humanity . . . not to be reminded of it when favorable circumstances present themselves, and to rise up.

Immanuel Kant (1798)

In German Idealism's interpretation of the French Revolution, the political emancipation of the bourgeoisie functions as the universal emancipation of humankind. The *citoyen* as the reasoning subject of the bourgeois constitutional state thus has to incorporate the roles of the *bourgeois* as the autonomous, self-interested owner of capitalistically functioning property and of the *homme* who is altruistically dedicated to the ideals of bourgeois humanism. In his commemorative essay honoring Herbert Marcuse in 1980, Habermas identified these ideals as the ones of "cognitive and moral universalism on the one hand" and of "expressive subjectivism on the other" (HAM 72).

In *Structural Transformation*, the former ideal is represented primarily by Kant and the latter primarily by Schiller. In 1990, Habermas specified in *Further Reflections* that this Enlightenment quest for universal truth and justice rests on the ideals of "rational formation of opinion and will" as well as of "political self-determination" (FRPS 442). Together they define the Kantian ideal of the political public sphere. On the other hand, the ideal of a cultivation of "subjectivity," "self-actualization," and "personal self-determination" finds its expression in the "saturated and free interiority" of the bourgeois family's intimate sphere (FRPS 442; STPS 28).

In 1985, in his *"Excursus on Schiller's 'Letters on the Aesthetic Education of Man'"* in *The Philosophical Discourse of Modernity*, Habermas explains that "Schiller conceived of art as the genuine embodiment of a communicative reason" and stressed the "communicative . . . force of art, which is to say, its *"public character"* (emphasis in the original) (PDM 48, 46). In other words, Schiller understood "art itself" as "the medium for the education [*Bildung*] of the human race to true political freedom" (PDM 45). The underlying "structure of communication" in this "aesthetic utopia" posits a personal sphere where the bourgeois individuals commune with themselves before they step out into the public sphere to communicate "with the whole race." (PDM 49)

Readers will now realize where *Structural Transformation*'s innovative concepts of an audience-oriented intimate sphere and a literary public sphere that prepares for participation in the political public sphere originated. Sections 4 to 7 do not introduce this context. Instead, they further obscure it by leaving out Koselleck's detailed analysis of Schiller's role in "The Process of Criticism" when drawing on *Critique and Crisis* for this blueprint. The reader can now also much better understand why, in an endnote to Section 9, Habermas adds that Schiller's drama *The Robbers* "belonged in its own way to the beginnings of political publicity" (STPS 264n41).

Habermas's reflection in 1985 that "Herbert Marcuse later specified the relationship between art and revolution in a manner similar to Schiller" (PDM 49), dovetails with his view of Marcuse's lecture at Frankfurt University in 1956, discussed above in chapter 1. Habermas's admiration of Marcuse's "courage to release utopian energies again, with the uninhibitedness of the eighteenth century" (quoted in HPSC 37) ties in with his overt valorization of Kant's moral-practical thought in a presentation to the German Philosophical Society in October 1960. Discussing the relationship between politics and morality at the heart of Kant's philosophy, Habermas declared that Kant's idea of the rational-critical discourse in the public sphere as "the principle of the rationalization of political domination" reflected "the great achievement of his century."

Readers have to be aware of Habermas's pronounced valorization of the Kantian ideals when studying, in the fifth step of this guide, *Structural Transformation*'s Section 13. For this degree of idealization plays a key role in his reconstruction of the "built-in moral categories" of bourgeois constitutions, specifically with regard to the postulated dissolution of political domination. In this regard his book from 1962 anticipates a central aspect of *Between Facts and Norms*, published three decades later. Given the importance of safeguarding constitutional rights in today's global crisis of liberal democracy, it is worth quoting Habermas's explanation from 2013, partially introduced above, in its entirety:

> The discourse theory of law and of the democratic rule-of-law state does not at all want to compete with political science in describing the political process, nor does it want to be a normative theory committed to designing, in the manner of Aristotle's *Politics*, the ideal framework of a 'well-ordered society'. Rather, it wants to rationally reconstruct (in Hegelian terms: reduce to the concept) the normative substance *already present* in the constitutions of existing democracies. (emphasis in original, quoted in Floridia 2017: 299–300)

Similarly, in 1962 *Structural Transformation*'s Section 11 claims as normative substance this "moral-practical thought" inherent in the "new constitutions, written and unwritten" of the bourgeois state, because they "refer to citizens and *human beings as such*, and indeed necessarily so, as long as the public sphere constitutes their organizational principle" (STPS 84–85, emphasis added). Applying Rockmore's analysis mentioned above, one can demonstrate that Habermas's reconstruction of Kant's ideal of the "public use of reason" follows this Hegelian approach. In this process, he analyzes the proposed rationalization of politics through the "moral-practical thought" inherent in the rational natural law that constitutes the bourgeois public sphere. His intention is to reconstruct Kant's "earlier, imperfect" theory of the public sphere "to better attain [its] goals."

The "imperfection" in Kant's ideal consists, in Habermas's interpretation from 1960, in its unresolved ambivalence regarding the world-historical process of establishing universal human rights through "the perfectly just" republican order of the bourgeois constitutional state. Will this order emerge out of "natural necessity," as the "official" version of Kant's philosophy of history and his political philosophy claim? Or does the implementation of political virtue *and* public welfare, that is, the entwinement of civic duty *with* the happiness of the citizens (VPM 98, 100) through the bourgeois constitution require "*both* natural necessity *and* moral politics" (STPS 115, emphasis in the original)—as Kant's "unofficial" version allegedly hints at?

Only in fall 1960, when presenting to the German Philosophical Society, did Habermas acknowledge to "certainly" go "beyond Kant" (VPM 99) in this theory reconstruction. In 2019, Yos would even call it a "thoroughly surprising Kant-reconstruction" (Yos 2019: 468). Nevertheless, this idealization of revolutionary practice "as a theoretically informed realization of human rights" (BFN 469) contains the "master key" to unlocking *Structural Transformation*'s intention when dialectically upending the narratives by Koselleck and Schmitt.

Needless to say, it is quite challenging for the reader to discover it when studying the rather complex argument in Section 13. For only in his 1960 conference presentation, titled "Über das Verhältnis von Politik und Moral" ["On the Relationship between Politics and Morality"] and published in 1962, did Habermas analyze this perceived ambivalence in Kant's political philosophy and his philosophy of history in more detail and early on in his deliberations. In comparison, Section 13 relegates a much shorter discussion of the alleged "*two* versions" of Kant's respective thought, the "official" one and the "unofficial" one (STPS 115, emphasis in the original), to pages thirteen and fourteen of its sixteen pages (STPS 115 to 116). Moreover, Section 13 no longer *explicitly* states "the interest of moral politics" in Kant's "unofficial" version (VPM 101). Namely, to conceptualize a philosophy of history that posits the rational-critical instruction of "moral-political action" (VPM 101) in order to impact the course of history itself.

Specifically, *Structural Transformation* avoids using the explicit term "moral-political action." The book also leaves out Habermas's observation in 1960 that "Kant, too, does not believe that he can expect any other beginning of a juridical condition than the one achieved by force" (VPM 98). Instead, Section 13 tasks the philosophy of history only with the guidance of the public in the process of establishing legality out of morality. Since "in this philosophy . . . the laws of reason are congruent with the requirements of welfare," it "must itself become public opinion" (STPS 115; SÖ 142).

In other words, *Structural Transformation* stops short of invoking the "moral-political action" of revolutionary practice that follows from such a public opinion. The book only posits that the "unofficial" version of Kant's thought allegedly "proceeds from the notion that politics first has to push for the actualization of a juridical condition" (STPS 115; SÖ 141). While it does not specify what kind of pressure needs to be applied in this process, it definitely deletes *Kant's reference to the use of force* quoted in the 1960 presentation. However, Section 13 otherwise adopts the identical wording and the same Kant quote used in 1960 to highlight this perceived causal relationship. Namely, the postulated impact of the philosophy of history on the course of history itself:

> Accordingly, a remarkable self-implication of the philosophy of history occurs. It takes into account the effect of a theory of history on the actual development of that history: "A philosophical attempt to work out a universal history according to a natural plan directed to achieving the perfect civic union of the human race, must be regarded as possible and, indeed, as contributing to this intention of nature." (VPM 101; STPS 116; SÖ 142)

Habermas takes this key quote from Kant's essay "Idea for a Universal History with a Cosmopolitan Purpose," which was published in the November 1784 issue of the *Berlinische Monatsschrift*. He then connects it directly to a text Kant published fourteen years later, namely, *Dispute of the Faculties* (1798), to claim a causal relationship between the two:

> *Consequently*, in the context of his 'prophetic history of humanity,' *Kant devotes a special paragraph* to the difficulties "of the maxims that apply to world progress (*zum Weltbesten*) with regard to their publicity." (VPM 101, STPS 116, emphasis added; SÖ 142)

To mitigate this lack of publicity for the maxims of Kant's universal history with a cosmopolitan purpose, free and independent instructors of rational natural law, namely, the philosophers, have to educate the nation in the political public sphere. In 1960, Habermas even added another Kant quote from his 1798 essay that reveals the intention of such moral politics: The public impact of philosophy is the precondition for "speeding up," through "our own rational orchestration," the advent of "the cosmopolitan condition," which will be "so beneficial for our descendants" (VPM 101).

Readers thus receive the mistaken impression that immediately upon publishing his essay from 1784, Kant called on the public philosophers of rational natural law to facilitate, in political practice, "the effect of a theory of history on the actual development of that history." Neither the German original nor the English translation of *Structural Transformation* contain the publication dates of Kant's essays. Overcoming this obstacle is even more time-consuming for the German-language public, because *Strukturwandel der* Öffentlichkeit only refers to the respective volumes in Ernst Cassirer's edition of Kant's Works (see SÖ 323n54).

Needless to say, this missing information is essential for understanding the relationship between Kant's philosophy and the French Revolution. For Kant's perspective on speeding up the actual development of history toward a cosmopolitan condition by entering the maxims of the philosophy of history into the reasoning of a public that seeks to enlighten itself *differed in 1798 from what it had been in November 1784*. After all, when publishing his signature answer to the question "What is Enlightenment?" only one month later, in the December 1784 issue of the *Berlinische Monatsschrift*, Kant included the following far-reaching statement that is *not* referred to in *Structural Transformation*:

> Thus a public can only achieve enlightenment slowly. A revolution may well put an end to autocratic despotism and to rapacious or power-seeking oppression, but it will never produce a true reform in *ways of thinking.* (quoted in HPSC 76, emphasis added)

Readers thus have to compare the theory reconstruction of Kant's "unofficial" philosophy in Section 13 to his essay from 1798 to find out how and why Habermas practiced an oscillating mode of selective reception and presentation. Since Kant's "unofficial" philosophy allegedly posits the rational-critical instruction of "moral-political action," the omission, in Section 13, of Kant's 1798 reference to speeding up the advent of the cosmopolitan condition through "our own rational orchestration," has to be surprising. Conversely, *Structural Transformation* paraphrases Kant's 1798 reference to the instructors of rational natural law as "precisely the philosophers who under the name of enlighteners are decried as *persons dangerous to the state*" (STPS 116, emphasis added). In Kant's words, "the very freedoms they allow themselves, are a stumbling block to the state, whose only wish is to rule."

Nevertheless, the fact that these "enlighteners" are "decried as a menace to the state" does not mean that their presentation of grievances "in *respectful* tones to the state, which is thereby implored to take the rightful needs of the people to heart" (emphasis in the original), can be equated with the reasoning of a "moral politics" which aims at the revolutionary realization of rational natural law. Instead, section 8 of *Dispute of the Faculties*, titled "The Difficulty of Making Maxims Directed toward the World's Progressive Improvement as Regards their Publicity," supports Kant's "official" philosophy of history, which predicts that this progress will occur out of "natural necessity," if the public use of reason is not prohibited. In turn, Section 13 seemingly supports this "official" version by only quoting Kant's *evolutionary* statement that "the prohibition of publicity impedes the progress of a people toward improvement" (STPS 116).

However, directly in the first sentence of *Structural Transformation*'s next paragraph readers are confronted with an unabashedly *revolutionary* statement: "The *system-exploding* consequences of a philosophy of history that implies its own political intent and effect come to the fore precisely in connection with the category of publicity" (STPS 116, emphasis added; SÖ 142-143). Only when analyzing the substantial differences between the above quoted section 8 of *Dispute of the Faculties* and section 7, titled "The Prophetic History of Humankind," will they realize that Section 13 mirrors the oscillating ambivalence of Kant's philosophy with regard to rationally instructing the "moral-political action" that otherwise remains mostly implicit in *Structural Transformation*.

In short, Habermas does not reveal why his Kant interpretation is seemingly justified to use language like the evocative wording "*system-exploding* consequences of a philosophy of history." Or to claim that in Kant's 1798 essay the "conflict of the faculties" marks "only the *center of the fire* from which the *flames of enlightenment* spread and where it finds ever new nourishment" (STPS 105, emphasis added; SÖ 130). The reader finds a justification only in two explicit passages in Kant's *Dispute of the Faculties*. Significantly, neither one is quoted either in *Structural Transformation* or in Habermas's 1960 conference presentation. Excerpts from the expressive first passage, culminating in the call "to rise up" if "favorable circumstances present themselves," are quoted as the keynote of this guide to reading Section 13. The second passage offers a comprehensive explanation for such enthusiasm on Kant's part:

> The *revolution of a brilliant people* which we have seen unfolding in our day may succeed or fail; it may be so filled with misery and atrocities that a right-thinking person who could have hopes of bringing it off successfully if he were to attempt it a second time would still never decide to do so, since the cost of the experiment would be too high.—This revolution, I say, finds in the minds of all those watching it . . . a wish to participate that borders on *enthusiasm*, and since

merely revealing this attitude could have dangerous consequences, it must be caused by a *moral disposition in the human race.* (quoted in Preuss 1990/1995: 41, emphasis added, translation by Deborah Lucas Schneider)

Only in his essay commemorating Michel Foucault which was translated into English in 1989 under the title "Taking Aim at the Heart of the Present: On Foucault's Lecture on Kant's *What Is Enlightenment?*" would Habermas *implicitly* acknowledge that Kant's "interpretation of revolutionary enthusiasm as a sign of historical progress toward the better" (TAHP 176) was a key motivating force for his theory reconstruction of Kant's "unofficial" philosophy of history. For such revolutionary enthusiasm seemed to provide the empirical evidence that free teachers of rational natural law could guide the public toward "moral-political action" to "speed up" the advent of the "cosmopolitan condition" as "the end state" of the "continual progress toward the better." Under this "cosmopolitan condition" a "republican constitution would ensure the rule of law internally as well as externally: both the autonomy of citizens under laws they had made for themselves and the elimination of war from international relations" (TAHP 175; see STPS 103).

Readers of *Structural Transformation* are not informed about Kant's "interpretation of revolutionary enthusiasm as a sign of historical progress toward the better." While the Tacit Model Case of French Revolutionary Development and of Kant's "Unofficial" Philosophy of History looms in the background throughout Section 13, any reference to the French Revolution is edited out with surgical precision. Literally so, as a comparison with Habermas's conference presentation from 1960 demonstrates. Both texts draw on two identical quotes from Kant's 1793 essay titled "On the Common Saying: This May Be True in Theory, but It Does Not Apply in Practice" (see STPS 271n61). They do so to tease out "the ambivalence" in Kant's philosophy of history (STPS 113). Both texts use identical wording to describe their findings and to introduce the first identical quote: "Besides the many statements that are in harmony with [Kant's] system *by exempting morality from progress*, limiting the latter to an increase in the products of legality, one also finds the *contradictory admission* 'that, since *the human race* is constantly progressing in cultural matters (in keeping with its natural purpose), it *is also engaged in progressive improvement in relation to the moral end of its existence*'" (VPM 99; STPS 113, emphasis added; SÖ 139).

In the second identical quote, Kant expands on his claim regarding the progressive improvement of morality. Moreover, he now adds that there is evidence to prove it. However, he does not yet identify this evidence:

Besides, various evidence suggests that in our age, as compared with all previous ages, the human race as a whole has really made considerable progress. (VPM 99; STPS 113; SÖ 139)

Exactly at this point in his argument from 1960, Habermas edits out the reference to the French Revolution when reusing his earlier text in *Structural Transformation*. It is contained in a quote from the same Kant essay "Common Saying." Significantly, Kant's argument from 1793 anticipates the one he will make in1798 in *Dispute of the Faculties*. Here it is, together with Habermas's introduction from 1960:

> As such evidence, *Kant* offers the interpretation of a great event, which reveals "the moral tendency of the human race," he *identifies the French Revolution.* (VPM 100, emphasis added)

Above all, even when closely reading Section 13 it is not possible to decipher that in Habermas's tacit interpretation the "true reform in *ways of thinking*," which Kant called for in 1784, finds, fourteen years later, "*expression precisely in enthusiasm* for the revolution that has since taken place" (TAHP 175, emphasis added). This underlying equation of morality and rationality further confirms *Structural Transformation*'s tacit privileging of "moral politics." The reader will recall from the discussion above, that Section 13 almost immediately introduces an observation (in brackets) that is as far-reaching as it is presented merely in passing. Namely, that in the eighteenth century the "'moral'" is "in any event thought as one with 'nature' and 'reason'" (STPS 103).

This valorization of the progressive improvement in the morality of the human race, which is facilitated by Kant's "unofficial" philosophy of history, informs Section 13 when it considers "the *citoyen*, the citizen eligible to vote, under the twofold aspect of legality *and* morality" (STPS 111, emphasis added). In this context, Habermas reminds the reader that the self-interpretation of the political public sphere in bourgeois society, which defines the citizen as "a morally free person," is "derived from the literary public sphere" (STPS 111). To illustrate his point, he could have included one of the most famous publications of the French literary public sphere in the second half of the eighteenth century. Namely, Rousseau's *Emile* (1762), the hybrid between a treatise on education and a domestic novel, which forms the original template for the *Bildungsroman* of the German classic period as the link between the bourgeois family's intimate sphere and the literary public sphere.

While Rousseau's two *Discourses* from 1750 and 1755 regard the trend toward alienation from altruism and communal life among the rising bourgeoisie as irreversible, Emile's tutor and a letter from Julie to Saint-Preux in Rousseau's *La Nouvelle Heloise* (1761) voice the possibility of a *return to universal goodness through "inevitable revolutions."* On one hand, Emile's tutor articulates Rousseau's prediction of "the state of crisis and the century of revolutions." On the other hand, Julie's romantic hope can be regarded as an expression of Rousseau's prophecy of "purely interior revelation": "I should think that a soul once corrupted is so forever, and no longer returns to goodness by itself; unless some *sudden revolution* . . . with a *violent shock*, helps it to recover a good position" (quoted in HPSC 68–69, emphasis added).

Kant famously interrupted his daily rituals to read Rousseau's lengthy *Emile* (HPSC 72). His pathos and enthusiasm when celebrating the revolutionaries for their "zeal and greatness of soul" certainly matches the expressive language displayed by the heroine Julie in Rousseau's other novel. Nevertheless, the reader has to wonder whether even a complete conflation of reason and morality, that would go *beyond* the construct of a "morally pretentious rationality," can falsify Kant's thesis from 1784 that "a public can only achieve enlightenment slowly."

Section 13 itself devotes three pages to the *process* of enlightenment by focusing on Kant's elaborations on his maxim "to think for oneself" (STPS 104), on "the public use of one's reason" (STPS 105), and on "the world of a critically debating reading public" (STPS 106). This process, in which "the *public* should enlighten itself, . . . if only freedom is granted" (STPS 104, emphasis in the original), has still faced great obstacles. After all, Kant introduces his thesis that "a public can only achieve enlightenment slowly" at the end of the very same paragraph which opens with the assertion that "enlightenment is almost sure to follow" (STPS 104), if freedom is granted. In *Structural Transformation* already Section 9 acknowledges that "the nobility in its *salons* was more receptive to the enlightened mode of thought of bourgeois intellectuals than the bourgeoisie itself" (STPS 68, see 6.1 above). And in "Natural Law and Revolution" the Abbe Sieyes is quoted as conceding in January 1789 that the "Third Estate is still far behind" regarding the knowledge of human rights based on rational natural law (NLR 88).

Joan McDonald's extensive analysis of French pamphlets, books, and speeches from 1762 to 1789 confirmed this fact in her book *Rousseau and the Revolution* (1965). In spite of Rousseau's revolutionary language about the sovereignty of the people, his *Contrat Social* (1762) did not influence the views of many bourgeois revolutionaries in 1789. Above all, his book was almost universally regarded as "extremely difficult" and "abstract"—thus almost impossible to understand (quoted in HPSC 71–72). In short, readers are faced with the question *how* "the concept of right alone" could produce in the bourgeois revolutionaries "that zeal and greatness of soul?"

Chapter Seven

The Achilles' Heel of Schiller's Moral Stage and *Structural Transformation*'s Moral Politics

A Dependency of Smith's Political Economy and Kant's Constitutional Law on Mandeville's Moral Paradox of Bourgeois Society

One of the key challenges when trying to understand Section 13 is caused by Habermas's cryptic reference to "Mandeville's slogan, 'private vices, public benefits,'" which is presented without any explanation either in the text itself or in an endnote (STPS 109). As stated above under 5.4, this "slogan" was the inspiration for Smith's famous dictum, first published in his *Theory of Moral Sentiments* in 1759, about the "invisible hand" that allegedly self-regulates all markets as well as the capitalist economy as a whole (see HPSC 211–212, 201–203). For readers who are not well-versed in eighteenth century British moral philosophy and political economy, the significance of *Structural Transformation*'s seemingly obscure reference to "Mandeville's slogan" must stand in an inverse ratio to the gravity of the rational natural law issue that hinges on the validity of this "slogan." Namely, Kant's challenge to find a "practical resolution" for his task of theoretically constructing the "perfectly just bourgeois constitution" (STPS 109; SÖ 134):

> Given a multitude of rational [human] beings demanding universal laws for their preservation, but each of whom is secretly inclined to exempt himself from them, to establish a constitution in such a way that, although their *private* intentions clash, they check each other, with the result that their *public* conduct is the same as if they had no such evil intentions. (STPS 109, emphasis in the original; SÖ 134–135)

In other words, readers have to try to comprehend why Habermas calls this principle underlying Kant's concept of the perfect republican constitution, published in *Perpetual Peace* (1795), a *variation* and Bernard Mandeville's fundamental moral paradox a *slogan*? Especially since in the late

1950s the latter term had gained currency in the West German language as an Anglicism (SÖ 135) used in "hard sell" political advertising that reduces the citizen to the status of a consumer, as Section 22 analyzes with regard to the West German parliamentary election of 1957. In short, how can the German Anglicism "*Slogan,*" even if it is retranslated into English as "formula," be used in the scholarly discourse of rational natural law?

7.1. THE "INVISIBLE HAND" AS THE "WHOLLY PERNICIOUS" TRUTH (SMITH) OF MANDEVILLE'S SATIRE

The answer can be found in a very widespread bipartisan consensus that has mostly ostracized Mandeville's book of more than 400 pages. This consensus first manifested itself in 1723, when a presentment of the "Grand Jury for the County of Middlesex" indicted the publisher of the second edition of *The Fable of the Bees; or Private Vices Publick Benefits*. Its charge reveals that Mandeville's satirical polemic identified the Achilles' heel of bourgeois morality: "The more effectually to carry on these Works of Darkness, studied Artifices and invented Colours have been made use of to run down Religion and Virtue as *prejudicial* to Society, and detrimental to the State; and to recommend Luxury, Avarice, Pride, and all kind of Vices, as being necessary to *Publick Welfare*" (quoted in HPSC 201, emphasis in the original).

In 1982, Habermas included Mandeville in his list of the "*dark* writers of the bourgeoisie—such as Machiavelli, Hobbes, and Mandeville" (EME 13, emphasis in the original). Already in 1944, Karl Polanyi had complained that Mandeville's "cheap paradox" about private vices creating public benefits should not have "exercised minds of the quality of a Berkeley, Hume, and Smith" (quoted in HPSC 203). In 1984, on the other end of the ideological spectrum, the neoconservative historian Gertrude Himmelfarb expanded on Polanyi's outrage: "The Fable of the Bees profoundly shocked contemporaries, provoking a frenzy of attacks . . . culminating in a ruling handed down by the grand jury of Middlesex." Finally, in 2004, sixty years after Polanyi, she still mirrored the liberal point of view: "Joining in the near-universal condemnation were most of the eighteenth-century greats—Bishop Berkeley, Francis Hutcheson, Edward Gibbon, Adam Smith" (quoted in HPSC 201).

However, Himmelfarb only gives a one-sided presentation of Smith's thought when she highlights that he "expressed the general sentiment in pronouncing Mandeville's theory . . . 'wholly pernicuous'" (quoted in HPSC 201). Smith himself started to present the other side in his *Theory of Moral Sentiments*. At the beginning of a long paragraph about Mandeville that covers almost two pages, he presents the following analysis:

But how destructive so ever this system may appear, it could never . . . have occasioned so general an alarm among those who are friends of better principles, *had it not in some respects bordered upon the truth.* (quoted in HPSC 201, emphasis added)

At the end of that paragraph Smith concludes that "the greatest falsehoods which he [Mandeville] imposes upon us must bear some resemblance to the truth, and must even have *a considerable mixture of truth in them*" (quoted in HPSC 202, emphasis added). More than a century later, the "Ex-President of the College of New Jersey, Princeton," James McCosh, a Doctor of Law and of Divinity, went even further in his voluminous book on *The Scottish Philosophy: Biographical, Explanatory, Critical: From Hutcheson to Hamilton* (1890):

Mandeville . . . advanced some . . . doubtful speculations as to private vices public benefits; showing that the power and grandeur of any nation . . . cannot be procured unless . . . the intemperance, luxury, and pride of men consume manufactures, and promote industry. The author has here caught hold of *a positive and important truth*, the explanation of which carries us into some of the deepest mysteries of Providence, in which we see *good springing out of vice*, and God ruling this world in spite of its wickedness, and by means of its wickedness, but without identifying himself with it. (quoted in HPSC 202, emphasis added)

In his introduction to the classic Modern Library edition of the *Wealth of Nations*, Edwin Cannan refers to the book's following famous quote to demonstrate that Smith "clearly believed" that the moral philosophy of his teacher Francis Hutcheson "did not give a sufficiently high place to self-interest": "It is not from the benevolence of the butcher, the brewer, or the baker, that we expect our dinner, but from their regard to their own interest. We address ourselves, *not to their humanity*, but to their self-love, and never talk to them of our necessities, but of their advantages. *Nobody but a beggar choses to depend chiefly upon the benevolence of his fellow citizens*" (quoted in HPSC 202, emphasis added). Cannan concludes that Smith did not "obtain the belief that self-interest works for the benefit of the whole economic community" from Hutcheson, but "was assisted by his study of Mandeville, a writer who has little justice done him in histories of economics" (quoted in HPSC 202, 203).

The seamless transition of Smith's concept of the "invisible hand" from the *Theory of Moral Sentiments* (1759) to the *Wealth of Nations* (1776) demonstrates the entwinement of his moral and his economic thought: "*The rich . . . in spite of their natural selfishness and rapacity, . . .* divide with the poor the produce of all their improvements. They are led by an invisible hand to make nearly the same distribution to the necessaries of life, which would have been made, had the earth been divided into equal portions among all inhabitants, and thus *without intending it, without knowing it, advance the interest of society*." In short, the rich person "neither intends to promote the *public interest*, nor knows how much he is promoting it" (quoted in HPSC 211, emphasis added).

This *unintentional* promotion of the public interest stands at the center of Smith's attention and reflections: "By pursuing his own interest, [the rich person] frequently promotes that of society *more effectually* than when he really intends to promote it." Finally, Smith concludes with the remarkable dictum that he has "never known much good done by those who affected to trade for the *public good*" (quoted in HPSC 212, emphasis added).

The reader needs this information to realize that Smith's analysis dovetails with Kant's thesis from 1784 that "nature employs the 'antagonism within society'" to develop "all the innate endowments of humanity in a "'bourgeois society that administers justice universally.'" Hence, the "'perfectly just bourgeois constitution'" mentioned above can "necessarily be no more than a 'pathologically enforced social union' representing a 'moral whole' *in appearance* only" (STPS 109, emphasis in the original; SÖ 134). Accordingly, the citizens assembled for rational-critical debate on the "affairs of the 'commonwealth'" can, in their "pathologically enforced" conduct, only *appear* as "morally free" persons. In short, they have to "behave outwardly, as if they were inwardly free persons" (STPS 107, 111; SÖ 132, 137).

At this point in Habermas's theory reconstruction, it becomes apparent for the reader that *Structural Transformation*'s concept of a morally pretentious rationality in the bourgeois public sphere stands and falls with the validity of natural laws of society posited by classical political economy. In Habermas's crucial words: "Under the social conditions that translate private vices into public virtues, a state of cosmopolitan citizenship and hence the subsumption of politics under morality is *empirically conceivable*" (STPS 111–12, emphasis added).

7.2. THE SOCIAL CONDITIONS FOR THE REIGN OF THE "INVISIBLE HAND"

By now the readers of this guide to Habermas's original public sphere concept are quite familiar with *Structural Transformation*'s dictum that the social conditions for the genesis of a rational-critical public opinion developed *only* in the last third of the eighteenth century when the Physiocrats were the first to detect the alleged "natural laws" of society. However, Section 13 does *not* connect Kant's liberal model of the public sphere in the bourgeois constitutional state to *the* Physiocratic theory of "laissez faire" capitalism, which Quesnay started to publish in the Encyclopedia in the late 1750s. Instead, in Habermas's theory reconstruction the specific social conditions that informed Kant's idea of the bourgeois public sphere are the ones referred to in Mandeville's moral paradox, first printed in 1705, expanded on in 1714, and finalized in 1724.

This is quite surprising, because the Industrial Revolution was already rapidly advancing when Kant presented in 1795 his Mandeville-like paradox quoted above about transforming evil private intention into good public conduct through the perfect republican constitution. Moreover, for "Natural Law and Revolution" it "is well known," that Quesnay "anticipated Adam Smith's insight of 'laissez faire.'" Habermas's essay even adds that [in 1767] the Physiocrat Le Mercier de la Riviere "celebrated" Quesnay's "laissez faire" theory as the "'glory of our century'" (NLR 100; NR 106).

Nevertheless, these specifics are all missing from the discussion in Section 13 regarding alleged natural economic laws as the foundation of the rational-critical public sphere. Just how outdated Kant's understanding of the role of the "laissez-faire" principle in classical political economy seemingly was, surfaces inadvertently in endnote 83 on page 272. Significantly, this is the only place where Section 13 discusses this important topic, which it also reduces to the status of a slogan ("*Schlagwort*") (STPS 272n83; SÖ 325n79).

Moreover, Section 13 itself erroneously assumes that only in 1798, when Kant made an "anecdotal reference" to it, was "the slogan, 'laissez-faire,' just put in currency." In reality, at that point in time, the "slogan" was already more than one hundred years old. In "the 1824 Supplement to the *Encyclopedia Britannica*," James Mill traced it back to opposition to French mercantilism after 1660. Since that time, "the memorable advice of the merchants to the meddling Colbert was well known, *Laissez nous faire*" (quoted in HPSC 116). In short, Kant grounds an important aspect of his eighteenth century rational natural law in seventeenth-century political economy:

> A minister of the French government summoned a few of the most eminent merchants and asked them for suggestions on how to stimulate trade. . . . After one had suggested this and another one that, an old merchant who had kept quiet so far said: "Build good roads, mint sound money, give us laws for exchanging money readily, etc.; but as for the rest, leave us alone." (STPS 272n83; SÖ 325n79)

According to *Structural Transformation*'s own criteria, this error in the chronology of bourgeois political economy's development in Section 13 is rather substantial. As Habermas would explain in "Natural Law and Revolution," "the classical economics of the eighteenth-century project into the natural basis of society the same natural laws which in the seventeenth century were still conceived as the norms of formal law." Specifically, this allowed Thomas Paine to identify "the natural *rights* of humankind" in Locke's political theory with "the natural *laws* of commodity exchange and social labor" in Smith's political economy (NLR 94, emphasis added; NR100). In other words, Kant *could* have drawn on the political economy of "the second half of the eighteenth century," which declared Locke's formal laws of the state to be "the natural laws of society itself" (see 5.4 above).

Conversely, the Kantian rational natural law argument in Section 13 is further weakened by its inability to draw on Say's Law like Section 11 had done in the context of the Reform Bill from 1832. As discussed above, eight years separate Kant's application of Mandeville's moral paradox in 1795 from the first printed sketch of Say's Law in 1803. Instead, Section 13 has to repeat itself and offer the reader three variations of Mandeville's "slogan" on pages 109, 111–12, and 116–17.

Arguably, the Achilles' heel of the Kantian discourse about a "subsumption of politics under morality" that is "empirically conceivable" becomes quite visible in Section 13. While the errors and omissions regarding the reception of classical political economy contribute to this weakness, it is mostly systemic and results from the rather existential challenge British moral philosophy had been faced with when trying to transform Mandeville's moral paradox from a negative into a positive. Smith's own rhetoric from 1759 clearly illustrates this. As quoted under 7.1 above, his argument started out quite cautiously by only acknowledging that Mandeville's satire "*bordered* upon the truth." He even added the qualifier "*in some respects.*" However, at the end of the same long paragraph he conceded that Mandeville's arguments "must even have *a considerable mixture of truth in them*" (quoted in HPSC 201, emphasis added).

More than 160 years after the "Grand Jury for the County of Middlesex" indicted the publisher of the *Fable of the Bees* to defend "Religion and Virtue" as well as Society and the State against Mandeville's alleged recommendation of "Luxury, Avarice, Pride, and all kind of Vices," McCosh interpreted Smith's "invisible hand" as the hand of God and a manifestation of the "deepest mysteries of Providence." Accordingly, he upgraded Smith's wording *considerable mixture of truth* by removing the last qualifiers and acknowledging the truth of Mandeville's observation. Moreover, McCosh valorized it as *a positive and important* truth. This Doctor of Law and Divinity, who was a former College President at Princeton and *not* a "dark writer of the bourgeoisie," thus ascribed to the "Seven Deadly Sins" a key role in the promotion of industry and the accumulation of capital.

To further complicate matters, readers will notice a tension in Section 13 regarding the explanation of just what "renders plausible the conflation of *bourgeois* and *homme*" (STPS 111, translation adjusted to SÖ 137). Since *Structural Transformation* references Mandeville three times, one would assume that this conflation is achieved by harnessing his moral paradox in order "to consider the *citoyen*, the citizen eligible to vote," not just under the aspect of legality but also under the one of morality (STPS 111). The following quote seems to confirm such an assumption. It directly connects Mandeville's moral paradox to the "*ordre naturel*" of the Physiocrats:

> The public sphere fit easily into the categories of the Kantian system only as long as . . . [it] can count on the social conditions of the liberal model of the public sphere, on the classic relationship of *bourgeois-homme-citoyen*, which is to say on bourgeois society as the *ordre naturel*, which converts private vices into public virtues. (STPS 116–117)

However, on page 111 Habermas identifies the "fiction of a justice immanent in free commerce," repeatedly discussed in this guide, as the explanation that "renders plausible" this conflation of "*bourgeois* and *homme*." Significantly, Smith's claim about an "invisible hand" in *The Wealth of Nations* neither invokes "justice" nor connects this ethical notion to his analysis of the alleged exchange of equivalents in the labor market. Since he ascribes *natural selfishness and rapacity* to the *rich*, as 7.1 above documents, there hardly is any room for justice.

In other words, Smith measures the validity of his thesis about an "invisible hand" solely, by the outcome of capitalist production and distribution. He claims that "without intending it," and "without knowing it," the rich "advance the interest of society." Allegedly, they "divide with the poor the produce of all their improvements."

In short, Smith's political economy only knows the selfish *bourgeois*. He does not ascribe any empirical validity to the role of the *homme*, because he has "never known much good done by those who affected to trade for the public good." Readers will immediately realize that this puts him at loggerheads with *Structural Transformation*'s claim that the representation of the economic interests of the rising bourgeoisie is "interpreted with the aid of ideas grown in the soil of the intimate sphere of the conjugal family" (STPS 51). Namely, love, altruism, and cultivation of the person (STPS 49, STPS 260-61n48).

7.3. SOCIOLOGICAL PRECONDITIONS FOR PRIVATE AUTONOMY IN THE POLITICAL PUBLIC SPHERE

Section 13 refers like Section 11 to the absolute importance of universal access to the bourgeois public sphere, which completely depends on an "effective mechanism of free competition" in all markets. Only "laissez faire" policies can, in the idea of the liberal public sphere, safeguard such "equal chances for the acquisition of property." In turn, the private autonomy that capitalistically functioning private property offers is needed to be "admitted to the public use of reason." For only the owners of private property are "their own masters." Only "they should be enfranchised to vote." (STPS 85, 110).

Based on Kant's reflections from 1793, Section 13 devotes a full page with two long quotes from his journal article in the *Berlinische Monatsschrift* to these complex preconditions for the bourgeois public sphere as "the organizational principle of the liberal constitutional state" and "as the method of enlightenment" (STPS 110, 107, 104). They are strikingly contemporary, as the beginning of the second quote immediately illustrates. Already Kant has to concede that the "free exchange of commodities may indeed 'over a series of generations create *considerable inequalities in wealth among the members of the commonwealth'*" (quoted in STPS 110, emphasis added; SÖ 136).

However, as long as the landowner or manufacturer does "'not prevent his subordinates from raising themselves to his own level if they are able and entitled to do so by their talent, industry and good fortune,'" the guarantee of "equal chances for the acquisition of property" and the universal access to the public sphere will *not* be violated. In this context, Kant emphasizes that, even if the subordinates do not achieve these goals, they have to be "'aware that. . . the fault lies either with [themselves] (i.e., lack of ability or serious endeavor) or with circumstances for which [they] cannot blame . . . the irresistible will of any outside party'" (quoted in STPS 110, emphasis added; SÖ 136).

The universal freedom from coercion is essential. If the property owner would be allowed "'to practice coercion without himself being subject to coercive counter-measures'" (STPS 110). Kant's idea of transforming all evil private intentions into good public conduct in the medium of the perfect republican constitution would be null and void. If systemic inequality regarding the acquisition of property and thus of private autonomy existed, not all evil private intentions could be mutually checked anymore. Already seventeenth century theorists of republican constitutions like James Harrington knew about the entwinement of economic and political power.

Kant posited this absolute need for a universal "*spirit of freedom*" also for Rousseau's "principle of popular sovereignty" itself (STPS 107, emphasis in the original). Section 13 very carefully analyzes the distinction that Kant makes regarding the "public law" as "the act of a public will" expressed by "the entire people." This act in which "all men decide for all men and each decides for himself" establishes only the necessary condition for a perfectly just legislative process. The sufficient condition for the realization of this principle of popular sovereignty can only be provided, if the "public use of reason" is guaranteed. For "'in all matters concerning universal human duties, each individual requires to be *convinced by reason* that the coercion which prevails is lawful.'" Crucially, Habermas emphasizes that in this context "the famous statement about the *freedom of the pen* as 'the sole sacred safeguard (*Palladium*) of the rights of the people' was made" (STPS 107, emphasis added; SÖ 132–133).

The great importance that Habermas himself has ascribed to these social preconditions can be gleaned from the fact that he revisited the topic in his *1986 Tanner Lectures on Human Values.* He also reprinted them in 1992 as an appendix to the German edition of *Between Fact and Norms*, titled "Law and Morals" (FG 541–599). Especially his second Tanner Lecture, titled "On the Idea of the Constitutional State (*Rechtsstaat*)," addressed their neglect in the social contract theories of rational natural law.

According to Habermas's perspective in 1986, not only the idealist variants of these contract theories but all of them had been conceptualized on a level that was too abstract. For they had not accounted for "the social presuppositions of their possessive individualism." He now posited that "they had not admitted to themselves that the fundamental institutions of private law (property and contract) . . . had only been able to promise justice, because the *fiction about a society of petty commodity producers* met them half-way" (FG 592, emphasis added).

In this quote from 1986, Habermas acknowledged for the first time in print that also the second one of the three "presupposition of classical economics" (see 5.4) on which *Structural Transformation*'s whole theory reconstruction rests, was a *fiction*. Namely, "the *model* of a society of petty commodity producers" with "relatively widely and evenly distributed ownership of means of production" (STPS 86, emphasis added). Moreover, while the third presupposition, Say's Law, turned out to be a fiction only when it "came to grief" in the global economic crisis of the early 1870s, this second one never had any foundation in reality.

Say's Law of Markets about the alleged equilibrium of all factors of production and reproduction was at least somewhat propped up by the unique *historical* condition of the British economy during the first half of the nineteenth century. Readers who track down Habermas's 1986 Tanner Lectures have to realize that no such unique *historical* condition existed in 1795, when Kant developed on the basis of his Mandeville-based principle of the constitutional state "the specific sociological conditions for a politically functioning public sphere" (STPS 109). One of these sociological conditions was the model of a society of petty commodity producers, as it was defined in Section 11. In 1986, Habermas newly classified the model as a fiction.

As *Habermas's Public Sphere: A Critique* analyzes, *Structural Transformation* does not alert the reader to this *sociological* fiction about a society of petty commodity producers. Tacitly drawing on Neumann's 1937 essay in the Frankfurt School's *Zeitschrift* für *Sozialforschung*, the book adopted Rousseau's social contract theory inherent in his draft for the Constitution of Corsica. As highlighted in chapter 1, Rousseau's "model of a society of petty commodity producers" posits a social structure with individual property "so weak and dependent" that "the government needs to apply hardly any force." It can lead the citizens "with the touch of a finger." Since there is "hardly any room for domination," Neumann concludes that in "Rousseau's system the law is the real sovereign" (quoted in HPSC 32).

In other words, Neumann anticipated in his analysis key elements of the wording and imagery that *Structural Transformation* uses in its ideology-critical thesis about the "objective meaning" of the political institutions of the bourgeois constitutional state. Namely, "the idea of the dissolution of domination into that *easygoing constraint* that prevails on no other ground than the compelling insight of a public opinion" (STPS 88, emphasis added). Arguably, this origin constitutes a fascinating trajectory in the intellectual history of the concept of the sovereignty of law as the dissolution of political domination: From "the touch of a finger" via "that easygoing constraint" to today's universal Habermas *bon mot* about the "uncoerced coercion of the better argument."

Significantly, *Structural Transformation* outlines the sociological pre-supposition of a society of petty commodity producers in Section 11—thus separating it from the discussion of Rousseau's social contract theory in Section 12. Accordingly, the reader who is told on page 96 that Rousseau provides "with all desirable clarity" the foundation "for the public's demo-cratic self-determination," will find it difficult to think back to page 86 and ground the ideas of the *Social Contract* (1762/1959) in the sociological presupposition of "a *relatively* widely and evenly distributed ownership of means of production" (emphasis added). Needless to say, it is even more challenging for the reader to think back to this second presupposition from page 109 in Section 13, where Rousseau's fiction becomes one of the spe-cific sociological conditions for Kant's idea of the political public sphere.

Especially since in Rousseau's ideas "relatively" is replaced by "abso-lutely." Beyond a purely bibliographical reference in endnote 36 on page 269, Habermas brackets Iring Fetscher's seminal study on Rousseau's polit-ical philosophy. It offered him in 1960 the description of a very remote farm-ing community in an absolute state of evenly distributed means of production. As Fetscher analyzed: "Rousseau's ideal is based on a largely self-sufficient, almost closed economy of petty farmers" (quoted in HPSC 32).

Structural Transformation's adoption of the sociological fiction of a society of petty commodity producers only follows Kant. As Fetscher points out, Rousseau's model clearly excludes the "high bourgeois" while Kant's liberal ideal includes him. Moreover, while there are only very limited exchange relations in Rousseau's image of an "almost closed economy of petty farmers," Kant situates his petty commodity producers in the context of a fully developed market economy (quoted in HPSC 32–33).

Nevertheless, the reader has to wonder why Section 13 did not immediately identify Kant's economic presupposition of petty commodity producers as a fiction? After all, it did so regarding the "fiction of a justice immanent in free commerce" that "renders plausible the conflation of *bourgeois* and *homme*" (STPS 111; SÖ 137). Above all, on the last page of that section Habermas even refers to a "*series of fictions*, in which the self-understanding of the bourgeois consciousness as 'public opinion' articulates itself." (STPS 117, emphasis added; SÖ 143).

7.4. THE FICTIONS OF THE KANTIAN SYSTEM AND HORKHEIMER / ADORNO'S CRITIQUE OF THE PHILOSOPHY OF HISTORY

Arguably, what motivated Habermas to write *Structural Transformation* not only against Koselleck's *Critique and Crisis* and Schmitt's *The Leviathan in the State Theory of Thomas Hobbes* but also against Horkheimer and Adorno's *Dialectic of Enlightenment* is condensed in their appended note titled "On the Critique of the Philosophy of History" (DE 222–25). While the one "On Philosophy and the Division of Labor" (DE 242–44) discussed above in 1.1 tacitly draws on Marcuse's seminal essay on Critical Theory from 1937, this one takes an almost diametrically opposed point of view. Such an extraordinary degree of tension within the same book certainly explains the subtitle *Philosophical Fragments*. Unfortunately, it is not included in the English edition from 1986.

It looks like Habermas has never publicly referenced "On the Critique of the Philosophy of History," let alone published about it. In this note, Horkheimer and Adorno hold the attempt by the philosophy of history to shift "the position of humane ideals as an active force into history itself," whether in idealism or in materialism, "responsible for the barbaric acts perpetrated in their name" (DE 224). Needless to say, *Structural Transformation* offers a textbook example to illustrate their claim. Habermas's book employs a Hegelian-Marxist philosophy of history to conceptualize a dialectic between the "ideals of bourgeois humanism" and "a constitutional reality that negates them" to fuel the "dynamic of historical development" (FRPS 442).

Conversely, their harsh critique directly and comprehensively contradicts the essence of *Structural Transformation*, starting with its reflections in Section 13 on the "theoretically fully developed form" of the idea of the bourgeois public sphere in Kant's philosophy of history. It is simply impossible to try to logically reconcile Horkheimer and Adorno's note with Habermas's theory reconstruction especially of the "unofficial version" of Kant's philosophy.

Specifically, *Structural Transformation*'s key theses rest exactly on that passage from Kant's essay about the "Idea for a Universal History with a Cosmopolitan Purpose," to which *Dialectic of Enlightenment* implicitly refers in its veiled critique of Kant's presupposition about "a plan . . . aimed at a perfect civil union of humankind" as nature's "immanent law." For this paradigmatic articulation of bourgeois idealism asserts that "a certain commitment of *heart* which the enlightened man cannot fail to make *to the good* he clearly understands, must step by step ascend to the thrones and even influence their principle of government" (quoted in HPSC 51, emphasis added). To which Horkheimer and Adorno respond that "*the goodness* which in reality remains at the mercy of suffering is *concealed* as the force which determines the course of history and ultimately triumphs." In short, it is idolized as the "*spirit of the world*" by Hegel or as an "*immanent law*" by Kant (DE 224, emphasis added).

Habermas first acknowledged in September 1989 that "*Structural Transformation* moved totally within the circle of a classical Marxist critique of ideology, at least as it was understood in the Frankfurt environment." This "ideology critique was linked to the background assumptions that were still somehow relying on some kind of a materialist philosophy of history" (CR 463). In March 1990, he wrote down two different reasons for distancing himself from *Structural Transformation*'s Hegelian-Marxist philosophy of history (FRPS 435, 442).

Only one of them can be interpreted as tacitly responding to Horkheimer and Adorno's above critique in *Dialectic of Enlightenment* which he had read in the very early 1950s (HB 70). Although he did not address the question of responsibility for "the barbaric acts" perpetrated in the name of the idealist and materialist philosophies of history, Habermas acknowledged that their background assumptions "have been refuted by the civilized barbarisms of the twentieth century" (FRPS 442). In short, he now implicitly referred to a thesis that Karl Loewith had published already in 1947 and with which he had been familiar since his studies at the University of Bonn (cf. HPSC 49).

However, Habermas did not address the larger issue of the civilized barbarisms intrinsic in the development of the capitalist mode of production in modernity. Even after his separation from the dialectical philosophies of history that viewed the destructive antagonisms in society as the forces that developed civilization, he only sharpened his critique of the book by Horkheimer and Adorno. In 1982, he called *Dialectic of Enlightenment* "their blackest, most nihilistic book." As he now emphatically stated, it even went beyond the "*dark* writers of the bourgeoisie—such as Machiavelli, Hobbes and Mandeville—[who] had always appealed to Horkheimer" (EME 13, emphasis in the original).

Horkheimer regarded Mandeville as a "somber" writer of the "bourgeois dawn," who "decried the egotism of the self" and "acknowledged in so doing that society was the destructive principle" (DE 90). Specifically, with "the development of the economic system in which control of the economic apparatus divides men, survival as affirmed by reason—the reified drive of the individual bourgeois—was revealed as destructive natural power. . ." (DE 90). It is in the context of this assessment that Horkheimer presented a memorable conclusion which is applicable to the substance of *Structural Transformation*'s "morally pretentious rationality." Arguably, it must have presented to Habermas a fundamental challenge, comparable to the one in the appended note which ascribes responsibility to the philosophies of history for "the barbaric acts" that were perpetrated in their name (DE 224):

> The root of Kantian optimism, according to which moral behavior is rational even if vile guile would prevail, is actually an expression of horror at the thought of reversion to barbarism. (DE 85–86, translation modified, DA 78)

When Adorno asked Habermas in December 1955 whether his *Merkur* essay from 1954 on "The Dialectic of Rationalization" had been influenced by *Dialectic of Enlightenment*, he wrote back stating that he had studied their book "so long ago that it 'only tacitly . . . directed and enriched his approach'" (HB 70). Nevertheless, as a refresher course on the way toward his decisive use of the book for his 1958 preface on "The Concept of Political Participation," he attended Adorno's lecture on *Dialectic of Enlightenment* in the winter term 1956. At that time, Adorno's wife Gretel shared with him the well-kept secret regarding which chapters had been written by whom (HB 78). Habermas thus learned that the author of the book's reflections on Mandeville was Horkheimer.

In that same chapter Habermas must have become aware of yet another challenge by Horkheimer when he read that "the utopia" which "gave the French Revolution hope," entered powerfully but helplessly into the philosophy of German Idealism with the result that the "established bourgeois order completely functionalized reason" (DE 88–89, translation modified; DA 80). It is difficult to imagine a starker contrast to the appended note in which Horkheimer and Adorno assert that philosophy "is immune to the suggestion of the *status quo* for the very reason that it accepts the bourgeois ideals without further consideration" (DE 243, emphasis added, DA 218; cf.

1.1 above). It would be enlightening for the reader to learn whether in 1958 Habermas used this Marcusean intrusion from 1937 as an entering wedge to upend *Dialectic of Enlightenment*. The excellent Habermas biographies by Müller-Dohm and Yos do not contain an answer. However, both biographers had exceptional access and might know.

After all, these bourgeois ideals were mostly identical with the Kantian fictions. Plus they form the substance of *Structural Transformation*'s "morally pretentious rationality." Moreover, not all of them were consciously counterfactual intrusions derived from Marcuse. Instead, the perhaps most stunning example was *inadvertently* contributed by none other than Horkheimer himself.

The reader finds it tucked away in endnote 48 on pages 260–61. Habermas uses it as another intrusion from 1930s Critical Theory. This long quote is contained in Horkheimer's essay "Authority and the Family" from 1936. *Structural Transformation* draws on it to back up its claims in one of the most important passages of the book. Namely, Section 6 on the bourgeois "ideals of freedom, love, and cultivation of the person" in the conjugal family's intimate sphere where allegedly "the experience of 'humanity' originates" (STPS 48, translation modified; SÖ 66).

Actually, this signature passage in Section 6 is a supreme blend of Horkheimer's and Marcuse's contributions to the "Golden Age" of the Frankfurt School. Readers can identify all key building blocks of *Structural Transformation*'s narrative introduced so far in this guide. They will first recognize Marcuse 1937: The three bourgeois ideals that the passage introduces are "surely more than just ideology." They can then deconstruct the intrusion of Marcuse 1937 into Horkheimer/Adorno 1944, as it was articulated by Habermas in 1958:

> As an *objective meaning* contained as an element in the structure of the *actual institution* [i.e., the bourgeois family], without whose *subjective validity* society would have not been able to reproduce itself, *these ideas are also reality.* (STPS 48, emphasis added, translation adjusted to the German original; SÖ 65)

Since *Structural Transformation* relegates Horkheimer 1936 to the endnote, readers themselves have to integrate the key points from that quote into Habermas's arguments presented above. First of all, Horkheimer explicates the bourgeois ideal of love by differentiating between "sexual love and, above all, . . . *maternal care.*" Secondly, he emphasizes that within "this unity . . . *the development and the happiness of the other is desired*" (STPS 260–61n48, emphasis added, SÖ 309n48).

Once readers enter Horkheimer's additional explications into Habermas's presentation, they will realize that the bourgeois ideal of love, which encompasses sexual love and *maternal care*, can become a reality as an element in the structure of the *actual institution* of the bourgeois family, because without the *subjective validity* of the experience that *the happiness of the other is desired*, society would have not been able to reproduce itself. The Horkheimer quote contains the information to further clarify this point. For he juxtaposes the "communal interest" in "bourgeois life" on one hand and in the intimate sphere of the bourgeois family on the other hand.

While in "bourgeois life" this "communal interest has an essentially *negative character*, concerning itself only with the defense against danger, it assumes *a positive character* in sexual love, and above all, in *maternal care*" (STPS 260-61n48, emphasis added, SÖ 309n48). In short, society needs *subjective validity* for *a positive character* of the "communal interest" in the intimate sphere of the bourgeois family to reproduce itself. For the *negative character* of the "communal interest" in "bourgeois life" in the private sphere of commodity exchange and social labor is insufficient to achieve this on its own. The following portion of the Horkheimer quote further details this juxtaposition between the intimate sphere of the bourgeois family and the private sphere of the market:

> *The reification of the human being in the economy as the mere function of an economic variable* is, of course, also continued in the family . . . . Nonetheless, *since relations inside the family are not mediated by the market* and individuals do not oppose one another to be competitors, human beings have always had the opportunity for acting not merely as determined by a function but as *human*. (STPS 260–61n48, emphasis added; SÖ 309n48)

The Horkheimer quote ends with a succinct summation of the utopian dimension of these ideals of bourgeois humanism in conjugal family life that *Structural Transformation* elaborates on in precise detail. Habermas writes:

> With this specific notion of humanity a conception of what exists is promulgated within the bourgeoisie which promises redemption from the constraints of what exists without escaping into a transcendental realm. The conception's transcendence of what is immanent is the element of truth that raises bourgeois ideology above ideology itself, most fundamentally in that area where the experience of 'humanity' originates, in the humanity of the intimate relationships between human beings who, under the aegis of the family, are nothing more than human. (STPS 48, translation adjusted to the German original; SÖ 66)

Horkheimer summarizes:

> … the bourgeois family leads not only to bourgeois authority but to a premonition of a better human condition. (STPS 260–61n48, emphasis added, SÖ 309n48)

Horkheimer's reference to "maternal care" is particularly productive for delineating the interconnection between the intimate sphere of the bourgeois family, which is oriented toward an audience, and the literary public sphere. Section 5 describes that already in seventeenth-century Germany the *Sprach-gesellschaften* (language societies) were among the first institutions of the literary public sphere. Since they sought to bring about "an equality and association among persons of unequal status," they "devoted their attention to the *Muttersprache* (mother tongue)." For this shared mother tongue was now interpreted "as the medium of communication and understanding between people in their *common quality as human beings and nothing but human beings*" (STPS 34, emphasis added, translation adjusted to the German original; SÖ 50).

While the English translation of *Structural Transformation* uses the term "native tongue," translating *Muttersprache* as "mother tongue" allows to connect the ideal of maternal care that Horkheimer highlights and the face-to-face communication of learning one's native language from one's mother. This connection can thus serve as a universal manifestation of "the humanity of the intimate relationships between human beings," that is, moral persons (STPS 48, 85). In turn, the bourgeois reading public that is based on the commonality of the "mother tongue" is thus naturally imbued with humanity as such.

As Habermas emphasizes, our natural ability to learn to speak our mother tongue, to generate our native language, simultaneously elevates us above nature. Accordingly, with its linguistic "structure rational autonomy [Mündigkeit] is posited *for us*" (Habermas 1965 / 1968: 163, emphasis in the original). Nevertheless, this rational autonomy can only be achieved through conscious action.

In 1965, in his inaugural address as Horkheimer's successor on the philosophy chair at Frankfurt University, Habermas praises German Idealism for defining reason as a linguistic unity of "will *and* consciousness." Specifically, he identifies the process of Enlightenment with the interest to achieve rational self-determination. In his 1968 reflections on "Critique as the Unity of Knowledge and Interest," he further elaborates on this idealist decision to define reason as rational will:

> The need for emancipation and an originally accomplished act of freedom have to precede all logic, so that human beings can rise up to the idealist standpoint of rational autonomy. (KHI 205–06, translation modified; EI 253)

7.5. SCHILLER'S BRAZEN MORAL STAGE AND *STRUCTURAL TRANSFORMATION'S* TACIT MORAL POLITICS

Before the ideals of bourgeois humanism can serve to legitimize the private owners of the capitalistically functioning means of production in the political public sphere, two steps of appropriation are necessary. First, these ideals have to achieve hegemony in the literary public sphere by appropriating Renaissance humanism and transforming it through the tenets of the Protestant Reformation and their transition from moral theology to moral philosophy. Second, once the bourgeoisie is in control of the literary public sphere, it functionally converts its "institutions of the public and the forums for discussion" into a sphere that facilitates the "critique of public authority." The private people do so by making public use of their reason to "appropriate the public sphere regulated by the authority of the state" (STPS 51; SÖ 69).

In the neohumanism of the German classic period, this appropriation was marked by three key publications in 1784 which paradigmatically presented the bourgeois ideals. Kant's classic examples of his *cognitive and moral universalism* in his two articles for the *Berlinische Monatsschrift* from November and December of that year ("Idea for a Universal History" and "What Is Enlightenment?") were discussed above. In June 1784, Schiller's address to the Palatinate German Society in Mannheim, titled "The Legitimate Theater as a Moral Institution," reflected on the role of *expressive subjectivism* in *moral-political action*. He was speaking from experience.

Already his very first play, *The Robbers*, polarized the public due to its emotionally charged critique of injustice, hypocrisy, and corruption of the political authorities in feudal society. Schiller was only twenty-two years old when his rebellious subjectivity exploded on the Mannheim stage in January 1782—causing his immediate arrest on orders from Karl Eugen, Duke of Württemberg. Conversely, during the French Revolution, *The Robbers* earned Schiller the honorary citizenship of the Republic (see HPSC 73, 65).

In a 1971 interview, Habermas retrospectively highlighted his interest in dramatic literature as a student, because it bridged the dichotomy between his philosophical and his political views. He could thus well imagine "that discourses on dramaturgy were the medium to discuss political issues on a higher level of generalization." In 1959, in a seemingly immediate response to Koselleck, Habermas pointedly reversed the order of *Critique and Crisis*: "Since the eighteenth century the power of criticism has been brought to bear against crisis." Above all, he equated the decisive "force" of criticism "in philosophy" since Kant and "in the theater" since Schiller.

Structural Transformation's Section 9 points out that the "young Schiller" received his "first political impulses" for his revolutionary dramaturgy from the martyrdom of the political journalist Christian Friedrich Schubart. Schubart had founded his *Deutsche Chronik* in 1774 in Germany's "darkest corner," Augsburg, "surrounded by despotism." Habermas's vivid portrayal with its horrifying details of Schubart's imprisonment climaxes in the very last sentence of Section 9. Its wording reminds readers of Schiller's own moral dramaturgy: "[Schubart] was broken in ten years' confinement in a fortress: brainwashing in the direct mode still existed" (STPS 73).

Readers of *Structural Transformation* have to turn back to the diagram in Section 4 (STPS 30) to realize that the book's grounding of the bourgeois intellectuals in the intimate sphere of the bourgeois family as "humanity's genuine site" morally elevates the significance of Schubart's despotic incarceration. It graphically turns it into a crime against humankind. However, these normative origins of universal human rights remain ambivalent. To this day, the struggle to safeguard these human rights also for *non-bourgeois* intellectuals in bourgeois society continues.

Nevertheless, on the eve of the bicentennial of the French Revolution, Habermas still highlighted the "anarchistic, hence *power-dissolving*, consequences of public discussion" (BFN 480, emphasis in the original). In Koselleck's words: "For Schiller the stage is a place of moral jurisdiction where, in majestic splendor, 'truth incorruptible . . . sits in judgment.' The moral stage provides an exalted view of the world divided into beauty and horror to subject the ruling politics to its criticism. The stage becomes a tribunal" (CC 100–01).

Schiller's seminal definition of the bourgeois theater's moral jurisdiction very precisely follows Locke's distinction between the "Law of Opinion or Representation" and the "Civil Law": "The jurisdiction of the stage begins at the point where the sphere of secular law ends" (quoted in CC 98). This strict separation gives "the stage the freedom to become the 'common channel through which the light filters down to the thoughtful, superior portion of the nation'" (quoted in CC 101).

Moreover, he directly applies to this central institution of the literary public sphere Locke's other definition of the "Law of Opinion or Reputation" as the "Measure of Virtue and Vice": "It punishes a thousand vices which [Civil Law] tolerates with impunity while a thousand virtues kept secret by the latter are recommended from the stage" (quoted in CC 99). In short: "Precisely this inadequacy . . . of political laws . . . determines the moral influence of the stage" (quoted in CC 100).

As a "moral institution" of the literary public sphere the bourgeois stage thus separates "the just from the unjust and in the course of this separation the 'mighty' and 'the rulers,' whose 'justice is blinded by gold and revels in the pay of vice,' are vanquished by the more just verdict of the stage" (CC 101). Accordingly, Schiller confirms *Structural Transformation*'s analysis by functionally converting the legitimate theater into a sphere that facilitates the "critique of public authority" (STPS 51). In this process, the "moral tribunal" becomes "political criticism" that unmasks "the political law" of "the rulers" as "immoral" (CC 102, 100).

Juxtaposing "freedom and despotism," Schiller holds up a mirror to "that 'peculiar group of people,' the politicians" (quoted in CC 102). Toward the end of a century that, in *Structural Transformation*'s narrative, began with the rising bourgeois public holding up a mirror to itself in the moral weeklies to learn about its own humanity originating in the conjugal family's intimate sphere, Schiller is ready to speak truth to power:

> Only [on the moral stage] do the great men of the world get to hear [what they otherwise] never or only rarely get to hear—truth; what they never or only rarely get to see, they see here—the human being. (quoted in CC 100; cf. HPSC 74)

Above all, Schiller confirms *Structural Transformation*'s implied inclusion of "moral-political action" in its theory reconstruction of Kant's "unofficial" quest for a "cosmopolitan condition." Unmasking "the great men of the world" as "wicked men" before the "moral tribunal" is not sufficient. Schiller thus issues "a call to action: 'We must evade them or meet them, we must undermine them or be vanquished by them'" (quoted in CC 102, 103).

Readers have to research this context on their own to fill in the key gaps in Habermas's reception of Koselleck's interpretation of the "Process of Criticism." Both authors arrive at the same destination, namely, the French Revolution, but with diametrically opposed intentions. For *Structural Transformation*, this development of a "morally pretentious rationality" terminates in the "sovereignty of reason," for *Critique and Crisis* in regicide and Condorcet's suicide.

Koselleck's open condemnation of the French Revolution is straightforward. Habermas's tacit celebration of it is rather enigmatic. After reading Habermas's 1960 discussion of "moral-political action" as a part of Kant's "unofficial" thought, one would have expected its inclusion in *Structural Transformation*—as well as the selection of Schiller's matching "call to action" quoted in Koselleck's 1959 book.

Instead, even the valorization of *The Robbers* as a contribution to the early political public sphere is relegated to an endnote. Making the connections between all three transparent, would have helped the reader to better understand key components of the concept of a "morally pretentious rationality." After all, Schiller emphasized in a letter to his patron, Prince Friedrich Christian, that in "the cardinal question of moral theory, [his] thought is completely Kantian" (quoted in HPSC 69).

Of course, Kant and Schiller's matching thoughts would follow different trajectories *after* the Jacobin phase of the French Revolution. In 1798, Kant would in spite of the potentially "dangerous consequences" still *publicly* reveal his moral attitude toward the French Revolution, that "borders on enthusiasm." Neither the "misery" nor the "atrocities" of the Jacobin Terror kept him from issuing his call "to rise up," when "favorable circumstances present themselves." For he never doubted that the Revolution is "intimately interwoven with the interests of humanity" (quoted in Preuss 1990/1995: 41 and in HPSC 27).

In stark contrast, by 1795 Schiller's moral-practical revolutionary spirit had been largely sublimated in his vision of an "aesthetic utopia." His withdrawal from the political public sphere to the merely literary one became apparent in his prospectus for his journal *Horae*, which invited "all the great names of German literature and philosophy." The degree of self-censorship in his prospectus was rather comprehensive. First, "there was to be no mention of 'anything related to established religion and the political constitution." Second, "the events of the Revolution and the war" were to be excluded (quoted in HPSC 233).

Interestingly, the post-revolutionary positions of Kant and Schiller thus would be the reverse from their pre-revolutionary ones. Only a few months after Kant published his respectful plea for the "free and open examination" of Church and State, Schiller would stage his rebellious play *The Robbers* that triggered both his arrest on orders from Prince Eugen and his honorary citizenship during the French Revolution. Conversely, the post-revolutionary Kant was willing to face the "dangerous consequences" of his public enthusiasm for the French Revolution while, at the same time, Schiller's *Horae* self-censored any reference to it.

7.6. SHAFTESBURY'S MORAL SENSE AND MANDEVILLE'S DISCOVERY OF CIVILIZED BARBARISM

"Further Reflections" explains that "the withdrawal of the ideals of bourgeois humanism" deeply affected Habermas's original public sphere concept. In the words of the translators of his 1990 preface to the new German edition of *Structural Transformation*, they were "cashed in" in the context of "the civilized barbarisms of the twentieth century." Without a commitment to these ideals that inform the "morally pretentious rationality" as the central norm of the bourgeois public sphere, ideology critique loses one side in its juxtaposition of constitutional norm and constitutional reality. Accordingly, it can no longer dialectically advance (FRPS 442).

As is apparent in "Juliette or Enlightenment and Morality," Horkheimer had a similar but even more intense experience between 1936 when he published "Authority and the Family" and 1944 when he wrote this "Excursus

II" in *Dialectic of Enlightenment*. When "the ocean of open violence really broke into Europe," political domination revealed itself as "archaic terror in a fascistically rationalized form" (DE 86, 87, translation modified; DA 78, 79). He thus witnessed the "civilized barbarisms" of World War II when the country that prided itself on the bourgeois ideals of Kant and Schiller unleashed its technologically advanced *Blitzkrieg*.

Small wonder that the appended note "On the Critique of the Philosophy of History," which he probably also authored, ascribed to the philosophy of German Idealism responsibility for the "barbaric acts" perpetrated by "the country of poets and thinkers." It is plausible that under such circumstances Horkheimer no longer could maintain his idealistic view that "the bourgeois family leads not only to bourgeois authority but to a premonition of a better human condition" (STPS 260-61n48, emphasis added, SÖ 309n48). However, he also *inadvertently* revealed why until then the civilized barbarisms of modernity which Mandeville discovered failed to strike a responsive chord with the bourgeoisie. To quote the memorable words of the leading founder of Critical Theory: "Previously, only the poor and the *savages* were exposed to the fury of the capitalist elements" (DE 86, emphasis added; DA 78).

As Thomas McCarthy analyzes in *Race, Empire, and the Idea of Human Development* (2009), Locke, as "an original shareholder in the Royal African Company" chartered in 1672, "famously . . . declared America to be a 'vacant land' occupied by nomadic *savages*, who had failed to heed God's command to cultivate the earth" as well as "Nature's law that conferred ownership upon those who did so." Accordingly, his political theory in his *Second Treatise* contrasts "the idle, irrational, '*wild Indian*' wandering the 'uncultivated waste' of America and the industrious, rational, civilized planter harvesting its bounty" (McCarthy 2009: 167, emphasis added).

As Eric Williams explains in his path-breaking study *Capitalism & Slavery* (1944), the Royal African Company, which between 1680 and 1686 had transported an annual average of 5,000 slaves, lost its monopoly in 1698. Instead, the business-oriented Modern Whigs established "the right of a free trade in slaves . . . as a fundamental and natural right of Englishmen." As a result, the Bristol slave traders alone shipped a total of 160,950 African slaves to the plantations between 1698 and 1707—thus more than tripling the annual average rate of the Royal African Company (Williams 1944/1994: 32, 33).

Most of the African slaves were shipped to sugar plantations. In *The Wealth of Nations*, Smith states: "In our sugar colonies . . . the whole work is done by slaves. . . . The profits of a sugar plantation in any of our West Indian colonies are generally much greater than those of any other cultivation that is known either in Europe or America." In another context of his bourgeois classic, Smith was even more specific: "It is commonly said, that a sugar planter expects that the rum and molasses should defray the expence of his cultivation, and that his sugar should be all clear profit" (Smith 1776/1994: 418–19, 180–81).

In *The British Seaborne Empire* (2004), Jeremy Black calculates that between the 1710s and the 1770s, average annual revenues from sugar shipments to England from the Caribbean rose from under 1 million pounds sterling to above 3 million. Similarly, the annual shipments of rum to England rose from 207 gallons in 1698 "to an annual average of 2 million gallons in 1771–5." Given the "considerable capital expenditure required for sugar production" (Smith), such "clear" sugar profits are astounding. Planters needed a "large, expendable and easily replaced labour force," because the "back-breaking work" under conditions of extreme heat, humidity, and frequent tropical diseases caused a "high death rate." Slavery provided that work force (Black 2004: 63).

Mandeville who was raised and educated in the Dutch Republic had witnessed the public debate about these ethical challenges even before settling in London. In *The Dutch Seaborne Empire, 1600-1800* (1965), J.R. Boxer quotes Count John Maurice of Nassau-Siegen, who, as governor of Netherlands Brazil from 1637 to 1644, tried to use free white labor in the sugar mills of Pernambuco. However, he soon concluded that "it is not possible to effect anything in Brazil without slaves." In other words, the needs of capital accumulation had to defeat ethical concerns: "if anyone feels that this is wrong, it is a futile scruple" (quoted in Boxer 1965: 239).

Nevertheless, this "futile scruple" initially exercised the Dutch "Calvinist consciences," as Lewis Feuer discusses in *Spinoza and the Rise of Liberalism* (1958). However, in the end it was economic necessity that forced the Dutch colonists in Brazil to use African slave labor, in spite of their qualms about "the trade in human flesh" (Feuer 1958: 42). That's why "the *savages* were exposed to the fury of the capitalist elements" (DE 86, emphasis added; DA 78) and the civilized barbarism of modernity developed already in the seventeenth century.

It is against this background that Mandeville wrote his satirical *Fable of the Bees*, when Anthony Cooper, Third Earl of Shaftesbury sought to replace his tutor Locke's moral relativism in his *Essay concerning Human Understanding* with the claim about an inner "moral sense" in "An Inquiry Concerning Virtue, or Merit" (1699). In the fully developed form of his intellectual construct, Shaftesbury asserted in his *Characteristics of Men, Manners, Opinions* (1711) that this *natural* "moral sense" distinguishes between right and wrong, *without* the need of any input from the rational-critical faculties. Regarding "the emancipation of bourgeois morality (*Sittlichkeit*) from moral theology" (STPS 43; SÖ 60), the moral weeklies now had a choice between Locke's moral philosophy with its reflections on moral relativity and the "optimistic doctrines of Lord Shaftesbury, that human nature is good and all is for the best in this harmonious world."

This is how J. B. Bury's *The Idea of Progress: An Inquiry into Its Origin and Growth* (1932/1987) sums up Shaftesbury's elaboration of a "moral sense" that is allegedly "implanted in our nature" and "inwardly joined to us." In 2004, Himmelfarb would still insist in *The Roads to Modernity: The British, French, and American Enlightenment* that Shaftesbury's claim about this "moral sense" was "not a Rousseauean idealization of human nature, of man before being corrupted by society." Conversely, Bury sees no difference between Rousseau and Shaftesbury's views in this regard. He thus posits, more than 70 years before Himmelfarb, that "Rousseau ... agreed with Shaftesbury as to the natural goodness of man," while agreeing with Mandeville that innocence of manners is incompatible with the conditions of a civilized society" (quoted in HPSC 203, 193).

Significantly, Shaftesbury's text deeply influenced the moral weeklies in the emerging literary public sphere. It served as the lodestar for "the cultivated refinement" that Addison and Steele's *The Spectator* sought to communicate to the rising bourgeoisie. Above all, its optimistic anthropology allowed them to bracket the barbarism of slavery as the main driver of the capital accumulation needed for advancing civilization. Addison's essay "Our *English* Merchant" can thus wax eloquent about the civilizing effects of global trade when the "Fruits of *Portugal* are corrected by the Products of *Barbadoes*" and the "Brocade Petticoat rises out of the Mines of Peru." Needless to say, he did not publish a single word about the barbaric working conditions on the sugar plantations of Barbados and in the mines of Peru (cf. HPSC 193, 196).

Chapter Eight

Habermas's Unexplained Methodology

A Complex
"Ideology-Critical Procedure"

Structural Transformation's methodology was more than five years in the making. As stated above under 1.2, its origins date back to Habermas's first research grant from the German Science Foundation. He received it in spring 1955 for his study on "The Concept of 'Ideology' and the Ideology-Critical Procedure" (Yos 2019: 154).

Almost a year before he became Adorno's assistant at the University of Frankfurt in February 1956, Habermas already set out to research the specific sociology the Frankfurt School in exile had developed in the United States during the 1930s. Only in the "winter term 1956–7" would he also attend Adorno's seminars about "The Dialectic of Enlightenment" and "The Concept of Ideology" (HB 78).

It took until 1958, when discussing the "Concept of Political Participation," before Habermas drew on the two-page note, titled "Philosophy and the Division of Labor," that is appended to *Dialectic of Enlightenment*. Only then would he adopt Horkheimer and Adorno's as well as Marcuse's Hegelian-Marxist critique of ideology. As mentioned above in chapter 1 and under 5.1, in 1971 he would specifically identify this introduction to the book "Student and Politics" as the forerunner of *Structural Transformation* regarding his analysis of "the historical interconnection between capitalist development and the origin and decomposition of the liberal public sphere" (TAP 4; TUP 11).

8.1. THE HEGELIAN-MARXIST CRITIQUE OF IDEOLOGY AND HEGEL'S DISCOVERY OF THE "PROFOUND SPLIT IN CIVIL SOCIETY"

In 1958, Habermas referred to the ideology-critical approach of detecting and accepting the bourgeois ideals as the "objective meaning of existing institutions" only when beginning the concluding part of his introductory essay. However, he introduced its key phrase "objective meaning of institutions" more than 40 pages earlier, in the second paragraph of his essay. He thus began his discussion of political participation by directly criticizing contemporary political science for reducing democracy to a purely technical method of arranging political decision-making. Instead, democratic practice should be deducted from the philosophical and legal principles of popular sovereignty and the constitutional state as "the objective meaning of institutions" (CPP 9).

Moreover, neither at the start nor toward the end of his essay did Habermas explain the methodological criteria used for identifying these ideals and bestowing validity on his analysis. Nevertheless, he at least quoted a key source for his ideology-critical method. Something he would no longer do in *Structural Transformation*. Accordingly, readers are very much on their own when trying to understand the methodological keywords "idea," "ideology," "more than ideology," "objective meaning of institutions," "fiction," "reality," "institutionalized," and "actually realized."

In light of the global distribution of his book, it is fair to assume that a huge number of readers have been puzzling over what Habermas exactly means when he writes in Section 6 about the intimate sphere of the bourgeois family that its "ideas of freedom, love, and cultivation of the person . . . are surely *more than just ideology*" and claims that as "an *objective meaning . . . of the actual institution* . . . these ideas are *also reality*" (STPS 48, emphasis added; SÖ 65, cf. 7.4 above). After all, on the preceding page they had just read that "the conjugal family's self-image of its intimate sphere collides even within the consciousness of the bourgeoisie itself with the *real* functions of the bourgeois family." For "it plays its precisely defined role in the process of the reproduction of capital" (STPS 47, emphasis added; SÖ 64).

Moreover, the bourgeois family "serves especially the task of that difficult mediation through which, in spite of *the illusion of freedom*, strict conformity with societally necessary requirements is brought about." Finally, even "the contractual form of marriage, imputing the autonomous declaration of will on the part of both partners, is largely a *fiction* (STPS 47, emphasis added; SÖ 64-65). In response, many readers will ask how the bourgeois intimate sphere's idea of freedom and autonomy can simultaneously be an *illusion* and also the *reality*?

In addition, readers have to take at face value not only the unexplained contradiction between the idea and the reality of the bourgeois intimate sphere in Section 6, but also the one defining the eighteenth-century institutions of the public sphere in Section 5. There they are first presented with the thesis that in "the *Tischgesellschaften, salons*, and coffee houses" social and political status is disregarded "altogether" to establish the "parity of 'common humanity'" on whose basis alone "the authority of the better argument can assert itself." Afterwards, one is directly confronted with the anti-thesis: "Not that this idea of the public is *actually realized* in earnest in the coffee houses, the *salons*, and the societies. . . ." Followed by the cryptic synthesis that through the establishment of these institutions of the public sphere this idea "has become *institutionalized* and thereby stated as an *objective claim*" (STPS 37, emphasis added; SÖ 52).

Readers thus have to wonder whether different criteria apply to the institution of the bourgeois family's intimate sphere compared to the bourgeoisie's institution of the literary public sphere? On one hand, *Structural Transformation* claims that the "ideas of freedom, love, and cultivation of the person . . . are surely *more than just ideology*," because as "an *objective meaning . . . of the actual institution . . .* these ideas are *also reality*." On the other hand, the book seems to introduce a distinction between an idea's *objective meaning* (*objektiver Sinn*) in Section 6 and its *objective claim* (*objektiver Anspruch*) in Section 5. The latter can thus become only *institutionalized*, but not *actually realized*. Does this mean that Habermas ranked the "ideas of freedom, love, and cultivation of the person" higher than the one about the "parity of 'common humanity,'" in which social and political status is disregarded "altogether" to establish a basis on which "the authority of the better argument can assert itself?" (STPS 48, SÖ 65; STPS 37, SÖ 52).

In any event, in 1982 Habermas would at least explain *Structural Transformation*'s dialectical method to his readers, even if only *indirectly* so: "Marx's critique of ideology . . . presupposed that there were two sides to the potential for reason articulated in the 'bourgeois ideals' and in the 'objective meaning of institutions.'" Primarily, this potential for reason "gives the ideologies of the ruling classes the deceptive appearance of persuasive theories." Hence, they can "claim to be in the interest of the general public," while actually only serving "a dominating segment of society." Beneath this deceptive appearance, however, the same potential for reason "provides a point of departure for an *immanent critique* of these ideas" (EME 20–21, emphasis added).

Thanks to this dialectical procedure, the critique of ideology can discover even in these "instrumentalized and abused ideas" a "rational kernel" (Marx). That is, "a piece of existing reason hidden to itself." In short, Habermas's explanation invokes the signature expression used in Critical Theory.

To access and harvest this "potential for reason articulated in the 'bour-geois ideals' and in the 'objective meaning of institutions,'" such an immanent critique has to follow Marx in his use of Hegelian dialectics. Only this dialectical method of analyzing historical developments makes it pos-sible for *Structural Transformation*'s "sociological investigation of historical trends" to define itself as proceeding "on a level of generality," on which concrete events and processes can only "be interpreted as instances of a more general social development" (STPS xviii). While such a "sociological procedure . . . seems less bound to the specifics of the historical material," Habermas claims that it nevertheless "observes *its own equally strict criteria* for the structural analysis of the interdependencies at the level of society as a whole." However, his "Author's Preface" does not explain these "*meth-odological preliminaries*" and their "strict criteria" any further (STPS xviii, emphasis added).

Hence, this guide has to again turn to "The Classical Doctrine of Politics in Relation to Social Philosophy," first presented in December 1961, where Habermas posits that Hegel, standing on the "level of modern science, . . . invokes the *methodologically certain* self-reflection of science" to develop "the methodological primacy of the *dialectical procedure* over the analytic in the investigation of the things themselves" (TAP 80, emphasis added; TUP 84). For Hegel's "dialectical procedure" provides *Structural Transforma-tion* with a methodological alternative to the "so-called structural-functional theory" in advanced "formal sociology" (STPS xviii). After all, by "com-prehending history dialectically" Hegel can "sublate scientifically based social philosophy into a dialectical theory of society." As a result, he has the freedom to "*select and develop the categories* in such a way that this theory at every step is guided and permeated by the self-consciousness of its own relationship to praxis" (TAP 80, 81, emphasis added; TUP 84).

Equipped with Hegelian-Marxist dialectics, *Structural Transformation* could seemingly turn the fictions in the Kantian system from a liability into an asset regarding the book's search for normative potential. Specifically, "it was possible to derive from [these fictions] the idea of the bourgeois public sphere *precisely* in its connection with the presupposition of a natural basis of the juridical condition" (STPS 117, emphasis added). In his lecture "Between Philosophy and Science: Marxism as Critique," presented in Zürich in 1960, Habermas draws on Bloch to take this approach one step further and literally look at fiction as the preferred object of interest for the bourgeois reading public. While Marx discovered the "utopian core" within the "ideological shell," Bloch can glean from his study of fictions also the "utopian surplus" of ideas:

. . . what arouses [Bloch's] interest is not the state, but *fiction* about the state, not the norms of law which are in force, but *theories* of justice. For obviously ideas will reveal their utopian surplus, that goes beyond ideology, all the more readily, *the more indirect the mediations that relate them to social conflicts*. . . (TAP 240, emphasis added; TUP 268)

Readers are forced to reflect on the power of such fictions after realizing that Habermas presented the essence of his thoughts on Kant and Hegel in Sections 13 and 14 *already in 1960* and *not* developed it only in 1961 as the Author's Preface from Autumn 1961 seems to suggest. For the preface states that these sections were not included in his *Habilitationsschrift* submitted early in 1961. Hence, readers might get the impression that Habermas had researched and added Hegel's fundamental critique of Kant's idea of the bourgeois public sphere to balance what in 1992 he would call *Structural Transformation*'s methodologically illegitimate idealizations especially in Sections 4 to 7 and 11 to 13 of the book.

However, Habermas's conference presentation from October 1960 reveals that, months before finishing *Structural Transformation*, he was already fully aware that *as early as 1821* Hegel's *Elements of the Philosophy of Right* "decisively destroyed the liberal pretenses upon which the self-interpretation of public opinion as nothing but plain reason rested" (STPS 118). In other words, more than a decade before in Section 11 the very same liberal pretenses would allegedly still "have credibility" — thus allowing the "Third Estate" to "be set up as the nation" in the British election reform of 1832 (STPS 87). Since the Section 14 endnote 98 on page 273 does not give the original German publication date of Hegel's classic, readers not familiar with it might indeed falsely assume that the liberal "self-interpretation of public opinion as nothing but plain reason" still had credibility in Section 11 *before* it was "decisively destroyed" in Section 14.

In October 1960, Habermas acknowledged already on the third page of his remarks, that "the bourgeois consciousness," which learned through the political function of the public sphere "to interpret itself as the public opinion, articulates itself in a series of fictions which extend into the Kantian system" (VPM 95). The key fiction of a justice inherent in free market exchanges facilitated at the time the common identification of private property owners with autonomous human beings as such. This fiction of the liberal bourgeoisie generated their "other identification of an opinion based on the public use of their reason with the tenets of rational natural law and the welfare of all." Only through the interconnection of both fictitious identifications can Kant guarantee the convergence of politics and morality within the politically functioning rational-critical public sphere (VPM 103).

Moreover, Habermas immediately added that Hegel's *Philosophy of Right* exploded all these fictions. Specifically, Hegel analyzed how the unregulated development of bourgeois society leads to an accumulation of wealth on one side and to the dependency and poverty of the laboring classes on the other. In this context, Habermas refers to Hegel's "famous phrase that in spite of its abundance of wealth, bourgeois society is not rich enough to ameliorate its abundance of poverty." According to Habermas, in this phrase "Hegel sums up his *empirical* arguments against Kant's conviction that, based on a legal condition sanctioned by rational natural law, reason can be politically realized through *moral* actions" (VPM 104, emphasis added).

Given *Structural Transformation*'s mining of fictions for normative potential, this focus on Hegel's *empirical* arguments is particularly relevant for the reader. Since Hegel referred to "the political economy of Smith, Say, and Ricardo as the manifestation of rationality," it was not a critique of their doctrines that "decisively destroyed" Kant's "liberal pretenses." Instead, it was his empirical "insight into the at once anarchic and antagonistic character" of the private sphere of commodity exchange and social labor as a "system of needs" that would falsify Kant's theses (STPS 118).

In stark contrast to Kant, whose attention to and knowledge of political economy was relatively limited, as Manfred Riedel explains in his seminal study from 1969 on the *Philosophy of Right*, Hegel had not only studied it but also followed the economic and financial news from England ever since he had been a tutor in the household of a Frankfurt businessman from 1797 to 1800. Specifically, he left annotated excerpts from parliamentary debates about the Poor Laws that document that he had analyzed the Speenhamland system of poor relief from 1795 as an attempt by the aristocracy to pacify restive masses lacking the means of subsistence. Already in his Jena lectures from 1805/1806, Hegel connects sudden unemployment in whole branches of industrial production, caused by changing fashions and new inventions, to the vast poverty he contrasts with the newly created great wealth (see HPSC 110).

On one hand, *Philosophy of Right*'s section 245, the climax of which Section 14 quotes (STPS 118-19), thus only sums up Hegel's analysis of the English example during the previous two decades. On the other hand, he now realizes that the logic of liberal capitalism has to keep the state from *productively* employing the "suffering classes"—a solution he had recommended in Jena. In short, he sketches, in Habermas's words, a "theory of underconsumption" (STPS 119) that "diagnoses a conflict of interest that discredits the common and *allegedly universal* interest of property-owning private people engaged in political debate as a *solely particular* one" (STPS 119, emphasis added; see HPSC 110).

Specifically, Hegel concludes that "to maintain the increasingly impoverished mass at its normal standard of living . . . their livelihood might be facilitated by work (that is, the opportunity to work) which would increase the volume of production; but it is precisely in overproduction and the lack of proportionate numbers of consumers who are themselves productive that the evil [Übel] consists . . . ." Only after this precise analysis does Hegel add his "famous phrase" that Habermas referred to *already* in 1960: "This shows that, despite an *excess of wealth*, civil society is *not wealthy enough*—that is, its own resources are not sufficient—to prevent an excess of poverty" (quoted in HPSC 110, emphasis in the original).

Just how knowledgeable and astute Hegel's reflections were can be demonstrated by a comparison with a similar analysis by the influential Whig politician Lord Henry Petty, Marquis of Lansdowne, in the House of Lords on November 30, 1819. As Barry Gordon quotes in his study *Political Economy in Parliament, 1819-1823* (1976), Lansdowne added another aspect that ties in with Hegel's examination of overproduction accompanied by underconsumption: "In the face of falling demand, 'the master-manufacturers lowered the rate of wages; this reduction induced the labourers to work a greater number of hours, and thus more goods were produced, which served only to add to the evil'" (quoted in HPSC 110–11).

Significantly, Hegel's empirical insights date from the same year as Lansdowne's. By 1819, Hegel had completed the draft of *Philosophy of Right*. However, he did not publish it. In September 1819, the Carlsbad conference of German states imposed censorship on all academic publications. Only after making revisions and composing a new preface in June 1820, did Hegel go ahead with the publication of his text early in 1821 (see HPSC 111).

Above all, Hegel's analysis of really existing liberal capitalism deconstructs Kant's claim from 1793 that all members of civil society can acquire property and thus private autonomy, provided they have sufficient "talent, industry, and good fortune" (quoted in STPS 110). Two centuries later, Hegel's conclusion that in civil society's liberalized markets the "natural inequality" is raised to "an inequality of skills and resources, and even to one of moral and intellectual attainment" (quoted in STPS 118), remains strikingly current. Already in the year his draft was finished, Hegel's discovery of this "profound split in civil society" (STPS 118) dovetailed with statements by several members of the House of Commons in parliamentary debate on December 9, 1819. In the memorable words of the Tory member of Parliament James Stuart Wortley: "Between the laboring mechanics and the master-manufacturers, there was an opposition of interests, and violent disputes which had lasted for years" (quoted in HPSC 111).

Readers will recall from studying Section 15 in the context of 5.4 above that identifying the origins of the "profound split in civil society" for a date even earlier than 1819 contradicts *Structural Transformation*'s claim, that "the coarser forms of violent conflict" developed in the British public sphere only with "the Chartist movement" (STPS 132, 131). For the *People's Charter* was launched only in 1838. And the leading newspaper of the Chartist movement, *The Northern Star*, had been founded by Feargus O'Connor just a few months earlier, in November 1837 (see HPSC 113). Needless to say, this contradiction also affects Habermas's assertion that in 1832 "the bourgeois class interest could be identified with the general interest" and thus the "Third Estate" be credibly "set up as the nation" (STPS 87).

However, readers will encounter a much larger and rather enigmatic contradiction when they compare the impact that Hegel's *Philosophy of Right* had on the credibility of Kant's liberal model of the public sphere with the one caused by the alleged demise of Say's Law *fifty years later*. Logically, one would assume that once Hegel "decisively destroyed the liberal pretenses upon which the self-interpretation of public opinion as nothing but plain reason rested" (STPS 118), *Structural Transformation*'s narrative could no longer employ Say's Law to posit an alleged freedom of civil society not only from domination but also "from any kind of coercion" (STPS 79). But this is exactly what Habermas does. Only in the early 1870s will in his narrative Say's Law "come to grief" (STPS 144, see 5.4 above). Even though Hegel had already revealed "the at once anarchic and antagonistic character" of civil society in Section 14, this private sphere of commodity exchange and social labor, with the intimate sphere of the bourgeois family at its core, is only "forced to relinquish even the flimsiest pretense of being a sphere in which the influence of power is suspended" in Section 16, *half a century later* (STPS 144).

8.2. EXTREME STYLIZATIONS: *STRUCTURAL TRANSFORMATION'S* RELIANCE ON DOBB'S HISTORICAL MATERIALISM

Readers may be inclined to ask how Habermas can rationally reconstruct the ideal-typical stylization of a society free from economic coercion and political domination, if Hegel discovered the "profound split in civil society" already for 1821, "On the Concept of Political Participation" unequivocally declares that such a society has never existed, and Section 15 joins the "liberalist apologetic" (STPS 130) in fundamentally questioning "the very presuppositions of a natural basis [for civil society] upon which the idea of a political public sphere rests" (STPS 131)?

The answer is complex and contradictory. For *Structural Transformation* is tasked with finding a substitute for the "natural" self-regulation of civil society through Say's Law. One that can plausibly explain how the political public sphere of the bourgeois constitutional state could be institutionalized in the 1832 Reform Bill *as if* this presupposition existed. To do so, one has to employ the Hegelian-Marxist ideology-critical procedure in a rather elaborate fashion.

Proceeding dialectically, Section 16 can discover this substitute in the unique "historical circumstances" of the model case of British development for the period between 1775 and 1875. For that purpose, it has to appropriate Maurice Dobb's historical-materialist stylizations as its ideology-critical procedure. However, readers encounter obstacles when trying to access and evaluate the claim by Dobb that from "the perspective of the overall development of capitalism the period between 1775 and 1875 appears to be no more than 'a vast secular boom'" (quoted in STPS 144).

For the German original of *Structural Transformation* falsely ascribes the crucial phrase "a vast secular boom" to Dobb himself. Moreover, while the English translation of the book correctly identifies the staunch "free market" advocate J. R. Hicks as its author, it still lacks a bibliographical reference to the publication that contains this quote. Clearly, readers need to know the source, *Value and Capital* (1939), because Dobb and Hicks work with very different understandings of the term "secular" (cf. HPSC 100–101).

Adding to this complexity is the fact that both interpretations are covered by *Webster's New Collegiate Dictionary*, which defines "secular" as "occurring once in an age or century." Obviously, Dobb implicitly uses the latter part of this definition to justify his choice of the boom's duration, namely, the *one hundred* years between 1775 and 1875. But in his decisive footnote in *Value and Capital*, Hicks does not leave any doubt that his argument is based not on "a century" but on an "age": "one cannot repress the thought that perhaps the whole Industrial Revolution of the last *two hundred* years has been nothing but a vast secular boom" (quoted in HPSC 101, emphasis added). In short, for Dobb the alleged vast boom already ended with the Great Depression of the 1870s, for Hicks only with the more severe one of the 1930s.

In "Further Reflections," Habermas himself alerts the reader to the "great risks" that are inherent in any sociological generalization, "especially for someone who, unlike the historian, does not go back to the sources but instead relies on the secondary literature" (FRPS 422–23). Whether it happened inadvertently or intentionally, it was enticing for Dobb's *Studies in the Development of Capitalism* (1946) to present this distortion of the analysis, which Hicks as a Austrian School economist published during the Great Depression of the 1930s. If even for a *laissez-faire* economist that "vast secular boom" terminated already in the first Great Depression of the 1870s, unimpeachable evidence existed for the critique of capitalism as an anarchic and destructive order of society.

Significantly, his sympathetic biographer Timothy Shenk acknowledges in *Maurice Dobb: Political Economist* (2013) that the ends of Dobb's Hegelian-Marxist philosophy of history could justify the means of its application in his scholarship. In this context, Shenk gives the following example:

> Dobb's primitive accumulation two-step did vital work for his analysis. . . . . The solution was attractive enough that he could dismiss concerns over its scanty empirical foundation. Having demonstrated that the process was "necessary" for capitalism's development, he assured his readers that it must have occurred. (quoted in HPSC 101)

For *Structural Transformation*, Dobb's interpretation of a vast secular boom triggered by the Industrial Revolution offers a functional substitute for Say's Law. Together with its history of decline in the first Great Depression, it also provides an economic parallel to the philosophical as well as political rise and fall of the bourgeois ideals in the liberal model of the public sphere in the bourgeois constitutional state. In Dobb's "golden age" of liberal capitalism (Shenk), it was "vigorous, prosperous and flushed with adventurous optimism." In other words, it matched the 1848 exclamation in *The Communist Manifesto* that "the bourgeoisie has played an extremely revolutionary role upon the stage of history." For it "was the first to show us what human activity is capable of achieving." Above all, capitalism "cannot exist without incessantly revolutionizing the instruments of production" (quoted in HPSC 101).

Readers will remember from studying Section 10 that such an emphatic valorization of liberal capitalism is reflected in Habermas's identification of it as the "one blissful moment in the long history of capitalist development" (STPS 79) that allegedly facilitated the "effective institutionalization" of a rational-critical public sphere as the organizational principle of the bourgeois constitutional state. Interestingly, it ties in with the assessment that W. W. Rostow published in 1960 in *The Stages of Economic Growth: A Non-Communist Manifesto* regarding the "take-off" of the capitalist economy in England between 1783 and 1802 (HPSC 104). An endnote to Section 16 includes a lengthy quote from Dobb that celebrates this unprecedented degree of economic growth. It partially reads as follows:

> An age of technical change which rapidly augmented the productivity of labour also witnessed an abnormally rapid increase in the ranks of the proletariat,

together with a series of events which simultaneously widened the field of investment and the market for consumption goods to an unprecedented degree. . . . . (quoted in STPS 277n4)

Once again, Dobb's stylization is inspired by a famous (and controversial) claim in *The Communist Manifesto*: "The bourgeoisie, by the rapid improvement of all instruments of production, by the immensely facilitated means of communication, draws all, even the most barbarian, nations into civilization" (quoted in HPSC 102). In light of these stylizations of liberal capitalism, readers can now see why its unique historical constellation can substitute for Say's Law in *Structural Transformation*'s narrative. After all, Say, unlike Dobb and Marx, could not bracket the "general glut" controversy. Confronted in 1820 with overwhelming empirical evidence against the validity of his Law of Markets, he felt compelled to compare himself to Copernicus and Galileo to seemingly prop up his counterfactual argument.

Of course, Marx thought dialectically and embraced the "system of commercial liberty" that Say advocated only as a *tactical* move. For "Free Trade" hastens "the Social Revolution" by pushing "to the extreme the antagonism between bourgeoisie and proletariat," as he declared in his address to the Democratic Association of Brussels in January 1848. Similar to "The Absolute Concept of the Constitution," Marx posited an absolute concept of the economy whose dialectic between the forces and the relations of production was fueled by conceiving them in the form of absolute generalizations. Accordingly, *The Communist Manifesto* juxtaposes the bourgeoisie's *incessant revolutionizing* of the productive forces that draws *even the most barbarian* nations into civilization with an equally absolute antagonism in the relations of production. In such an extreme stylization, the "commercial crises" seemingly can "by their periodical return put on trial, *each time more threateningly*, the *existence of the entire* bourgeois system" (quoted in HPSC 103, emphasis added).

For Dobb the start of the first Great Depression thus marked "the watershed between two stages of Capitalism." Since from his perspective it would have to eventually revolutionize itself into oblivion, its second stage was "more troubled, more hesitant and some would say, already bearing the marks of senility" (quoted in HPSC 102). This context can explain for the reader the ambivalence Section 15 ascribes to the liberalist interpretation of the bourgeois public sphere. In *Structural Transformation*'s narrative, the theory of liberalism "does not admit to itself the structural conflict of society whose very product it is" (STPS 130). In short, the "anarchic and antagonistic character" of the sphere of commodity exchange and social labor that Hegel had already diagnosed in 1821 (STPS 118).

8.3. AGAINST FACTICITY: HABERMAS'S TACIT USE OF MARCUSE'S "VARIANT OF CRITICAL THEORY"

Without Marcuse's 1937 essay in the *Zeitschrift für Sozialforschung*, Habermas could not have developed his methodology for *Structural Transformation*. Indirectly, he hinted at that fact in his written interview conducted in November 1984 by Dews and Anderson. There he acknowledged using an "inherited theoretical framework" for his 1962 book. Moreover, within this framework he "felt a special affinity with the existentialist, i.e., the Marcusean variant of Critical Theory." Above all, he also confirmed having read in "Frankfurt, from 1956 in other words . . . a few articles from the *Zeitschrift für Sozialforschung*." Finally, in a follow-up interview with Dews and Andersen in Starnberg in December 1984, he specifically referred to Marcuse's essays in the *Zeitschrift*: ". . . while I was working on the concept of ideology . . . I came across Marcuse's early articles" (AS 152, 150, 194; cf. HPSC 230, 241–42).

That confirmation was surprising news when the first interview was published in 1985 and the second one in 1986. For in a German-language interview in 1981, Habermas did not yet acknowledge that he had read Marcuse's 1930s articles after his arrival at Frankfurt's Institute for Social Research in 1956. Instead, he emphasized twice that "they didn't exist," because "Horkheimer had a great fear that we would get to the crate in the Institute's cellar that contained a complete set of the *Zeitschrift*." Although Habermas added that an equally complete set "could have been obtained from [Professor] Carlo Schmidt at the Institute [of Political Science]," that was located not far away, readers of the 1981 interview were left with the impression that he did not access the *Zeitschrift* during his assistantship with Adorno. This impression was reinforced by the use of the above quote from the 1981 interview in the seminal work about *The Frankfurt School* (1986/1994) by Wiggershaus and as recently as 2010 in Specter's intellectual biography of Habermas (AS 95; Wiggershaus 1986/1994: 544; Specter 2010: 31).

This mystery of Horkheimer's shipping crate, which remained unopened after its arrival from the Institute in exile on Morningside Heights in New York City, adds even more suspense to the colorful (academic) politics surrounding the genesis of *Structural Transformation*. For Schmidt's assistant Wilhelm Hennis, a conservative Social Democrat and future informal advisor to Chancellor Helmut Kohl, a Christian Democrat, had acquired the set of the *Zeitschrift* from an antiquarian in Paris to expose Horkheimer, who, situated during the McCarthy era in the heart of United States Occupation Zone, tried to hide his past in a crate in the basement. For good reason. In 1957, the American sociologist Edward Shils, a translator of works by Max Weber, would attack Horkheimer and Adorno in the *Sewanee Review*, alleging that they had been "Marxist socialists." Moreover, in the same year in which the conservative Chancellor Konrad Adenauer won an absolute majority in Parliament by denouncing his Social Democratic opponents with the slogan that "All Roads of Marxism Lead to Moscow," Shils accused these two leading members of the Frankfurt School of veiling their "refined Marxism" in their scholarly work (Shils 1957: 588–89).

When developing his methodology for *Structural Transformation*, Habermas was only too aware of this context. In 1958, when writing about the "objective meaning of institutions" in his essay on political participation, he still included a reference to *Dialectic of Enlightenment*. However, Horkheimer wrote to Adorno that the essay, which was designed as the introduction to an empirical study conducted by their Institute, was too radical and refused to have it published under the auspices of the Institute. By March 1960, in the final version of his critique of *Critique and Crisis* for *Merkur*, Habermas would only cryptically refer to an "objective intention of the public sphere: "Since conflating, on one hand, private views and public opinion, while, on the other hand, discrediting the principle of public debate as one of civil war, Koselleck has to be unable to comprehend *the objective intention of the public sphere*, which, on the basis of a bourgeois society emancipating itself from the [directives of the] state, develops as the new sphere first in England and then in France" (KUK 358, emphasis added). As analyzed above, he continued this veiling of his Marxist ideology critique in his 1962 book.

Interestingly, Horkheimer and Adorno seemingly served as his role models in that regard. In December 1960, he pointed out that such an approach can often be found among "the older scholars who are still connected to the Marxist tradition" and classified it as *"tacit orthodoxy*: the categories of the Marxist theory of labor reveal themselves when used for cultural critique, without being identified as such" (TAP 203; TUP 235, emphasis in the German original). In retrospect, Habermas would indirectly confirm that during the political climate of the 1950s he had consciously engaged in such a tacit use of Marxist methodology. When responding to a question about *Structural Transformation* during a 1979 interview with the philosophers Detlef Horster and Willem van Reijen, Habermas stated that he was "shocked" when after the book's publication the philosopher Karl-Otto Apel, his friend and former mentor at the University of Bonn, "publicly called [him] a Neo-Marxist" (AS 78).

In 1982, Habermas observed that Horkheimer and Adorno's references from 1947 to "the objective meaning of existing institutions" and to accepting "the bourgeois ideals without further consideration" read "like an intrusion from the earlier period of Critical Theory" (EME 20). With regard to the sources quoted in *Structural Transformation*, this observation applies primarily to Horkheimer's text from 1936 about *Authority and Family*. However, regarding its unidentified sources, Marcuse's 1937 essay "Philosophy and Critical Theory" stands out. In 1980, Habermas emphasized that it forms "the center of the Frankfurt School's theory" (quoted in HPSC 37).

As highlighted above in chapter 1, readers can find in Marcuse's concept of ideology, which he develops in this essay, key elements of *Structural Transformation*'s methodology. The level of abstraction which is the hallmark of the book's analyses, is systematically rooted in Marcuse's following thesis:

> The truth which is contained in the philosophical categories, was won by abstracting from the concrete status of the human being; it exists only on that level of abstraction. Reason, spirit, morality, knowledge, happiness are not only categories of bourgeois philosophy but matters of the human race. They have to be preserved as such, even won anew. (PCT 640)

Significantly, readers can locate in Marcuse's essay a key influence for Horkheimer and Adorno's reference to "the objective meaning of existing institutions," which, in spite of all the "distortion" and "manipulation" they have been subjected to, "are still recognizable." For his programmatic essay states that "when Critical Theory deals with the philosophical doctrines in which it was still allowed to speak about the human being, it first addresses the concealments and misinterpretations, which defined the discourse about humanity in the bourgeois period" (PCT 640). Even the title of Horkheimer and Adorno's appended note, namely, "Philosophy and the Division of Labor," reflects a key statement in Marcuse's essay: "Once reason—that is, the rational organization of humankind—has been realized, philosophy will lose its subject matter. For *philosophy*, provided it was more than a business or a discipline within the given *division of labor*, so far existed, because reason had not yet become reality" (PCT 632, emphasis added).

Dialectic of Enlightenment was completed in 1944, before the liberation of the German concentration camps and the dropping of atomic bombs on Hiroshima and Nagasaki informed a global public about these advancements in the civilized barbarism of modernity. In 1980, in his commemorative lecture at Berkeley, Habermas pointed out that soon thereafter Marcuse adopted Horkheimer and Adorno's critique of instrumental reason and later prefaced the English edition of "Philosophy and Critical Theory" as follows: "That . . . this was written before Auschwitz deeply separates it from the present. What was correct in it has become, perhaps not false, but a thing of the past. . . . The end of a historical period and the horror of the one to come were announced in the simultaneity of the civil war in Spain and the trials in Moscow" (quoted in HPSC 50).

Habermas placed this quote, which summarizes a present that was worse than the "bad facticity" in 1937 when Marcuse coined the phrase (PCT 635), in the middle of his lecture. However, he ended it on a very carefully constructed note that selectively quotes Marcuse in a discussion with students at the Free University in Berlin in 1967 to tacitly revive perhaps *the* key dictum in Marcuse's essay from 1937: The individual who "reflects on the idea about the human being has to think in a countermove against facticity. . . . Of course, together with the concrete, with the facticity the thinking subject keeps the misery at bay" (PCT 640).

It is worth looking at Habermas's rational reconstruction of Marcuse's thoughts and arguments in 1967 in detail, because it implicitly illuminates his own motivation when writing the normative essence of *Structural Transformation* "in a countermove against facticity." In this classic example of "the painful hesitations of moral-practical reasoning," Marcuse first responds to a question about humanitarian arguments after Horkheimer's *Eclipse of Reason* (1947): "As to your suspicion about humanitarian arguments. . . . We must finally relearn what we forgot during the fascist period . . . that humanitarian and moral arguments are *not merely deceitful ideology*. Rather, they can and must become central social forces" (quoted in HPSC 50, emphasis added).

Habermas introduced this exchange by setting the scene and providing context for the reader: "Marcuse was exposed to a situation where he knew that *every single word could have irrevocable consequences*. He was invited to talk about the *use of violence*. . ." (HAM 76, emphasis added). The next student question about "the right of resistance" thus could have been dynamite. Habermas builds up to it by placing the student in the intellectual company of *A Dangerous Mind* (Jan-Werner Müller), i.e., Schmitt: "Another student countered [Marcuse's] straight answer with a *moral skepticism* which in my country *often reveals the strong influence of Carl Schmitt* even on the left" (HAM 76, emphasis added; cf. Müller 2003).

In response, Marcuse displayed the "painful hesitations of moral-practical reasoning," which are Habermas's own: "In this moment, Marcuse decided to be *inconsistent rather than irresponsible. He swept aside his own doubts* on a corrupted practical reason which supposedly had been absorbed into a totality of instrumental reason." In Habermas's rendition of a classic example of self-determined will-formation, Marcuse's "answer was *clear, without the slightest ambiguity*." He opened by placing the student's question in context: ". . . appealing to the right of resistance is an appeal to a higher law, which has *universal validity* . . ." Accordingly, "there really is a close connection between the right of resistance and *natural law*." Marcuse then stood his ground:

Now you will say that such a universal higher law simply does not exist. I believe that it does exist. Today we no longer call it *Natural Law* . . . If we appeal
to humanity's right to peace, to the right to abolish exploitation and oppression,
we are . . . talking about . . . in fact, interests demonstrable as *universal rights.*
(quoted in HAM 70–71, emphasis added)

In "Further Reflections," Habermas returns to these "universalistic discourses of the bourgeois public sphere" (FRPS 429) as the core of "the
normative theory of democracy" (FRPS 439), which he started to develop
in *Structural Transformation*. This normative theory posits "public opinion
"as a "fictitious construct of constitutional law," which is "endowed with the
unitariness of a *counterfactual* entity" to conceptualize democratic self-determination and rational-critical will-formation in spite of the "bad facticity"
(Marcuse) of a constitutional reality distorted by the powers that be (FRPS
439, emphasis added). While we no longer call it *Natural Law* when we appeal to humanity's right to peace, as Marcuse explained in 1967, this search
for utopian potential remains grounded in rational natural law constructions
like the ones in Kant's *Perpetual Peace*.

In 1937, Marcuse emphasized that the "utopian element has for a long time
been the only progressive element in philosophy." To exemplify his thesis, he
pointed to "the philosophical constructions of the best [constitutional] state . .
. and of perpetual peace" (PCT 637). In 2010, Habermas expressed this continuity in his thought in a lecture at the Princeton University Center for Human
Values, titled "The Utopian Surplus of Human Rights" (see HPSC 49).

8.4. BEFORE *STRUCTURAL TRANSFORMATION'S* IDEOLOGY-CRITICAL TURN: HABERMAS'S PREFERENCE FOR FACTICITY OVER NORMATIVITY WHEN ANALYZING THE LIBERAL CONSTITUTIONAL STATE IN 1958

Significantly, the English-language global readership of *Structural Transformation* would encounter a truly enigmatic contradiction, if the book's forerunner "Zum Begriff der politischen Beteiligung" were finally translated and
actually became "On the Concept of Political Participation." If that happened,
readers would not only have to ask why Habermas presented Kant's idea of
"the public sphere as the organizational principle of the bourgeois constitutional state" as still credible in 1832 (STPS 87), even though he had publicly
stated months before finishing his book that Hegel "decisively destroyed"
Kant's underlying liberal pretenses already in 1821? But also how he could
conceptualize *Structural Transformation*'s narrative *after* he had denied in
1958 any validity for "the guarantee of free competition," for "the model of a

society of petty commodity producers," and for Say's Law (STPS 86) at any point in the history of liberal capitalism?

Readers will recall from studying Section 11 (see 5.4 above), that only if these three "presuppositions of classical economics" are valid will all members of civil society have "an equal chance" to acquire "property and education" as the prerequisite for being admitted as private people to the public sphere (STPS 86, 87). In other words, without the validity of these three presuppositions it would be impossible to conceptualize *Structural Transformation*'s narrative. After all, Section 11 highlights that the "bourgeois public sphere stands or falls with the principle of *universal access*" (STPS 85, emphasis added; SÖ 107).

Without identifying them as such, Habermas had previously introduced the same three presuppositions of classical political economy in "On the Concept of Political Participation." In 1958, they served as the requirement for the realization of the idea of democracy in the tradition of 1930s Critical Theory. As discussed in chapter 1, Neumann reintroduced the bourgeois ideals of rational autonomy and political self-determination into his democratic theory, which he outlined in his essay "The Concept of Political Freedom" (1957).

In 1958, Habermas reflected on the relationship between this idea of democracy and the "liberal constitution," which "is visibly oriented toward the interests of the bourgeoisie," To do justice to the idea of democracy, it thus has to safeguard the material existence of all citizens. Otherwise they could not "actually and equally realize their constitutional liberties." For in a liberal constitution the realization of political rights depends on economic presuppositions (CPP17). They are the same three that readers are familiar with from *Structural Transformation*. Only the order is different. In 1958, he started by describing "the model of a society of petty commodity producers." He then referenced "the guarantee of free competition." Finally, he not only introduced the essence of Say's Law but also emphasized the need that it actually fulfilled its function:

> As a matter of fact, [the liberal constitution] requires a society of independent citizens with equally distributed private property; all of them must be given an equal opportunity to reproduce their life mediated by the market. Under conditions of completely unfettered competition, the market actually has to fulfill the function of rational self-regulation that is ascribed to it. (CPP17)

As immediately pointed out above in chapter 1, Habermas's initial response from 1958 to these economic presuppositions for the realization of political rights guaranteed in the liberal constitution was direct and succinct:

> *Of course, such a society has never existed.* (CPP 17, emphasis added)

As the long footnote documents, Habermas's assessment is based on the critique of these three economic presuppositions in Heller's constitutional state theory. For Heller, these economic ideas represent in reality a "grand veiling of a situation that is just the opposite." While they do not have "the conscious purpose" to "provide a good conscience for bourgeois society," they nevertheless function that way:

> For the real bourgeois society knows no free exchange of commodities in the market, no free competition, no free self-determination and responsibility for oneself, Above all, it does not know any uncoerced formation of society as a whole through the free and equal play of forces. (CPP 17n15)

Significantly, the reader who tries to understand the development of Habermas's complex ideology-critical procedure culminating in *Structural Transformation*'s methodology is faced with an unfathomable tension between key statements in the first and in the last part of "On the Concept of Political Participation." While the latter immediately emphasizes that the essay follows the methodology of Critical Theory for its analysis of the bourgeois constitutional state, the fundamental critique of the economic presuppositions in the former prevents it from trying to access the potential for reason articulated in the "bourgeois ideals" and in the "objective meaning of institutions." Instead of using the "instrumentalized and abused ideas" delineated by Heller as a point of departure for an *immanent critique* of the liberal constitution based on those economic presuppositions, Habermas focuses primarily on the falsehoods it proclaims—thus reiterating the critique of the sociology of knowledge:

> The development of liberal democracy took place within the rigid hierarchy of a stratified society. Factually, the participation in political will-formation was restricted to an upper stratum. *The real basis of the liberal state was never an arrangement of [freely] competing citizens with equal chances*, but a stable . . . social order secured by the ranks of property and education. (CPP 17, emphasis added)

In 1958, Habermas *still privileges facticity over normativity*. While he introduces the methodology of Critical Theory toward the end of his text, in its first parts he only applies its Hegelian-Marxist thought in a very limited fashion. Instead of trying to glean from bourgeois ideology the "objective meaning of existing institutions," he uses a historical perspective that is not yet permeated by the philosophy of history to explain the development of the contradictions in the liberal constitution.

Implicitly selecting the history of the French Revolution as his template, he argues that the Third Estate, due to its "revolutionary origins, with its struggle for a liberal, constitutional state of bourgeois society, had to declare itself not only as the representative of the nation, but as the nation itself." Accordingly, the "liberal law-based state (*Rechtsstaat*) posits the identification of the bourgeoisie with the people as its presupposition." For the Third Estate "no longer interprets itself as one estate among other ones, but as the [civil] society, which, on principle, does not exclude anybody and which is open for everybody who subjects the reproduction of his life to the laws of the market" (CCP 17–18).

However, as analyzed by Heller and expanded on by Habermas, these laws of the market do not guarantee free competition and equal chances for all citizens as well as a harmonious self-regulation of the economy. In short, the bourgeois claim about the validity of these economic presuppositions represents a falsehood. Without applying the ideology-critical procedure and searching for the "objective meaning" of these economic ideas as the presuppositions for the liberal constitution, Habermas can only confirm the contradiction between its representation of the bourgeois interests and its democratic claim about the identification of the bourgeoisie with the people:

> The contradiction, namely, to *proclaim the idea of democracy*, to also *institutionalize it in a certain fashion*, but to factually organize a democracy of [propertied] minorities based on a social hierarchy, is characteristic for the liberal constitutional state. (CPP18, emphasis added)

Similarly, Habermas's 1958 emphasis on historical facticity still kept his focus on the Belgian Constitution of 1831 with its classic separation of powers. Lorenz von Stein's seminal constitutional theory regarded it as the "true ideal type of the bourgeois state" (CT 332). Only in *Structural Transformation* would he introduce the revolutionary ideal of an "absolute normative quality" of the constitution that abolishes all domination.

His 1958 essay thus barely mentions England's 1832 parliamentary reform, which would play such a key role in Sections 10 and 11. Instead, he emphasizes that the Belgian Constitution "implemented Montesquieu's doctrines in exemplary fashion for continental Europe" Before introducing the absolute normativity of a rational *consensus* in the interest of all that replaces the political decision, Habermas regarded the *compromise* between the propertied classes as the typical expression of liberal constitutionalism in the nineteenth century. It was implemented as the separation of political powers. As summarized above in chapter 1, the economically dominant bourgeoisie gained significant influence in the legislature while the politically dominating feudal forces retained their control over executive power (CPP 15n11).

Specifically, "the *separation* of the legislature from the executive branch" of government "actually gave the bourgeoisie the right to themselves make the laws, on the basis of which in the future the monarch was allowed to intervene regarding the status of the property and freedom of citizens." Moreover, "the *separation* of the judiciary from the executive safeguards the judge's independence from administrative command." Finally, it "guarantees that a system of universal constitutional norms posited according to the will of bourgeois society is effective and cannot be violated" (CPP 16–17, emphasis added).

In short, for Habermas in 1958 the liberal concept of a constitutional monarchy based on "Montesquieu's doctrines" represented the "true ideal type of the bourgeois state." However, for Section 15 in *Structural Transformation* this implementation of the separation of powers and of "the compromise between competing private interests" (STPS 132) proved that the "no longer liberal bourgeoisie, converting to liberalism" had now abandoned Kant's idealist "philosophy of history in favor of a commonsense meliorism" and "become 'realistic'" (STPS 138, 131). Given the fact that Kant's idea of a republican constitution *did* include the separation of powers, this critique actually refers to Habermas's theory reconstruction of Kant's "unofficial" philosophy of history in Section 13 (see chapter 6 above).

By comparing "On the Concept of Political Participation" and Section 15 of *Structural Transformation*, readers can reconstruct exactly how Habermas utilized his ideology-critical procedure, grounded in the Hegelian-Marxist philosophy of history, to shift the focus of his research from facticity to normativity. Clearly, in 1958 he already introduces the outline of his idealist theory of democracy. However, he does not yet systematically present his thesis as the "objective meaning of existing institutions." Moreover, there is no reference that would indicate his future theory reconstruction of Kant's idea of the bourgeois public sphere:

> The parliamentary democracies of the West, even pseudo-parliamentary authoritarian regimes like Portugal and France, are dependent on the consciousness of their citizens that political authority is mediated through the rational self-determination of enlightened human beings. (CPP 13)

Above all, the concrete historical references to existing political regimes *at that time* allow the reader to immediately identify the degree of idealization inherent in his thesis. On one hand, it equates Portugal's dictatorship with the authoritarian government in France. On the other hand, it contains a peculiar omission of Spain's dictator Franco. Significantly, Schmitt's "civil war topos" was influential among the Spanish ruling elite, because it legitimized *auctoritas*.

Similarly, Habermas's claim that all these political regimes thus "have to be intent on creating and maintaining such a consciousness, even by using means of opinion management" (CPP 13), is still sufficiently concrete to be accessible to empirical review. For comparing the state of freedom of the press under these respective governments would reveal whether "the rational self-determination of enlightened human beings" *can* take place. And a content analysis of influential media in the political public spheres of these nations would allow to assess whether it *did* take place.

8.5. *WITHOUT FURTHER CONSIDERATION:* SHIFTING FROM FACTICITY TO NORMATIVITY BY DIALECTICALLY APPROPRIATING SCHMITT'S "ABSOLUTE CONCEPT OF THE CONSTITUTION"

Perhaps the clearest indicator for the still ambivalent and relatively undeveloped state of the ideology-critical procedure in "On the Concept of Political Participation" is the prevalence of Heller's constitutional theory over Schmitt's. While there is a reference to the latter, the switch from Heller's critique of bourgeois ideology to Schmitt's ideal-typical reconstruction of the absolute concept of the bourgeois constitution immediately in section 1 had not yet taken place. That section's focus on the absolute rationalism of the French Revolution with its valorization of the bourgeois constitution as a *"unified, closed system of highest and ultimate norms"* (CT 62) would become emblematic for Habermas's theory reconstruction in *Structural Transformation*.

Nonetheless, readers can already discover in his text from 1958 key building blocks for his future book, even if they are neither systematically connected nor clearly identified as the "objective meaning" of the liberal constitution in the Kantian sense, enhanced by his "unofficial" philosophy of history. Expanding on Neumann's 1957 idea of democracy, Habermas claims that it will become possible to "transform personal into rational authority to the degree, in which enlightened citizens under the condition of a politically functioning public sphere will, through informed delegation of their will and through effective control of its implementation, take the organization of their social life into their own hands" (CCP 12).

While this crucial role of the "politically functioning public sphere" is not expressly included in the following quote from Heller's constitutional theory, it contains the seeds for the future keywords regarding a civil society free from coercion and the dissolution of domination in the political public sphere. All that is still needed is the application of the ideology-critical procedure and of Kant's "unofficial" philosophy of history with its "remarkable self-implication" that "takes into account the effect of a theory of history on the course of the history itself" (STPS 116, see 6.1 above).

In short, an immanent critique in the Hegelian-Marxist sense will accomplish this task. It can take Heller's analysis of the foundational legitimation of bourgeois society and its liberal constitution as a point of departure. This move will facilitate access to the potential for reason in this ideological construct to develop the central theses in *Structural Transformation*. Here, again, is this key quote that was immediately introduced under 1.2 above:

> According to its foundational legitimation, bourgeois society functions as the uncoerced interaction of equal forces. Essentially, it thus cannot justify any (political) domination, least of all a domination based on class rule. (quoted in CCP 13)

Readers can find the genesis of *Structural Transformation*'s narrative in this quote. All the forensic evidence presented above suggests that three years into his research on "Ideology and the Ideology-Critical Procedure" Habermas decided to adopt Critical Theory's key maxim and accept the bourgeois ideals serving the "foundational legitimation" of civil society and the bourgeois constitutional state *without further consideration*. Schmitt's ideal-typical stylization of "The Absolute Concept of the Constitution" (Section 1), "The Legal Concept of the Law-Based State (*Rechtsstaat*)" (Section 13), and of "Concepts to Be Derived from the Concept of the Constitution" (Section 11) in *Constitutional Theory* provided one set of basic building blocks in this regard—*if read selectively*.

As analyzed above under 8.1, the Hegelian-Marxist critique of ideology allowed to do this. Once Habermas decided to comprehend "history dialectically," he inherited Hegel's freedom to "select and develop the categories in such a way that this theory at every step is guided and permeated by the self-consciousness of its own relationship to praxis" (TAP 80, 81). Chapter 6 above discussed that this freedom informed Habermas's theory reconstruction of Kant's "unofficial" philosophy of history which "takes into account the effect of a theory of history on the course of the history itself."

Kant, Rousseau, and Schiller are the three main sources for the bourgeois ideals that inform *Structural Transformation*'s theory reconstruction of a "morally pretentious rationality" as the hallmark of the bourgeois public sphere. It looks like Habermas's selection of Kant was primarily influenced by Schmitt's *Constitutional Theory* and the new introduction to *Perpetual Peace* that the philosopher Karl Jaspers published in 1958. Schmitt emphasized already in 1928 that Kant's concept of the republican constitution contains the "clearest and final expression of the principal ideas of the bourgeois

Enlightenment, which so far have not been replaced by a new ideal foundation" (CT 170, VL 126).

Around 1957, Habermas "tackled *Das Kapital* seriously," as he stated in November 1984 in a written interview with Perry Anderson, editor of the *New Left Review*, and the philosopher Peter Dews. Already in late 1956, he had researched the philosophical discussion about Marx and Marxism. Following Hegel's philosophy which posits "the methodological primacy of the dialectical procedure over the analytic in the investigation of the things themselves" (TAP 80, TUP 84), Habermas could use the Hegelian-Marxist method of the immanent critique to find "a piece of existing reason hidden" to Kant's philosophy itself.

Selecting Kant also allowed Habermas to introduce a distinction between Kant's *liberal* ideal of the bourgeois public sphere with its "unofficial" dissolution of political domination into "pure reason" and John Stuart Mill's *liberalist* interpretation of the political public sphere, which only posits a "division" of political domination. In short, "public opinion becomes a mere limit on power" (STPS 136; SÖ 166). Since Mill is in agreement with Kant who in *Perpetual Peace* "moves entirely within the concept of the bourgeois constitutional state with its division of powers" (CT 183, VL 141), Habermas has to use the "dialectical procedure" to reconstruct Kant's liberal ideal by drawing mainly on "The Absolute Concept of the Constitution."

As analyzed above under 5.2 and 6.1, to dialectically replace the division of powers with their dissolution, Habermas has to extract the Marxian "rational kernel" from "the ideal of the law-based state to encompass all possible state activities in a system of norms, thus binding the state" (CT 190: VL 150). Specifically from its core fiction that "constitutional norms . . . are sovereign" (CT 154-155) which, in turn, presupposes "the binding of all state activity to a system of norms legitimated by public opinion" (STPS 82). This "piece of existing reason hidden" in Kant's republican constitution thus "already aims at abolishing the state as an instrument of domination altogether" (STPS 82; SÖ 104).

In this context, readers can study how Habermas used his Hegelian freedom to "select and develop [his] categories." Arguably, when searching within the ideal-typical construct of Schmitt's *Constitutional Theory* for a potential for reason, he found it in connection with the "fiction of the absolute normative quality" of the bourgeois constitution. To maintain this fiction, the law-based bourgeois state has to develop for the in reality "inevitable acts of sovereignty a method for apocryphal acts of sovereignty" (CT 155, VL 108).

This explanation by Schmitt offers the opportunity for its rational reconstruction to better attain the goal of Kant's republican constitution, namely, to substitute the truth of the law for the authority of the sovereign—thus reversing Hobbes. By thinking dialectically, one can turn this challenge for the "fiction of the absolute normative quality" of the bourgeois constitution into an opportunity. For the fact that "a method for apocryphal acts of sovereignty" has to be developed to maintain the logical consistency of this fiction points to a normative potential. While Schmitt emphasizes the *contradiction* between this fiction and the "inevitable acts of sovereignty" when governing, Habermas focuses on the *normative power* of that fact. Yes, there is a contradiction. But once one develops a method for implementing those acts, one implicitly and simultaneously acknowledges that they *are* regarded as apocryphal *within* this fiction.

8.6. THE METHODOLOGICAL CHALLENGES OF LIBERAL AMBIVALENCE: FROM KANT'S "RATIONAL AUTONOMY" TO NIETZSCHE'S "SELF-DESTRUCTION OF REASON"

In *Civil Society and Political Theory* (1992), Jean L. Cohen and Andrew Arato would critique *Structural Transformation* for following "the internal logic of the liberal conception of the public sphere to such a point that the only form of effective social control of the state that seems to be logically possible is its abolition . . . and its replacement by a closed system of legal norms" (Cohen/Arato 1992: 222–23). In their eyes, Habermas in 1962 did "not seem to understand that the idea of the public as the abolition of political power involves a renunciation of the need to limit all power through the only means possible, the establishment of counterpowers and organizations" (Ibid., 230). In other words, they inadvertently demonstrate just how challenging it is to correctly understand the ideology-critical procedure in Habermas's "perplexing and ambivalent book," as Peter Uwe Hohendahl called it in 2001, after three decades of research and publications on *Structural Transformation* (Hohendahl 2001: 7).

Like Condorcet, Habermas regarded a public opinion enlightened by rational natural law with its universal understanding of truth and justice as a greater check on all powers than "the establishment of counterpowers and organizations" could possibly provide. He critiqued Mill and Tocqueville's "liberalist interpretation of the bourgeois constitutional state" as "reactionary," because it "reacted to the power of *the idea of a critically debating public's self-determination*, initially included in its institutions," once "the inability to resolve rationally the competition of interests in the public sphere" became evident. From Habermas's point of view, this happened as soon as the rational-critical bourgeois public "was subverted by the propertyless and uneducated... masses" (STPS 136, 135, emphasis added).

Readers have to realize that it is this "power of the idea of a critically debating public's self-determination" that fuels Habermas's critique of Mill and Tocqueville in Section 15 and his presentation of Marx in Section 14. Contrary to Cohen and Arato's reading of these sections, his "preference for Marx over Mill and Tocqueville in the further development of the normative model" is more ambivalent and contradictory than "obvious" (Cohen/Arato 1992: 230).

Since Mill and Tocqueville cannot contribute any normative potential to Habermas's ideology-critical search for the conditions conducive to the dissolution of domination, he has to turn to Marx. In stark contrast, Marx took the idea of the bourgeois public sphere seriously and used it to critique Hegel's philosophy of the state with its attempt to control the antagonism in bourgeois society with a constitution "based on neo-estates" (STPS 123). Hegel's philosophy certainly lost any normative potential after he declared that "to be independent of public opinion is the first formal condition of achieving anything great or *rational* whether in life or in science" (quoted in STPS 121, emphasis added).

It was their focus on rationality in the public sphere of a political society in the tradition of the Physiocrats and the absolute rationalism advocated by Condorcet and others in the French Revolution that let Habermas apply his ideology-critical procedure to a "counter-model" offered by Marx and Engels. In their concept, "the public sphere is supposed to be able to realize in earnest what it always promised—subjecting political domination, as the domination of human beings over human beings, to reason" (STPS 127-128, SÖ156). Readers will notice the parallel to his reflections in "On the Concept of Political Participation," when Habermas paraphrases the dictum by Engels that in such a counter-model "the administration of things and direction of production-processes will take the place of the rule over human beings." In other words, "the associated producers" will "*rationally* regulate their natural reproduction" instead of being ruled by it "as a blind force" (quoted in STPS 128, emphasis added).

In this socialist counter-model, "autonomy is no longer based on private property; . . . but has to have its foundation in the public sphere itself." Accordingly, "the identity of *bourgeois* and *homme* is replaced by that of *citoyen* and *homme.*" Specifically, this "autonomous public" of "citizens in society" (*Gesellschaftsbürger*), secures for its members as "private persons" a "sphere of personal freedom" through "the planned organization of a state being absorbed into society" (STPS 129, SÖ 157). In short, the concept of "autonomy" developed by Rousseau and Kant in their respective rational natural law constructions provides the normative potential that Habermas is searching for.

When comparing Sections 14 and 15, readers encounter a remarkable difference between a detached, abstract argument in the former and a concrete, judgmental one in the latter regarding essentially the same topic. First, they will read that as soon as "the mass of non-owners make the general rules governing social transactions into a topic of *their* public debate, the reproduction of social life as such becomes a universal concern" (STPS 127, emphasis in the original, SÖ 155). Then they will be confronted with the assertion that the public sphere "becomes an arena of competing interests fought out in the coarser forms of violent conflict," once "group needs that cannot expect to be satisfied by a self-regulating market tend to favor regulation by the state" (STPS 132; SÖ 160–61).

While Section 14 implies that "the reproduction of social life as such" can become a universal concern in rational-critical debate, Section 15 fears that once the interests of the mass of non-owners are placed on the public agenda, the "reasonable consensus of publicly debating private persons" will be replaced by a "compromise between competing interests" (STPS 132; SÖ 161). For Habermas, already the Chartist movement is thus incompatible with the rational autonomy of a critically debating public's self-determination inscribed in the institutions of the bourgeois constitutional state.

Cohen and Arato analyze that *Structural Transformation*'s narrative "represents a species of *Verfallsgeschichte*, a history of decline" (Cohen/Arato 1992: 211). Their conclusion is based on the social and political transformation of the bourgeois public sphere that the book describes. However, readers have to realize that for Habermas this decline also, and perhaps above all, occurred in the realm of German philosophy. Specifically, it was caused by the challenge to the philosophy of Idealism presented in the last third of the nineteenth century by the philosopher of nihilism, Friedrich Nietzsche.

In 1958, Habermas set out to apply in his ideology-critical procedure the ideals of bourgeois humanism, no matter how distorted they had become in the meantime. In 1973, when publishing the German original of *Legitimation Crisis*, he vehemently critiques "the cynicism" of a "self-denying bourgeois consciousness" that it "has been possible to observe" for "more than a hundred years" (LC 122). In a paragraph that is almost one page long, Habermas singles out Nietzsche for radicalizing "the experience of the retrenchment of the ideas with which reality could be confronted" and quotes him as follows:

> For why has the advent of nihilism become necessary? Because the values we have had hitherto thus draw their final consequence; because *nihilism represents the ultimate logical conclusion of our great values and ideas*—because we must experience nihilism before we can find out what value those "values" really had. (quoted in LC 122, emphasis added)

Specifically, Habermas analyzes how "Nietzsche assimilated the *historical loss of force of normative validity claims* as well as the Darwinian impulses to a *naturalistic self-destruction of reason*" (LC 122, emphasis added). Significantly, Habermas reflects on the impact of nihilism on the bourgeois reading public toward the end of the nineteenth century: "Nietzsche counted on the shock effect of his revelations." Just how personal this shock effect still is for Habermas as the most important philosopher of German Idealism in the second half of the twentieth century, can be gleaned from the evocative wording he uses to convey the magnitude he ascribes to this terminal act in the decline of the bourgeois ideals: Nietzsche's "heroic style also reveals the pain that cutting the umbilical cord to the *universalism of the Enlightenment* caused him after all" (LC 122, emphasis added).

Habermas certainly refers to himself when he concludes his long paragraph by criticizing the contemporary impact of Nietzsche, more than a decade *before* he would feel compelled to attack French post-structuralism in *The Philosophical Discourse of Modernity*:

> Anyone who still discusses the admissibility of truth in practical questions is, at least, old-fashioned. (LC 123)

Similarly, the political transformation that *Structural Transformation*'s narrative presents is primarily informed by the "revocation of bourgeois ideals . . . in the retrograde development of democratic theory" (LC 123). Explicitly stated only in 1973, this critique already served as the background for Section 15 with its distinction between the *liberal* ideal of the bourgeois public sphere and its "relativized form" (STPS 131) once liberalism had liberated it from its "natural-law idealism" (LC 123). To emphasize its retrograde character, Habermas puts "bourgeoisie" in italics when highlighting that the *liberalist* form of "the *bourgeois* public sphere" is determined to conserve its bourgeois character by strictly narrowing access. Section 15 seeks to prove this point by selecting from *On Liberty* a passage, in which Mill "advocated 'that political questions be decided not by a direct or indirect appeal to the insight or the will of an uninformed multitude, but only by appeal to views, formed after due consideration, of a relatively small number of persons specially educated for this task" (quoted in STPS 136).

Section 15 also emphasizes that "Tocqueville shares Mill's conception of 'Representative Government': public opinion determined by the passions of the masses is in need of purification through the authoritative insights of materially independent citizens." While Tocqueville regards the press as an "important instrument of enlightenment," it alone cannot accomplish this task. Only a "social hierarchy" can provide a basis for "political representation." However, he is aware that "corporative powers of pre-bourgeois society," among which especially "the landed estates" were distinguished by "birth, education, and wealth" and thus "destined to command," cannot be "recreated overnight from the soil of bourgeois society." Lacking this "natural born aristocracy," bourgeois society has to rely on educated and powerful citizens "to form an elite public, whose views determine public opinion" (quoted in STPS 136–137; SÖ 166–167).

Not only Cohen and Arato, but also Ira Katznelson in his discussion of Section 15 in "On Liberal Ambivalence" (2012) regards Habermas's reading of Mill and Tocqueville as selective and one-sided (cf. Hofmann 2021: 962–63). Readers can find one explanation for this selectivity in *Legitimation Crisis.* There, in the context of analyzing "the retrograde development of democratic theory," Habermas expands on his 1958 critique of political scientists like Seymour Martin Lipset and William Kornhauser (see CPP 10 and 44).

While the "sober pathos" of the retrograde "theory of mass democracy" by Joseph Schumpeter and Max Weber "still reflects the sacrifice that a purportedly better insight into a pessimistic anthropology seems to demand," a "new generation of cocky (*forscher*) elite theorists" allegedly "already stands beyond [Nietzsche's] cynicism and [Schumpeter and Weber's] self-pity" (LC 123; LS 169).The following sentences reveal to the reader why Habermas, even though he otherwise valorizes Tocqueville as a staunch advocate for the "sovereignty of the constitution," is inclined to primarily think of him as the forerunner of these elite theorists:

> They adopt *Tocqueville as an honorable precursor* and *recommend the new elitism in good conscience* as the simple alternative to the dark night of totalitarianism in which all cats are grey. . . . [They no longer understand as "democracy"] "the conditions under which all legitimate interests can be fulfilled by way of *realizing the fundamental interest in self-determination and participation.* . . . [For them], "Democracy no longer has the goal of *rationalizing authority through the participation of citizens in discursive processes of will-formation.* (LC 123, emphasis added; LS 169–170)

In 1958, when he accepted the bourgeois ideals *without further consideration* for his immanent critique of bourgeois society's foundational legitimation regarding uncoerced interaction and absence of political domination, Habermas's motivation was this decline in the emancipatory character of bourgeois political theory and practice since the middle of the nineteenth century. "On the Concept of Political Participation" largely adopted Schmitt's discussion of the deteriorating commitment of the French bourgeoisie and the German Liberal Party to the liberal idea of the republican constitution after 1848. While *Constitutional Theory* drew on analyses by Lorenz von Stein, Marx, and Friedrich Julius Stahl, Habermas only quoted in full the latter one by this "conservative theoretician of the constitutional monarchy" (CPP 42n62).

Published in 1863, Stahl's analysis falls into the decade which *Structural Transformation* selected as the beginning of the terminal decline of the bourgeois public sphere. 1867 marks the turning point due to the publication of *Das Kapital* and the second Election Reform Bill, which opens access for non-bourgeois members and ends what not only the bourgeoisie in England but also the one in Germany and France regarded as the "classic epoch" of British parliamentarism. Finally, the first cyclical economic crisis on a global scale, followed by the start of the first "Great Depression" in 1873 (STPS 143) terminate "even the flimsiest pretense" that in bourgeois society "the influence of power is suspended" (STPS 144).

Stahl's book is based on his lectures from 1850 to 1857 about the "Parties in Church and State" (CT 333). Schmitt and Habermas open their identical quotes with Stahl's observation that with regard to "positively carrying out the ideas of popular sovereignty" by "installing the entire people in power on equal terms," the Liberal Party "installs in power only the middle class, the wealthy, the educated, that is, just itself." According to Stahl, the Liberal Party uses the same approach when claiming "the idea of equality against the nobility, against all estates as such, because, due to the [ideological] basis of the Revolution, it cannot admit an organic formation [of society]." However, "should equality be positively instituted, should the propertyless class receive the same rights as the middle class, it forfeits the idea [of equality] and politically makes legal distinctions in favor of the wealthy property owners." Specifically, Stahl observes that the Liberal Party "wants a census for representation and security deposits for the press, *allows only the fashionable into the salon*, does not extend to the poor the honor and polite treatment it does to the rich" (quoted in CT 333, emphasis added, VL 309–310; CPP 42n62). In conclusion, Stahl highlights the essence of his analysis as follows:

> It is this *partial execution of the principles of the Revolution* that characterizes the party position of the Liberals. (quoted in CT 333, emphasis in the original; CPP 42n62)

Schmitt quoting Stahl guided *Structural Transformation*'s narrative toward the end zone of its political public sphere's downward trajectory. Schmitt quoting Marx implicitly offered Habermas the high points of this trajectory, namely, the abolition of the French monarchy in September 1792 and Condorcet's presentation of the "Gironde" constitution in the French National Convention in February 1793. Although the Marx quote introduces the Stahl quote in *Constitutional Theory*, "On the Concept of Political Participation" omits it when referencing Marx's writings on the class struggles in France from 1848 to 1850 and on the usurpation of power by Napoleon III in December 1851 (CT 333, CPP 42n62):

> Karl Marx . . . mocks the bourgeois [political] parties, which from the "sole possible form of their united power, from the most dominating (*gewaltigsten*) and complete form of their class rule, the constitutional republic, flee back to their subaltern, incomplete, weaker form of the [constitutional] monarchy." (CT 333, VL 309)

Nevertheless, the liberal bourgeoisie's flight back from its political self-determination during the French Revolution to its subordination in the constitution of the Belgian monarchy from 1831 as the new "ideal type of the bourgeois constitutional state," is clearly reflected in the transition from the liberal idea of the public sphere to its liberalist diminution in Section 15. The reader thus realizes how Habermas can align in his "history of decline" the weakening of the ideals of the Enlightenment in bourgeois philosophy *and* in the political public sphere of the bourgeois constitutional state. In other words, switching from Heller's constitutional theory to Schmitt's to reconstruct the undistorted bourgeois ideals inscribed in the latter's ideal-typical stylization of "The Absolute Concept of the Constitution," allowed Habermas to shift his focus from the Belgian constitution of 1831 in "On the Concept of Political Participation" to the constitutional debates during the French Revolution in *Structural Transformation* as the realization of the Kantian idea of a rational-critical discourse in the political public sphere.

Chapter Nine

The Result of *Structural Transformation*'s Dialectical Use of Schmitt's "Civil War *Topos*" and Koselleck's "Process of Criticism"

A Tension between Developmental History and Ideology-Critical Procedure

9.1. THE SCHMITT/KOSELLECK TEMPLATE: FROM "MORAL INNER SPACE" TO BOURGEOIS PUBLIC SPHERE

Readers of this guide are now aware of the three key components in *Structural Transformation*'s theoretical framework that allowed Habermas to dialectically appropriate and upend Schmitt and Koselleck's conservative critique of the process of Enlightenment criticism culminating in Kant's cognitive and moral universalism as well as in Schiller's expressive subjectivism. The first one is Horkheimer and Adorno's admonition from 1944 that Critical Theory accepts the ideals of bourgeois humanism without further consideration, which is based on Marcuse's 1937 essay. The second one is Marcuse's 1937 dictum that when reflecting on the idea of the human being one has to think in a countermove against facticity and abstract from the concrete misery of the status quo. The third is Horkheimer's 1936 application of the Hegelian-Marxist critique of ideology to his study on *Authority and the Family*, which concludes that the existing institution of "the bourgeois family leads not only to bourgeois authority but to a premonition of a better human condition" (quoted in STPS 261n48, see 7.4 above).

Since Horkheimer grounded the bourgeois family's utopian potential for a better human condition in the love of the spouses and maternal care, Habermas can use "the conjugal family's intimate sphere" to fill the "moral inner space" that Hobbes, according to Schmitt, excised from the Absolutist State. As analyzed under 5.2 above, this distinction between inward and outward already implies the *superiority of the inward* over the outward and hence *of the private* over the public, due to the "authority" of the moral conscience as "an uncon-

199

quered remnant of the state of nature" (Koselleck). Accordingly, *Structural Transformation* can designate the intimate sphere of the bourgeois family as the historical point of origin for "privateness in the modern sense of a saturated and free interiority" *and* for a moral superiority of "the inner-worldly opposition of a privatized society to political authority." This dualism allows Habermas to construct a unity of expressive subjectivism and universalistic discourses in the transition from the literary to the political public sphere. In turn, the unity of the ideals of bourgeois humanism guides the moral politics of the bourgeois revolutionaries when implementing rational natural law.

Arguably, using the Hegelian-Marxist critique of ideology to dialectically appropriate Schmitt's unique blending of constitutional theory and intellectual history has to be regarded as the most complex stage in Habermas's research on and application of the ideology-critical procedure between 1955 and 1960. Specifically, it informs his selection of Bayle's *Dictionnaire Historique et Critique* as the starting point in his dialectical adoption of Koselleck's stylization of the "Process of Criticism." For Bayle, under the guise of a harsh critique, broke the enforced silence about the atheist philosophy of Baruch Spinoza who in Schmitt's reading successfully subverted Hobbes's theory of the Absolutist State.

According to *The Leviathan in the State Theory of Thomas Hobbes*, the "modern 'neutral' state" originated in the "distinction between private and public," between "inner faith and outer confession." This "leaves to the individual's private reason whether to believe or not to believe." In Schmitt's and Koselleck's view, this distinction which created the "moral inner space" was exploited by the philosophers of the Enlightenment, specifically by Spinoza, to construct the "modern, individualistic right of freedom of thought and conscience" and the "characteristic individual freedoms embodied in the structure of the liberal constitutional system" (quoted in HPSC 88n126).

While Koselleck defined this theoretical construct as the "the entry point" (*Einsatzpunkt*) of Enlightenment," his translator seemingly expressed Schmittian sentiments when sharpening the language to "Enlightenment's specific point of attack" (CC 38). For Schmitt's anti-Semitic conspiracy theory, in which "a liberal Jew noticed the barely visible crack in the theoretical justification of the sovereign state," charges Spinoza's *Tractatus Theologico-Politicus* (1670) with subverting "public peace" and the absolute state's "sovereign power." Spinoza allegedly does so by inverting individual freedom of thought from an "implicit right open only as long as it remained private" into the "form-giving principle," which facilitates "the rise of the liberal constitutional state" from *within* the Old Regime (quoted in HPSC 88n126).

Beyond deciphering Habermas's ideology-critical appropriation of Schmitt's theoretical construct, readers face the challenge posed by his equally tacit renunciation of it in 1986. While his adversarial review of *Critique and Crisis* in 1960 contains the acknowledgment that "we owe the seminal conceptualization of the civil war *topos*" to Carl Schmitt, in 1986 he would reduce its status to the level of a "scenario." In between, *Structural Transformation* took its *structure* at face value while upending its *content*.

Nevertheless, "The Horrors of Autonomy: Carl Schmitt in English" (1986/1989) for the first time contains an explanation of Schmitt's concept. Moreover, Habermas's choice of words clearly signals his adversarial stance. Above all, the last sentence of his following quote tacitly points to Koselleck's stylization of Condorcet's death during the Jacobin phase of the French Revolution:

> The state consists of the ongoing prevention of civil war. Its dynamic consists of the crushing of revolt, the containment of a chaos inherent in the evil nature of individuals. Individuals press for their *autonomy* and would perish in the terrors of their emancipation if they were not rescued through the *facticity* of a power that overcomes every other power. (HA 130, emphasis added)

In other words, the "bad facticity" of the oppressed individual's concrete misery. Clearly, Habermas in 1960 refers to Schmitt's civil war *topos* as underlying *Critique and Crisis* when he accuses Koselleck of "discrediting the principle of public debate as one of civil war." Schmitt's student does indeed follow his teacher's denunciation of the process of criticism, in which "the subversive forces appear under the name of truth and justice." To protect his sovereignty, the absolute ruler thus reserves "the power to define what is publicly held to be true or just." In short, his "decision power is the source of all *validity*." Hence, the "state alone determines the *public* creed of its citizens" (HA 131, emphasis added).

What Habermas in 1986 downgraded to a scenario had in 1959 informed Koselleck's chapter 2 on "Hobbesian Rationality and the Origins of Enlightenment," which, in turn, would determine the chronology and trajectory in *Structural Transformation*'s stylization of the *rising* bourgeois public sphere. However, "Horrors of Autonomy" now declared that Schmitt's scenario "completely disregards the fact that *from the beginning* Hobbes had developed his concept of sovereignty in connection with the development of positive law." Accordingly, "Hobbes's idea of a sovereign legislator who is bound to the medium of positive law already contains the seed of the development of the constitutional state," that Schmitt "tries to derive from the neutralization of state power vis-à-vis the powers of private religious belief. . ." (HA 131, emphasis in the original).

In stark contrast, in *Structural Transformation*'s Section 12 Hobbes "took a momentous step when he identified 'conscience' . . . with 'opinion'" and defined religion as "a private matter." For this allowed him to conceptualize "the religious civil war" as coming "to an end under the dictate of a *state authority neutralized in religious matters.*" (STPS 90, emphasis added). In other words, in Habermas's interpretation from 1962 Schmitt not only "tries to derive" the constitutional state "from the neutralization of state power vis-à-vis the powers of private religious belief." Schmitt also still succeeds in doing so.

Far from treating this "civil war *topos*" as merely a Schmittian scenario, Habermas in 1962 ascribed the validity of facticity to it. In his view, it was "well known" that "Hobbes was guided by the experiences of the religious civil war. . ." (STPS 90). Three years earlier, Koselleck had used even stronger language:

> *Unequivocally, Hobbes's doctrine of the State grew out of the historical situation of civil war.* For Hobbes, who had experienced the formation of the Absolutist State in France, having been there when Henri IV was assassinated, and again when La Rochelle surrendered to the troops of Richelieu—*for Hobbes there could be no other goal than to prevent the civil war he saw impending in England.* . . (CC 23, emphasis added)

Section 12 neither refers to Schmitt nor calls it a "logical error" that Hobbes's doctrine only subjected "public worship" to "state control" (HA 131). Nevertheless, it reaches the same conclusion regarding the consequences. Namely, that "the privatization of religion" and "the *emancipation of civil society's private people from the semi-public bonds of the Church.* . . increased the importance of these people's private opinions even more" (STPS 91, emphasis added).

Clearly, readers would have been greatly helped, if the following Habermas quote from 1986 had been included in Section 12. Needless to say, with two crucial changes. Namely, the substitution of "*gradually unfold their morally pretentious rationality*" for "gradually unfold their subversive forces." And the acknowledgment by Habermas that he uses this Schmittian template to express his diametrically opposed view:

> In Schmitt's view, the space Hobbes reserved for private religious belief is the gate through which the subjectivity of bourgeois conscience and private opinion make their entrance and *gradually unfold their subversive forces.* For *this private sphere is turned inside out and extends to become the bourgeois public sphere.* (HA 131, emphasis added)

Moreover, the fact that "Horrors of Autonomy" identifies "the development of the constitutional state" with the unfolding of "the bourgeois public sphere" facilitates another revealing insight for the reader. For it directly connects to Section 13, where Kant would conceive one of the two functions "of 'the public sphere'. . . . as the principle of the legal order" (STPS 104). After Section 10 had already asserted the *status of facticity* for this *normative principle* thirty pages earlier, *without* identifying its Kantian origins:

> . . . it was not by accident that the public sphere assumed a central place. It became the *very organizational principle of the bourgeois constitutional states* that feature parliamentary forms of governance as, for example, Great Britain after the great Reform Bill of 1832. . . (STPS 74, emphasis added)

Amazingly, tacitly terminating the use of Schmitt's civil war *topos* in 1986 retroactively takes the structure out of *Structural Transformation*. For Habermas in 1962 needed Schmitt's claim about a "moral inner space" as Koselleck had discussed it in his book's chapter 2 in 1959 (CC 38-39). Otherwise he could not have conceptualized the three-step development of a morally pretentious rationality beginning with the "cultivation of the person" in the intimate sphere of the bourgeois family. And continuing in a literary public sphere, which contrary to Section 4 does have *one* "autochthonously bourgeois" origin (STPS 29). Namely, the moral weeklies that were "an immediate part of coffee house discussions and considered themselves literary pieces," as Section 5 emphasizes (STPS 42).

Accordingly, the moral weeklies illustrate *how* "the private sphere is turned inside out and extends" in its first *public* step toward becoming the bourgeois public sphere. As discussed above under 1.2 and 5.2, in this process of the "self-enlightenment of individuals" the evolving bourgeois public "held up a mirror to itself." The "wellspring" of this "specific subjectivity" was exactly that "moral inner space." For it "had its home, *literally*, in the sphere of the patriarchal conjugal family," as Section 6 highlights (STPS 43, emphasis added).

"Horrors of Autonomy" praises Schmitt as "a good writer who could combine conceptual precision with surprising and ingenious associations of ideas" (HA 133). Readers have to keep in mind that Habermas adopted this intellectual technique when writing *Structural Transformation*. For he tends to only present the results of ingeniously associating ideas without making these thought processes transparent.

Schiller's "romantic picture" of the "*human beings pure and simple*" (STPS 56, emphasis in the original) quietly communing with themselves in their *private* huts before stepping out into the *public* square and communicating "with the whole race" (PDM 49) is a prime example. For it informs Sections 4 to 7 but is introduced to the Habermas reader with a delay of more than two decades in the *Philosophical Discourse of Modernity*. Schiller's reflections on this "structure of communication" in an "aesthetically reconciled society"

(PDM 49) would have illuminated why the "bourgeois reading public" of the eighteenth century found "genuine satisfaction" in the "domestic novel, the psychological description in autobiographical form." Its "early and for a long time most influential example" was the "mediocre" *Pamela* (1740), which catered to the same taste as the moral weeklies. (STPS 43, 49).

In short, a reference in *Structural Transformation* to Schiller's "On the Aesthetic Education of Man" would have provided to the reader the *necessary* explanation why in Section 6 "the privatized individuals stepped out of the intimacy of their living rooms into the public sphere of the *salon*." However, it would not have been *sufficient* to explain the connection between the coffee houses and the *salon* as the "most imposing room in the distinguished bourgeois home" (STPS 45). To understand the other root of the literary public sphere, the one that was not "autochthonously bourgeois," the reader has to remember from Section 4 that the "bourgeois avant-garde of the educated middle class learned the art of critical-rational public debate through its contact with the . . . courtly-noble society" (STPS 29).

Only in these French *salons* would "the nobility and the *grande bourgeoisie* of finance and administration" meet "with the 'intellectuals' on an equal footing" (STPS 29). But in spite of a wealth of facticity in Sections 5 to 9, culminating in the detailed description of the lion's head attached to the west side of Button's Coffee House "through whose jaws the reader threw his letter" (STPS 42), *Structural Transformation* does not explain the relationship between these two rather different origins of the literary public sphere. On one hand, various topics discussed in the moral weeklies demonstrate how the bourgeois intimacy of the conjugal family could be "played off against courtly conventions" (STPS 35). On the other hand, the urban nobility congregating in the *salons* of Paris and setting "the standard for the rest of Europe, . . . despised the bourgeois family life turned in on itself" (STPS 44).

Nevertheless, the roles of both literary public spheres as the forerunners of the political public sphere manifesting itself at the end of the eighteenth century would have been obsolete, if "Hobbes's idea of a sovereign legislator who is bound to the medium of positive law already contains the seed of the development of the constitutional state." Interestingly, Habermas tacitly acknowledged this at the Chapel Hill conference, three years *after* the publication of "Horrors of Autonomy." It is plausible to assume that his broad and implicit acknowledgment responded to the conference presentation by the historian David Zaret.

Zaret posits that the *political* public sphere in modernity originated during the English Revolution. In his view, "Parliament's appeals to public opinion" and the printing of speeches by members on the floor of the House in the 1640s have to be regarded as unprecedented modes of directly addressing the public. He systematically expanded on his thesis in his well-documented study *Origins of Democratic Culture: Printing, Petitions, and the Public Sphere in Early Modern England* (2000).

In comparison, *Structural Transformation*'s stylization of a rising bourgeois public sphere presents a very different chronology. Only in 1750, more than a century later, would the bourgeois public sphere begin to transition from a literary to a *political* public sphere. At the end of Section 6, Habermas identifies the new medium for this transition. Namely, "the press and its professional criticism" (STPS 51).

In stark contrast, in Zaret's chronology the "low cost in printing simple texts facilitated the deluge of *political* declarations, replies, ordinances, petitions" already "during the 1640s" (Zaret 2000: 151, emphasis added). In short, years *before* Hobbes's *Leviathan* (1651) would create in intellectual history the "moral inner space" at the center of Schmitt's civil war *topos*. However, without this construct of a "moral inner space" *Structural Transformation* could not have conceptualized "the patriarchal conjugal family's intimate sphere that was oriented toward a public" as the "*historical and social location*," in which the rise of the bourgeois public sphere originated (STPS 85, emphasis added).

In this normative concept that is given the appearance of facticity, the property owners in their roles as human beings pure and simple *literally* step out of their private homes, where they experience and reflect on their bourgeois intimacy, and walk to a new social space like Button's Coffee House where they can throw their letters containing their autobiographical notes through the lion's mouth. After completing this first phase of a process, in which the "moral inner space" is turning itself "inside out," they congregate inside the coffee houses. There they will enter into face-to-face communication to achieve their goal of self-enlightenment. They accomplish this task by *jointly* reflecting on their autobiographical observations, which were now printed in the new moral weeklies.

In the next phase of this evolving literary public sphere, these private letters written with the public in mind take on a public life of their own. Two years after Richardson created with *Pamela* the model for domestic novels written in letters, another new social institution, the "first public library," was founded. Once "book clubs, reading circles, and subscription libraries shot up" and "the sale of the monthly and weekly journals" accelerated (STPS 51), the bourgeois reading public emerged toward the middle of the eighteenth century.

At that point in *Structural Transformation*'s narrative, this reading public "had long since grown out of early institutions like the coffee houses, *salons* and *Tischgesellschaften*." It was no longer restricted to specific locations and could establish itself nationwide through the medium of the printed press.

However, even in this third phase of turning inside out "the public sphere of a rational-critical debate in the world of letters" remained tethered to its roots in the "moral inner space." As Section 6 emphasizes, in this rational-critical debate "the subjectivity originating in the interiority of the conjugal family, by communicating with itself, attained clarity about itself" (STPS 51).

Without progressing through all these stages of turning inside out, the subjectivity of bourgeois conscience and private opinion cannot gradually acquire its morally pretentious rationality. In other words, neither "a psychological emancipation" of the bourgeoisie nor "the political-economic one" could have occurred. In short, the commodity owners could not have viewed "themselves as autonomous" and the "fiction of a justice immanent in free commerce" could not have triumphed over force (STPS 46, 111). Small wonder then that Habermas has responded to critics like Zaret as follows:

> I have some doubts about how far we can push back the very notion of the public sphere into the sixteenth and seventeenth centuries *without somehow changing the very concept of the public sphere to such a degree that it becomes something else.* (HPS 465, emphasis added)

Zaret's analysis of the political public sphere of the 1640s could not have been included in *Structural Transformation*'s stylization, because there is no way to fit it into the chronology and trajectory of Habermas's narrative. In Schmitt's interpretation, it would take almost two decades before Spinoza detected the crack in *Leviathan*'s armor and another two before Locke found a way to tame Spinoza's atheism by introducing moral relativism in his *Essay Concerning Human Understanding* (1690). In Koselleck's description, Locke, whom he calls the "spiritual father of the bourgeois Enlightenment," started writing his *Essay* in 1670, "under the rule of the Absolutist Stuarts," and "finished his voluminous work in Holland, during his six-year exile," before publishing it "in England after the fall of James II" (CC 53).

Without any reference to Spinoza, *Structural Transformation*'s Section 12 follows this trajectory in intellectual history from Hobbes to Locke, thus connecting "the medium of positive law" that "already contains the seed of the development of the constitutional state" to the process of Enlightenment. For without this connection the positive law would have only contained "the *formal* criteria of generality and abstractness" without also acquiring the "*substantive* rationality" that Habermas introduces in Section 7 (STPS 55, emphasis added). In other words, the morally pretentious rationality of Kant's rational natural law underlying his concept of the republican constitution.

Section 11 makes this quite clear when it juxtaposes the concept of law as an expression of the *will* of the absolute ruler as "a sovereign legislator" with the one in which law is grounded in *reason* (STPS 81; HA 131). For the bourgeois public sphere that could have sprouted out of the Hobbesian seeds for the development of the constitutional state would have been restricted to *only one* of its two Kantian functions. Namely, to serving as the organizational principle of the constitutional state. Without also providing the medium for rational-critical Enlightenment with Kant's "public use of reason" as its method.

To this day, Habermas has been an advocate for what he calls the "typically bourgeois idea" that "the rule of law aims at dissolving domination altogether" (STPS 81). He thus remains tethered to Aristotle's definition of the "sovereignty of the laws" in book IV, chapter 4 of his *Politics*: "In democracies that are bound to the law, no demagogue emerges. . . . However, where the laws do not have the highest authority, demagogues arise. For there the people become a monarch, specifically a many-headed one." Readers have to be aware of this fact, because *Structural Transformation* leaves out this classical source for the idea of law as "something rational-universal; not *voluntas* but *ratio*," when Section 11 quotes from the paragraph that references Aristotle in Schmitt's *Constitutional Theory*, which "Horrors of Autonomy" classifies as a "brilliant" book (STPS 81; CT 182; VL 139; HA 133; HPSC 46).

This omission must surprise the reader. After all, *Structural Transformation*'s Section 1 immediately highlights the "peculiarly *normative power*" of the political public sphere in ancient Greece "in the stylized form of Greek self-interpretation" (STPS 4, emphasis added). Moreover, the idea of law as "something rational-universal" informs Kant's rational natural law.

Above all, transforming Hobbes's dictum that "authority not truth makes the law" into the claim that reason prevails and thus truth will make the law defines the process of criticism as it is stylized in *Structural Transformation*. Significantly, Section 7 about the relationship of the literary and the political public sphere primarily discusses "the controversy in constitutional law over the principle of absolute sovereignty" from Hobbes, via Locke, to Montesquieu. In this context, the development of a rational-critical discourse in the rising bourgeois public sphere served "the promotion of legislation based on *ratio*" (STPS 53).

In intellectual and constitutional law history, the Enlightenment rationality "in which what is right converges with what is just" (STPS 53) developed in the interplay between Locke and Bayle as well as between Rousseau and the Physiocrats before culminating in the morally pretentious rationality of Kant's rational natural law. Habermas could not have reconstructed this trajectory without deriving its structure from Koselleck's rendition of the "Process of Criticism" and using it as his template. In turn, Koselleck implicitly highlighted the necessity of Schmitt's civil war *topos* when conceptualizing the starting point for this process of Enlightenment: "As [Locke] demonstrated quite empirically, the *bourgeois moral laws* originated in the *interior of the human conscience*, in the *space which Hobbes had exempted from the realm of the State* (CC 54-55, emphasis added).

Locke's moral "Law of Opinion or Reputation," the "Measure of Virtue and Vice," was implemented "by a secret and tacit consent" of "private men who have not authority enough to make a law" (quoted in STPS 91, CC 54). While Section 12 valorizes it as the first important expression of "secularized morality," it did not contribute to critical debate. Accordingly, the process of criticism only starts with Bayle who weds "the concept of criticism to that of reason" (CC 108). Nevertheless, "rational criticism and moral censure" remain interconnected throughout the eighteenth century (CC 57n15).

Regarding the development of rational-critical debate, Koselleck and Habermas present a clear trajectory from Bayle in 1695 via the Encyclope-dists after 1751 as well as the Physiocrats around 1767 to Kant's seminal concept of "the public use of reason" in 1784. Koselleck points out that in the course of this development reason "becomes a critical process of the search for truth" (CC 108n29). His following quote from the translation of Ernst Cassirer's seminal work about the *Philosophy of the Enlightenment* (1951) helps readers to better understand Section 12:

> The whole eighteenth century understands reason in this sense; not as a sound body of knowledge, principles, and truths, but as a kind of energy, a force which is fully comprehensible only in its agency and effects. (quoted in CC 108n29)

Nevertheless, the relevance of Schmitt and Koselleck's concept of a "moral inner space" resurfaces with Rousseau. Especially since *Structural Transfor-mation*'s thesis that "Locke's 'Law of Opinion' became sovereign by way of Rousseau's *Contrat Social*" (STPS 97) is only partially correct. As discussed above under 7.6, it was primarily Shaftesbury's concept of a *natural* moral sense, not Locke's tacit moral censure of private men, that inspired Rousseau.

The year 1750, when Rousseau published his *Discourse on the Arts and Sciences* and Diderot his *Prospectus*, the prepublication announcement for the *Encyclopedie* "that was soon echoed throughout Europe" (STPS 263n26), marks the transition point from a *literary* to a *political* public sphere in the chronology of *Structural Transformation*'s stylization. Such a structural demarcation is also applied to the English development as its delineation at the end of Section 6 illustrates. However, readers will realize this only in hindsight when they learn about Rousseau's introduction of his moral but uncritical concept of *opinion publique* in Section 12. There it is contrasted to the enlightened public of the Encyclopedists (STPS 93, 95). One then has to connect this information to Section 9 where Habermas emphasizes that "only at the stage of its encyclopedic publication did the moral intent of the *philosophes* develop into a political one, at least indirectly" (STPS 68).

Significantly, he is aware that Montesquieu's constitutional theory, highlighted in Section 7 as a key step toward reversing "Hobbes's theory of the state" (STPS 53), does not fit neatly into his claim that in "the first half of the century, the criticism of the *philosophes* was preoccupied . . . with religion, literature, and art . . ." (STPS 68). He thus had to inject into that sentence the qualifier "Montesquieu notwithstanding." The ideology-critical logic inherent in *Structural Transformation*'s theory reconstruction seemingly allowed him to exclude *Esprit des Lois* (1735) from the encyclopedic process of criticism that "Robespierre could celebrate . . . later as 'the introductory chapter of the Revolution'" (STPS 68–69). This introductory chapter began in earnest with the publication of d'Alembert's *Preliminary Discourse* (1751), which Habermas praises as "a brilliant outline of the entire work." Expressly addressed to the enlightened public, the *Encyclopedie* "was a publicist undertaking in the grand style" (STPS 68, 263n26).

Readers have to keep in mind that for Habermas the turn in the development of modern constitutional law toward Kant's rational natural law could only occur after the Physiocrats had seemingly discovered the "natural laws of society" which informed the construction of Kant's republican constitution. In stark contrast, Montesquieu was still bound to Locke's traditional natural law, which Condorcet would reject as "unenlightened." As Schmitt points out in his *Constitutional Theory*, "[u]nder the influence of Bolingbroke, Montesquieu drafted an ideal image of the English constitution. . ." (CT 221).

However, for Rousseau even Montesquieu's "unenlightened" rationality was already too estranged from the "naturalness" of "the opinion of the people." As *Structural Transformation* highlights in Section 12, Rousseau's *Contrat Social* from 1762 critiqued Montesquieu, because for him "the spirit of the constitution" was "anchored in the hearts of the citizens," in their mores and their customs (quoted in STPS 97). After all, it was their "moral sense," implanted in them by nature, that guided their natural *opinion publique*.

In other words, until Schiller would apply in 1784 the criteria of Locke's moral laws to the political dramaturgy of his "moral stage" and, under Kant's influence, develop a rational morality, Rousseau's privileging of a "moral sense" in his constitutional theory had an outsize influence on the discourse in the political public sphere. In 1767, the Physiocrat Le Mercier de la Reviere used the presupposition of "natural laws of society" to introduce a rational-critical concept of *opinion publique*. Afterwards the meaning of the term *opinion publique* "became particularly polarized in prerevolutionary France," as Habermas emphasizes in Section 12 (STPS

99). One has to remember Kant's interpretation of the French Revolution as a historical sign for the moral progress of the human race to understand how *Structural Transformation* seeks to dissolve this polarization of morality and rationality. Namely, by interpreting the Constitution of 1791 with its Declaration of Human and Civil Rights, which grew out of the rational-critical discourse in the National Assembly, as the revolutionary manifestation of a morally pretentious rationality.

The preceding analysis demonstrates that there is no substitute in intellectual history for Schmitt's civil war *topos*, as it informs Koselleck's stylization of the eighteenth century "Process of Criticism," if *Structural Transformation* wants to maintain the structure of its trajectory and chronology from Locke and Bayle to Schiller, Kant, and the French Revolution. Indirectly, the reader will realize this when confronted with the book's structural gap of more than forty years between the French Revolution and Great Britain's "great Reform Bill of 1832" (STPS 74). The book's tacit switch to section 25.1 in *Constitutional Theory*, which presents the most important dates of the historical development of "the Parliamentary System" in England (CT xii), remains insufficient. Already the limited structural relevance of the starting point that Habermas could glean from Schmitt's text for *Structural Transformation*'s "Model Case of British Development" illustrates this shortcoming. For the relevance of the reference in Section 8 that the introduction in 1695 of "the first cabinet government marked a new stage in the development of Parliament" (STPS 58), which Schmitt received from Wilhelm Hasbach's seminal text on the topic from 1919 (CT 343), pales greatly in comparison to the crucial importance of the publication of Bayle's *Historical and Critical Dictionary* in the same year. Even the "elimination of the institution of censorship," also in 1695, traditionally highlighted in the Whig Interpretation of History, remains tangential to the development of the bourgeois public sphere's signature morally pretentious rationality, which the civil war *topos* allows to conceptualize.

Needless to say, Schmitt's civil war *topos* remains equally controversial and relevant. It "dates from 1938 and was published in the middle of the Nazi period." As Habermas points out, it "leads us to the center of Schmitt's intellectual world" (HA 129), whose conception of the totalitarian state first oriented itself toward Mussolini's Italy, then toward Hitler's Germany, and finally toward Franco's Spain. There can be little doubt that today Schmitt, a connoisseur of state power and decisive action, would be impressed by the sovereignty of political will and the strict regulation of rational autonomy in China's totalitarian capitalism. Especially since its Stalinist leadership faithfully follows the crucial instruction by Hobbes that the "state alone determines the *public* creed of its citizens" (HA 131, emphasis added).

9.2. BEFORE THE CIVIL WAR *TOPOS: STRUCTURAL TRANSFORMATION'S* METHODOLOGICAL CONTRADICTION BETWEEN ITS DEVELOPMENTAL AND ITS IDEOLOGY-CRITICAL HISTORY OF THE BOURGEOIS PUBLIC SPHERE

Habermas's explanation from March 1990 that only "on a superficial glance would it have appeared possible to write *Structural Transformation* along the lines of a developmental history in the style of Marx and Max Weber" (FRPS 442) is correct with regard to Sections 4 to 7 and 10 to 13. For these eight sections select their sources and their respective data from intellectual, constitutional, social, and political history according to the criteria of Habermas's ideology-critical procedure. However, as the reader knows by now, all these sections do not wear the dialectical structure of this approach on their sleeves (FRPS 442).

In stark contrast, Section 3 "On the Genesis of the Bourgeois Public Sphere" as well as Sections 8 and 9 lack this dialectical structure, because the book's ideology-critical procedure is not applied to them. Instead, they present a developmental structure, which for Section 3 covers the time period from the thirteenth to the eighteenth century. Moreover, even for the years that do overlap with the unfolding of the civil war *topos*, from Locke's *Essay* in 1690 to the French Revolution in 1789, does Section 3 remain mostly focused on the facticity of the historical development. Although its presentation is selective and incomplete.

The same can be said for Section 8, which covers the time period from 1694 to 1834. In this case, readers are even retroactively alerted to the break between that section's developmental history and the ideology-critical version of history presented in Sections 10 and 11, even though the underlying dialectical procedure remains unidentified. As was discussed under 5.3 and 5.4, the ideology-critical Section 10 immediately emphasizes that "the kind" of political function that "the public sphere takes on . . . during the eighteenth century" can *not yet* "be grasped" (STPS 73) in Section 8.

As analyzed above under 5.5, Section 8 states in a straightforward manner that with the first issue of *The Craftsman* in November 1726 "the press was for the first time established as a genuinely critical organ of the public engaged in critical political debate: as the fourth estate" (STPS 60). However, Section 10 tacitly withdraws *Structural Transformation*'s assessment in Section 8 and implies that Bolingbroke's "publicist platform of the opposition" in Parliament could *not yet* be "genuinely critical" after all. For only about forty years later would the political economy of the Physiocrats purify *opinion publique* "through *critical* discussion in the public sphere to constitute a *true* opinion" (STPS 95, emphasis added). In other words, in 1726 even "genuinely critical" was *insufficiently* critical compared to Physiocratic *opinion publique* after 1767.

To briefly recap: the Physiocrats could accomplish this purification only after Quesnay had first discovered "the natural laws of society" starting in the late 1750s. And after they had defined in 1767 the role that the press would have to play in educating the public about these *social* presuppositions of a *political* society. Secondly, Kant had to ground the rational *natural* law of his republican constitution in these *natural* economic laws. In comparison, Bolingbroke remained tethered to Locke's traditional natural law and even passed it on to Montesquieu who thus had to remain "unenlightened" in Condorcet's eyes.

Above all, according to the ideology-critical logic that informs Section 10, the question whether the press can take on the political function of a "fourth estate" can only be decided "in relation to the developmental history of civil society as a whole in which commodity exchange and social labor became largely emancipated from government directives" (STPS 73-74). In short, after the decisive role of Free Trade in all markets that Adam Smith's political economy had advocated for since 1776 would have been fully implemented.

Logically, this leaves even the trajectory of the unfolding of the civil war *topos* in a feeder role toward allegedly achieving justice immanent in all market exchanges and the private autonomy of the property owner. Namely, as the economic preconditions for the *telos* of a morally pretentious rationality as the hallmark of the critical discourse in the bourgeois public sphere. Hence, the founding of the Bank of England as the economic Section 8 starting point of this trajectory (STPS 58) can only serve as a means toward achieving this end. In other words, its rivalry with the South Sea Company, which triggered the first global financial crisis, delayed the start of the Industrial Revolution by half a century, resurrected the failed politician Walpole as the most important statesman of the eighteenth century, created "a systematic opposition" in Parliament (STPS 63), and spawned the publication of *The Craftsman*, has to be largely neglected because these historical events do not fit into the civil war *topos* trajectory and occurred strangely prematurely according to the logic of *this* Marxist critique of ideology (cf. HPSC 171–88).

This methodological contradiction between *Structural Transformation*'s developmental and its ideology-critical history of the bourgeois public sphere manifests itself in the tension between its main normative theses introduced under 1.1 and 1.2 and its central historical thesis about the role of the modern public sphere as the organizational principle of the rules governing the sphere of commodity exchange and social labor at the outset of Section 4. Since the latter is presented in an ideology-critical context where normativity is privileged, readers do not learn *where and when* the public of private property owners "*soon* claimed the public sphere regulated from above against the public authorities themselves" (STPS 27, emphasis added). Only after having reached the end of Section 13 can one be certain that *Structural Transformation* refers to France and Prussia in the last third of the eighteenth century.

This triggers the question why Great Britain was designated as a "model case?" After all, the "Glorious Revolution," in which England's leading private property owners outsourced the political leadership of their parliamentary system to the monarch of the most advanced capitalist nation on the globe, had already imported all the Dutch know-how necessary to develop the governing rules for the Financial Revolution, which facilitated the monetary framework for the capital accumulation needed for the Industrial Revolution. Moreover, readers will search in vain in the developmental history of Section 8 for a description of this crucial event in modernity, because it occurred two years *before* Locke published his *Essay* and the unfolding of the civil war *topos* could begin.

As this guide analyzes directly at the beginning of chapter 6, the French Revolution is granted a monopoly in *Structural Transformation*. There is no mention of the Dutch, English, and American Revolutions included in the developmental history of Section 3. While Habermas references "the *traffic in commodities and news* created by early capitalist long-distance trade" from Northern Italy to "Dutch centers for staple good" (STPS 15, emphasis in the original, 14), which spawned the development of news as a commodity (STPS 21), readers will find only in an endnote to Section 9 the acknowledgment that the newspapers of the Dutch Republic "earned the reputation" as "Europe's least censored papers" already in the seventeenth century. They also maintained this reputation "throughout the eighteenth century" (STPS 263n23).

This omission in Section 3 becomes even more pronounced, if one connects information in the same endnote about the censorship of these *Gazettes de Hollande* by Louis XIV in 1679, 1683, and 1686 to extended references in Section 3 to newspapers as "preferred instruments of governments" in London and Paris at around the same time. Not a word about the wealth of newspapers published during the Commonwealth period that Zaret would later analyze, but "the *Gazette of London* that appeared from 1665 on under Charles II" is recognized (STPS 22). In short, neither the English Revolution that used the printing presses to create a democratic culture nor the Dutch Revolution, which had done the same even earlier, are mentioned. In Spinoza's words about the Dutch Republic from 1670:

> [W]e have the rare happiness of living in a republic, where everyone's judgment is free and unshackled . . . without such freedom, piety cannot flourish nor the public peace be secure. (quoted in HPSC 155)

Perhaps the clearest expression of the methodological contradiction between *Structural Transformation*'s developmental and its ideology-critical
history of the bourgeois public sphere can be recognized in the *twofold* inability of Section 3 to deliver what its title promises. Namely, a description of the
genesis of the *bourgeois* public sphere. For readers will be challenged to find
a single reference to this central category of *bourgeois* society (cf. STPS 5).

Section 3 contains only two references to *bourgeois*, one with quotation
marks and the other without. The first one refers to an "initial assimilation
of *bourgeois humanism* to a noble courtly culture ... during the rise of Flo-
rentine Renaissance society" (STPS 14–15, emphasis added). The second
one identifies "the 'capitalists,' the merchants, bankers, entrepreneurs, and
manufacturers" as belonging "to that group of 'bourgeois' who . . . was *the
real carrier of the public,* which from the outset was a *reading public*" (STPS
23, emphasis added).

However, the single reference to "the new domain of a *public sphere*" does
not classify it as a bourgeois institution. Instead, it states that its "decisive
mark was the *published word*" (STPS 16, emphases added). In other words,
this new domain could also be a state or even a royal institution.

Specifically, this could be the case with regard to the "first journals in the
strict sense." Namely, the "'*political journals*'" that "appeared weekly at
first, and *daily as early as the middle of the seventeenth century*" (STPS 20,
emphasis added). Significantly, the regular use of "the press for the purposes
of the state administration," like publishing "instructions and ordinances,"
would "genuinely" turn "*the addressees*" of these announcements into "'*the
public' in the proper sense*" (STPS 21, *emphasis added*).

If, as quoted above, *the real carrier of the public,* which from the outset was a *reading public,* were the merchants, bankers, entrepreneurs, and
manufacturers, then the members of this first public "in the proper sense"
were merely *passive recipients* of *administrative orders* to follow specific
instructions. Worse, instead of holding up "a mirror to itself" (STPS 43),
like the bourgeois reading public would do in London's coffee houses early
in the eighteenth century when perusing and debating the moral weeklies,
this public had to direct its gaze upward toward their aristocratic superiors
or royal rulers. For these political journals did not only publish state instructions: "From the beginning, [they] had reported on the journeys and returns
of the princes, on the arrival of foreign dignitaries, on balls, 'special events'
at court" (STPS 21).

This administrative and royal perspective from above prevails in Section 3.
For it ends with the long quote from the "rescript of Frederick II from 1784"
mentioned under 5.1 above. In it, the monarch admonishes the private persons
in no uncertain terms that they have "no right to pass *public* and perhaps even

disapproving judgment" on any instruction issued by the state (STPS 25, emphasis in the original).

Again, readers will find it difficult to fathom that for the same year, in which Kant publishes his famous essay on the "public use of reason" and Schiller gives his address about the "moral stage," Section 3 primarily pays attention to a royal address. The only hopeful sign for a future emancipation of the bourgeoisie through their public use of reason is the observation on page 24 that "official interventions into the privatized household finally came to constitute the target of a developing critical sphere." Specifically, these interventions "provoked the *critical judgment* of a public making use of its reason" (STPS 24, emphasis added).

Apart from etymological reflections on the term "public" and its variations, Section 3 ends with the statement that seemingly until 1784 the bourgeois reading public in Prussia had "without question ... counted as a sphere of *public authority.*" However, it "was now casting itself loose as a forum in which the private people, come together to form a public, readied themselves to compel *public authority* to legitimate itself before public opinion" (STPS 25-26, emphasis added). Needless to say, such an *intention* alone is insufficient to constitute "the Genesis of the Bourgeois Public Sphere."

Moreover, Section 3 does not inform the reader that in *Structural Transformation's* stylization the *really normative* "Genesis of the Bourgeois Public Sphere" will take place in the last third of the eighteenth century in prerevolutionary France. This will be facilitated through an ideology-critical reading of the unfolding of the civil war *topos*. For the French Revolution had "less stability" (STPS 70) than the parliamentary development after the "Glorious Revolution." In short, the normativity inherent in the French Constitution of 1791 will have to be privileged over the "bad facticity" of the Jacobin Terror.

Finally, *Structural Transformation's* dependency on Schmitt's civil war *topos* as well as on Koselleck's interpretation of the "Process of Criticism" in modernity prevented its Section 3 from using its developmental history to explore the *really existing* genesis of the bourgeois public sphere in the seventeenth century Dutch Republic in interplay with England during its Commonwealth period. For that purpose, it could have employed the book's main thesis about the rational-critical public sphere as a central category of bourgeois society from the perspective of facticity. *Habermas's Public Sphere: A Critique* has demonstrated in its chapter 4, titled "From the Dutch Republic to the Fiscal-Military State of the Modern Whigs," that such an approach is viable (cf. HPSC 155–88).

However, this perspective would have necessitated treating the analysis of this category as an end in itself. Instead of subsuming its social and political history under the norms inherent in constitutional law and intellectual history.

And following Hegel in comprehending "history dialectically." As discussed in section 8.1 above, this normative and dialectical perspective gave Habermas the freedom to select the "specifics of the historical material" (STPS xviii) with which to study the public sphere as the organizational principle of the bourgeois constitutional state that regulates the sphere of commodity exchange and social labor.

Small wonder that most historians "have been and still are skeptical about the validity of Habermas's master narrative on the causes of the transformation of the public sphere," as the historian Andreas Gestrich observed in his essay "The Public Sphere and the Habermas Debate" (2006). Nevertheless, in spite of this skepticism the English edition of *Structural Transformation* has acquired "the status of a global classic" and "unleashed an astonishingly lively and long-lasting debate amongst historians on his theory of the historical development of political public spheres in western European societies," as Gestrich also emphasizes.

Based on its interdisciplinary approach, this guide intends to assist this lively debate by clarifying *Structural Transformation*'s dialectical and counterfactual treatment of the specifics of the historical material. Once readers have taken off the "moral inner space" blinders of Schmitt's civil war *topos* that since Section 4 had restricted their perspective on the origins of the public sphere, they will realize just how selective and tenuous the historical material that propped up the book's "master narrative" was. That's why Habermas in his Zurich lecture from December 1960 granted the fictions of classical political economy, which Kant and Marx both relied on, only a "*certain* fundamentum in re" even during the liberal phase of capitalism (TUP 265, emphasis added).

Among the key criticisms that Gestrich summarizes, the one from early communication history about "the driving forces behind the early modern transformation of the public sphere" stands out. While *Structural Transformation*'s stylization assesses "the institutions and circles of communication" that constitute "a new critical public sphere" as "bourgeois in character," these historical studies document "how socially varied the participation in these circles was." But this finding should not have come as a surprise. As discussed above in chapter 6, Habermas himself acknowledged that in pre-revolutionary France "the nobility in its *salons* was more receptive to the enlightened mode of thought of bourgeois intellectuals than the bourgeoisie itself (STPS 68).

Similarly, as late as January 1789 Sieyes had to acknowledge just how "far behind" the bourgeois consciousness of the third estate still was (NLR 88). Even Tocqueville's claim, tacitly adopted by Habermas, that Rousseau's *Contrat Social* was treated as the "canonical" text during the French Revolution does not survive the scrutiny of empirical research. Arguably, Habermas could have sensed that when he described the preferences of the bourgeois reading public as follows: "When Rousseau used the form of the novel in letters for *La Nouvelle Heloise* and Goethe for *Werthers Leiden*, there was no longer any holding back" (STPS 49–50).

For *La Nouvelle Heloise* achieved an estimated one hundred editions and illegal reprints before 1800. In short, the novel outsold his paean to natural rights and popular sovereignty by a considerable margin. In 1910, when Daniel Mornet introduced empirical methods into the study of literary history, he discovered stunning evidence. In his analysis of the contents of *five hundred* private libraries that were auctioned off between 1750 and 1780, he found only one copy of the *Contrat Social* but, in stark contrast, 185 copies of *La Nouvelle Heloise* (cf. HPSC 66).

Conclusion

Renewing the Human Rights Perspective in the Political Public Sphere

Although a "statesman-like optimism pervades the pages of *Between Facts and Norms*," as Benhabib diagnosed in 1997, in his close reading of the book Forbath nevertheless detected as early as 1998 Habermas's warning that the public sphere remains vulnerable to "the repressive and exclusionary effects of unequally distributed social power . . . and systematically distorted communication." Significantly, Habermas added the demand that "the general public must rest on a society 'that has emerged from the confines of class and thrown off the millennial-old shackles of social stratification and exploitation.'" In short, Habermas defined such a "societal basis" as the presupposition for "equal rights of citizenship" and a rational-critical public discourse (BFN 307–08; cf. Forbath 1998: 283–84).

Unfortunately, these essential reminders have only occasionally been taken into account. Like Scheuerman did in 2012 when reflecting in *Political Theory* on the undercurrent of radical reformism that connects *Structural Transformation* with *Between Facts and Norms*. However, as the political theorists Veith Selk and Dirk Jörke pointed out in *Constellations* in 2019, in the past thirty years "many social scientists in general, and theorists of democracy in particular" have instead focused on Habermas's 1992 dictum that "a modern, market-regulated economic system" cannot be subjected to "democratic decision making, without threatening its performance capacity" (FRPS 436). Hence, "the widespread belief about the complexity and self-contained character of the economic system has become a self-fulfilling prophecy" (Selk/Jörke 2019).

Needless to say, Silicon Valley's promise of a "new economy" with equal access and prosperity for all through an exponentially improving cost/benefit ratio for digital technologies (Moore's Law) strengthened this libertarian trust in the resurrection of "Say's Law of Markets." The cult-like following for a visionary entrepreneur like Steve Jobs even attached a rock star aura to the new digital capitalism. Above all, initial public offerings of start-up stocks seemed to erase the old antagonism between capital and labor. They could not only turn employers in their twenties but also a few of their employees into instant billionaires.

Emblematic for this libertarian celebration of the "performance capacity" of "a modern, market-regulated economic system" was the high-profile product launch of the Apple Macintosh personal computer early in 1984 with an attention-grabbing commercial on the Super Bowl TV broadcast, the most-watched television show in the United States. Liberating the individual from the domination of the IBM mainframe computer was expressed in this TV spot as a dramatic act of highly stylized empowerment. Sprinting through the center aisle of a movie theater populated by robotic serfs gazing up to their oppressor on the screen, is a scantily clad female runner. At the climax of this commercial, she releases Thor's mythical weapon to destroy "Big Brother" with the ultimate hammer blow. In the year that George Orwell selected for his prediction about totalitarianism in his dystopian novel *1984*.

While this visualization of a triumphant "performance capacity" vividly employs the "expressive subjectivism" of a Rousseau novel written in a state of "flaming ecstasy," Apple's global marketing campaign targeted, for example, the West German reader with the low-key approach of Kantian contemplation. In September 1984, the business section of the *Süddeutsche Zeitung* featured a two-page ad that placed the image of an Apple Macintosh next to enlarged images of books by, from left to right, Mao Tse-Tung, Engels, Lenin, Karl Marx, and Trotsky—with *Das Kapital* taking center stage. Unfazed by the works of these communist heavy hitters, the computer screen displays a friendly "Hello" to announce the message, in small print, that "Apple invented the Macintosh." While the ad's headline reads, in similarly understated type: "It is high time that, for once, a capitalist changes the world" (*SZ*, no. 203, 9/3/1984, 20–21).

THE "FRIEDMANITE" TURN AND THE HEGEMONY OF "ECONOMIC AUTONOMY" IN THE NEOLIBERAL PUBLIC SPHERE

As a historian of ideas and a public intellectual writing in *The New York Review of Books*, Mark Lilla has offered incisive analyses of the convergence of left and right versions of Libertarianism during the 1980s and 1990s, carrying over into the new millennium. In a variation of Paul Berman's thesis in his *A Tale of Two Utopias: The Political Journey of the Generation of 1968* (1996), he posited in

1998 the "indivisible" unification of the 1960s cultural revolution for "private autonomy" with the 1980s "Reagan revolution" for "economic autonomy." In 2010, he would reiterate his argument by noting that during "the Clinton years the country edged left on issues of private autonomy (sex, divorce, casual drug use) while continuing to move right on economic autonomy (individual initiative, free markets, deregulation)." To illustrate his claim, he asserted already in 1998 that especially young Americans "see no contradiction in holding down day jobs in the unfettered global marketplace. . . and spending weekends in a moral and cultural universe shaped by the Sixties" (Lilla 2010: 53; Lilla 1998: 4).

To a certain extent Lilla's juxtaposition between employment in the deregulated global marketplace and self-realization outside the workplace mirrors Habermas's distinction between system and lifeworld which he systematically introduced in 1981 in his *Theory of Communicative Action*. What Lilla subsumes under his term "economic autonomy," Habermas more precisely identifies as the "substantial autonomy" of the economic system in which money functions as the steering mechanism for global market exchanges. In his reflections from 2004 on the "Kantian Project and the Divided West," he would identify such "substantial autonomy" with rationality when writing about an "autonomously, i.e., rationally formed will of a bourgeois society" with a republican constitution (DW 132).

Specifically, the "economic autonomy" Lilla refers to becomes truly substantial when the deregulated market, liberated from government interventions like rulings by the Federal Communications Commission, can fully reward the "individual initiative" of Silicon Valley entrepreneurs. The Reagan Revolution thus restored and secured for them as the owners of "the means of production" the social "power, sanctioned in civil law, to appropriate surplus value and to use it privately and *autonomously*" (LC 26, emphasis added). Only such a neoliberal order could seemingly safeguard the "kind and measure of *rationality*" in "exchange relations," which Max Weber defined as the implementation of "calculable expectations" for "profit opportunities" (STPS 80, emphasis added).

"The Social Responsibility of Business Is to Increase Its Profits." In September 1970, this headline above a *New York Times Magazine* article in which Milton Friedman spelled out his "doctrine" was as attention-grabbing as it was controversial. Only six years after his crushing defeat as Goldwater's economic advisor in the 1964 election, when his plan to privatize Social Security was not only attacked by the Democrats but also by the Rockefeller Republicans, the *Times* granted his libertarian doctrine exposure on *the* liberal Establishment platform. Fifty years later, the *Times* published a commemorative section dedicated to what it called "arguably the most consequential idea of the latter half of the 20th century." Under the title "Greed Is Good. Except When It's Bad," the section implicitly credited the *Times* with having launched Friedman's "call to arms for free market capitalism that influenced a generation of executives and political leaders, most notably Ronald Reagan and Margaret Thatcher" (NYT, 9/13/2020).

As discussed throughout this guide to reading *Structural Transformation*, Habermas's 1962 classic defines the function of the modern public sphere as facilitating the rational-critical discourse about "the general rules governing relations in the basically privatized but publicly relevant sphere of commodity exchange and social labor" (STPS 27). Significantly, Friedman published *Capitalism and Freedom* (1962), the first book-length presentation of his libertarian economics, in the same year. Both books agreed that the "specifically bourgeois science" of "political economy" (STPS 29) informs this public discourse about the general rules governing all exchange relations in modernity. However, only Friedman claimed that the eighteenth-century doctrines presented by Adam Smith were still valid.

Moreover, there is a distinct difference between Habermas's public use of reason and Friedman's. As *New York Times* columnist Paul Krugman, winner of the 2008 Nobel Prize in Economics, pointed out in his commemorative essay from 2007 in the *New York Review of Books*, only the professional rigor of Friedman's "technical, more or less apolitical analyses of consumer behavior and inflation" made him the proverbial "economist's economist." However, as the "great popularizer of free-market doctrine" he used "looser, sometimes questionable logic" and engaged with his trademark "single-mindedness" (Krugman 2007: 27, 29). Above all, his energy imbued his arguments with a "revolutionary fervor," as the journalist Naomi Klein highlighted in her book *The Shock Doctrine* (Klein 2007: 60).

In short, Friedman's tireless advocacy for the teachings of the University of Chicago's Economics Department channeled the rhetoric and supreme confidence of the author of Say's Law. In Klein's words, for Friedman "the economic forces of supply, demand, inflation and unemployment were like the forces of nature, fixed and unchanging." Once markets were truly free, these nature-like forces would exist "in perfect equilibrium, supply communicating with demand the way the moon pulls the tides" (Klein 2007: 61).

Like Reagan had honed his free market rhetoric for many years as the spokesman for General Electric, Friedman would become such a powerful debater that he dominated the public presentations of all other members of the Chicago School of Economics. In retrospect, even the *New York Times* overlooks the fact that it was Friedrich Hayek whose writings first convinced Thatcher to adopt the Chicago teachings. Already "during a visit to the Conservative Party's research department in the mid-1970s" did she announce her plan to implement these teachings which Hayek had espoused at the London School of Economics since 1932 before joining the Chicago School after the success of his anti-Keynesian manifesto *The Road to Serfdom* (1944). According to a colorful description published by the Hoover Institute at Stanford University, Thatcher "slammed" a copy of Hayek's *The Constitution of Liberty* (1960) on the table and declared: "This is what we believe" (quoted in Cassidy 2000: 7).

Structural Transformation's Section 15 discusses how after the mid-nineteenth-century political economy's propositions about natural laws for the harmonious organization of society lost their "objective guarantee of a concordance of interests in society." In short, "the rational demonstrability of a universal interest as such" (STPS 135). Logically, these propositions then had to assume the character of a faith as Thatcher's wording unwittingly indicates. However, Section 15 and the remaining sections of Habermas's classic omit that they did so *successfully*. Looking back from his perspective in 1936, Keynes observed that classical economics in the tradition of Adam Smith's dictum about self-regulating markets had "conquered England as completely as the Holy Inquisition conquered Spain" (quoted in Krugman 2007: 27).

Krugman equally refers to the realm of religion when describing the uphill battle that Keynes had to fight with his professional peers in spite of the fact that "classical economics offered neither explanations nor solutions for the Great Depression." Keynes thus had to play "the role of Martin Luther, providing the intellectual rigor needed to make heresy respectable." Regarding the inevitable counterreformation, Krugman largely neglects Hayek's influence and ascribes the role of "Ignatius of Loyola, founder of the Jesuits," solely to Friedman. Accordingly, Friedman's disciples formed a disciplined army of the faithful that spearheaded "a broad, but incomplete, rollback of Keynesian heresy" (Krugman 2007: 27).

Krugman's analogies to the controversies in the history of religious thought are justified, because the absolute rationalism that informed the classical economics of the late eighteenth century ended after Condorcet's death during the Jacobin Terror of the French Revolution. In turn, its termination coincided with the rapid accumulation of overwhelming empirical evidence for the horrific exploitation of child labor in England during the Industrial Revolution (cf. HPSC 114–15). Afterwards, the "free-market orthodoxy" had to be defended against all "heresies." Even David Ricardo was subjected to James Mill's policing of the speakers in the Political Economy Club once he revised himself and acknowledged in 1821 that the introduction of machinery could be detrimental to the interest of the laboring classes. In the eyes of free-market orthodoxy, "Ricardo's recantation was tantamount to a surrender of Say's Law" (cf. HPSC 96, 123, 148n66). As Krugman points out, before Keynes such heresies "were always suppressed" (Krugman 2007: 27).

Regarding today's growing influence of *Structural Transformation*, Krugman's analysis that the "rollback of Keynesian heresy" was "incomplete" has gained in significance due to the global financial crisis of 2008, the following "Great Recession," and the "Great Supply Chain Disruption" in the wake of the global Covid-19 pandemic and Russia's invasion of Ukraine. Nevertheless, readers have to keep in mind that most corporate leaders in Silicon Valley share a "Friedmanite" view of their social responsibility regarding social media and the digital economy. Emblematic for this libertarian hegemony that informs the *new* structural transformation of the public sphere was the emphatic confession to be a "Friedmanite" by the last Treasury Secretary in the Clinton administration, Lawrence H. Summers, who played a key role in the termination of the New Deal safeguards against financial crises. For his chief of staff, Sheryl Sandberg, would go on to create Google's and Facebook's business models of extracting personal data to sell their precision-targeted digital ads, generating a combined revenue total of about 325 billion dollars in 2021.

In November 2006, Summers eulogized Friedman in the *New York Times* under the title "The Great Liberator" as a "great man" who "freed markets and minds." He thus "lost his hero," even though he "grew up in a family of progressive economists," where "Milton Friedman was a devil figure." In short, his 1970s rebellion against parental authority coincided with Friedman's consequential valorization of the profit motive in the *New York Times*. During his undergraduate studies "in the early 1970s," Friedman was still regarded as one of "a few . . . dissidents" from mainstream economics. However, when Summers started "teaching undergraduates a decade later, Mr. Friedman's heresies [!] had become the new orthodoxy." Less than two years before the onset of the global financial crisis Summers concluded: ". . . any honest Democrat will admit that we are all Friedmanites" (Summers 2006: 13).

Already in 1973 Habermas provided the criteria for analyzing what this new bipartisan valorization of increasing profits as capital's social responsibility means, when he pointed out that "the *social power* of the capitalist is institutionalized as an exchange relation in the form of the private labor contract" (LC 25–26, emphasis in the original). Since the political discourse in the modern public sphere determines the general rules governing all exchange relations in the sphere of social labor, such a bipartisan definition of the *private* interest of the proverbial 1 percent as their *social* responsibility opened in all three branches of government the floodgates for an unprecedented tidal wave of legislative votes, executive orders, and juridical rulings that exponentially advanced the "unequally distributed social power " in the United States. As the historian Kevin Boyle succinctly sums up the key finding in *The Rise and Fall of the Neoliberal Order: America and the World in the Free Market Era* (2022) by Gary Gerstle, an emeritus at Harvard University where the proud "Friedmanite" Summers would serve as its president after Clinton's vice president Al Gore lost the 2000 presidential election:

> . . . Clinton claimed neoliberalism as his own, proudly proclaiming the globalization of manufacturing, the deregulation of banking and telecommunication, and a fiscal policy designed to convince investors that they could make as much money under a Democratic government as they could under a Republican one. (NYT Book Review, 4/5/2022)

HABERMAS'S WARNING ABOUT "UNEQUALLY DISTRIBUTED SOCIAL POWER" AND THE NEED FOR AN "ANTI-OLIGARCHY CONSTITUTION"

Habermas's timeless insight that the state of a democracy can be assessed by listening to the heartbeat of its political public sphere illuminates the urgent need for political change when applied to the present status quo in the United States. On one hand, Gerstle's prediction of a fall of the neoliberal order seems to be rather premature given the extent to which "the repressive and exclusionary effects of unequally distributed social power" have become solidly entrenched. On the other hand, the results of the comprehensive research project by constitutional law theorists Joseph Fishkin and William E. Forbath on the *The Anti-Oligarchy Constitution: Reconstructing the Economic Foundations of American Democracy* (2022) demonstrates that we are in the process of losing our republican form of government due to the rise of American oligarchs and their increasing stranglehold on economic and political power.

Fishkin and Forbath analyze that the United States Constitution was designed to protect against the same threat that Habermas identifies, namely, the hollowing out of the "equal rights of citizenship" due to "unequally distributed social power." Specifically, they analyze that already in the public discourse about the framing of Virginia's state constitution Noah Webster emphasized that the "equality of property" is "the very *soul* of *a republic.*" A proposition that can be traced back to seventeenth century Republican thought when James Harrington posited that "power follows property" (Fishkin/Forbath, February 2022, 5; cf. HPSC 15, 191, 237).

Significantly, in Virginia's constitutional debate Jefferson anticipated the requirements that *Structural Transformation* highlights for admission to the political public sphere, namely, property and education. To allow all citizens to meet them, he "argued that it was essential to block the intergenerational transmission of large, landed estates, to make sure that 'every person' had at least 'fifty acres' of land, and to build a system of public schools." The Jacksonians did expand on these "constitutional arguments about political economy" when they focused on the need to avoid "an unconstitutional concentration of special privileges and power" in the hands of a "moneyed aristocracy."

Structural Transformation's basic grounding of the modern public sphere in the political economy of the bourgeois constitutional state finds a parallel in Fishkin and Forbath's concept of constitutional political economy that informed the New Deal legislation. Specifically, Franklin D. Roosevelt argued that passing the 1935 Social Security Act was "the federal government's 'plain duty' under the general welfare clause and 'a right which belongs to every individual and every family." Similarly, Senator Robert Wagner, sponsor of the National Labor Relations Act, called legislating these rights "fundamental to 'democratic self-government' in an industrial society" (Fishkin/Forbath 2022, 8).

Arguably, the New Deal Democrats only took the first steps toward finally fulfilling the promise that Woodrow Wilson's Democratic administration had given to convince blue collar workers that World War I was a "people's war" to "make the world safe for democracy." As the historian Michael Kazin observed in *War against War: The American Fight for Peace, 1914-1918* (2017), "Wilson's government enticed the loyalty of immigrant workers . . . with the promise of achieving 'industrial democracy.'" Moreover, under the heading "Professor Dewey of Columbia on War's Social Results," the *New York World* in July 1917 quoted him as forecasting this social change in even starker terms: "Industrial democracy is on the way . . . the domination of all upper classes, even of what we have been knowing as 'respectable society,' is at an end" (quoted in Hofmann 2019: 60).

However, this vision of constitutional political economy would only gain ground almost two decades later when FDR, as Fishkin and Forbath point out, critiqued a "new oligarchy of 'economic royalists'" for using their social power "to construct 'a new despotism wrapped in the robes of legal sanction.'" Memorably, FDR argued that political equality is "meaningless in the face of economic inequality . . . freedom is no half-and-half affair." Accordingly, workers needed the rights "to strike and organize, to join unions and bargain collectively" as "grounded in the First, Thirteenth, and Fourteenth Amendments, along with the Constitution's guarantee of a 'Republican Form of Government'" (Fishkin/Forbath 2022, 8).

Already in 1998, Forbath quoted Habermas's observation in *Between Facts and Norms* that it takes binding rules to achieve justice in exchange relations. Specifically, such regulations must ensure against outcomes in which "exploited parties . . . contribute more to the cooperative effort than they gain from it" (Forbath 1998: 285). Emblematic for the neoliberal domination of this regulatory process has been the inability of the U.S. Senate to raise the federal minimum wage above $7.25 per hour. It thus remains below the amount that President Truman signed into law in 1949. Adjusted for inflation, those 75 cents per hour translate into $9.21 per hour in 2022. Moreover, if it had been raised to reflect not only some of the cost of living increases but also the general gains in productivity, like it was until 1968, it would today stand at about $24 per hour.

In his legendary letter from a Birmingham jail, 1964 Nobel Peace Prize winner Martin Luther King observed that justice too long delayed is justice denied. This truth is as valid for exchange relations in the political economy of the bourgeois constitutional state as it is for race relations. Almost four decades after Apple's iconic ad the results are in. Digital capitalism has indeed changed the world. However, the outcomes are debatable.

The next few years will reveal whether the functionality of the political public sphere is still sufficient. Can rational-critical debate develop solutions to the existential problems either caused or amplified by implementing the neoliberal doctrine in the process of globalization? This reckoning, to use a signature *New York Times* term that encapsulates the liberal public sphere's morally pretentious rationality, can be quite personal. After countless fawning "Corner Office" columns about "Friedmanite" chief executive officers, the *Times*'s business journalist David Gelles published a book titled *The Man Who Broke Capitalism: How Jack Welch Gutted the Heartland and Crushed the Soul of Corporate America—and How to Undo His Legacy* (2022).

Welch's tenure as General Electric's CEO reached from Reagan's inauguration in 1981 to China's admission to the WTO in 2001—thus spanning the decisive phase of globalization. His business strategy of downsizing, outsourcing, and offshoring took center stage in public discourse and became the dominant template that was used by a wide range of corporations from Boeing to Home Depot and Kraft Heinz. Right from the beginning his relentless downsizing was highly controversial. Ranking the productivity of all GE employees and eliminating the lowest-performaning 10 percent every year earned him in public debate the epithet "Neutron Jack."

Nevertheless, his outsize creation of "negative externalities," the economic term for "all the unfortunate consequences of businesses running roughshod over their communities" (David Gelles), did not prevent him from finding 10 million buyers for his best seller and from receiving a retirement package worth more than 400 million dollars. In comparison, the seven-part series "The Downsizing of America" (1996) in the *New York Times* received a

George Polk Award for investigative reporting but could enjoy only a fraction of Welch's readership. Equally, the book *The Disposable American: Layoffs and Their Consequences* (2006) by the co-author of this 1996 series, *Times* economics reporter Louis Uchitelle, did not sell millions of copies.

REGULATING SOCIAL MEDIA'S DESTRUCTIVE POWER IN THE POLITICAL PUBLIC SPHERE: THE CASE OF FACEBOOK

The crucial test case for the political public sphere's viability to facilitate the regulatory debates about digital capitalism's "negative externalities," including its systemic threat to the democratic process, will be the proposed but not yet initiated antitrust proceedings against the domination of the Facebook, Whats-App, and Instagram connection. Such an interdisciplinary case study will be in a unique position to assess whether the uncoerced coercion of the better argument can prevail in democratic practice. Rarely has the political public sphere encountered so many high-profile witnesses whose credibility is derived from their insider knowledge. Not to mention the forensic evidence contained in thousands of pages of internal documents which contain multiple versions of the proverbial "smoking gun."

The most recent public discourse about such antitrust proceedings began in 2018 after Cambridge Analytica's breach of privacy regarding 87 million Facebook accounts and the release of 250 pages of internal Facebook emails by a British parliamentary committee. These documents included exchanges between Zuckerberg and Sandberg about methods to veil the collection of personal data from user accounts and to strategically employ access to it to reward partners and punish competitors. Against this background the early Facebook investor Roger McNamee, who in 2008 had connected Sandberg to Zuckerberg for the position of Facebook's chief operating officer, published *Zucked: Waking Up to the Facebook Catastrophe* (2019).

Only two weeks after McNamee had declared in the *Columbia Journalism Review* that "Facebook is the biggest problem we have for democracy," Facebook co-founder Chris Hughes announced in a long lead article for the May 12, 2019 "Sunday Review" section of the *New York Times* that "It's Time to Break Up Facebook." In his personal reckoning Hughes acknowledged that he helped build a social media company that "is a threat to our economy and democracy." The *Times* generated maximum attention for his Op-Ed piece by publishing it online already on Thursday morning, May 9 and by building up suspense in Friday's print edition with a lengthy article in the Business section that announced a response from Facebook's vice president for global affairs and communication,

Nick Clegg, who as leader of the British Liberal Party had once served in a coalition government with the conservative prime minister David Cameron.

Arguably, one has to regard it as an expression of Facebook's social power that Clegg's response was not just printed as a "Letter to the Editor" and thus limited in length. Instead, it was awarded the same status of an "Opinion" article. Moreover, it was included within the layout of Hughes's essay under the heading "Breaking Up Facebook Is Not the Answer," with Facebook's corporate message succinctly highlighted: "Better regulation is the way to fix social media. Not punishing success."

As Clegg's choice of self-confident and assertive language indicates, Facebook's social power was even greater than Mobil Oil's in 1977 when it successfully used the *Times*'s op-ed page to influence public opinion against the "Windfall Profits" tax on oil companies planned by the Carter administration. Although Mobil's economic influence was big enough to have the *Times* change its policy and print Mobil's messages in the bottom right-hand corner, it still had to pay for that space. In stark contrast, Facebook not only received free prime advertising space but also had its corporate message veiled as an editorial.

Above all, Facebook received this uniquely preferential treatment less than two weeks after the *Times* had published an opinion column that called the Federal Trade Commission's likely fine for Facebook's role in the Cambridge Analytica scandal "trivial." Under the heading "When $5 billion Is a Slap on the Wrist," it argued that such a fine for Facebook "would mean the government isn't just deferential to the company, but that it doesn't truly understand its power." For "in just one hour of after-hours trading after signaling its impending $3-billion-to-$5-billion fine, Facebook's market capitalization increased by $40 billion."

Repeatedly, McNamee's own reckoning reads like a confessional. As early as March 2011 did he listen to a talk titled "Beware Online 'Filter Bubbles'" at a TED conference. It analyzed how Facebook's algorithmic filters reinforced user preferences even if their "friend list included a balance of liberals and conservatives." If one clicked more often on liberal links, the filter algorithms would "prioritize such content, eventually crowding out conservative content entirely" (McNamee 2019: 67, 66).

Although McNamee emphasizes that he was "gobsmacked" by this analysis and after the talk introduced himself to the presenter, he did not follow up with Zuckerberg. His explanation? He no longer informally advised him on a regular basis. His confession in retrospect: "All I could do was hope that Zuck and Sheryl would have the sense not to use [the filter bubbles] in ways that would harm users" (McNamee 2019: 66, 67).

In October 2019, more than eight years after this TED Talk warning, Zuckerberg himself could use for free the bottom half of page 3 in a "Sunday Review" section of the *New York Times* to present his Opinion piece titled "Facebook Can Help the News Business." It announced the launch of "Facebook News" as a tab outside the main "News Feed" in a multiyear partnership with several national news outlets including the *Times*. Seemingly, Facebook finally responded to growing public concern about the filter bubbles and echo chambers its algorithms created. For "a team of diverse and seasoned journalists" will curate "the most important and highest-quality stories" to be shown at "the top in Facebook News."

However, below those curated top stories "will be a wider selection of stories that are personalized algorithmically." Readers who asked themselves whether Facebook News marked a genuine attempt to break up echo chambers with diverse news could find the answer on page A5 in the same issue of the *New York Times*. For Facebook had bought its use for a full-page ad that introduced Facebook News. Significantly, the ad did not contain any reference to the curated selection of top stories that Zuckerberg highlighted on page SR3. Instead, it reassured Facebook users that on this "better space for news" they "can be confident that every story [they] see is relevant, personalized to [their] interests. . . ."

In Facebook usage, the word "relevant" signifies an Orwellian euphemism that Sandberg brought with her from Google's search engine advertising. It asserts that if one enters a specific search term, one must be "in the market" for all goods or services that can be possibly connected to it. Given this market logic of commodifying as a virtual shopping mall the originally promised free Internet data base, all these online ads have to be automatically "relevant" for Google users.

Obviously, Facebook has much broader and deeper access to the most intimate data of its "friends." It can even find out what will be "relevant" for them in the future and monetize their desires in the bud. Given this "deep dive" knowledge about its "friends," the Facebook News algorithm can personalize its story selection to their interests with pinpoint accuracy. Since the social media company has to hold and monetize the full attention of its "friends" for as long as possible, creating personalized echo chambers is a systemic demand of Facebook's business model.

As McNamee explains, when "users pay attention, Facebook calls it *engagement*, but the goal is behavior modification that makes advertising more valuable" (McNamee 2019: 9). Since its algorithms are designed "to nudge user attention in directions that Facebook wants," speaking of user engagement is another Orwellian sleight of hand. In this subtle and invisible process of manipulation, such an Orwellian use of the term engagement reassures Facebook's "friends" that they are actively engaging in self-determined choices. In short, it covers up that they are actually watching "at attention."

McNamee's and Hughes's urgent warnings that Facebook's algorithms can be exploited to undermine the democratic process are based on their knowledge how such steering capabilities function. When citizens consciously remain dispassionate in order to solve complex issues in rational-critical discourse, they are of "relatively little value to Facebook." Its algorithms thus have to "choose posts calculated to press emotional buttons." While the ubiquitous videos of cute puppies and babies indicate that generating joy can serve as a powerful "emotional button," "fear and anger produce a more uniform reaction and are more viral in a mass audience." As the winning votes for Brexit and Trump in 2016 demonstrated, "Facebook may confer advantages to campaign messages based on fear or anger over those based on neutral or positive emotions" (McNamee 2019: 8, 9).

Friedman ended his 1970 manifesto with the reminder that it is the social responsibility of business to increase profits provided "it stays within the rules of the game." To do so, it has to engage "in open and free competition without deception fraud." As McNamee sums up based on many years of business conversations with him, Zuckerberg "did not believe in data privacy and did everything he could to maximize disclosure and sharing [of user data]." In pursuit of growth on an unprecedented scale, Facebook thus "embraced invasive surveillance, careless sharing of private data, and behavior modification" (McNamee 2019: 5).

In short, deception of its "friends" has been Facebook's standard operating procedure with regard to data collection at least since 2007, when it introduced Beacon, "a system that gathered data about user activity on external websites to improve Facebook ad targeting." For example, if a Facebook user bought a product on a Beacon partner website, this purchase would automatically show up in the user's News Feed. Since Facebook did not give its "friends" any warning about these postings and "did not give them any ability to control Beacon," the harm it inflicted reached all the way from spoiling surprise gifts to exposing the most intimate desires to public view. Not surprisingly, users "thought Beacon was creepy." After a protest campaign was started and class action lawsuits were filed, Facebook withdrew Beacon within "less than a year after launch" (McNamee 2019: 60).

It took more than a decade of such deceptive practices, which triggered Federal Trade Commission rulings against Facebook in 2011 and 2019, before McNamee would publish his book and Hughes would follow up with his opinion article in the *New York Times*. As Hughes concluded: "Mark . . . needs to have some check on his power." Specifically, he recommended that the "American government needs to . . . break up Facebook's monopoly and regulate the company to make it more accountable to the American people."

The originality (and complexity) of *Structural Transformation*'s concept of the bourgeois public sphere results from its integration of the stylized template of the ancient *polis* into the modern sphere of commodity exchange and social labor, that is, into civil society in the original Hegelian sense. This conceptual transformation moved the cultivation of the person, the process in which human beings as such develop their humanity, from the political public sphere to the intimate sphere of the bourgeois family at the core of capitalist society. Achieving this humanity through self-determination, self-realization, and self-actualization is only possible, if the intimate sphere, and the literary public sphere emanating from it, are "emancipated from the constraints of survival requirements" (FRPS 442; STPS 160). In short, if these social spheres can become the realm of freedom and autonomy "in the Greek sense" of the *polis* (STPS 160).

Today, Facebook's News Feed plays a key role in structuring the intimate sphere of about two billion users around the globe. As Zuckerberg emphasized in October 2019, most Facebook users even "want to see more updates from their friends, families and communities." Given this impact and the fact that Facebook's intrusive surveillance techniques like its Beacon project can wreak havoc in a family's life, the regulatory need to "make Facebook more accountable to the American people," as Hughes demands, is self-evident.

Structural Transformation's Section 18, in which Habermas critiques the transformation of a culture-debating public into a culture-consuming one, emphasizes that the cultivation of the personal autonomy of family members and their friends depends on their interaction as "'human beings' and only as such" (STPS 164). Once the systemic need of commercial media for ratings and circulation structure the channels of communication, these interactions are subjected to "the exchange relations of the market" (STPS 164). In short, the sales criteria of mass culture will set clear boundaries for self-determination, self-realization, and self-actualization (STPS 165).

Worse, Facebook not only limits the private autonomy of family members and friends by permeating even their intimate sphere with the sales pitches of an online shopping mall. It also manipulates and harms them through the use of algorithms which privilege fear and anger artificially generated by personalized disinformation. That's why Habermas now focuses on the analysis of a new structural transformation of the public sphere generated by the convergence of digital platforms and social media. As McNamee delineates, Zuckerberg for the longest time tried to shirk his social responsibility by claiming that Facebook due to its technology platform was only a neutral "social utility" and not simultaneously a social media publisher.

Of course, "social responsibility" is a term that all "Friedmanites" can feel free to reduce to the pursuit of maximum profits for shareholders. Moreover, in all the years of his interactions with Zuckerberg, McNamee could not detect a key outcome of the cultivation of one's humanity, namely, empathy (McNamee 2019:4). Accordingly, it is unlikely that the "negative externalities" caused by Facebook's algorithms will one day convince Zuckerberg to reassess his social media company's business model *on his own*.

CUTTHROAT COMPETITION, MORAL RELATIVISM, AND THE ETHICAL COMPASS OF THE UNITED NATIONS UNIVERSAL DECLARATION OF HUMAN RIGHTS

Significantly, the *New York Times*'s Gelles explains his reckoning with his close-up and personal look at the "negative externalities" that Boeing's management generated by zealously following a "carbon copy" of Welch's playbook. As is well known, in its cutthroat competition with Airbus for global market share Boeing decided against taking the time to design and build a safe new plane. Instead, it tried to graft some new technology onto an outdated design while hiding the risks it was taking from the regulators who had to conduct the safety inspections of the 737 Max.

In the aftermath of the two Boeing 737 Max crashes that killed several hundred people, Gelles had a visceral experience when he interviewed relatives of the victims. Specifically, one woman commented to him that Boeing's management committed "corporate manslaughter." As Gelles explained in the business newsletter *The Ink*:

> I'll never forget those words because this was a company that had been cel-
> ebrated for years and years. And at the end of the day, I understood what she was
> saying. At this point, Boeing was a company that had completely lost its ethical
> compass. . . (Quoted in Giridharadas 2022)

Adopting the ancient template of the *polis* as the realm of freedom from any kind of coercion, *Structural Transformation*'s theory reconstruction of Kant's ideal of the liberal public defines the "human being as such" as "a moral person." The modern genesis of this "formless humanity" required the "historical and social location" of "the patriarchal conjugal family's intimate sphere that is oriented to a public" (STPS 85). In this ideal-typical self-interpretation of the "bourgeois family," the "private autonomy" of the spouses as free individuals denies "its economic origins" in the power of its private property in market relations (STPS 46). For in their consciousness they must be "emancipated" from their "private interests of the reproduction"

of their own lives (STPS 160), if they want to cultivate a "morally pretentious rationality," solely grounded in the communicative "power of the better
argument" (STPS 54).

What separates in 1962 *Structural Transformation* from Friedman's
Capitalism and Freedom, which the *New York Times* would make respectable in the liberal public sphere eight years later, is Habermas's denial of a
systemic validity for Say's Law of self-regulating markets "free from any
kind of coercion" (STPS 79). Instead, he only ascribes to it a temporary
historical validity, which in his interpretation from 1962 would end with
the beginning of the last third of the nineteenth century. However, without
a systemic validity of Say's Law, the private property owner can no longer
be genuinely convinced of a "justice immanent in free commerce" that will
"triumph over force" in all "market exchanges" (STPS 111, 46). In short,
he will lose the ethical compass to guide the cultivation of his humanity.

Friedman seemingly offered a solution for this challenge. By sharing
"Adam Smith's skepticism about the benefits that can be expected from
'those who affected to trade for the public good,'" he could reject the feasibil-
ity of "civic virtue" as the political concept that informs a republican constitution. Moreover, he went beyond Smith who tacitly switched Mandeville's
ethical critique of capitalism as an economic system, in which even socially
harmful private interests can grow the gross domestic product, from a
liability into an asset. For his doctrine of extreme individualism allowed
him to engage in moral relativism. As he would claim in 1970: ". . . one
man's good is another's evil" (Friedman 1970).

Two years before the publication of *Structural Transformation*, the
political philosopher Iring Fetscher emphasized that Rousseau's critique
primarily targeted "the developing *bourgeois* society" instead of "the obsolete feudal society" (Fetscher 1960: xv, emphasis in the original). Specifically, Rousseau addressed the dialectic of competition which already in the
era of liberal capitalism not only leads to "the most awesome exertions of
individual energy," but also to a "poisoning of the soul" and a "destruction
of the community"—thus going against the grain of the human rights orientation claimed by the philosophy of the Enlightenment. For Rousseau, all
progress in the mode and relations of production in bourgeois society is accompanied by a loss of morality, because these technological innovations and
increases in productivity result not only from individual achievement but also
from "stifling and damaging" the competitor (quoted in Fetscher 1960: 3).

Anybody who has worked and lived long enough in a global center of
capitalism like New York City, is thoroughly familiar with the streetwise
saying that "competition brings out the best in products and the worst in
people." Only that in the case of Boeing it also brought out the 737 Max with

its worst-case scenario of avoidable plane crashes. The question is whether a Congressional inquiry based on two dozen interviews with key employees at Boeing and at the Federal Aviation Administration as well as on an estimated 600,000 pages of internal documents will be sufficient to avoid future worst-case scenarios like this one. On one hand, the Democratic majority on the House Transportation and Infrastructure Committee concluded in its September 2020 report that Boing prioritized profits over safety. On the other hand, the Republican minority on the committee demanded that any new regulatory response to address this issue must be based on expert recommendations and not on what it immediately critiqued as a "partisan investigative report."

Increasingly, it looks like the steering mechanisms of power for the political system and of money for the economic system are not sufficient to avoid the loss of human lives. After the release of the committee report, the widow of an U.S. Army Captain who died in one of the two crashes commented: "Boeing cut corners, lied to regulators, and simply considers this the cost of doing business." For the company had only exchanged as its CEO one alumnus from Welch's General Electric days for another Welch disciple. When Gelles interviewed him in March 2020, he seemed to insinuate that the pilots of the crashed planes had mishandled the malfunctions of the 737 Max software. After witnessing this and another attempt by the new Boeing CEO to shift blame, Gelles concluded, as he would write in the *New York Times* under the heading "Boeing's Saga of Capitalism Gone Awry" in November 2020: "It seemed that inside Boeing, little had changed" with regard to "Friedmanite" and Welchian thinking. One year later, this conclusion was confirmed in *Flying Blind: The 737 Max Tragedy and the Fall of Boeing* (2021) by Peter Robison, an investigative reporter at Bloomberg business news. While a Boeing test pilot was criminally charged for deceiving the Federal Aviation Administration regarding the safety issues with the plane's software, the corporate managers "never paid any price." Although Boeing's board replaced the CEO who was primarily responsible for the construction of the unsafe plane, he nevertheless received a $60 million severance package.

Reading *Structural Transformation* offers an ethical compass at a time when the apparent pathologies of neoliberalism and globalization are spiraling out of control. Habermas's classic is infused with Enlightenment's advocacy of human rights that culminated in their declaration in the French and United States Constitutions. It took the Social Darwinism of nineteenth-century sweatshop capitalism and the civilized barbarism of two twentieth-century world wars before this revolutionary commitment to protect the common humanity of all individuals would be revived with the approval of the Universal Declaration of Human Rights by the United Nations General Assembly almost 160 years later (Hunt 2007: 203).

As head of the United Nations Human Rights Commission, Eleanor Roosevelt saw to it that the social and economic rights secured in New Deal legislation served as the blueprint for Articles 22 to 25 of the Universal Declaration of Human Rights, keeping in mind her husband's dictum quoted above that political equality is "meaningless in the face of economic inequality." Expanding on the commitment to economic equality in Jacksonian, Populist, and Progressive democracy that Fishkin and Forbath discuss, FDR's "New Deal" legislation implemented the genius of the Declaration of Independence that exchanged "pursuit of happiness" for "property" in Locke's original human rights wording "life, liberty, property." While still bracketing racial and gender equality, the "New Deal" Democrats at least initiated the process of transforming this individual "pursuit of happiness" into the "American Dream" for all citizens.

GLOBALIZATION AND THE LOSS OF HUMAN RIGHTS ON THE FACTORY FLOOR

After four decades of neoliberalism and globalization, "the American Dream is a cruel joke." This is how most "Factory Town" citizens in ten American Heartland states summed up their experiences with downsizing and outsourcing in polling and focus group research conducted in 2021. These blue-collar voters vividly remembered the results of Clinton championing NAFTA and China's admission to the WTO as well as the Obama administration bailing out Wall Street bankers during the 2008 financial crisis with their bonuses intact. After witnessing the same bankers foreclose on their homes throughout their neighborhoods, these union members and former Democrats concluded that property rights only prevail for the 1 percent, a term that they were thoroughly familiar with.

Under the neoliberal order, similar restrictions apply to access to the human rights of life and liberty. Emblematic for these economic restrictions is the experience of Guatemalan workers in a candle factory, some undocumented, when their Kentucky town was hit in December 2021 by an unseasonal tornado with wind speeds of up to 150 miles per hour, most likely facilitated by global warming. When the warning sirens went off inside the factory, about 100 workers huddled in a safe area for a few minutes until supervisors instructed them to return to work. Alerted again by the warning pings of their cell phones, several asked to leave their shift. However, some were told that they had already missed too much work and risked losing their jobs. When the tornado hit, the roof peeled off and the brick walls collapsed. Dozens of workers were buried under the rubble, eight were killed, and another eight remained missing two days later.

One survivor who had been buried alive for six hours under a pile of bricks told a *New York Times* reporter five days later that she heard her cell phone ring when her family called but could not reach it to guide rescuers to her location. Still traumatized after her release from the hospital, she described how she witnessed her co-worker on the production line, buried next to her, die. Nevertheless, she "wished nothing more" than seeing the factory reopen. When she was hired three years earlier for $7.50 an hour, she had "thanked God for the opportunity." Now, she "would gladly return," because she "depended on that work." In short, "not having it is scary" for her (Sandoval and Fausset 2021).

In neoliberal orthodoxy, nothing must interfere in the global marketplace with the price points for different commodities which serve as the steering mechanism for a "self-regulating" economy. After its admission to the WTO, these price points were primarily set in China. In December 2004, *Business-Week* presented a special report on "The China Price" as "the three scariest words in US industry." That report quoted a business professor at Ohio State University who recommended to "get out now rather than bleed to death," if "you still make anything labor intensive." Of course, while those price points originated *in* China, they were primarily set *by* U.S. importers like Walmart. Since the largest buyers could even demand quarterly price cuts, the *Wall Street Journal* wrote already in 2003 about the "survival of the cheapest" in China's export manufacturing sector (quoted in Harney 2008: 2, 3, 40).

Accordingly, the Kentucky candle factory could only survive, because U.S. tariffs on "cheap imports from China" provided a lifeline. Nevertheless, workers had to commit to 10- to 12-hour shifts with mandatory overtime. Further cost-cutting was achieved by contracting with the local government for the labor power of inmates from the county jail. Obviously, the *New York Times* reporters were familiar with the economic pressure emanating from the China Price. However, while the *Wall Street Journal* quoted Walmart's vice president in global procurement as acknowledging that "yeah, we try to take advantage of it," the *Times* presented the neoliberal mantra of *anonymous* market forces. Ethically concerned that wages at the candle factory started "close to the minimum wage," the paper euphemistically framed them as "a *concession* to the brutal realities of the global labor market" (NYT, 12/17/2021, A 14, emphasis added).

It took a tornado in December to literally expose the state of human rights on the shop floor of an American factory dependent on non-unionized immigrant labor. It also took a free press, protected under the First Amendment, to report on these violations of Articles 22 and 23 in the non-binding Universal Declaration of Human Rights (see Introduction, VI). Even if the *Times* did not identify them as such due to its still predominant "blind spot"

(Walter Lippmann) regarding the pathologies of "free trade" (cf. Hofmann 2018: 12).

But it takes the federal authority of the Occupational Safety and Health Administration to access the shop floor to investigate whether this loss of life could have been avoided. Moreover, only the subpoena power of a Congressional committee secures access to the business documents of the candle factory to analyze which economic factors contributed to the deadly extent of this tornado damage. In other words, what is needed for an informed rational-critical discourse in the public sphere is the cooperation of a political system whose steering mechanism is either power exercised to serve special interests or a democratic process of decision-making in the interest of all that safeguards the checks and balances of a republican constitution.

It is self-evident that politicians who acquired the public power of their offices based on the social power of oligarchs will only cooperate according to their own political interest and the private interests they are beholden to. However, the neoliberal hegemony in the U.S. Congress and in the White House has allowed them for decades to present the shareholder interest as the general interest. Only after the "negative externalities" caused by the most powerful shareholders had "gutted the heartland" (David Gelles), did even Fukuyama in *Liberalism and Its Discontents* (2022) concede that neoliberalism became "something of a religion" and resulted in "grotesque inequalities."

RICARDO'S RECKONING AND SILICON VALLEY'S DEFAMATION OF THE LUDDITES

This guide to *Structural Transformation* has analyzed that liberal political economy has been a kind of secular religion from the beginning. As such, the template for neoliberalism was actually inaugurated already in 1821 with a debate that today reads as strikingly contemporary. It did anticipate key arguments Silicon Valley used in the 1990s to promise an allegedly crisis-free "new economy" in which digital technologies opened up an abundance of job opportunities for all. The debate erupted in dramatic fashion when Ricardo's fellow political economists were completely blindsided by his sudden turn against Say's Law mentioned above. For in the first two editions of his classic *Principles of Political Economy and Taxation* from 1817 and 1819 as well as in his December 1819 speech in the British Parliament, Ricardo had maintained "that machinery did not lessen the demand for labour" (quoted in HPSC 148n66). He would still confirm his words nearly verbatim in a letter to his disciple J.R. McCulloch from March 1820.

When McCulloch expanded on Ricardo's dictum one year later in the *Edinburgh Review*, he did not yet know that his following words would become a key element in the template still used 150 years later by Friedman: "no improvement of machinery can possibly diminish the demand for labour, or reduce the rate of wages" (quoted in HPSC 123). But only a few weeks later, Ricardo withdrew in a new chapter "On Machinery" in the third edition of *Principles* his thesis that the introduction of machinery would *not* result in a reduction of wages as "erroneous." He now emphasized "that the substitution of machinery for human labour, is often very injurious to the interests of the class of labourers." Although it increased "the net revenue of the country," it could simultaneously "render the population redundant, and deteriorate the condition of the labourer" (quoted in HPSC 123).

The damage that Ricardo inflicted on economic orthodoxy was twofold. It put the rising bourgeoisie on the defensive vis-à-vis the aristocracy as well as the class of laborers. First of all, Ricardo's reversal helped the landed interest, because it supported the view of the prominent dissenting political economist Thomas Malthus who argued that vast productive investments in machinery had resulted in overproduction and a global glut of unsold commodities. Due to the increase in technological unemployment, many laborers no longer received the wages to buy any of these goods. To solve this severe economic crisis, the aristocracy's unproductive use of capital for spending on luxuries should be increased.

Secondly, his reversal would soon help "the laboring classes" as Malthus warned Ricardo in July 1821. While Malthus had initially enjoyed Ricardo's inadvertent support for his thesis about overproduction, he soon became alarmed. For Ricardo's following acknowledgment was tailor-made for a critical political economy that defended the interest of the laborers:

> . . . the opinion entertained by the laboring class, that the employment of machinery is frequently detrimental to their interests, is *not founded on prejudice and error*, but is *conformable to the correct principles of political economy.* (quoted in HPSC 123, emphasis added)

Worse for economic orthodoxy, in his June 1821 reply to a thunderstruck McCulloch he doubled down on his reversal. Ricardo now even ascribed to it mathematical precision and a validity akin to the natural sciences. Exactly like Say had claimed for his law of markets. In Ricardo's words:

> These truths appear to me as demonstrable as any of the truths in geometry, and I am only astonished that I should so long have failed to see them. (quoted in HPSC 148n66)

In other words, Ricardo just brushed aside McCulloch's argument that was particularly valid during the (first) Industrial Revolution and that is still relevant today during the third one, in which Silican Valley has played a key role. If Ricardo's reversal represents correct economic science, McCulloch argued, then "the laws against the Luddites are a disgrace to the Statute book" (quoted in HPSC 148n66). At least the "Luddites" would have had a brilliant defense in court, if they could have argued that none other than the eminent banker, political economist, and Member of Parliament David Ricardo had confirmed that the introduction of machinery injured their interests and deteriorated their condition.

For more than three decades, Silicon Valley's predominant first response to any question about the social good produced by the "disruptions" in the wake of new digital technologies has been to call the critic a "Luddite." Arguably, the use of this epithet has been the most successful bourgeois tactic to denigrate in public discourse the machine-breaking in uprisings by laborers as acts of blind barbarism that only destroy the technology needed to employ them. It took William Safire, then the conservative *New York Times* columnist and former speech writer in the Nixon administration, to set the record straight in his column "On Language" when Microsoft attacked Justice Department lawyers as "Luddites" for questioning its monopoly practices regarding its Internet browser. As Safire clarified, the "Luddites" were not against technological progress as such. On the contrary, they would have happily used the new machinery, if they had received their fair share of these productivity increases. Instead, they witnessed how the new technology was used to lower their wages (Safire 1998: 34).

Since *Structural Transformation* leaves out this crucial debate in the intellectual as well as institutional history of bourgeois political economy, it misses *the* decisive nineteenth century manifestation of ideal-typical bourgeois humanity as the identity of the autonomous property owner and the morally free human being that facilitates the morally pretentious rationality of the bourgeois public sphere (STPS 46, 56, 85, 111, 54). Namely, Ricardo's reckoning as an act of self-determination and self-realization more than two years before his death in September 1823. It is plausible to speak of a reckoning, because he had known what he called the mathematically precise truths about the "often very injurious" substitution of machinery for human labor since June 1817 but "failed to see them."

In his 1821 chapter "On Machinery," Ricardo gives as the reason for his reversal the analysis by John Barton titled *Observations on the Circumstances which Influence the Condition of the Labouring Classes of Society* (1817). Ricardo had been familiar with Barton's book since its publication. One month earlier, in May 1817, he had exchanged letters with Barton on that topic (cf. HPSC 148n67).

Arguably, he did not even mention Barton's book when he had the opportunity to do so in the second edition of his *Principles* in 1819, because at that point in time his views were still diametrically opposed to Barton's. Although 1819 was marked by a depression in manufacturing, with "very injurious" conditions for laborers, he argued in Parliament as a member of the Poor Laws committee against passing the proposed Poor Rates Misapplication Bill which sought to replace direct cash payments to the destitute parents of large families with the more economical solution of placing their children "in institutions where they would be put to work and educated." For Ricardo was concerned that the bill would further increase overpopulation at a time of very high technological unemployment. Why? In his reasoning parents would feel assured "that an asylum would be provided for their children in which they would be *treated with humanity and tenderness*" (quoted in HPSC 120, emphasis added).

Less than two years later, Ricardo finally introduced a human rights perspective into his *Principles of Political Economy* when analyzing the substitution of machinery for human labor. He thus violated the Political Economy Club rules, drafted by James Mill, which tasked its members with policing public discourse to prevent the spread of "any doctrines hostile to sound views on Political Economy" (quoted in HPSC 124). In comparison, Say never experienced a reckoning like Ricardo did.

Even the April 1815 letter from the Physiocrat Dupont de Nemours could not change Say's narrow orthodoxy. In vain did Dupont remind him that *political* economy had originally been conceptualized as "a science of constitutions." Only after the French Revolution had political *economy* been reduced to a "science of wealth." In other words, Dupont failed to convince Say to "leave the counting house" and to not "imprison" himself in the ideas and the language of those "who value a man only by the money he spends" and who were now excluding "morals, justice and the *droits des gens*" from the public discourse (quoted in HPSC 113).

With Ricardo's reversal this tension between the property rights of capital accumulation and all other human rights enshrined in republican constitutions became highly visible as a topic for political debate in the bourgeois public sphere. After all, in the eyes of the rising bourgeoisie Ricardo represented the greatest political economist since Adam Smith. Moreover, Ricardo was closely aligned with Say in the "general glut controversy," spearheading the manufacturing and financial interests against the "Sismondi-Malthus school" whose analysis of the "insufficiency of effective demand" Keynes would valorize in 1936 as "a scientific explanation of unemployment" (cf. HPSC 122, 121).

In 1821, Ricardo essentially terminated classical political economy when he denied the validity of Say's Law for the labor market and acknowledged the interest of laborers as separate from and potentially opposed to the manufacturing interest. In 1825, McCulloch would turn the original edition of Ricardo's *Principles* from 1817 into a key template for the neo-classical (or neoliberal) political economy that has dominated to this day—with the notable exception of the Keynesian interlude from the late 1930s to late 1970s. Defiantly declaring that he stood with the first edition of Mr. Ricardo's book, not with its third, he included his unchanged article from March 1821 on machinery when his book *The Principles of Political Economy with a Sketch of the Rise and Progress of the Science* (1825) was published (cf. 148n66).

When reading *Structural Transformation*'s Section 15, one thus has to keep in mind that "the liberalist apologetic" in the history of bourgeois political economy was introduced not only "around the middle" of the nineteenth century but more than two decades earlier. In short, before 1832 when it allegedly was still credible to identify "the interest of the bourgeois class . . . with the general interest" (STPS 130, 87). Conversely, this neoliberal apologetic did *not* question "the fundamental presuppositions" regarding a "natural basis" for the laws of political economy as Habermas states (STPS 130, 131). Anticipating Friedman, neo-classical political economists from McCulloch to John Stuart Mill claimed the validity of natural sciences for their assertion "that all machinery that displaces workers simultaneously, and necessarily, sets free an amount of capital adequate to employ precisely those workers displaced," as Marx sums up (quoted in HPSC 148n66).

Since *Structural Transformation* leaves out John Stuart Mill's *Principles of Political Economy* (1848), readers are not alerted to the tension between his orthodox economic liberalism and his celebrated political liberalism in *On Liberty* (1859). Certainly his open-minded dictum in *On Liberty*, quoted in Section 15, that "only through diversity of opinion is there . . . a chance of fair play to all sides of the truth" is not reflected in his political economy (STPS 135). In his highly influential *Principles*, there is no room for a human rights orientation like John Barton's. Regarding Say's Law, his *Principles* exclude all questions about its validity. Instead, he followed in his father's footsteps and assumed the role of its advocate in his correspondence with fellow political economists. To him, Say's "doctrine of Free Trade" was as solid as the human rights "principle of individual liberty." Above all, Dupont's 1815 critique of Say for reducing political economy from a "science of constitutions" to a "science of wealth" is equally applicable to Mill in 1848 and beyond. For he prided himself for treating political economy as the "science of man considered 'solely as a being who desires to possess wealth'" (quoted in HPSC 25n48, 23).

ECONOMIC VERSUS POLITICAL LIBERALISM IN "CRISIS-PRONE CAPITALIST DEMOCRACIES" (HABERMAS): A PARTIALITY FOR REASON AS THE STEERING MECHANISM FOR A HUMANE POLITICAL ECONOMY

The privileging of economic over political liberalism even by Mill as the author who since his publication of *On Liberty* has been commonly identified with the latter, is emblematic for the fundamental challenges that governments face when they try to safeguard a stable development of "crisis-prone capitalist democracies" (Habermas 2021:498). Given today's plethora of global crises, these challenges have only grown since 1823 when already the first professor of political economy at the University of Cambridge, George Pryme, proudly announced that while his narrow focus on economics "may seem less interesting than Political Philosophy its utility is more extensive, since it is applicable alike to a despotism and to a democracy." Almost 140 years later, Friedman could point out just how extensive the *utility* of bracketing the political philosophy dimension in political economy had become. Concluding that capitalism is only the necessary but not the sufficient condition for political freedom, he emphasized that nation states can have "economic arrangements that are fundamentally capitalist and political arrangements that are not free" (cf. HPSC 114).

In other words, the safeguarding of political freedom in the public sphere no longer is a systemic need of the corporate world once "economic arrangements that are fundamentally capitalist" have become institutionalized and are legally guaranteed. That's why the future of democratic governance will be decided in the political public sphere as well as by its ability to influence the political power structure. Logically, the more authoritarian governmental decision-making is, the greater the pressure on a free press will become. Under such circumstances, the active engagement for human rights in the public discourse will take on an existential dimension with regard to defending the democratic process.

Since there are no natural laws of political economy, neither a Friedmanite valorization of the price mechanism nor a Marxist analysis of the value form (LC 26) can discover the steering mechanism for a just, equal, and harmonious organization of society. It is the enduring strength of *Structural Transformation* that Habermas touched on this fundamental insight in Section 15. However, his book does not expand on it. Instead, *Structural Transformation*'s narrative uses a veiled Marcusean variant of ideology critique for its counterfactual stylization of a rise and fall of the bourgeois public sphere.

Habermas's reflections in "Natural Law and Revolution" indicate that, on one hand, *Structural Transformation*'s theory reconstruction of Kant's ideal of the bourgeois public is informed by the absolute rationalism of an all-encompassing political society conceptualized especially in Condorcet's

"Social Mathematics" (Keith Michael Baker). On the other hand, already his footnote in his 1960 critique of Koselleck and Kesting signals the influence by Engels and his counter-model dialectically projected to this concept of the Physiocrats. It explains that Engels famously followed up on a saying by Saint Simon (originating in this French intellectual tradition) to declare the future dissolution of the political realm: "The governing of persons will be replaced by administering things" (quoted in KK 358).

Without the existence of natural laws of society for a harmonious regulation of all human interaction, not only this elaborate edifice evaporates. But also the validity of a Hegelian-Marxist philosophy of history upon which Marcuse's dialectical critique of bourgeois ideology rests. It is unfortunate for its readers that *Structural Transformation* does not post this necessary disclaimer up front or at least *explicitly* in Section 15. As pointed out in this guide, Section 16 puts the burden on the reader to assess the consequences once Habermas declares that Say's Law is incorrect when claiming "an automatic tendency toward the equilibration of production and consumption on the level of the economy as a whole" (STPS 144).

If such an automatic tendency is not a function of "the system [of liberal capitalism] as such," Say's Law loses its validity as one of the three "presuppositions of classical economics" that determine whether each person will "have an equal chance" to gain access to the bourgeois public sphere (STPS 144, 86–87). Accordingly, if granting such an equal chance to acquire property and education as the entrance qualification is not facilitated by a systemic function of liberal capitalism, the defining "principle of universal access" will remain unrealized. Such a public sphere will be "less than merely incomplete." It will not be "a public sphere at all" (STPS STPS 85, 86–87).

In other words, there will not be a bourgeois public sphere as such but only a *bourgeois segment* in the public sphere of a civil society defined by commodity exchange and social labor. Equally, bourgeois deliberations in this segment will not be able to anticipate "in principle that all human beings belong to it" (STPS 85). In short, without the validity of Say's Law *bourgeois* humanism is unable to establish the *hegemony* it claims for itself.

However, readers will not find this logical conclusion in *Structural Transformation*. It is also absent from Habermas's *Further Reflections* published a decade *after* he had liberated his theory in 1981 from the "ballast" of Historical Materialism. While he now acknowledges the social segmentation and cultural as well as political pluralization of the modern public sphere, he still claims, quoting the research by Lottes about the London Jacobins, *hegemony* for a bourgeois public sphere. But while these members of the London Corresponding Society (L.C.S.) adopt its "emancipatory potential," they develop it "in a new social context"—thus voiding especially its social precondition of property ownership. Nevertheless, this "plebeian" public sphere allegedly "assumes shape" next to, "and interlocked with, the *hegemonic* public sphere" of the bourgeoisie "in the very process of [the latter's] emergence" (FRPS 426, emphasis added). In other words, at the time of the French Revolution, after the French Constitution of 1791 had established press freedom as the precondition for a political public sphere (STPS 99).

Structural Transformation asserts that, compared to "the practice of historiography," the "sociological procedure . . . seems less bound to the specifics of the historical material" (STPS xviii). Once Habermas formally renounced his use of a Marxist methodology, he lost this freedom to select his empirical material according to the "objective" trajectory structured by a philosophy of history. Nevertheless, *Further Reflections* still practices this liberty of selecting the evidence for an "interlocked" development of a "plebeian" public sphere and the *hegemonic* public sphere" of the bourgeoisie. Accordingly, Habermas neither mentions that the L.C.S. was outlawed already in 1799 under the Combination Act nor that William Pitt's "Two Acts" from 1795 allowed to repeatedly persecute its public meetings as "seditious" and "treasonable." Moreover, high stamp taxes put reading the newspapers out of individual reach for most laborers. They could only afford to share them in public places. But the authorities could shut those down as "disorderly houses" (cf. HPSC 237, 105, 106). In short, it is difficult to see how such a degree of naked repression could have advanced the *hegemonic* interest of the bourgeois public sphere.

Since the bourgeoisie does not have a monopoly on the public use of reason, *Structural Transformation*'s stylization of the patriarchal conjugal family's intimate sphere as the historical and social location in which humanity as such originated cannot do justice to the extent and the diversity of the modern public sphere's history. The rational-critical discourse of the political public sphere in Western democracies is rooted in all aspects of the intellectual tradition that reaches from the Greek *polis* and Renaissance humanism via the Republican political philosophy of the seventeenth century to the process of Enlightenment which culminated in the Declaration of Human and Civil Rights that was revived by the United Nations assembly in its Universal Declaration from 1948. To essentially restrict this wealth of intellectual achievements to the period from 1694 to 1832, with postscripts by Tocqueville, Mill, and Marx, and to further narrow its analysis by primarily selecting the perspective of Protestant morality, limits the emancipatory potential that such a study could have uncovered.

Nevertheless, Habermas's theory reconstruction of Kant's liberal ideal of the bourgeois public sphere clarifies that among the human rights the French and American constitutional revolutions had declared, not only Mill's political economy but also his political philosophy in *On Liberty* privilege the rights of private property. Specifically, Mill's signature commitment to "diversity of opinion" and "fair play to all sides of the truth" (quoted in STPS 135) reaches its limits of the possible once the self-determination of "a critically debating" bourgeois public "is subverted by the propertyless and uneducated masses" (STPS 136). In Mill's words quoted by Habermas in Section 15, these "masses do not take their opinions from dignitaries in Church or State, from above average leaders or books." Instead, "their thinking is done for them by men much like themselves who address them on the spur of the moment through the newspapers" (quoted in STPS 133; SÖ 163).

As quoted under 2.2 above, Kant in 1781 regarded "the opinions from dignitaries in Church or State" as objects of critique in the process of Enlightenment, not as much needed defenses of the propertied classes against critical opinions voiced by the propertyless in public discourse as Mill does. If religion sought to exempt itself from critique "through its sanctity" and "law-giving through its majesty," Kant would treat them with "just suspicion" and withhold his "sincere respect." Only if the institutions of Church and State are able "to sustain the test of free and open examination" can the reason of enlightened citizens accord them such sincere respect (quoted in CC 121). Today, Silicon Valley and Wall Street as the new institutions of social and political power should be subjected to the same free and open examination. Moreover, Kant's quest for a republican constitution should find its equivalent in today's political debate about the anti-oligarchy constitution.

This guide to reading *Structural Transformation* has emphasized that there is a striking similarity between the seminal Kant quote from 1781 and a crucial wording in Milton's plea for the liberty of unlicensed printing from 1644. Both want to subject religion and politics to reason in their search for truth—Milton in a "free and open encounter," Kant through the "free and open examination" discussed above. Both argue for the decisive human and civil rights of freedom of speech and of the press that became the crowning achievements of the constitutional revolutions (cf. HPSC 44).

At a time when the rational-critical search for truth in public discourse is under siege, it is hardly possible to overstate the existential importance of these human and civil rights for the future of democratic governance. It is truly remarkable that today Milton's reasoning from 1644 and Kant's from 1781 is more relevant than ever before. The clash between the First Amendment as the guarantee for a self-determined discourse in the political public sphere and the property right of social media owners who have largely turned the Internet into a virtual shopping mall that is occupying and manipulating the intimate sphere of billions, will only intensify.

Zuboff's warning that the ongoing "abdication of our information and communication spaces to surveillance capitalism" increasingly "obstructs solutions to all other crises" and "has become the meta-crisis of every republic" (Introduction, VII), has informed the focus of this guide to Habermas's rational reconstruction of Kant's concept of the public use of reason. By discussing the historical context for the development and global reception of Habermas's classic, it has become apparent why *Structural Transformation* is his most widely distributed and quoted work. Its comprehensive analysis of the public sphere as a central category of state and society in modernity confirms that reason is a more constructive steering mechanism for finding solutions to the existential challenges threatening the future of humankind than money and political power.

Bibliography

Arendt, Hannah. *The Human Condition.* Chicago: University of Chicago Press, 1958.

Bagehot, Walter. *The English Constitution.* First published in 1867. London: Oxford University Press, 1963.

Baker, Keith Michael. *Condorcet: From Natural Philosophy to Social Mathematics.* Chicago: University of Chicago Press, 1975.

———. *Inventing the French Revolution: Essays on French Political Culture in the Eighteenth Century.* Cambridge: Cambridge University Press, 1990.

———. "Defining the Public Sphere in Eighteenth–Century France: Variations on a Theme by Habermas." In *Habermas and the Public Sphere*, edited by Craig Calhoun. Cambridge, MA: MIT Press, 1992, 181–211.

Barton, John. *Observations on the Circumstances Which Influence the Condition of the Labouring Classes of Society.* London: John and Arthur Arch, 1817.

Baynes, Kenneth. *Habermas.* New York: Routledge, 2016.

Bell, Daniel. *The End of Ideology: On the Exhaustion of Political Ideas in the Fifties.* Glencoe, IL: Free Press, 1960.

Bengali, Shashank, and Marc Santora. "2021 Nobel Prize, Peace: Journalists in Philippines and Russia Are Cited for Courage." *The New York Times*, October 9, 2021, A 4.

Benhabib, Seyla. "Models of Public Space: Hannah Arendt, the Liberal Tradition, and Jürgen Habermas." In *Habermas and the Public Sphere*, edited by Craig Calhoun. Cambridge, MA: MIT Press, 1992, 73–98.

———. Book Review of *Between Facts and Norms: Contributions to a Discourse Theory of Law and Democracy* by Jürgen Habermas. Cambridge, MA: MIT Press, 1996. *American Political Science Review* 91, no. 3 (September 1997): 725–26.

Berlin, Isaiah. "My Intellectual Path" (1996), *The New York Review of Books* 45, no. 8 (May 14, 1998): 54–55.

Bernstein, Richard J. "The Normative Core of the Public Sphere." *Political Theory* 40, no. 6 (2012): 767–78.

Bird, Kai. *The Color of Truth: McGeorge Bundy and William Bundy, Brothers in Arms*. New York: Simon & Schuster, 1998.

Blaug, Mark. *Ricardian Economics: A Historical Study*. New Haven, CT: Yale University Press, 1958.

Blitzer, Charles. *An Immortal Commonwealth: The Political Thought of James Harrington.* New Haven, CT: Yale University Press, 1960.

Brewer, John. *The Sinews of Power: War, Money and the English State, 1688–1783*. New York: Alfred A. Knopf, 1989.

Bundy, McGeorge. *Danger and Survival: Choices About the Bomb in the First Fifty Years*. New York: Random House, 1988.

Bury, J. B. *The Idea of Progress: An Inquiry into its Origin and Growth*. With an introduction by Charles A. Beard. First published in 1932. New York: Dover Publications, 1987.

Butterfield, Herbert. *The Whig Interpretation of History.* First published in 1931. London: G. Bell and Sons, 1963.

Calhoun, Craig. ed. *Habermas and the Public Sphere*. Cambridge, MA: MIT Press, 1992.

———. "The Reluctant Counterpublic" (with Michael McQuarrie). In *The Roots of Radicalism: Tradition, the Public Sphere, and Early Nineteenth–Century Social Movements*. Chicago: University of Chicago Press, 2012, 152–80.

———. "The Problematic Public: Revisiting Dewey, Arendt, and Habermas," delivered at the University of Michigan, April 11, 2013. *The Tanner Lectures on Human Values* 33, edited by Mark Matheson. Salt Lake City: University of Utah Press, 2014, 65–107.

Cassidy, John. "The Hayek Century." *Hoover Digest*, no. 3 (2000). www.hooverdigest.org, accessed 9/27/2007.

Censer, Jack Richard. *Prelude to Power: The Parisian Radical Press, 1789–1791*. Baltimore: Johns Hopkins University Press, 1976.

———. ed. *The French Revolution and Intellectual History*. Chicago: Dorsey Press, 1989.

Chartier, Roger. *The Cultural Origins of the French Revolution*. Translated by Lydia G. Cochrane. Durham, NC: Duke University Press, 1991.

Clegg, Nick. "Breaking Up Facebook Is Not the Answer." *The New York Times*, May 12, 2019, SR 3.

Cohen, Jean L., and Andrew Arato. *Civil Society and Political Theory*. Cambridge, MA: MIT Press, 1992.

Cohen, Roger, Sui–Lee Wee, and Anton Troianovski. "2021 Nobel Prize, Peace: Recognizing the Growing Repression of the News Media by Governments." *The New York Times*, October 9, 2021, A 5.

Condorcet (Marquis de), Marie Jean Antoine Nicolas Caritat. "The Influence of the American Revolution on Europe." First published in 1786. Translated and edited by Durand Echeverria from the 1788 edition. *The William and Mary Quarterly* 25, no. 1 (1968): 85–108.

———. *Selected Writings*, edited with an introduction by Keith Michael Baker. Indianapolis: Bobbs–Merrill, 1976.

————. *Sketch for a Historical Picture of the Progress of the Human Mind.* Original French edition published in 1795. Translated by J. Barraclough. London: Weidenfeld and Nicolson, 1955.

Corchia, Luca, Stefan Müller–Doohm, and William Outhwaite, eds. *Habermas global. Wirkungsgeschichte eines Werks.* Berlin: Suhrkamp, 2019.

Crowley, Michael, and Zolan Kanno–Youngs. "At Summit on Democracies, Questions About Participants, and Host." *The New York Times*, December 10, 2021, A 6.

Darnton, Robert. *The Business of Enlightenment: A Publishing History of the Encyclopedie, 1775–1800.* Cambridge, MA: The Belknap Press of Harvard University Press, 1979.

Defoe, Daniel. *Giving Alms No Charity, and Employing the Poor: A Grievance to the Nation: Addressed to the Parliament of England.* London: Booksellers of London and Westminster, 1704. (Reproduction published in the series "Classic English Works on the History and Development of Economic Thought." London: S.R. Publishers; New York: Johnson Reprint Corporation, n. d.).

Dewey, John. *The Public and Its Problems.* New York: Henry Holt, 1927.

Diamond, Edwin, and Stephen Bates. *The Spot: The Rise of Political Advertising on Television*, third edition. Cambridge, MA: MIT Press, 1993.

Dickson, P.G.M. *The Financial Revolution in England: A Study in the Development of Public Credit.* London: Macmillan, 1967.

Doyle, William. *Origins of the French Revolution.* First published in 1980. Third edition. Oxford: Oxford University Press, 1999.

Elemia, Camille. "In Philippines, Fertile Ground for Political Lies." *The New York Times*, May 7, 2022, B 6.

Eley, Geoff. "Nations, Publics, and Political Cultures: Placing Habermas in the Nineteenth Century." In *Habermas and the Public Sphere*, edited by Craig Calhoun. Cambridge, MA: MIT Press, 289–339.

Ellis, Aytoun. *The Penny Universities: A History of the Coffee–Houses.* London: Secker & Warburg, 1956.

Ellis, Markman. *The Coffee House: A Cultural History.* London: Weidenfeld & Nicolson, 2004.

Ellsberg, Daniel. *The Doomsday Machine: Confessions of a Nuclear War Planner.* New York: Bloomsbury, 2017.

Engels, Friedrich. *The Condition of the Working–Class in England: From Personal Observation and Authentic Sources.* Original German edition published in 1845. With 1845, 1887, and 1892 prefaces. New York: International Publishers, 1973.

Fetscher, Iring. *Rousseaus Politische Philosophie: Zur Geschichte des demokratischen Freiheitsbegriffs.* First published in 1960. Second enlarged edition. Neuwied: Luchterhand, 1968.

Feuer, Lewis. *Spinoza and the Rise of Liberalism.* Boston: Beacon Press, 1958.

Fielden, John. *The Curse of the Factory System.* First published in 1836. Second edition with a new introduction by J. T. Ward. New York: Augustus M. Kelley, 1969.

Fishkin, Joseph, and William E. Forbath, *The Anti–Oligarchy Constitution: Reconstructing the Economic Foundations of American Democracy.* Cambridge, MA: Harvard University Press, 2022.

————. "How Progressives Can Take Back the Constitution." The Atlantic, February 8, 2022. www.theatlantic.com/ideas/archive/2022/02/progressives-constitution-oligarchy-fishkin-forbath/621614/ Accessed: 6/9/22.

Floridia, Antonio. *From Participation to Deliberation: A Critical Genealogy of Deliberative Democracy.* Colchester: European Consortium for Political Research Press, 2017.

Forbath, William. "Short–Circuit: A Critique of Jürgen Habermas's Understanding of Law, Politics, and Economic Life." In *Habermas on Law and Democracy*, edited by Michael Rosenfeld and Andrew Arato. Berkeley: University of California Press, 1998, 272–86.

Fox–Genovese, Elizabeth. *The Origins of Physiocracy: Economic Revolution and Social Order in Eighteenth–Century France*. Ithaca, NY: Cornell University Press, 1976.

Fraser, Nancy. "Rethinking the Public Sphere: A Contribution to the Critique of Actually Existing Democracy." In *Habermas and the Public Sphere*, edited by Craig Calhoun. Cambridge, MA: MIT Press, 1992, 109–42.

————. "The Theory of the Public Sphere: The Structural Transformation of the Public Sphere (1962)." In *The Habermas Handbook*, edited by Hauke Brunkhorst, Regina Kreide, and Christina Lafont. First published in German in 2009. New York: Columbia University Press, 2017, 245–55.

Friedman, Milton. *Capitalism and Freedom*. Chicago: University of Chicago Press, 1962.

————. "A Friedman doctrine—The Social Responsibility of Business Is to Increase Its Profits." *The New York Times*, September 13, 1970.

Fuchs, Christian. "Social Media and the Public Sphere." In *Culture and Economy in the Age of Social Media*. New York: Routledge, 2015, 315–71.

Fukuyama, Francis. *Liberalism and Its Discontents*. New York: Farrar, Straus & Giroux, 2022.

Galbraith, John Kenneth. *American Capitalism*. Boston: Houghton Mifflin, 1952.

Gay, Peter. *The Party of Humanity: Essays in the French Enlightenment.* New York: Alfred A. Knopf, 1964.

Gayer, Arthur D.; with W.W. Rostow and Anna Jacobson Schwartz. *The Growth and Fluctuation of the British Economy, 1790–1850: An Historical, Statistical, and Theoretical Study of Britain's Economic Development.* Two volumes. Oxford: Clarendon Press, 1953.

Gelles, David. *The Man Who Broke Capitalism: How Jack Welch Gutted the Heartland and Crushed the Soul of Corporate America—and How to Undo His Legacy.* New York: Simon & Schuster, 2022.

Gerstle, Gary. *The Rise and Fall of the Neoliberal Order: America and the World in the Free Market Era*. New York: Oxford University Press, 2022.

Gestrich, Andreas. "The Public Sphere and the Habermas Debate." *German History* 24, no. 3 (July 2006): 413–30.

Giridharadas, Anand. "Like Capitalism Itself, Business Journalism Is Broken. Can It Be Fixed?" (Interview with *New York Times* business reporter David Gelles). *The. Ink*, May 31, 2022. www.the.ink.com. Accessed on June 9, 2022.

Gitlin, Todd. *The Sixties: Years of Hope, Days of Rage*. New York: Bantam 1987.

———. "Public Sphere or Public Sphericules?" In *Media, Ritual, and Identity*, edited by Tamar Liebes and James Curran, London: Routledge, 1998, 168–74.

Goldstein, Gordon M. *Lesson in Disaster: McGeorge Bundy and the Path to War in Vietnam*. New York: Times Books / Henry Holt and Company, 2008

Gordon, Barry. *Political Economy in Parliament, 1819–1823*. London: Macmillan, 1976.

Gray, John. *False Dawn: The Delusions of Global Capitalism*. New York: New Press, 1998.

Gribbin, John. *The Fellowship: Gilbert, Bacon, Harvey, Wren, Newton, and the Story of a Scientific Revolution*. Woodstock, NY: Overlook Press, 2005.

Gripsrud, Jostein, Hallvard Moe, Anders Molander, and Graham Murdock, eds. *The Idea of the Public Sphere: A Reader*. Lanham: Lexington Books / Rowman & Littlefield, 2010.

Guizot, Francois. *The History of the Origins of Representative Government in Europe*. Original French edition published in 1851. First English edition published in 1861. Translated by Andrew R. Scoble. Indianapolis, IN: Liberty Fund, 2002.

Habermas, Jürgen. "Die Dialektik der Rationalisierung: Vom Pauperismus in Produktion und Konsum." *Merkur* 8, no. 8 (1954): 701–24.

———. "Literaturbericht zur philosophischen Diskussion um Marx und den Marxismus" (1957). In *Theorie und Praxis. Sozialphilosophische Studien*. First published in 1963. Fourth edition, corrected, enlarged, and with a new preface. Frankfurt am Main: Suhrkamp, 1971, 387–463.

———. "Zum Begriff der politischen Beteiligung" (1958). First published in *Student und Politik*. Neuwied: Luchterhand, 1961. Reprinted in *Kultur und Kritik. Verstreute Aufsätze*. Frankfurt am Main: Suhrkamp, 1973, 9–60.

———. "Verrufener Fortschritt—verkanntes Jahrhundert. Zur Kritik an der Geschichtsphilosophie. Replik R. Koselleck und H. Kesting. " *Merkur* 14, no. 147 (1960): 468–77. Revised reprint in *Kultur und Kritik* (1973), 355–64.

———. "Ein marxistischer Schelling. Zu Ernst Blochs spekulativem Materialismus." *Merkur* 14, no. 153 (1960): 1078–91.

———. "Ernst Bloch: A Marxist Schelling" (1960). In *Philosophical–Political Profiles*. Cambridge, MA: MIT Press, 1983, 61–77.

———. "Über das Verhältnis von Politik und Moral." In *Das Problem der Ordnung. Sechster Kongress für Philosophie München 1960*, edited by Helmut Kuhn and Franz Wiedmann. Meisenheim am Glan: Hain 1962.

———. "Der deutsche Idealismus der jüdischen Philosophen." In *Porträts deutsch–jüdischer Geistesgeschichte*, edited by Thilo Koch. Köln: Westdeutscher Rundfunk, 1961.

———. "The German Idealism of the Jewish Philosophers" (1961). *Philosophical–Political Profiles* (1983), 21–43.

———. *Strukturwandel der Öffentlichkeit. Untersuchungen zu einer Kategorie der bürgerlichen Gesellschaft*. First published in 1962. Fifth edition. Neuwied: Luchterhand, 1971.

———. *The Structural Transformation of the Public Sphere: An Inquiry into a Category of Bourgeois Society* (1962). Translated by Thomas Burger with the assistance of Frederick Lawrence. Cambridge: Polity Press, 1989.

———. *Theorie und Praxis. Sozialphilosophische Studien.* First published in 1963. Fourth edition, corrected, enlarged, and with a new preface. Frankfurt am Main: Suhrkamp, 1971.

———. *Theory and Practice* (1963). Translated by John Viertel. Boston: Beacon Press, 1973.

———. "Verwissenschaftlichte Politik und öffentliche Meinung" (1964). *Technik und Wissenschaft als "Ideologie."* Frankfurt am Main: Suhrkamp, 1968, 120–45.

———. "The Scientization of Politics and Public Opinion" (1964). *Toward a Rational Society: Student Protest, Science, and Politics.* Translated by Jeremy J. Shapiro. Boston: Beacon Press, 1970, 62–80.

———. "Erkenntnis und Interesse." June 28, 1965 Inaugural Address at Frankfurt University. First published in 1965. *Technik und Wissenschaft als "Ideologie,"* 146–68.

———. "Arbeit und Interaktion. Bemerkungen zu Hegels Jenenser 'Philosophie des Geistes.'" First published in 1967. *Technik und Wissenschaft als "Ideologie,"* 9–47.

———. "Technik und Wissenschaft als 'Ideologie.'" First published in July and August 1968 in *Merkur* to honor Herbert Marcuse on his 70th birthday. *Technik und Wissenschaft als "Ideologie,"* 48–103.

———. "Technology and Science as 'Ideology'" (1968). *Toward a Rational Society: Student Protest, Science, and Politics* (1970), 81–122.

———. *Erkenntnis und Interesse.* First published in 1968. With a new afterword. Frankfurt am Main: Suhrkamp, 1973.

———. *Knowledge & Human Interests* (1968). First English edition published in 1972. Translated by Jeremy J. Shapiro. Cambridge: Polity Press, 1987.

———. *Kultur und Kritik. Verstreute Aufsätze.* Frankfurt am Main: Suhrkamp, 1973.

———. *Legitimationsprobleme im Spätkapitalismus.* Frankfurt am Main: Suhrkamp, 1973.

———. *Legitimation Crisis* (1973). Translated by Thomas McCarthy. Boston: Beacon Press, 1975.

———. *Zur Rekonstruktion des Historischen Materialismus.* Frankfurt am Main: Suhrkamp, 1976.

———. "Toward a Reconstruction of Historical Materialism." In *Jürgen Habermas on Society and Politics: A Reader*, edited by Steven Seidman. Boston: Beacon Press, 1989, 114–41.

———. "Hannah Arendt's Communications Concept of Power," translated by Thomas McCarthy, *Social Research* 44, no. 1 (1977): 3–24.

———. "Psychic Thermidor and the Rebirth of Rebellious Subjectivity" (1980). First published in the *Berkeley Journal of Sociology.* In *Habermas and Modernity*, edited by Richard J. Bernstein. Cambridge: Polity Press, 1985, 67–77.

———. *Theorie des kommunikativen Handelns.* Band 2. *Zur Kritik der funktionalistischen Vernunft.* Frankfurt am Main: Suhrkamp, 1981.

———. *The Theory of Communicative Action.* Volume 2. *Lifeworld and System: A Critique of Functionalist Reason* (1981). Translated by Thomas McCarthy. Boston: Beacon Press, 1987.

———. "The Entwinement of Myth and Enlightenment," translated by Thomas Y. Levin. *New German Critique*, no. 26 (Spring–Summer 1982): 13–30.

———. "A Reply to My Critics," translated by Thomas McCarthy. In *Habermas: Critical Debates*, edited by John B. Thompson and David Held. Cambridge, MA: MIT Press, 1982, 219–83.

———. *Der philosophische Diskurs der Moderne. Zwölf Vorlesungen.* Frankfurt am Main: Suhrkamp, 1985.

———. *The Philosophical Discourse of Modernity: Twelve Lectures* (1985). Translated by Frederick Lawrence. Cambridge: Polity Press, 1987.

———. *Autonomy & Solidarity.* Interviews with Jürgen Habermas, edited and introduced by Peter Dews. London: Verso, 1986.

———. "Sovereignty and the *Führerdemokratie.*" *Times Literary Supplement*, September 26, 1986, 1053–54. Reprinted under the title "The Horrors of Autonomy" in Jürgen Habermas. *The New Conservatism: Cultural Criticism and the Historians' Debate*, edited and translated by Shierry Weber Nicholson. Introduction by Richard Wolin. Cambridge, MA: MIT Press, 1989, 128–39.

———. "The Idea of the University—Learning Processes," translated by John R. Blazek. *New German Critique*, no. 41 (Spring–Summer 1987): 3–22.

———. "Volkssouveränität als Verfahren: Ein normativer Begriff von Öffentlichkeit." *Merkur* 43, no. 6 (1989): 465–77.

———. "Taking Aim at the Heart of the Present: On Foucault's Lecture on Kant's *What Is Enlightenment?*" Originally translated by Sigrid Brauner and Robert Brown. *The New Conservatism: Cultural Criticism and the Historians' Debate*, edited and translated by Shierry Weber Nicholson. Introduction by Richard Wolin. Cambridge, MA: MIT Press, 1989, 173–79.

———. "Vorwort zur Neuauflage 1990." *Strukturwandel der Öffentlichkeit. Untersuchungen zu einer Kategorie der bürgerlichen Gesellschaft.* Frankfurt am Main: Suhrkamp, 1990, 11–50.

———. "Further Reflections on the Public Sphere." Translation by Thomas McCarthy of the 1990 preface. *Habermas and the Public Sphere* (1992), edited by Craig Calhoun, 421–61.

———. *Faktizität und Geltung. Beiträge zur Diskurstheorie des Rechts und des demokratischen Rechtsstaats.* Frankfurt am Main, 1992.

———. *Between Facts and Norms: Contributions to a Discourse Theory of Law and Democracy.* Translated by William Rehg. Cambridge, MA: MIT Press, 1996.

———. "Carl Schmitt in the Political Intellectual History of the Federal Republic." First published in *Die Zeit*, December 3, 1993. In *A Berlin Republic: Writings on Germany.* Translated by Steven Rendall. Introduction by Peter Uwe Hohendahl. Lincoln: University of Nebraska Press, 1997, 107–17.

———. "Reply to Symposium Participants, Benjamin N. Cardozo School of Law." In *Habermas on Law and Democracy*, edited by Michael Rosenfeld and Andrew Arato. Berkeley: University of California Press, 1998, 381–452.

————. "Learning by Disaster: A Short Look Back on the Short 20th Century," translated by Hella Beister. *Constellations* 5, no. 3 (September 1998).

————. "Das Kantische Projekt und der gespaltene Westen. Hat die Konstitutionalisierung des
Völkerrechts noch eine Chance?" *Der gespaltene Westen. Kleine Politische Schriften X.* Frankfurt am Main: Suhrkamp, 2004, 113–93.

————. "The Kantian Project and the Divided West: Does the Constitutionalization of International Law Still Have a Chance?" *The Divided West*, edited and translated by Ciaran Cronin. Cambridge: Polity Press, 2006, 113–93.

————. "Public Space and Political Public Sphere: The Biographical Roots of Two Motifs in My Thought." Transcript of lecture given at the Lifetime Achievement Award ceremony, Inamori Foundation, Kyoto, November 11, 2004. www.habermasforum.dk. Accessed on September 20, 2005.

————."Öffentlicher Raum und politische Öffentlichkeit. Lebensgeschichtliche Wurzeln zweier Gedankenmotive." *Neue Zürcher Zeitung*, December 11, 2004.

————. "Political Communication in Media Society: Does Democracy Still Enjoy an Epistemic Dimension? The Impact of Normative Theory on Empirical Research." *Communication Theory* 16, no. 4 (2006): 411–26.

————. "Der Hermann Heller der frühen Bundesrepublik. Wolfgang Abendroth zum 100. Geburtstag" (2006). In *Ach Europa. Kleine politische Schriften XI*. Frankfurt am Main: Suhrkamp, 2008, 11–14.

————. "Überlegungen und Hypothesen zu einem erneuten Strukturwandel der politischen Öffentlichkeit." In *Ein neuer Strukturwandel der Öffentlichkeit?* Edited by Martin Seeliger and Sebastian Sevignani. *Leviathan*, Special Issue 37. Baden–Baden: Nomos, 2021, 470–500.

————. "Krieg und Empörung." *Süddeutsche Zeitung*, April 29, 2022. Excerpts in
"Habermas on the war in Ukraine." https://habermas–rawls.blogspot.com/2022/04. Accessed on May 16, 2022.

————. *Ein neuer Strukturwandel der Öffentlichkeit und die deliberative Politik.* Berlin: Suhrkamp, 2022.

Hakim, Eleanor. "The Tragedy of Hans Gerth." In *History and the New Left: Madison, Wisconsin, 1950–1970*, edited by Paul Buhle. Philadelphia: Temple University Press, 1990, 252–63.

Halberstam, David. *The Best and the Brightest.* New York: Random House, 1972.

————. *The Fifties.* New York: Random House, 1993.

Hamilton, Alexander; James Madison, and John Jay. *The Federalist Papers.* First published in 1788. New York: New American Library, 1961.

Hammer, Joshua. "Maria Ressa's Dangerous Battle for the Truth." *The New York Times Magazine.* Published October 15, 2019. Updated October 9, 2021. www.nytimes.com. Accessed on June 9, 2022.

Harney, Alexandra. *The China Price: The True Cost of Chinese Competitive Advantage.* New York: Penguin Press, 2008.

Harrington, James. *The Political Writings of James Harrington.* Edited with an introduction by Charles Blitzer. New York: Liberal Arts Press, 1955.

Haugen, Frances. "I Blew the Whistle on Facebook. Europe Showed Us the Next Step." *The New York Times*, April 29, 2022, A 20.

Hegel, Georg Wilhelm Friedrich. *Philosophy of Right.* Edited by Allen W. Wood. Translated by H.B. Nisbet. Original German edition published in 1821. Cambridge: Cambridge University Press, 1991.

———. *Hegel's Political Writings*. Translated by T. M. Knox. London: Oxford University Press, 1964.

Heller, Henry. *The Bourgeois Revolution in France, 1789–1815.* New York: Berghahn Books, 2006.

Heller, Hermann. *Staatslehre*. Edited by Gerhart Niemeyer. First published in 1934 by A.W. Sijthoff, Leiden, Netherlands. Second edition with an afterword by the editor. Tübingen: J. C. B. Mohr (Paul Siebeck), 1992.

Himmelfarb, Gertrude. *On Liberty and Liberalism: The Case of John Stuart Mill.* New York: Alfred A Knopf, 1974.

———. *The Idea of Poverty: England in the Early Industrial Age.* New York: Alfred A. Knopf, 1984.

———. *The Roads to Modernity: The British, French, and American Enlightenments.* New York: Alfred A. Knopf, 2004.

Hobbes, Thomas. *Leviathan*. First published in 1651. Edited with an introduction by C.B. Macpherson. London: Penguin Books, 1968.

Hobsbawm, Eric J. *The Age of Revolution: Europe, 1789–1848.* London: Weidenfeld and Nicolson, 1962.

Hofmann, Michael. *Habermas's Public Sphere: A Critique.* Lanham: Fairleigh Dickinson University Press / Rowman & Littlefield, 2017.

———. "Habermas's Public Sphere versus Trump's Twittersphere: Citizenship in a World of Social Media." *The Journal of Communication and Media Studies* 3, no. 4 (2018): 1–19.

———. "Theoretische und praktische Wirkungen des akademischen Bestsellers *Strukturwandel der Öffentlichkeit* in den USA." In *Habermas global. Wirkungsgeschichte eines Werks*, edited by Luca Corchia, Stefan Müller–Doohm, and William Outhwaite. Berlin: Suhrkamp, 2019, 339–61.

———. "Deliberation in Dysfunctional Democracies: The Global Need for Critically Renewing Habermas's Public Sphere Concept." *The Journal of Communication and Media Studies* 4, no. 3 (2019): 47–67.

———. Review "Political Theory and History of Ideas": Roman Yos. *Der junge Habermas. Eine ideengeschichtliche Untersuchung seines frühen Denkens, 1952–1962* (2019). *Politische Vierteljahresschrift / German Political Science Quarterly* 61, no. 2 (June 2020): 377–79.

———. "Theoretical and Practical Influences of Habermas's Global Academic Best Seller 'Structural Transformation of the Public Sphere' in the United States." *Kybernetes* 50, no. 4 (2021): 955–68.

———. Review "Political Theory and History of Ideas": *Ein neuer Strukturwandel der Öffentlichkeit?* Edited by Martin Seeliger and Sebastian Sevignani. *Leviathan*, Special Issue 37 (2021). *Politische Vierteljahresschrift / German Political Science Quarterly* 63, no. 1 (March 2022): 125–28.

Hohendahl, Peter Uwe. "An Introduction to Habermas' 'The Public Sphere' (1964)." *New German Critique* 1, no. 3 (Fall 1974): 45–48.

———. "Critical Theory, Public Sphere, and Culture." *New German Critique* 6, no. 16 (Spring–Summer 1979): 89–118.

———. "Habermas' Critique of the Frankfurt School." *New German Critique*, no. 35 (Spring–Summer 1985): 3–26.

———. "Recasting the Public Sphere." *October*, no. 73 (Summer 1995): 27–54.

———. "From the Eclipse of Reason to Communicative Rationality and Beyond." In *Critical Theory: Current State and Future Prospects*, edited by Peter Uwe Hohendahl and Jaimey Fisher. New York: Berghahn Books, 2001, 3–28.

Hohendahl, Peter Uwe, Russell A. Berman, Karen Kenkel, and Arthur Strum. *Öffentlichkeit: Geschichte eines kritischen Begriffs*. Stuttgart / Weimar: J.B. Metzler, 2000.

Hohendahl, Peter Uwe, and Jaimey Fisher eds. *Critical Theory: Current State and Future Prospects*. New York: Berghahn Books, 2001

Hollander, Jacob H. *David Ricardo: A Centenary Estimate*. Baltimore: Johns Hopkins Press, 1910.

Hollander, Samuel. *The Economics of David Ricardo*. Toronto: University of Toronto Press, 1979.

———. *Jean–Baptiste Say and the Classical Canon in Economics: The British Connection in French Classicism*. London: Routledge, 2003.

Holub, Robert C. *Jürgen Habermas: Critic in the Public Sphere*. London, UK: Routledge, 1991.

Hont, Istvan, and Michael Ignatieff, eds. *Wealth and Virtue: The Shaping of Political Economy in the Scottish Enlightenment*. Cambridge: Cambridge University Press, 1983.

Hopkins, Valerie. "Accepting Nobel Prize, Two Journalists Warn of Perils to Democracy." *The New York Times*, December 11, 2021, A 9.

Horkheimer, Max. *Critical Theory: Selected Essays*. Translated by Matthew J. O'Connell and others. New York: Herder and Herder, 1972.

Horkheimer, Max, and Theodor W. Adorno. *Dialektik der Aufklärung. Philosophische Fragmente*. Completed in 1944. First published in 1947. Frankfurt/Main: S. Fischer, 1969.

———. *Dialectic of Enlightenment*. Translated by John Cumming. First English edition published in 1972. London: Verso, 1986.

Horne, Thomas A. *The Social Thought of Bernard Mandeville: Virtue and Commerce in Early Eighteenth–Century England*. New York: Columbia University Press, 1978.

Horster, Detlef, and Willem van Reijen. "Interview mit Jürgen Habermas am 23. März 1979 in Starnberg." In: Detlef Horster. *Habermas zur Einführung*. Hannover: SOAK, 1980, 70–94.

Hounshell, Blake. "Democrats Weigh a Comeback Strategy in Factory Towns." *The New York Times*, June 7, 2022, A 18.

Hubbard, Ben. "Hopes for Justice Dim as Turkey Ends Khashoggi Killing Inquiry." *The New York Times*, March 28, 2020, A 19.

Hughes, Chris. "It's Time to Break Up Facebook." *The New York Times*, May 12, 2019, SR 1–4.

Hunt, Lynn. *Inventing Human Rights: A History*. New York: W.W. Norton, 2007.

IMP Media. "Roarings of the Lion: The Starbucks that's on the site of social media history." www.impmedia.co.uk/single–post/2017/03/11. Accessed on April 13, 2020.

Israel, Jonathan I. *Dutch Primacy in World Trade, 1585–1740*. Oxford: Oxford University Press, 1989.

Jacoby, Russell. *The Last Intellectuals: American Culture in the Age of Academe*. New York: Farrar, Straus & Giroux, 1987.

Jamieson, Kathleen Hall. *Packaging the Presidency: A History and Criticism of Presidential Campaign Advertising*, 3rd edition. New York: Oxford University Press, 1996.

Jardine, Lisa. *Going Dutch: How England Plundered Holland's Glory*. New York: HarperCollins, 2008.

Jay, Martin. *The Dialectical Imagination: A History of the Frankfurt School and the Institute of Social Research, 1923–1950*. Boston: Little, Brown and Company, 1973.

———. *Reason after Its Eclipse: On Late Critical Theory*. Madison: University of Wisconsin Press, 2016.

Kahan, Alan S. *Aristocratic Liberalism: The Social and Political Thought of Jacob Burckhardt, John Stuart Mill, and Alexis de Tocqueville*. New York: Oxford University Press, 1992.

Kaminski, Margot E., and Kate Klonick. "Speech in the Social Public Square." *The New York Times*, June 27, 2017, A 23.

Kang, Cecilia. "Ex–Insider Says Facebook Hid Efforts to Hook Users: Senate Panel Is Told How Platforms Profit From Spread of Harmful Content." *The New York Times,* October 6, 2021, A 1.

Kant, Immanuel. *Kant's Political Writings*. Edited with an introduction and notes by Hans Reiss. Cambridge: Cambridge University Press, 1970.

———. *Was ist Aufklärung? Ausgewählte kleine Schriften*. First published in 1914. Edited by Horst D. Brandt. With an introductory text by Ernst Cassirer from 1923. Hamburg: Felix Meiner, 1999.

Kaplan, Steven L. *Bread, Politics, and Political Economy in the Reign of Louis XV*. Two volumes. The Hague: Martinus Nijhoff, 1976.

Kates, Steven. *Say's Law and the Keynesian Revolution: How Macroeconomic Theory Lost Its Way*. Cheltenham: Edward Elgar, 1998.

———, ed. *Two Hundred Years of Say's Law: Essays on Economic Theory's Most Controversial Principle*. Cheltenham: Edward Elgar, 2003.

Kazin, Michael. *War against War: The American Fight for Peace, 1914–1918*. New York: Simon & Schuster, 2017.

Keane, John. *The Media and Democracy*. London: Polity Press, 1991.

———. *Tom Paine: A Political Life*. London: Bloomsbury, 1995.

Kellner, Douglas. "Kulturindustrie und Massenkommunikation. Die Kritische Theorie und ihre Folgen."In *Sozialforschung als Kritik. Zum sozialwissenschaftlichen*

Potential der Kritischen Theorie, edited by Wolfgang Bonss and Axel Honneth. Frankfurt am Main: Suhrkamp, 1982, 482–515.

———. "Habermas, the Public Sphere, and Democracy: A Critical Intervention." In *Perspectives on Habermas*, edited by Lewis Edwin Hahn. Chicago and La Salle: Open Court, 2000: 259–88.

Kendrick, Alexander. *Prime Time: The Life of Edward R. Murrow*. Boston: Little Brown and Co., 1969.

Kennedy, Ellen. "Carl Schmitt and the Frankfurt School." *Telos*, no. 71 (Spring 1987): 37–66.

———. "Carl Schmitt and the Frankfurt School: A Rejoinder." *Telos*, no. 73 (Fall 1987): 101–16.

Kern, Montague, Patricia W. Levering, and Ralph B. Levering. *The Kennedy Crises: The Press, the Presidency, and Foreign Policy*. Chapel Hill: The University of North Carolina Press, 1983.

Kesting, Hanno. *Geschichtsphilosophie und Weltbürgerkrieg. Deutungen der Geschichte von der Französischen Revolution bis zum Ost–West–Konflikt*. Heidelberg: Carl Winter, 1959.

Keynes, John Maynard. *The General Theory of Employment, Interest, and Money*. First published in 1936. San Diego: Harvest / Harcourt, 1964.

Klein, Naomi. *The Shock Doctrine: The Rise of Disaster Capitalism*. New York: Henry, Holt, and Company / Metropolitan Books, 2007.

Koselleck, Reinhart. *Kritik und Krise. Eine Studie zur Pathogenese der bürgerlichen Welt*. First published in 1959. Third edition. Frankfurt am Main: Suhrkamp, 1979.

———. *Critique and Crisis: Enlightenment and the Pathogenesis of Modern Society*. Translation by Berg Publishers Ltd. Cambridge, MA: MIT Press, 1988.

Kramnick, Isaac. *Bolingbroke and His Circle: The Politics of Nostalgia in the Age of Walpole*. Cambridge, MA: Harvard University Press, 1968.

Kraus, Sidney, ed. *The Great Debates: Kennedy vs. Nixon, 1960*. A Reissue. First published in 1962. Bloomington, IN: Indiana University Press 1977.

Kristol, Irving. *Two Cheers for Capitalism*. New York: Basic Books, 1978.

Krugman, Paul. "Who Was Milton Friedman?" *The New York Review of Books* 54, no. 2 (February 15, 2007): 27–30.

Lilla, Mark. "A Tale of Two Reactions." *The New York Review of Books* 45, no. 8 (May 14, 1998): 4–7.

———. "The Tea Party Jacobins." *The New York Review of Books* 57. no. 9 (May 27, 2010): 53–56.

———. *The Reckless Mind: Intellectuals in Politics*. New York: New York Review Books, 2001.

Lippmann, Walter. *Public Opinion*. First published in 1922. New York: Free Press, 1965.

Locke, John. *An Essay Concerning Human Understanding*. First published in 1690. Edited by Alexander Campbell Fraser, with "Prolegomena: Biographical, Critical, and Historical." Two volumes. Oxford: Clarendon Press, 1894.

Lottes, Günther. *Politische Aufklärung und plebejisches Publikum: Zur Theorie und Praxis des englischen Radikalismus im späten 18. Jahrhundert.* München: Oldenbourg, 1979.

Luttwak, Edward N. *The Endangered American Dream*: New York: Simon & Schuster, 1993.

Lux, Mike. "Winning Back The Factory Towns That Made Trumpism Possible (Research Report, 2021)." www.americanfamilyvoices.org. Accessed on June 9, 2022.

Macpherson, C.B. *The Political Theory of Possessive Individualism: Hobbes to Locke.* London: Oxford University Press, 1962.

Mandeville, Bernard. *The Fable of the Bees: Or, Private Vices, Publick Benefits.* First published in 1705. Reissued in 1714 with an essay on "The Origin of Moral Virtue" and additional "Remarks." Reprint of the further enlarged edition published in 1724. With a "Commentary Critical, Historical, and Explanatory" by F. B. Kaye. Two volumes. Oxford: The Clarendon Press, 1924.

Marcuse, Herbert. *Reason and Revolution: Hegel and the Rise of Social Theory.* First published in 1941. With a new preface by the author: "A Note on Dialectic." Boston: Beacon Press, 1960.

———. *Studies in Critical Philosophy.* Writings from 1932 to 1969. Translated by Joris de Bres. London: New Left Books, 1972.

Marsh, James L. *Unjust Legality: A Critique of Habermas's Philosophy of Law.* Lanham / Oxford: Rowman & Littlefield, 2001.

Martin, Jonathan. "Democrats Lost the Most in Midwestern 'Factory Town,' Report Says." *The New York Times*, October 5, 2021.

Marx, Karl. *On Freedom of the Press and Censorship.* Writings from 1842 to 1871. Edited, translated, and introduced by Saul K. Padover. New York: McGraw–Hill, 1974.

———. *Das Kapital. Kritik der politischen Ökonomie.* Volume One: *Der Produktionsprozess des Kapitals.* Original German edition published in 1867. Berlin: Dietz, 1969.

———. *Capital: A Critique of Political Economy.* Volume One. Translated by Ben Fowkes. London: Penguin Books, 1976.

Marx, Karl; and Friedrich Engels. *The Communist Manifesto.* Original German edition published in London in 1848. First English translation by Helen Macfarlane published in 1850. New English translation by Samuel Moore, with a preface by Friedrich Engels, published in 1888. With an introduction by Eric Hobsbawm. London: Verso, 1998.

Matustik, Martin Beck. *Jürgen Habermas: A Philosophical–Political Profile.* Lanham: Rowman & Littlefield, 2001.

McCarthy, Thomas. *The Critical Theory of Jürgen Habermas.* Cambridge, MA: MIT Press, 1978.

———. *Ideals and Illusions: On Reconstruction and Deconstruction in Contemporary Critical Theory.* Cambridge, MA: MIT Press, 1991.

———. Book Review of *Unjust Legality: A Critique of Habermas's Philosophy of Law* by James Marsh. Oxford: Rowman & Littlefield, 2001. *Mind* 112, no. 448, 762–65.

————. *Race, Empire, and the Idea of Human Development*. Cambridge: Cambridge University Press, 2009.

————. "Herb Stempel, 93, Contestant Who Admitted Quiz Show Was Fake, Dies." *The New York Times*, June 1, 2020, D 7.

McNally, David. *Political Economy and the Rise of Capitalism: A Reinterpretation*. Berkeley: University of California Press, 1988.

McNamara, Robert S., James G. Blight, and Robert K. Brigham. *Argument Without End: In Search of Answers to the Vietnam Tragedy.* New York: Public Affairs, 1999.

McNamee, Roger. *Zucked: Waking Up to the Facebook Catastrophe*. New York: Penguin Press, 2019.

Mendieta, Eduardo, and Benjamin Randolph. "Vom Eklektizismus zur Rekonstruktion der kommunikativen Vernunft: Habermas in den Vereinigten Staaten." In *Habermas global. Wirkungsgeschichte eines Werks*, edited by Luca Corchia, Stefan Müller–Doohm, and William Outhwaite, Berlin: Suhrkamp, 2019, 315–338.

Mill, John Stuart. *Principles of Political Economy: with Some of Their Applications to Social Philosophy*. Two volumes. First published in 1848. Introduction by V.W. Bladen. Toronto: University of Toronto Press, 1965.

————. *On Liberty*. First published in 1859. London: Watts & Co., 1929.

————. *Autobiography*. Edited by Helen Taylor. First published in 1873. New York: Liberal Arts Press, 1957.

Miller, James. *Rousseau: Dreamer of Democracy*. New Haven, CT: Yale University Press, 1984.

————. *"Democracy Is in the Streets": From Port Huron to the Siege of Chicago*. New York: Simon & Schuster, 1987.

Mills, C. Wright. *The Power Elite*. First published in 1956. With a new afterword by Alan Wolfe. New York: Oxford University Press, 2000.

————. "The Sociology of Mass Media and Public Opinion." In *Power, Politics, and People: The Collected Essays of C. Wright Mills*, edited by Irving Louis Horowitz. New York: Oxford University Press, 1963, 577–98.

Milton, John. "Areopagitica." (First published in 1644.) *Complete Prose Works of John Milton*. Volume II (1643–1648). Edited and introduced by Ernest Sirluck. New Haven, CT: Yale University Press, 1959, 480–570.

Morgenson, Gretchen, and Joshua Rosner. *Reckless Endangerment: How Outsized Ambition, Greed, and Corruption Led to Economic Armageddon*. New York: Henry, Holt and Company / Times Books, 2011.

Morrison, Joan, and Robert K. Morrison, eds. *From Camelot to Kent State: The Sixties Experience in the Words of Those Who Lived It*. First published by Times Books/Random House in 1987. Updated edition. New York: Oxford University Press, 2001.

Müller, Jan-Werner. *A Dangerous Mind: Carl Schmitt in Post–War European Thought.* New Haven, CT: Yale University Press, 2003.

Müller-Doohm, Stefan. *Habermas: A Biography*. First published in German as *Jürgen Habermas. Eine Biographie*. Berlin: Suhrkamp, 2014. Translated by Daniel Steuer. Cambridge: Polity Press, 2016.

Murphy, Heather. "Facebook Pushes Back On Co–Founder's Op–Ed." *The New York Times*, May 10, 2019, B 3.

Neumann, Franz. "Der Funktionswandel des Gesetzes im Recht der bürgerlichen Gesellschaft." *Zeitschrift für Sozialforschung* 6 (1937): 542 – 96.

———. "The Concept of Political Freedom." *Columbia Law Review* 53, no. 7 (1953): 901 – 35.

———. *The Democratic and the Authoritarian State: Essays in Political and Legal Theory*. Edited and with a preface by Herbert Marcuse. Glencoe, IL: Free Press, 1957.

New York Times Editorial. "Facebook Is Not the Public Square." *The New York Times*, December 26, 2014, A 20.

———. "A Record Number of Journalists Jailed." *The New York Times*, December 19, 2021, SR 8.

O'Brien, D. P. *J. R. McCulloch: A Study in Classical Economics*. New York: Barnes & Noble, 1970.

O'Gorman, Frank. *The Long Eighteenth Century: British Political and Social History, 1688–1832*. London: Arnold, 1997.

Owen, Robert. *Observations on the Effect of the Manufacturing System: With Hints for the Improvement of Those Parts of It Which Are Most Injurious to Health and Morals; Dedicated Most Respectfully to the British Legislature*. London: Richard and Arthur Taylor, 1815.

Paine, Thomas. *Rights of Man*. Part One first published in 1791. Part Two first published in 1792. With an introduction by Eric Foner. Harmondsworth: Penguin Books, 1985.

———. *The Age of Reason*. First published in 1794. Edited by Moncure Daniel Conway. Reprint of the 1896 edition by G.P. Putnam's Sons. Mineola, NY: Dover, 2004.

Pang, Amelia. *Made in China: A Prisoner, an SOS Letter, and the Hidden Cost of America's Cheap Goods*. New York: Algonquin Books, 2021.

Peters, John Durham. "Distrust of Representation: Habermas on the Public Sphere." *Media, Culture and Society* 15 (1993): 541–71.

Plumb, John Harold. *The Growth of Political Stability in England, 1675–1725*. London: Macmillan, 1967.

Polanyi, Karl. *The Great Transformation*: Rinehart & Company, 1944.

Popkin, Jeremy D. *The Right–Wing Press in France, 1792–1800*. Chapel Hill: University of North Carolina Press, 1980.

———. *Revolutionary News: The Press in France, 1789–1799*. Durham, NC: Duke University Press, 1990.

Preuss, Ulrich K. "Carl Schmitt und die Frankfurter Schule: Deutsche Liberalismuskritik im 20. Jahrhundert. Anmerkungen zu dem Aufsatz von Ellen Kennedy." *Geschichte und Gesellschaft* 12, no. 3 (1986): 400–18.

———. "The Critique of German Liberalism: A Reply to Ellen Kennedy." *Telos*, no. 71 (Spring 1987): 97–110.

———. *Constitutional Revolution: The Link between Constitutionalism and Progress*. Translated by Deborah Lucas Schneider. First published in German in 1990. Atlantic Highlands: Humanities Press, 1995.

Read, Donald. *Peterloo: The "Massacre" and Its Background.* Manchester: Manchester University Press, 1958.

Ressa, Maria, and Mark Thompson. "The Free Press Needs Our Help." *The New York Times*, December 12, 2021, SR 3.

Ricardo, David. *On the Principles of Political Economy and Taxation*. First published in 1817. Third Edition. London: John Murray, Albemarle–Street, 1821. *The Works and Correspondence of David Ricardo*. Volume One. Edited by Piero Sraffa with the collaboration of M. H. Dobb. Cambridge: Cambridge University Press, 1951.

Riedel, Manfred. *Zwischen Tradition und Revolution: Studien zu Hegels Rechtsphilosophie.* First published in 1969. New and expanded edition. Stuttgart: Klett–Cotta, 1982.

———. *Between Tradition and Revolution: The Hegelian Transformation of Political Philosophy*. Translated by Walter Wright. Cambridge: Cambridge University Press, 1984.

Riordon, William L. *Plunkitt of Tammany Hall*. First published in 1905. New York: E.P. Dutton, 1963.

Robison, Peter. *Flying Blind: The 737 Max Tragedy and the Fall of Boeing*. New York: Doubleday, 2021.

Rockmore, Tom. *Habermas on Historical Materialism*. Bloomington: Indiana University Press, 1989.

Rorty, Richard. *Achieving Our Country: Leftist Thought in Twentieth–Century America.* Cambridge, MA: Harvard University Press, 1998.

Rosen, Jay. *What Are Journalists For?* New Haven, CT: Yale University Press, 1999.

Rosenfeld, Michael, and Andrew Arato, eds. *Habermas on Law and Democracy*. Berkeley: University of California Press, 1998

Rothschild, Emma. *Economic Sentiments: Adam Smith, Condorcet, and the Enlightenment*. Cambridge, MA: Harvard University Press, 2001.

Safire, William. "On Language; Return of the Luddites," *The New York Times Magazine*, December 6, 1998, 34.

Sandoval, Edgar, and Richard Fausset. "In a Kentucky Town, A Lifeline Ripped to Pieces." *The New York Times*, December 17, 2021, A 1.

Sanger, David E. "Biden Stakes Out His Challenge With China: 'Prove Democracy Works.'" *New York Times*, March 27, 2021, A 10.

Say, Jean–Baptiste. *Letters to Mr. Malthus on Several Subjects of Political Economy and on the Cause of the Stagnation of Commerce*. Revised and expanded translation by John Richter of Say's letters first published in the *New Monthly Magazine*. London: Sherwood, Neely & Jones, Paternoster–Row, 1821. Reprints of Economics Classics. New York: Augustus M. Kelley, 1967.

———. *A Treatise on Political Economy*. Original French edition published in 1803. Translation of the fourth edition of 1821. Philadelphia: Grigg R. Elliott, 1834.

Scheuerman, William E. "Between Radicalism and Resignation: Democratic Theory in Habermas's *Between Facts and Norms*." In *Habermas: A Critical Reader*, edited by Peter Dews. Oxford: Blackwell, 1999, 153–77.

———. "Good–Bye to Radical Reformism?" *Political Theory* 40, no. 6 (December 2012): 830–38.

———. "Habermas and the Fate of Democracy." Review of *Habermas: A Biography* by Stefan Müller–Doohm. *Boston Review*, April 12, 2017.

Schiller, Friedrich. *On the Aesthetic Education of Man: In a Series of Letters*. Original German edition published in 1795. English translation with an introduction by Reginald Snell published in 1954. Seventh printing. New York: Frederick Ungar, 1983.

Schmitt, Carl. *Die Diktatur. Von den Anfängen des modernen Souveranitätsgedankens bis zum proletarischen Klassenkampf.* First published in 1921. Seventh edition. Berlin: Duncker & Humblot, 2006.

———. *Die geistesgeschichtliche Lage des heutigen Parlamentarismus.* First published in 1923. With a preface to the second edition (1926): "Über den Gegensatz von Parlamentarismus und Demokratie." Eighth edition. Berlin: Duncker & Humblot, 1996.

———. *The Crisis of Parliamentary Democracy.* With a preface to the second edition (1926): "On the Contradiction between Parliamentarism and Democracy." Translated and introduced by Ellen Kennedy. With a foreword by Thomas McCarthy. Cambridge, MA: MIT Press, 1985.

———. *Verfassungslehre.* First published in 1928. Ninth edition. Berlin: Duncker & Humblot, 2003.

———. *Constitutional Theory.* Translated and edited by Jeffrey Seitzer. Foreword by Ellen Kennedy. Durham, NC: Duke University Press, 2008.

———. *Der Leviathan in der Staatslehre des Thomas Hobbes. Sinn und Fehlschlag eines politischen Symbols.* Hamburg: Hanseatische Verlagsanstalt, 1938.

———. *The Leviathan in the State Theory of Thomas Hobbes: Meaning and Failure of a Political Symbol.* Translated by George Schwab and Erna Hilfstein. Foreword and introduction by George Schwab. Westport, CT: Greenwood Press, 1996.

Schudson, Michael. "Was There Ever a Public Sphere? If So, When? Reflections on the American Case." In *Habermas and the Public Sphere*, edited by Craig Calhoun. Cambridge, MA: MIT Press, 1992, 143–63.

Schuessler, Jennifer. "After History's End, Still Plugging Along." *The New York Times*, May 11, 2022, C 1.

Seeliger, Martin and Sebastian Sevignani, eds. *Ein neuer Strukturwandel der Öffentlichkeit? Leviathan*, Special Issue 37. Baden–Baden: Nomos, 2021.

Seelye, Katherine Q. "Max Cleland, Vietnam War Veteran and Former Senator, is Dead at 79." *The New York Times*, November 10, 2021, B 10.

Selk, Veith, and Dirk Jörke. "Back to the Future! Habermas and Dewey on Democracy in Capitalist Times." *Constellations* 27, no. 1 (March 2020): 36–49.

Seltz, Herbert A., and Richard D. Yoakam. "Production Diary of the Debates." In *The Great Debates: Kennedy vs. Nixon, 1960*, edited by Sidney Kraus. A Reissue. First published in 1962. Bloomington, IN: Indiana University Press 1977, 73–126.

Shear, Michael D. "Biden to Name Qatar as Major Non–NATO Ally, Deepening Ties to U.S." *The New York Times*, February 1, 2022, A 9.

Shenk, Timothy. *Maurice Dobb: Political Economist*. New York: St. Martin's Press/ Palgrave Macmillan, 2013.

Shils, Edward. "Daydreams and Nightmares: Reflections on the Criticism of Mass Culture." *Sewanee Review* 45, no. 4 (1957).

Simonde de Sismondi, J.C.L. *Political Economy*. First published in Brewster's *Edinburgh Encyclopedia* in 1815. Reprints of Economic Classics. New York: Augustus M. Kelly, 1966.

Smith, Adam. *The Theory of Moral Sentiments*. First published in 1759. Reprint of the sixth, enlarged edition published in 1790. Lincoln–Rembrandt Publishing, n. d.

———. *An Inquiry into the Nature and Causes of The Wealth of Nations*. First published in 1776. Edited, with an introduction, notes, marginal summary, and enlarged index by Edwin Cannan. Modern Library Edition. New York: Random House, 1994.

Sola Pool, Ithiel de. *Technologies of Freedom*. Cambridge, MA: Harvard University Press, 1984.

Sowell, Thomas. *Say's Law: An Historical Analysis.* Princeton, NJ: Princeton University Press, 1972.

———. *On Classical Economics*. New Haven, CT: Yale University Press, 2006.

Specia, Megan, and Charlie Savage. "U.K. Court Rules Assange, WikiLeaks Founder, Can Be Extradited." *The New York Times*, December 11, 2021, A 9.

Specter, Matthew G. *Habermas: An Intellectual Biography*. Cambridge: Cambridge University Press, 2010.

Speier, Hans. "The Historical Development of Public Opinion." (First published in 1950). *Social Order and the Risks of War: Papers in Political Sociology*. New York: George W. Stewart, 1952, 323–38.

Stephens, Mitchell. "The Theologian of Talk; The Question Is Whether Justice Exists and Reason Can Benefit Society, It's Postmodern to Say No, But Jürgen Habermas, a German Philosopher, Disagrees." *Los Angeles Times Magazine*, October 23, 1994. Published online: http://www.nyu.edu/classes/stephens/Habermas%20page .htm (12 pages). Accessed: 8/21/2008.

Stockman, Farah. *American Made: What Happens to People When Work Disappears*. New York: Random House, 2021.

Summers, Lawrence H. "The Great Liberator." *The New York Times*, November 19, 2006, "Week in Review," 13.

Swisher, Kara. "Too Late To Shutter Social Media." *The New York Times*, April 23, 2019, A 23.

Tarnoff, Ben. "What Would a More Egalitarian Internet Actually Look Like?" *The New York Times*, May 29, 2022, SR 10.

Thompson, E. P. *The Making of the English Working Class*. First published in 1963. Revised edition published in 1968. Reprinted with a new preface. Harmondsworth: Penguin Books, 1980.

Thompson, John B. "The Theory of the Public Sphere." *Theory, Culture & Society* 10 (1993): 173–89.

Thompson, John B., and David Held, eds. *Habermas: Critical Debates*. Cambridge, MA: MIT Press, 1982.

Thompson, Noel. *The People's Science: The Popular Political Economy of Exploitation and Crisis, 1816–34*. Cambridge: Cambridge University Press, 1984.

Thorpe, Vanessa. "How a Soho coffee house gave birth to the New Left." *The Guardian*, April 22, 2017.

Timur, Safak, and Ben Hubbard. "Turkey Sends Trial for Journalist's Killing to Saudi Arabia, Most Likely Dooming It." *The New York Times*, April 8, 2022, A 6.

Tocqueville, Alexis de. *Democracy in America*. Original French edition published in 1835 (First Part) and 1840 (Second Part). First English translation by Henry Reeve. Revised translation by Francis Bowen in 1862. Edited, with further corrections and an historical essay by Phillips Bradley. New York: Alfred A. Knopf, 1945.

———. *The Old Regime and the Revolution*. Volume One: The Complete Text. Original French edition published in 1856. Edited and with an introduction and critical apparatus by Francois Furet and Francoise Melonio. Translated by Alan S. Kahan. Chicago: University of Chicago Press, 1998.

———. *The Old Regime and the Revolution*. Volume Two: *Notes on the French Revolution and Napoleon*. Edited and with an introduction and critical apparatus by Francois Furet and Francoise Melonio. Translated by Alan S. Kahan. Chicago: University of Chicago Press, 2001.

Tufekci, Zeynep. "Beware the Smart Campaign." *The New York Times*, November 17, 2012, A 23.

Uchitelle, Louis. *The Disposable American: Layoffs and Their Consequences*. New York: Alfred A Knopf, 2006.

Vries, Jan de; Ad van der Woude. *The First Modern Economy: Success, Failure, and Perseverance of the Dutch Economy, 1500–1815*. Cambridge: Cambridge University Press, 1997.

Warzel, Charlie, "The Privacy Project: When $5 Billion Is a Slap on the Wrist." *The New York Times,* April 29, 2019, A 18.

Weber, Max. *The Protestant Ethic and the Spirit of Capitalism*. Original German journal article published in two parts in 1904–1905. Revised edition published in 1920–21. Translated by Talcott Parsons. With an introduction by Anthony Giddens. London: Routledge, 1992.

———. *The Methodology of the Social Sciences*. Edited and translated by Edward A. Shils and Henry A. Finch. With a foreword by Edward A. Shils. New York: Free Press, 1949.

Whatmore, Richard. *Republicanism and the French Revolution: An Intellectual History of Jean–Baptiste Say's Political Economy.* Oxford: Oxford University Press, 2000.

Wiggershaus, Rolf. *Die Frankfurter Schule. Geschichte, Theoretische Entwicklung, Politische Bedeutung.* München: Carl Hanser, 1986.

———. *The Frankfurt School: Its History, Theories, and Political Significance.* Translated by Michael Robertson. Cambridge, MA: MIT Press, 1994.

———. *Jürgen Habermas.* Reinbek bei Hamburg: Rowohlt, 2004.

Williams, David. *Condorcet and Modernity*. Cambridge: Cambridge University Press, 2004.

Williams, Eric. *Capitalism & Slavery*. First published in 1944. With a new introduction by Colin A. Palmer. Chapel Hill, NC: University of North Carolina Press, 1994.

Williams, Raymond. *Culture and Society, 1780–1950*. First published in 1958 by Chatto & Windus. New edition with a postscript. Harmondsworth: Penguin, 1963.

Willis, Derek. "Campaigns Use Facebook Tool To Deliver Targeted Political Ads." *The New York Times*, September 11, 2014, A 3.

Wirsching, Andreas. *Parlament und Volkes Stimme. Unterhaus und Öffentlichkeit im England des frühen 19. Jahrhunderts*. Göttingen: Vandenhoeck & Ruprecht, 1990.

Yos, Roman. *Der junge Habermas. Eine ideengeschichtliche Untersuchung seines frühen Denkens, 1952–1962*. Berlin: Suhrkamp, 2019.

Zaret, David. *Origins of Democratic Culture: Printing, Petitions, and the Public Sphere in Early–Modern England*. Princeton, NJ: Princeton University Press, 2000.

Zuboff, Shoshana. *The Age of Surveillance Capitalism: The Fight for a Human Future at the New Frontier of Power*. New York: Public Affairs, 2019.

———. "Facebook Is Targeting You." *The New York Times*, November 14, 2021, SR 8.

Zuckerberg, Mark. "Facebook Can Help the News Business." *The New York Times*, October 27, 2019, SR 3.

Index

absolute concept of constitution, 179;
of Condorcet, 132–33; Habermas on,
131–32; of Schmitt, 78, 130, 189–92,
198; on social natural laws and
capitalism, xv, 189

absolute rationalism: of Condorcet,
117, 129, 132, 193, 223, 243–44; of
French Revolution, 79, 129, 189; of
Royer–Collard, 79

Addison, Joseph, 80, 83–84, 104, 125–
26, 167

Adenauer, Konrad: authoritarianism of,
40–42, 58–59; Germany of, 39, 181;
Habermas on, 44–47, 52, 58–59;
media manipulation by, 44–45; Nazis
and, 57; on nuclear weapons, 43–44

Adorno, Theodor W.: book of, 20–22,
24, 30, 59, 155–61, 169, 182, 199;
Dialectic of Enlightenment of, 20,
22, 155–58, 164–65, 169, 181–82;
Habermas and, 155–56, 169, 180;
"Philosophy and the Division of
Labor" by, 182; Shils on, 180–81

"against facticity": bad facticity and,
183–84, 201, 215; explanation of,
35–36; Habermas using, 25, 34, 39,
180–89, 202; by Marcuse, 24, 31,
35–36, 180, 199; normativity and, 6,
70, 73, 84–85, 95, 184–92, 203, 205

alternative facts, xviii–xix

American Revolution, 117; French
Revolution and, 120–21

Anglo–Saxon, 58, 61

apocryphal acts of sovereignty, 77, 130–
32, 191–92

apolitical culture, 39, 44, 76–77, 83, 89,
95, 222

Arato, Andrew, 192–94, 196

Arendt, Hannah, 8–9, 43, 70

Areopagitica (Milton), 96

Aristotle, 136, 207

authoritarianism: Adenauer and, 40–42,
58–59; on free press, 243; populism
of, 2; voting manipulated by, 42–47,
53, 57

autonomy: of citizens, xv, 12, 14, 19–20,
59, 66, 102, 141, 232; concept of,
9–10, 117–18; as economic, 92–95,
99, 220–25; Facebook on, 228–33;
freedom and, 170; Habermas on, 117–
18; "Horrors of Autonomy," 201–4,
207; Kant on, 175; as private and
public, 9, 13–14, 81, 87–93, 95, 151–
55, 175, 212, 220–21, 233; property
ownership and, 193, 212, 240

Bacon, Francis, 10

Barton, John, 240–42

About the Author

Michael Hofmann, professor of communication and multimedia studies at Florida Atlantic University, holds a PhD in communication (summa cum laude) from the Free University of Berlin. He was a Harkness Fellow of the Commonwealth Fund and received an Airlift Memorial Fellowship as well as a Fulbright Fellowship. He was Co-Director of Research on Media Associates (Rome/Berlin/London/Paris) and published in the fields of communication and media theory as well as public and commercial broadcasting research. His recent publications include *Habermas's Public Sphere: A Critique* (Fairleigh Dickinson University Press/Rowman & Littlefield, 2017; paperback: 2019), a chapter in the Suhrkamp—*Festschrift Habermas global* (2019) commemorating Jürgen Habermas's 90th birthday, the *Journal of Communication and Media Studies* articles "Habermas's Public Sphere versus Trump's Twittersphere: Citizenship in a World of Social Media" (2018) and "Deliberation in Dysfunctional Democracies: The Global Need for Critically Renewing Habermas's Public Sphere Concept" (2019), and the *Kybernetes* essay "Theoretical and Practical Influences of Habermas's Global Academic Best Seller *Structural Transformation of the Public Sphere* in the United States" (2021).

www.ingramcontent.com/pod-product-compliance
Lightning Source LLC
Chambersburg PA
CBHW031351290326
41932CB00044B/955